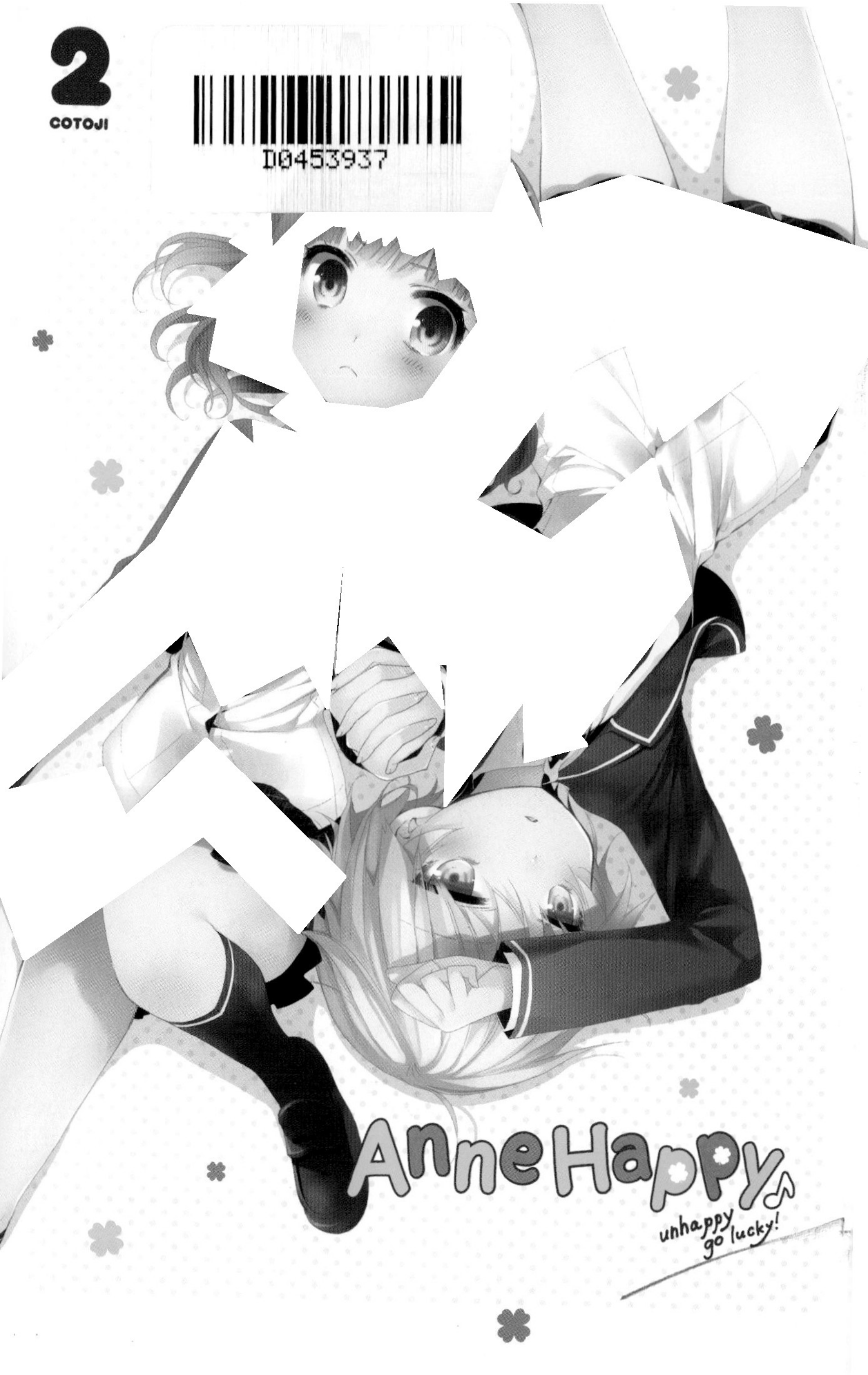
2
COTOJI
Anne Happy
unhappy go lucky!

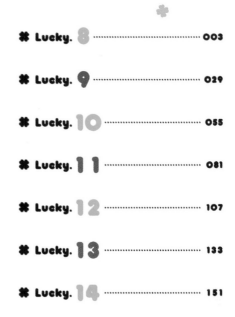

CONTENTS
ANNE HAPPY
VOLUME TWO
COTOJI

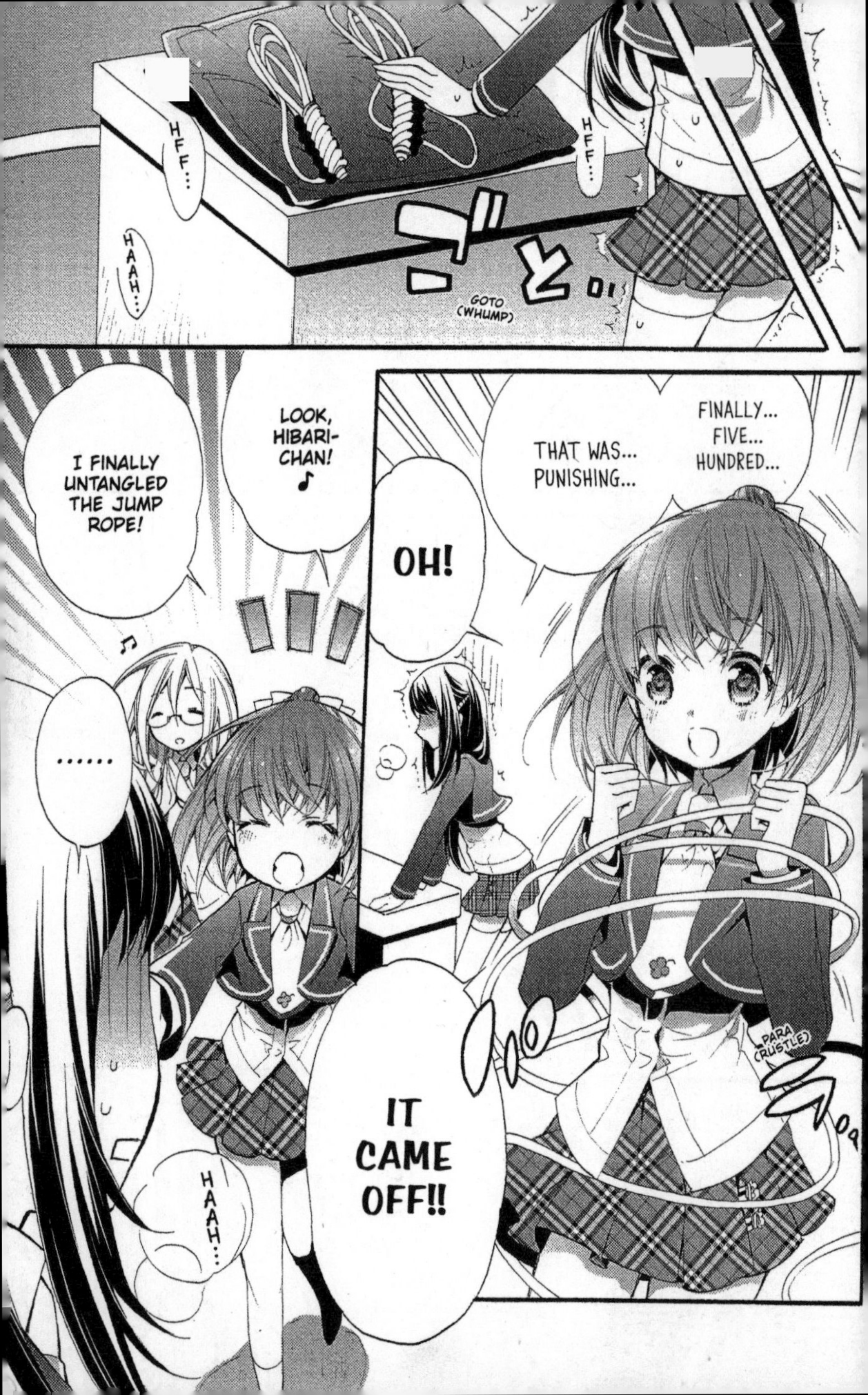
HFF...
HFF...
HAAH...
GOTO (WHUMP)
FINALLY... FIVE... HUNDRED...
THAT WAS... PUNISHING...
OH!
PARA (RUSTLE)
IT CAME OFF!!
LOOK, HIBARI-CHAN! ♪
I FINALLY UNTANGLED THE JUMP ROPE!
......
HAAH...

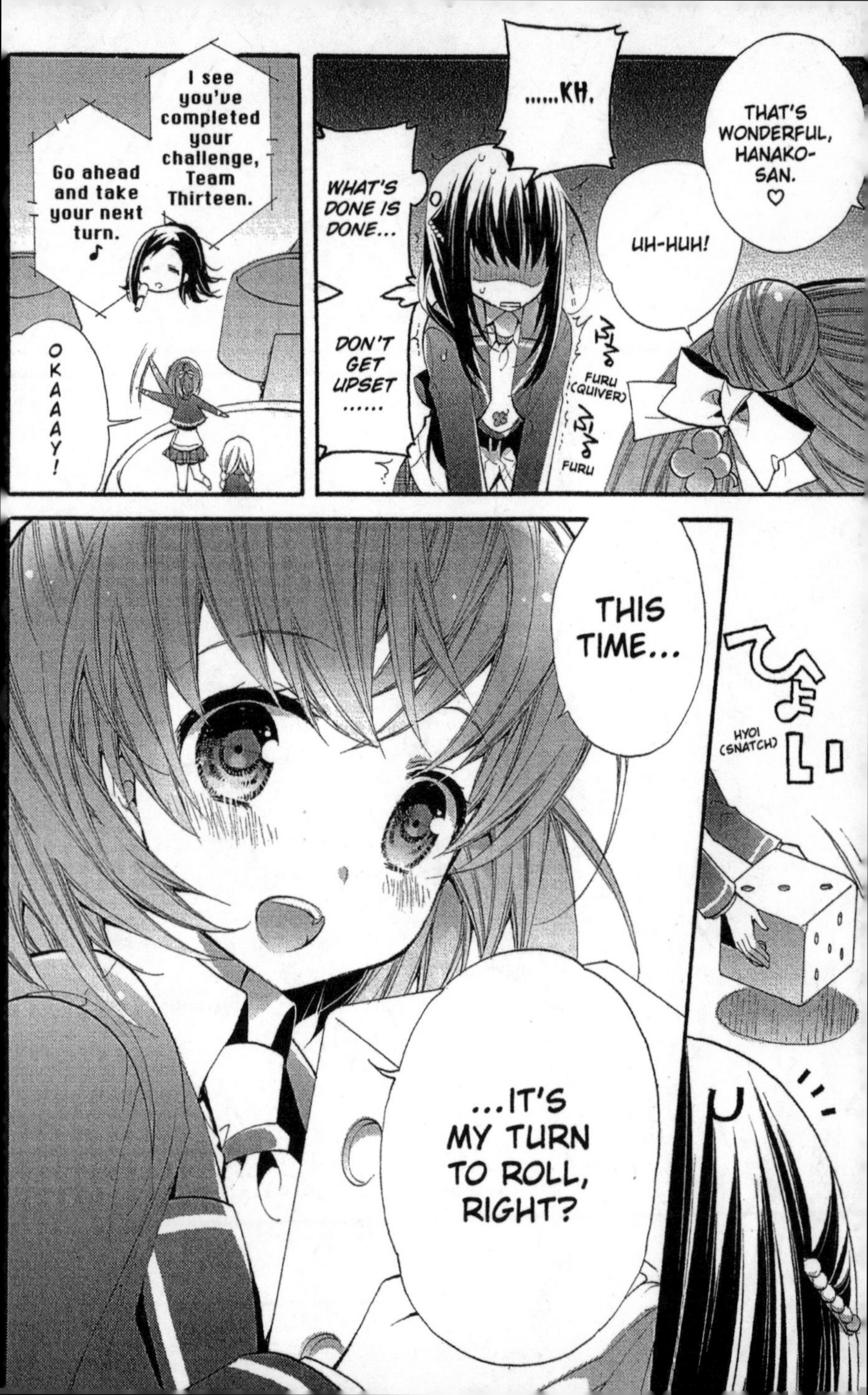
THAT'S WONDERFUL, HANAKO-SAN. ♡
UH-HUH!
......KH.
WHAT'S DONE IS DONE...
DON'T GET UPSET ......
FURU (QUIVER)
FURU
I see you've completed your challenge, Team Thirteen.
Go ahead and take your next turn. ♪
OKAAAAY!
HYOI (SNATCH)
THIS TIME...
...IT'S MY TURN TO ROLL, RIGHT?

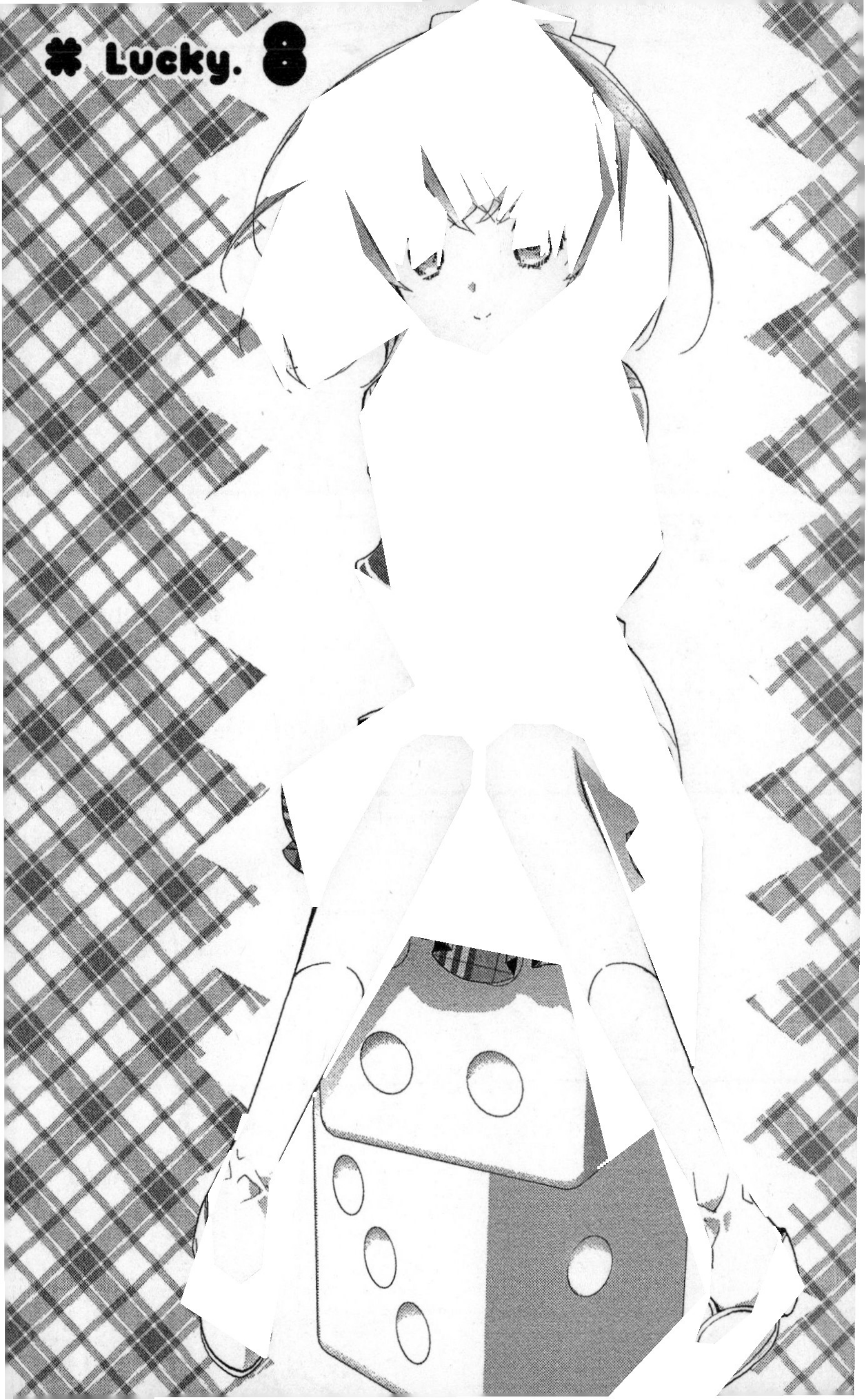
Lucky. 8

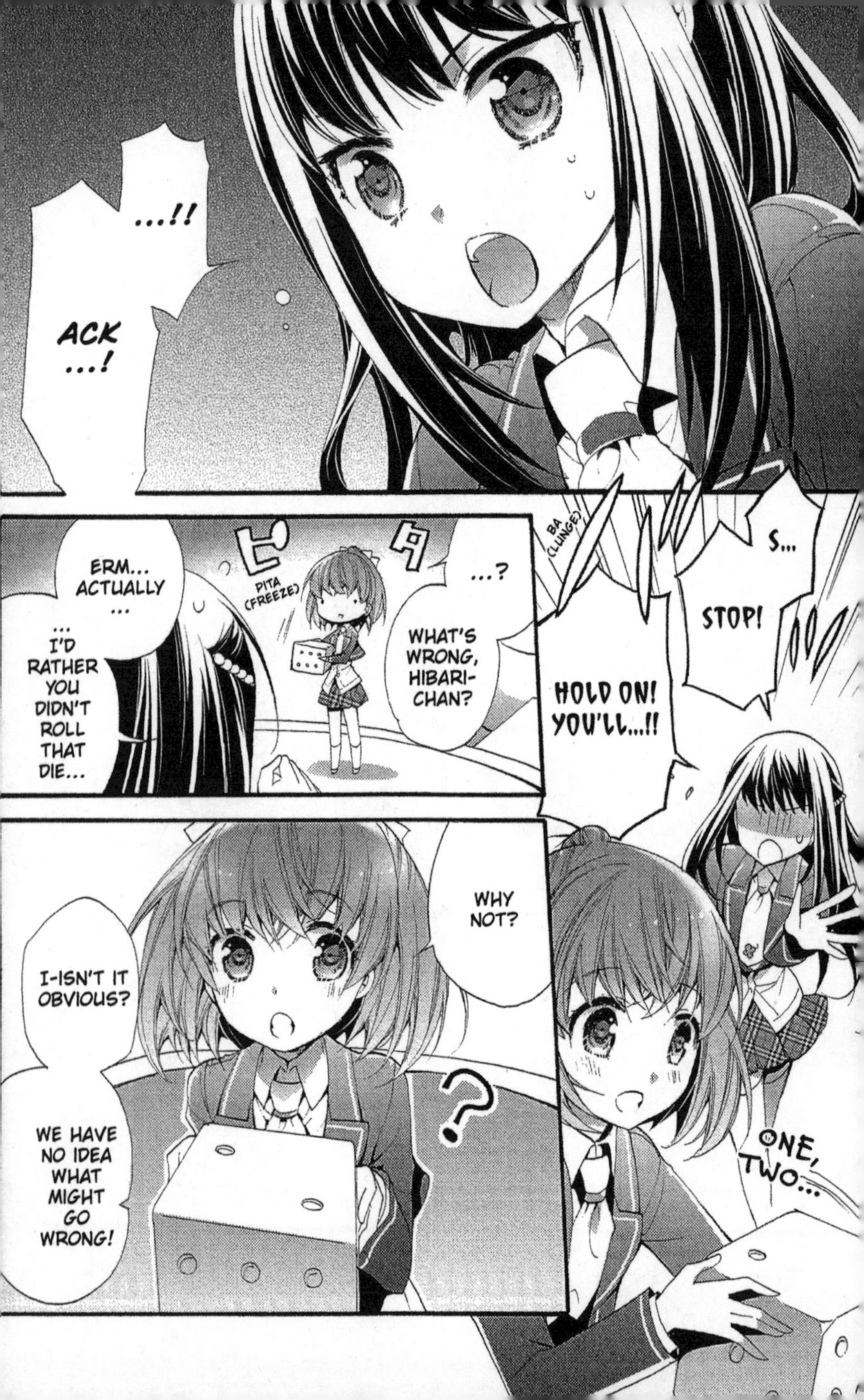

...!!
ACK ...!
S...
STOP!
BA (LUNGE)
HOLD ON! YOU'LL...!!
ONE, TWO...
...?
WHAT'S WRONG, HIBARI-CHAN?
PITA (FREEZE)
ERM... ACTUALLY...
...I'D RATHER YOU DIDN'T ROLL THAT DIE...
WHY NOT?
I-ISN'T IT OBVIOUS?
WE HAVE NO IDEA WHAT MIGHT GO WRONG!

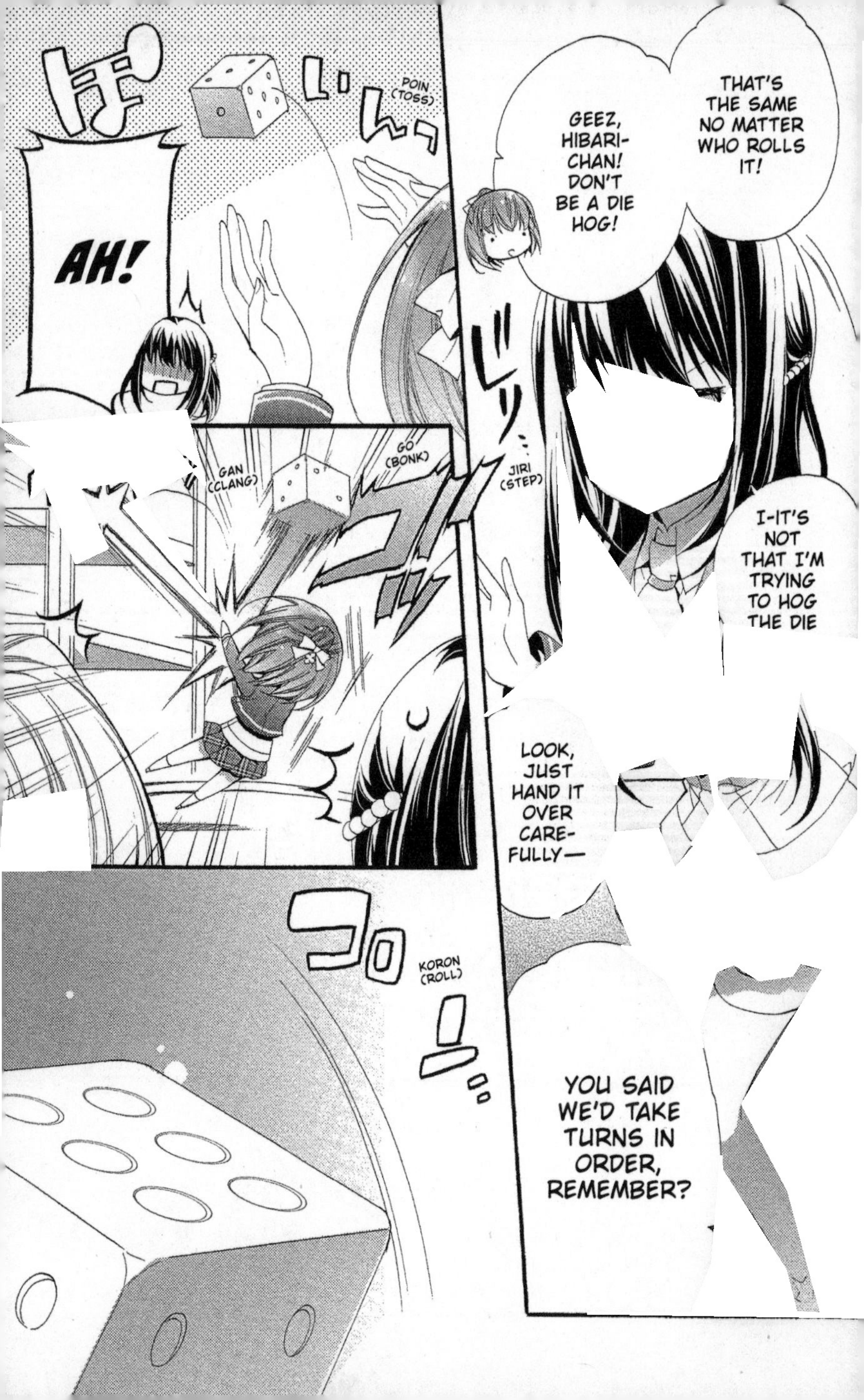
THAT'S THE SAME NO MATTER WHO ROLLS IT!
GEEZ, HIBARI-CHAN! DON'T BE A DIE HOG!
JIRI (STEP)
I-IT'S NOT THAT I'M TRYING TO HOG THE DIE
LOOK, JUST HAND IT OVER CARE-FULLY—
YOU SAID WE'D TAKE TURNS IN ORDER, REMEMBER?
POIN (TOSS)
AH!
GO (BONK)
GAN (CLANG)
KORON (ROLL)

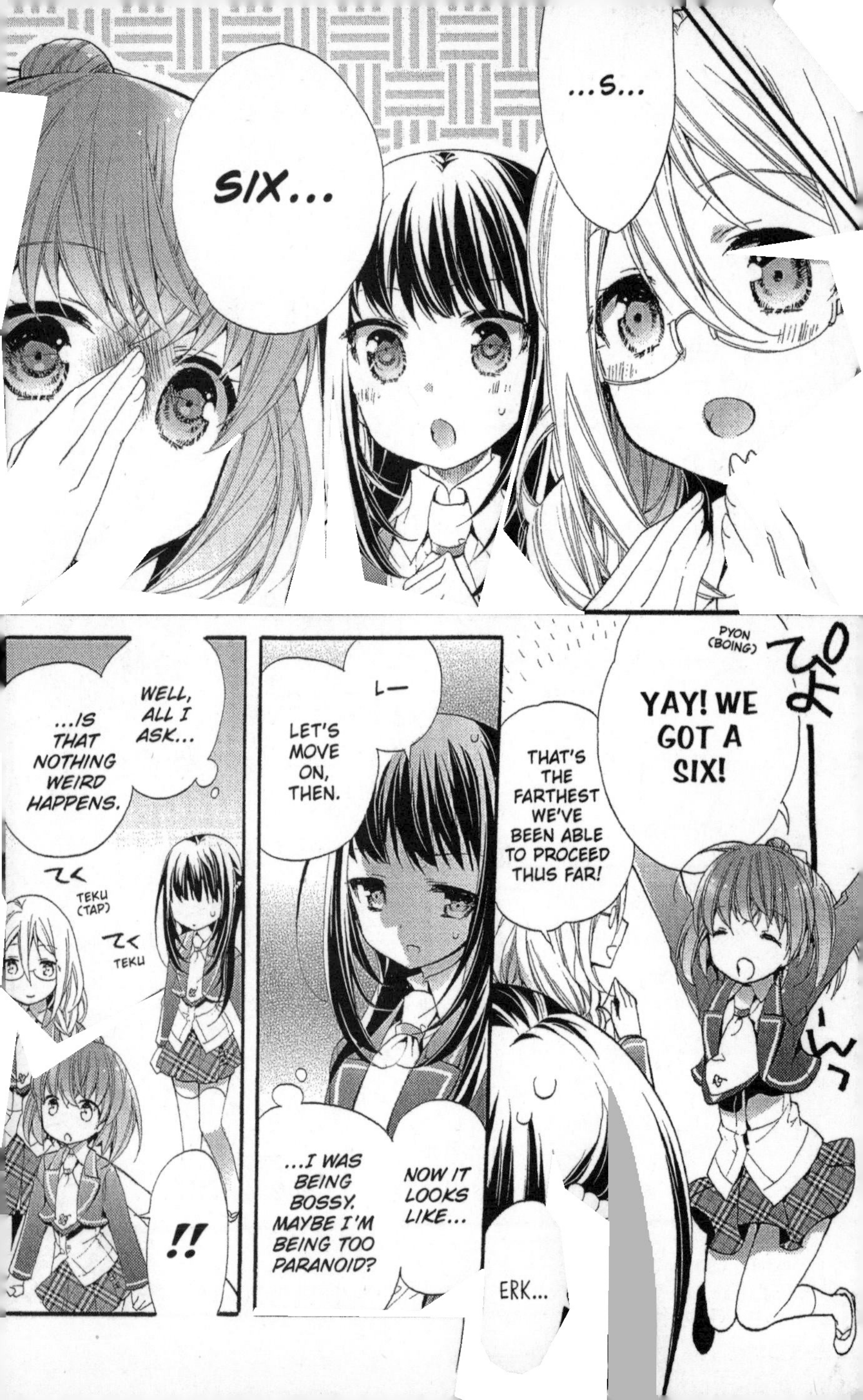
...S...
SIX...
PYON (BOING)
ぴょ
YAY! WE GOT A SIX!
THAT'S THE FARTHEST WE'VE BEEN ABLE TO PROCEED THUS FAR!
ーん
L—
LET'S MOVE ON, THEN.
ERK...
NOW IT LOOKS LIKE...
...I WAS BEING BOSSY. MAYBE I'M BEING TOO PARANOID?
WELL, ALL I ASK...
...IS THAT NOTHING WEIRD HAPPENS.
てく
TEKU (TAP)
てく
TEKU
!!

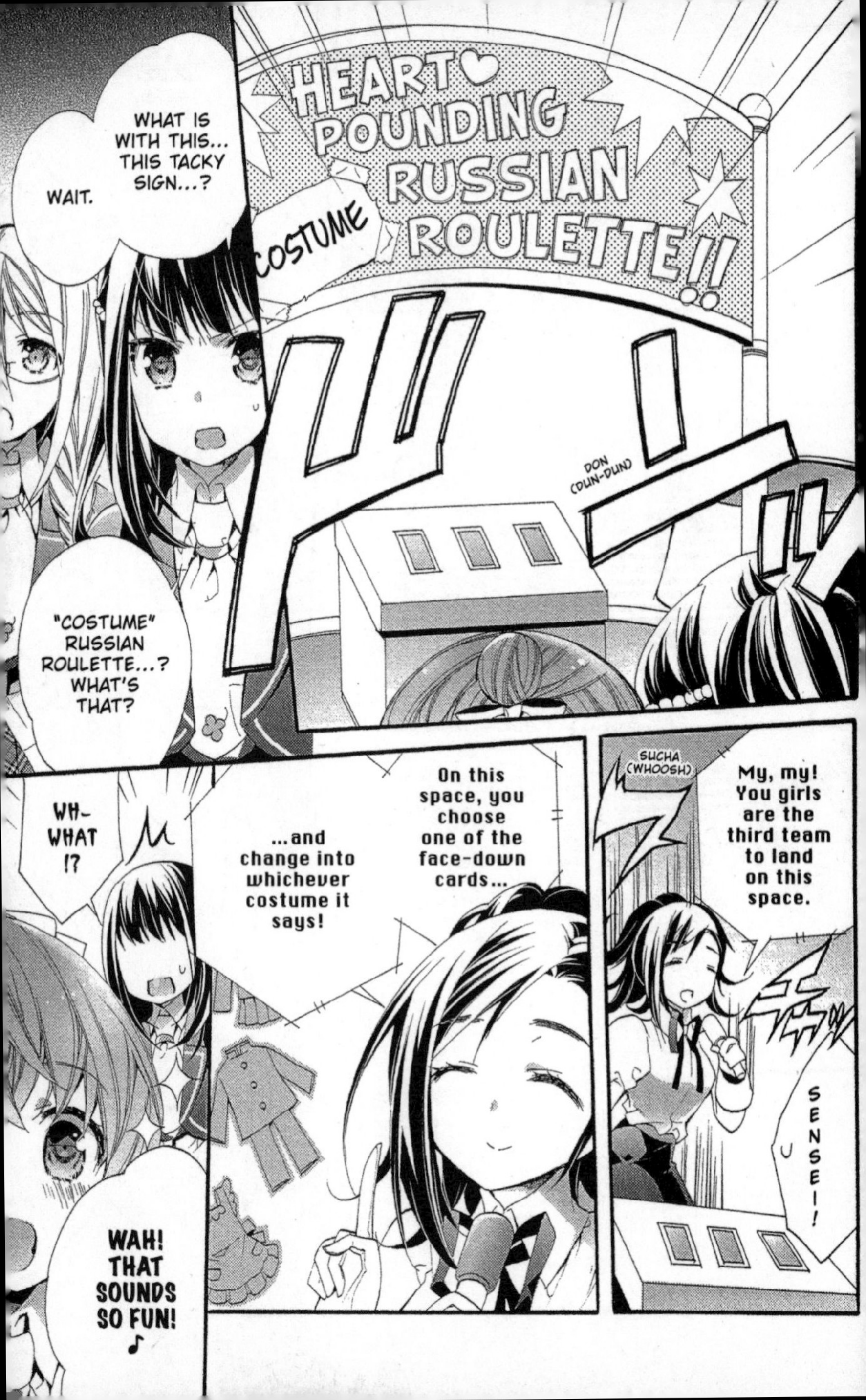

HEART♥ POUNDING RUSSIAN ROULETTE!!
COSTUME
WHAT IS WITH THIS... THIS TACKY SIGN...?
WAIT.
DON (DUN-DUN)
"COSTUME" RUSSIAN ROULETTE...? WHAT'S THAT?
SUCHA (WHOOSH)
My, my! You girls are the third team to land on this space.
SENSEI!
On this space, you choose one of the face-down cards...
...and change into whichever costume it says!
WH-WHAT!?
WAH! THAT SOUNDS SO FUN! ♪

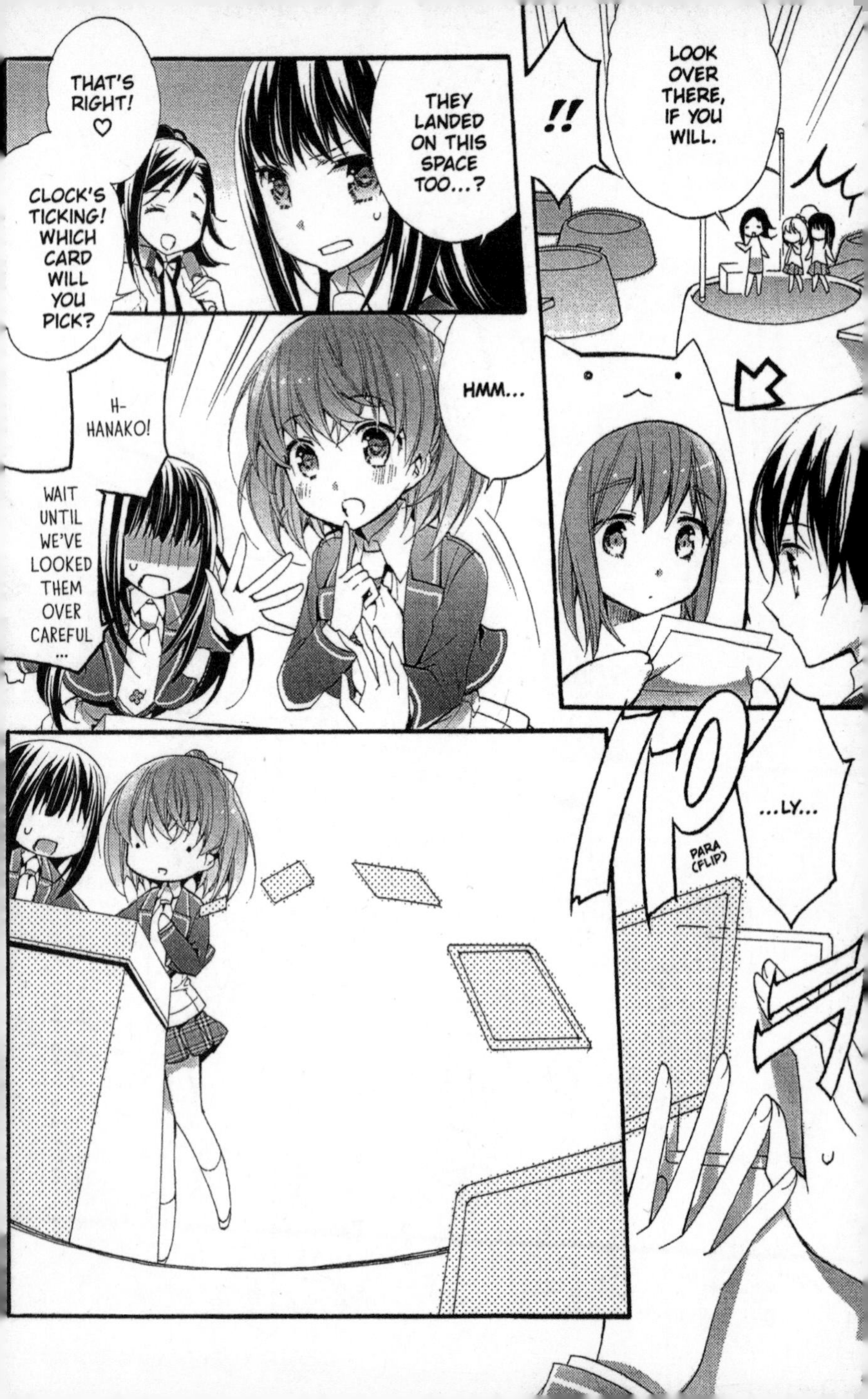
LOOK OVER THERE, IF YOU WILL.
!!
THEY LANDED ON THIS SPACE TOO...?
THAT'S RIGHT! ♡
CLOCK'S TICKING! WHICH CARD WILL YOU PICK?
HMM...
H-HANAKO!
WAIT UNTIL WE'VE LOOKED THEM OVER CAREFUL...
...LY...
PARA (FLIP)

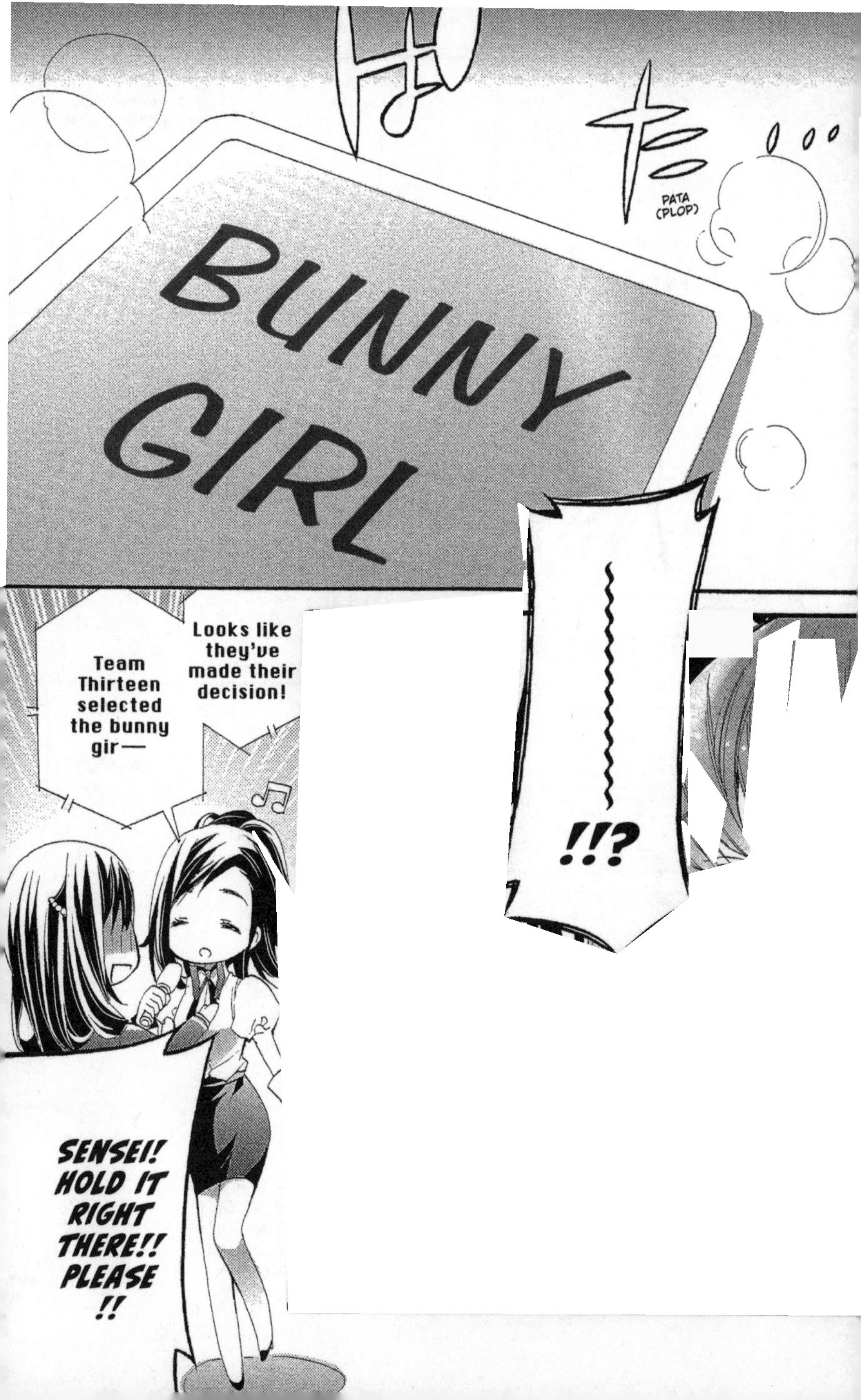
PATA (PLOP)
BUNNY GIRL
!!?
Looks like they've made their decision!
Team Thirteen selected the bunny gir—
SENSEI! HOLD IT RIGHT THERE!! PLEASE!!

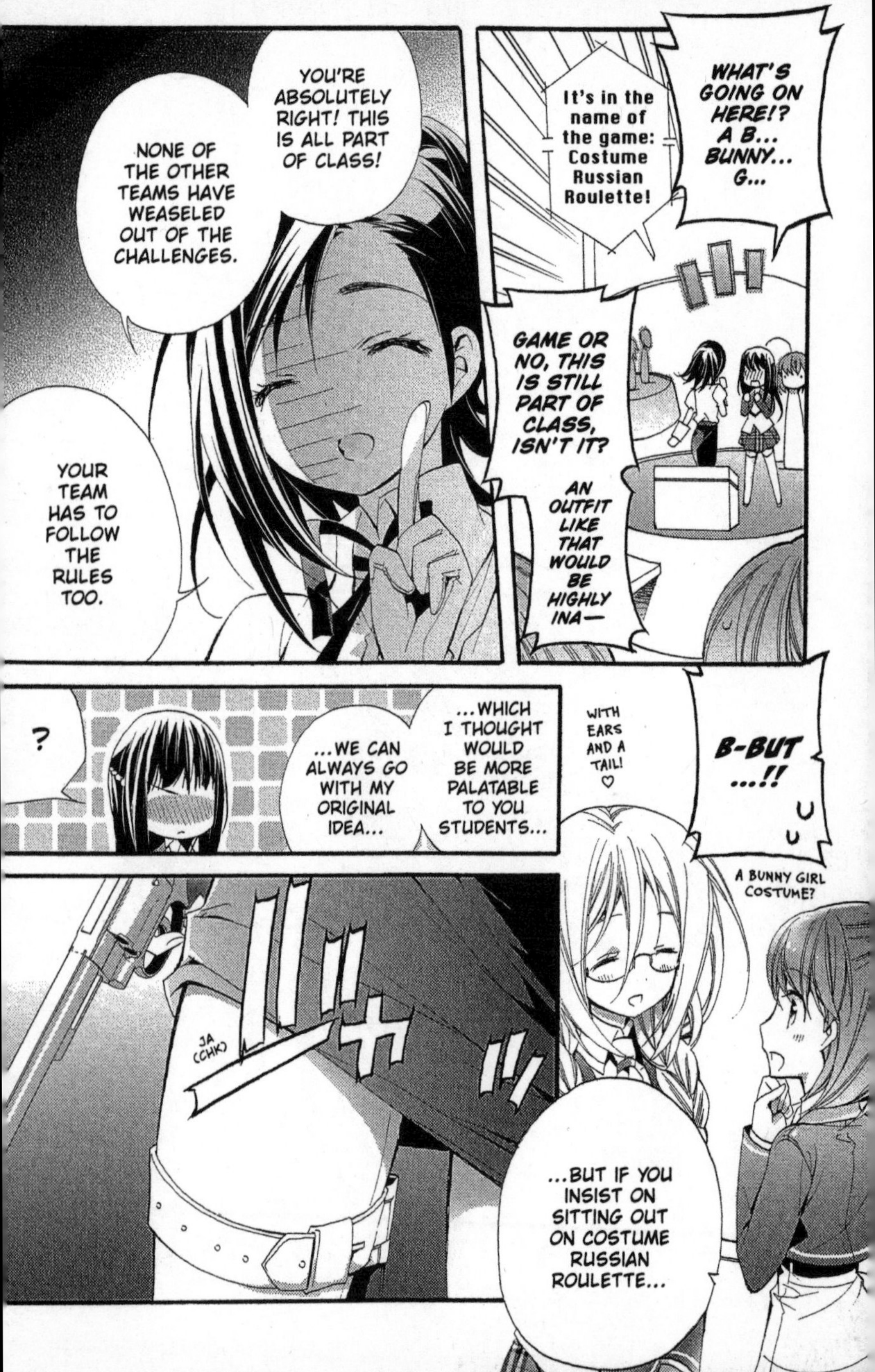
WHAT'S GOING ON HERE!? A B... BUNNY... G...
It's in the name of the game: Costume Russian Roulette!
GAME OR NO, THIS IS STILL PART OF CLASS, ISN'T IT?
AN OUTFIT LIKE THAT WOULD BE HIGHLY INA—
YOU'RE ABSOLUTELY RIGHT! THIS IS ALL PART OF CLASS!
NONE OF THE OTHER TEAMS HAVE WEASELED OUT OF THE CHALLENGES.
YOUR TEAM HAS TO FOLLOW THE RULES TOO.
B-BUT ...!!
A BUNNY GIRL COSTUME?
WITH EARS AND A TAIL! ♡
...BUT IF YOU INSIST ON SITTING OUT ON COSTUME RUSSIAN ROULETTE...
...WHICH I THOUGHT WOULD BE MORE PALATABLE TO YOU STUDENTS...
...WE CAN ALWAYS GO WITH MY ORIGINAL IDEA...
?
JA (CHK)

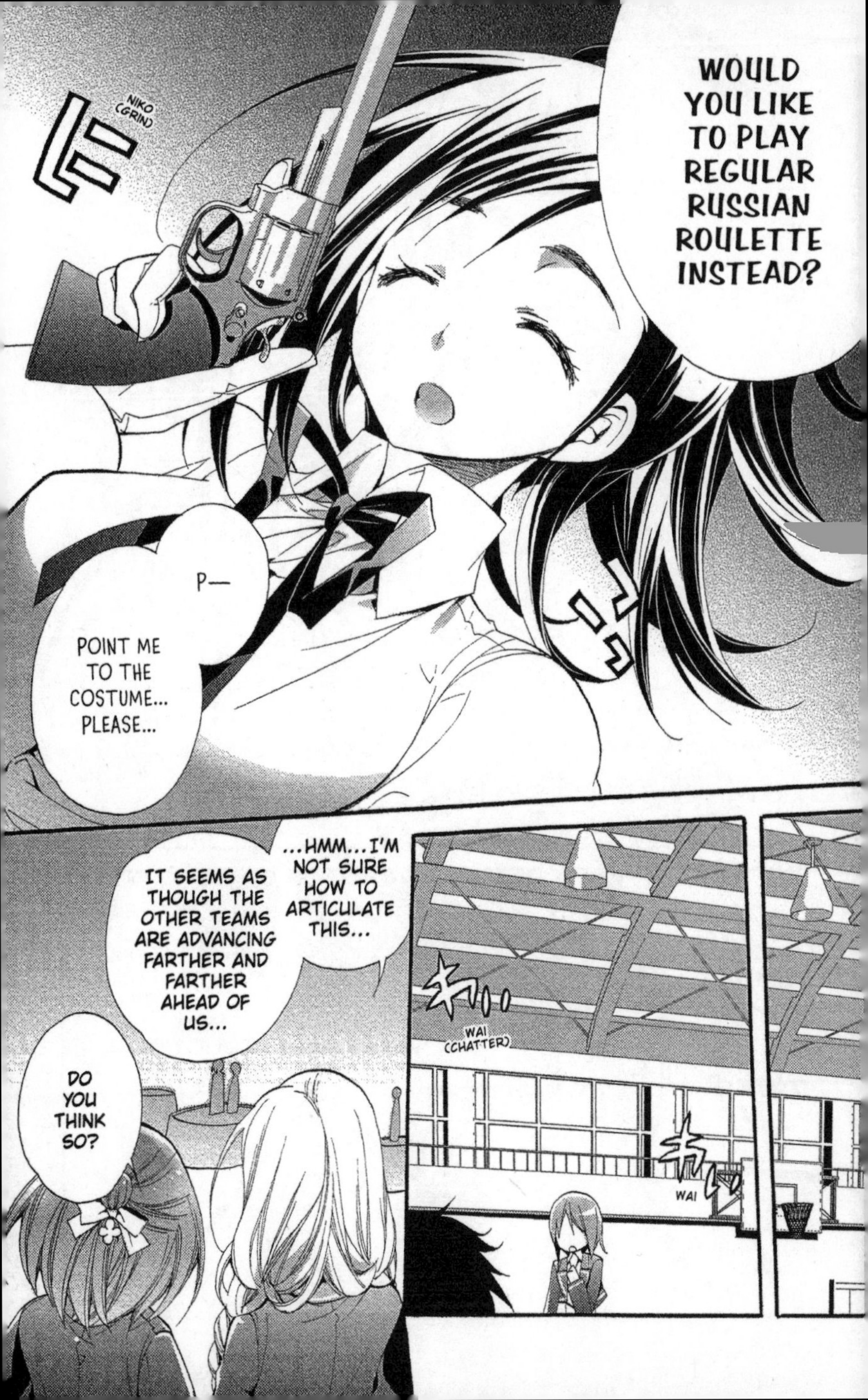
WOULD YOU LIKE TO PLAY REGULAR RUSSIAN ROULETTE INSTEAD?
NIKO (GRIN)
P—
POINT ME TO THE COSTUME... PLEASE...
WAI (CHATTER)
WAI
...HMM...I'M NOT SURE HOW TO ARTICULATE THIS...
IT SEEMS AS THOUGH THE OTHER TEAMS ARE ADVANCING FARTHER AND FARTHER AHEAD OF US...
DO YOU THINK SO?

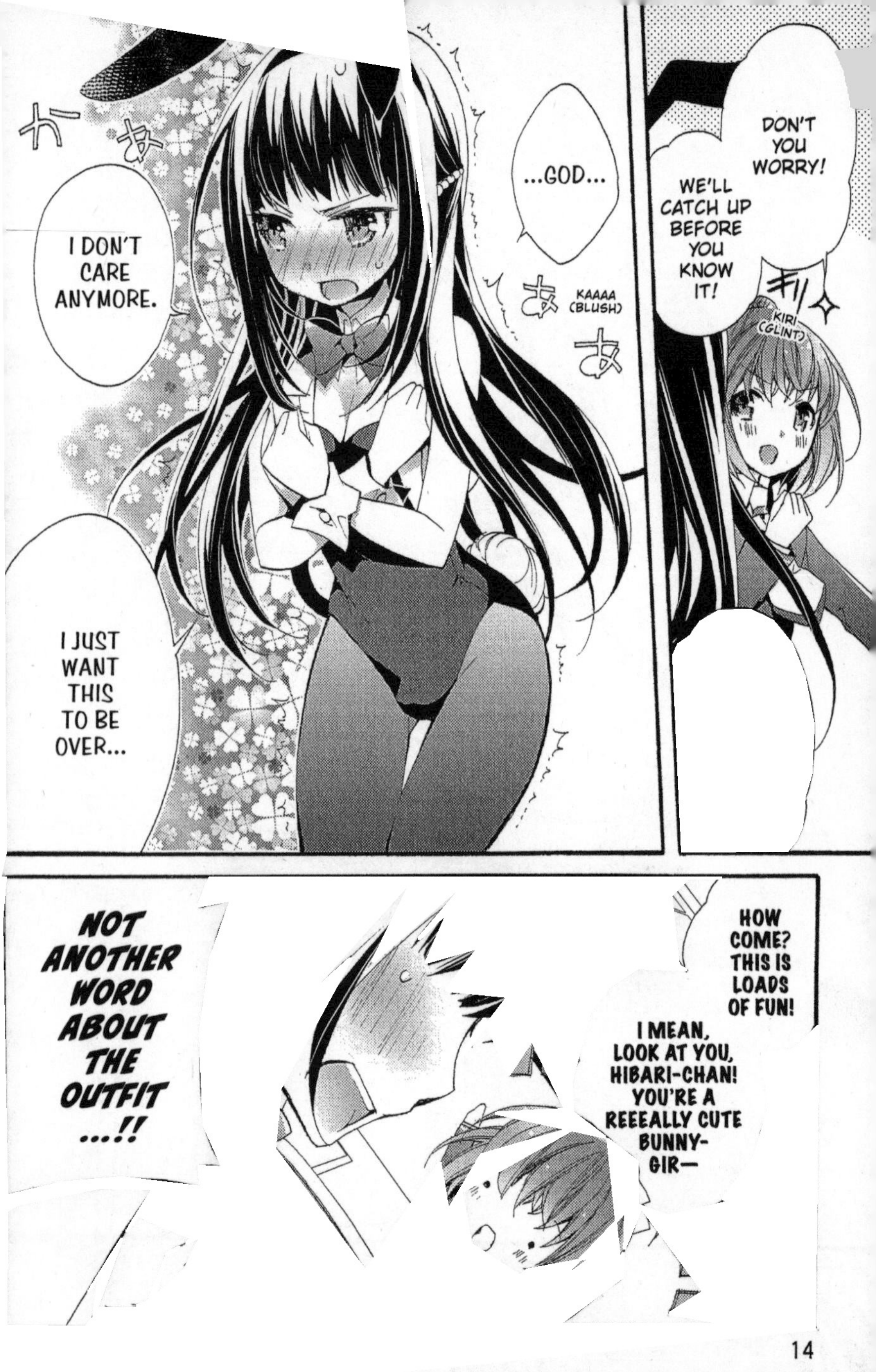
DON'T YOU WORRY!
WE'LL CATCH UP BEFORE YOU KNOW IT!
KIRI (GLINT)
...GOD...
KAAAA (BLUSH)
I DON'T CARE ANYMORE.
I JUST WANT THIS TO BE OVER...
HOW COME? THIS IS LOADS OF FUN!
I MEAN, LOOK AT YOU, HIBARI-CHAN! YOU'RE A REEEALLY CUTE BUNNY-GIR—
NOT ANOTHER WORD ABOUT THE OUTFIT...!!

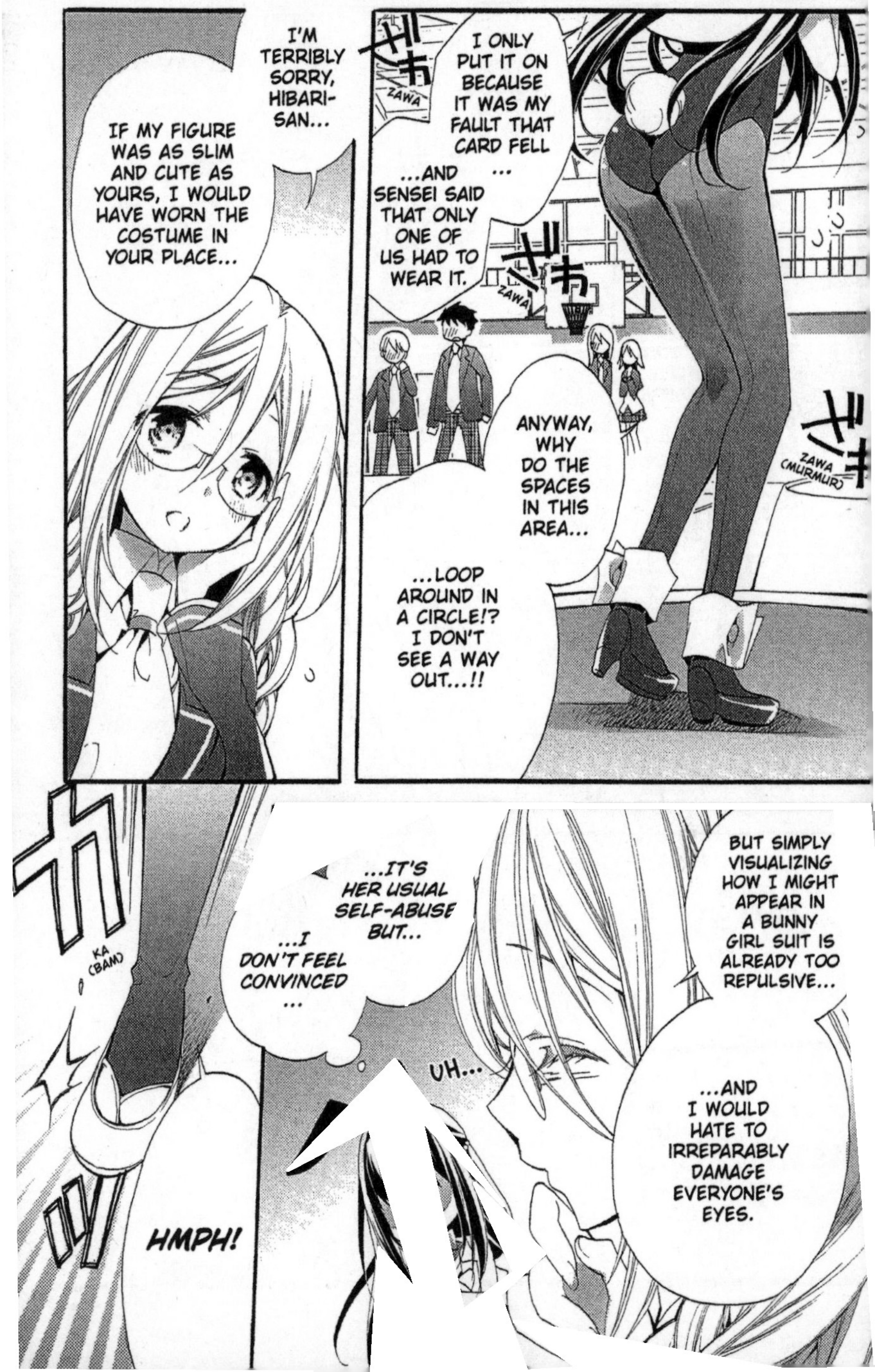
ZAWA (MURMUR)
I ONLY PUT IT ON BECAUSE IT WAS MY FAULT THAT CARD FELL ...
...AND SENSEI SAID THAT ONLY ONE OF US HAD TO WEAR IT.
ZAWA
ZAWA
ANYWAY, WHY DO THE SPACES IN THIS AREA...
...LOOP AROUND IN A CIRCLE!? I DON'T SEE A WAY OUT...!!
I'M TERRIBLY SORRY, HIBARI-SAN...
IF MY FIGURE WAS AS SLIM AND CUTE AS YOURS, I WOULD HAVE WORN THE COSTUME IN YOUR PLACE...
BUT SIMPLY VISUALIZING HOW I MIGHT APPEAR IN A BUNNY GIRL SUIT IS ALREADY TOO REPULSIVE...
...AND I WOULD HATE TO IRREPARABLY DAMAGE EVERYONE'S EYES.
UH...
...IT'S HER USUAL SELF-ABUSE BUT...
...I DON'T FEEL CONVINCED ...
KA (BAM)
HMPH!

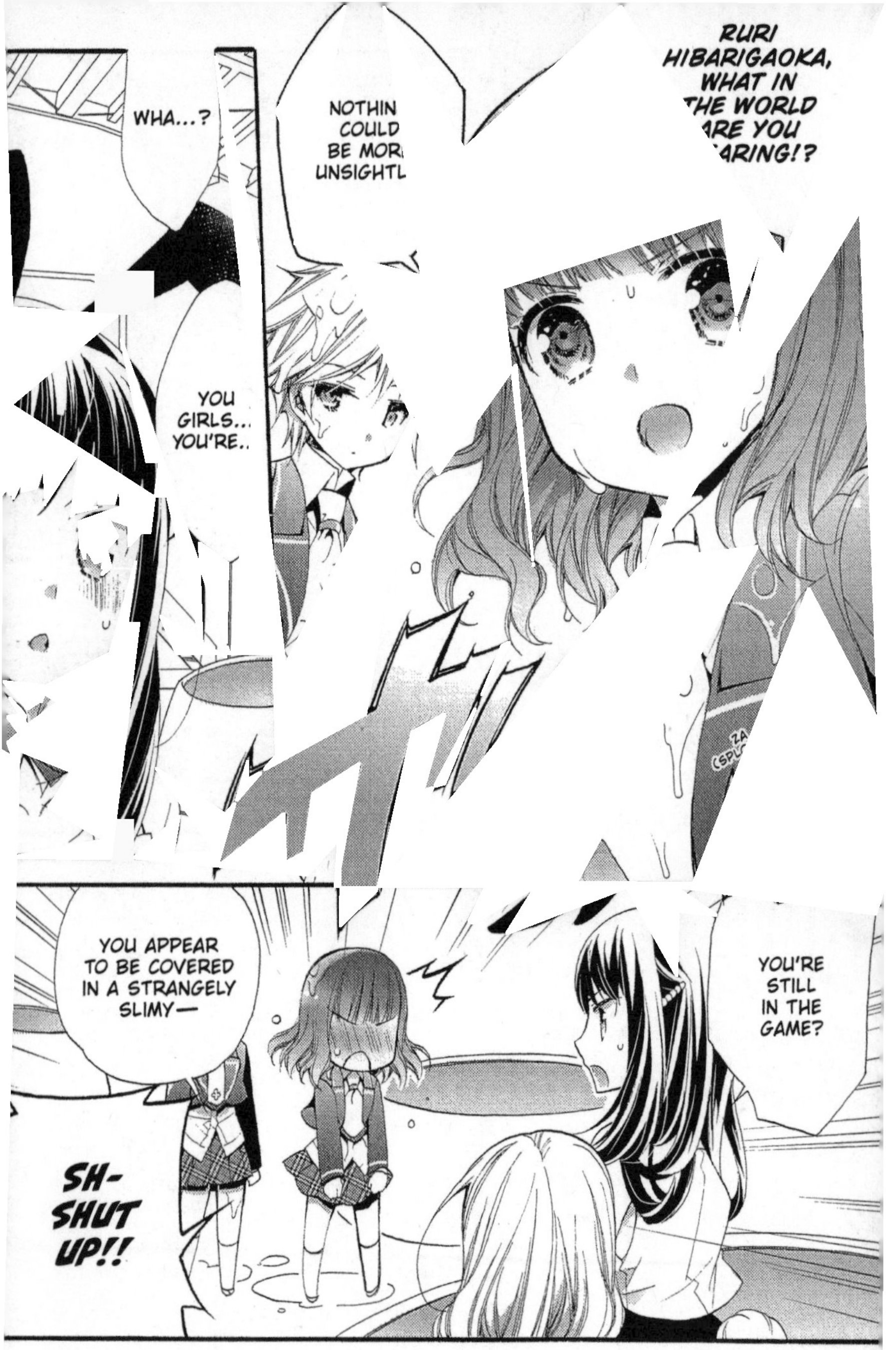
RURI HIBARIGAOKA, WHAT IN THE WORLD ARE YOU EARING!?
NOTHIN COULD BE MOR UNSIGHTL
WHA...?
YOU GIRLS... YOU'RE..
ZA
YOU'RE STILL IN THE GAME?
YOU APPEAR TO BE COVERED IN A STRANGELY SLIMY—
SH-SHUT UP!!

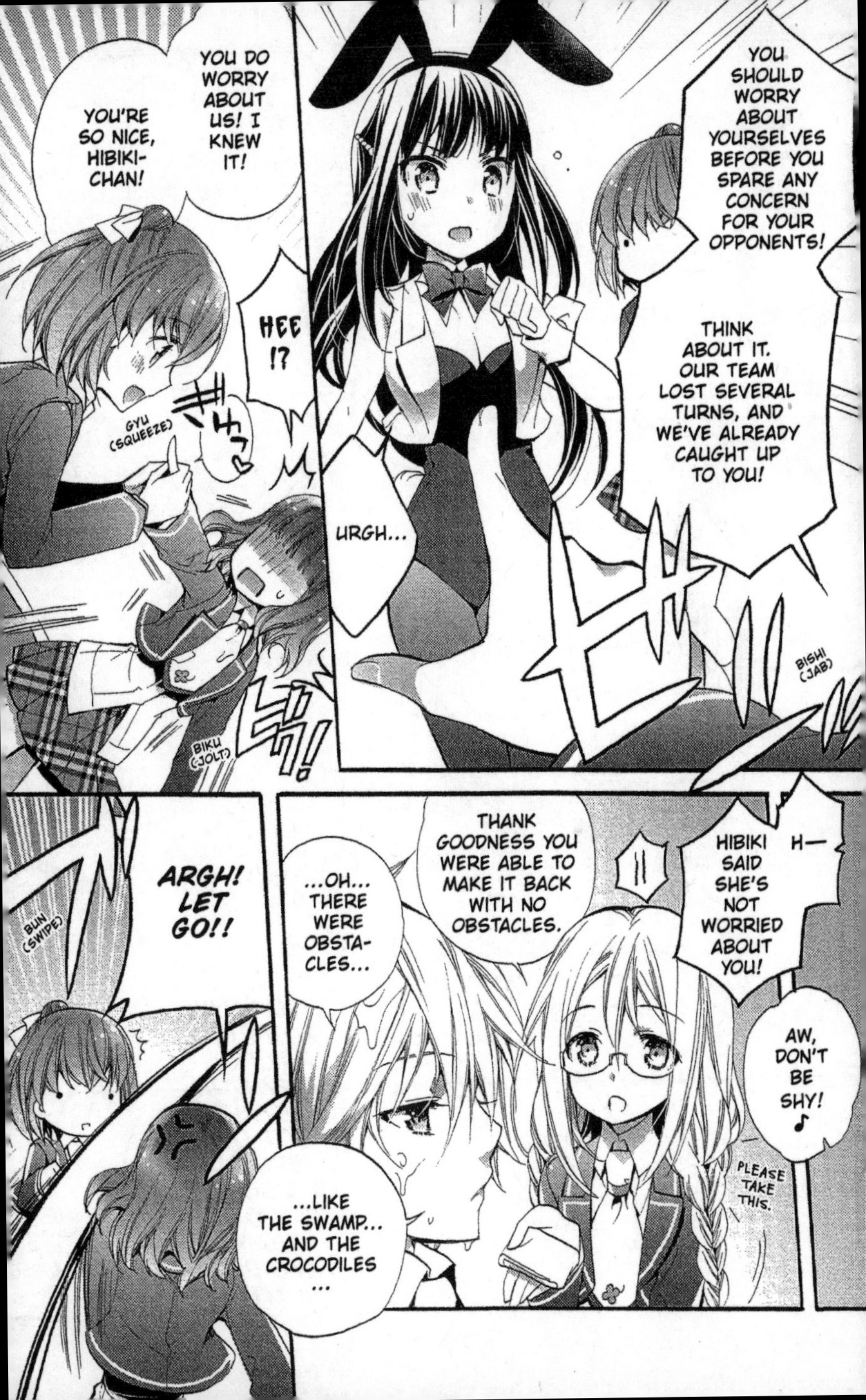
YOU SHOULD WORRY ABOUT YOURSELVES BEFORE YOU SPARE ANY CONCERN FOR YOUR OPPONENTS!
THINK ABOUT IT. OUR TEAM LOST SEVERAL TURNS, AND WE'VE ALREADY CAUGHT UP TO YOU!
BISHI (JAB)
URGH...
YOU DO WORRY ABOUT US! I KNEW IT!
YOU'RE SO NICE, HIBIKI-CHAN!
HEE !?
GYU (SQUEEZE)
BIKU (JOLT)
H—
HIBIKI SAID SHE'S NOT WORRIED ABOUT YOU!
AW, DON'T BE SHY! ♪
!!
THANK GOODNESS YOU WERE ABLE TO MAKE IT BACK WITH NO OBSTACLES.
...OH... THERE WERE OBSTACLES...
PLEASE TAKE THIS.
...LIKE THE SWAMP... AND THE CROCODILES ...
ARGH! LET GO!!
BUN (SWIPE)

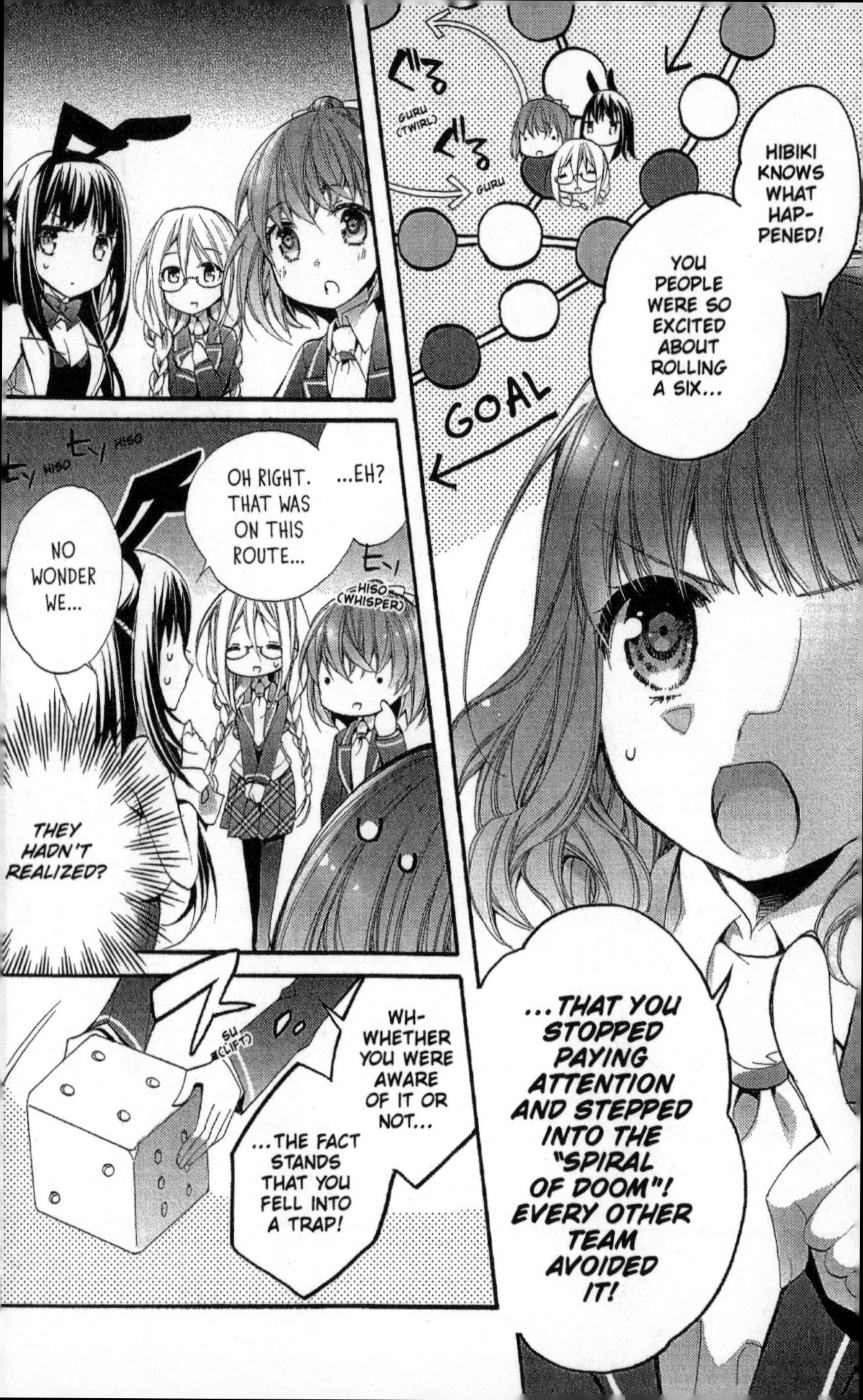

GURU (TWIRL)
GURU
GOAL
HIBIKI KNOWS WHAT HAP-PENED!
YOU PEOPLE WERE SO EXCITED ABOUT ROLLING A SIX...
...THAT YOU STOPPED PAYING ATTENTION AND STEPPED INTO THE "SPIRAL OF DOOM"! EVERY OTHER TEAM AVOIDED IT!
...EH?
OH RIGHT. THAT WAS ON THIS ROUTE...
HISO (WHISPER)
HISO
HISO
NO WONDER WE...
THEY HADN'T REALIZED?
WH-WHETHER YOU WERE AWARE OF IT OR NOT...
SU (LIFT)
...THE FACT STANDS THAT YOU FELL INTO A TRAP!

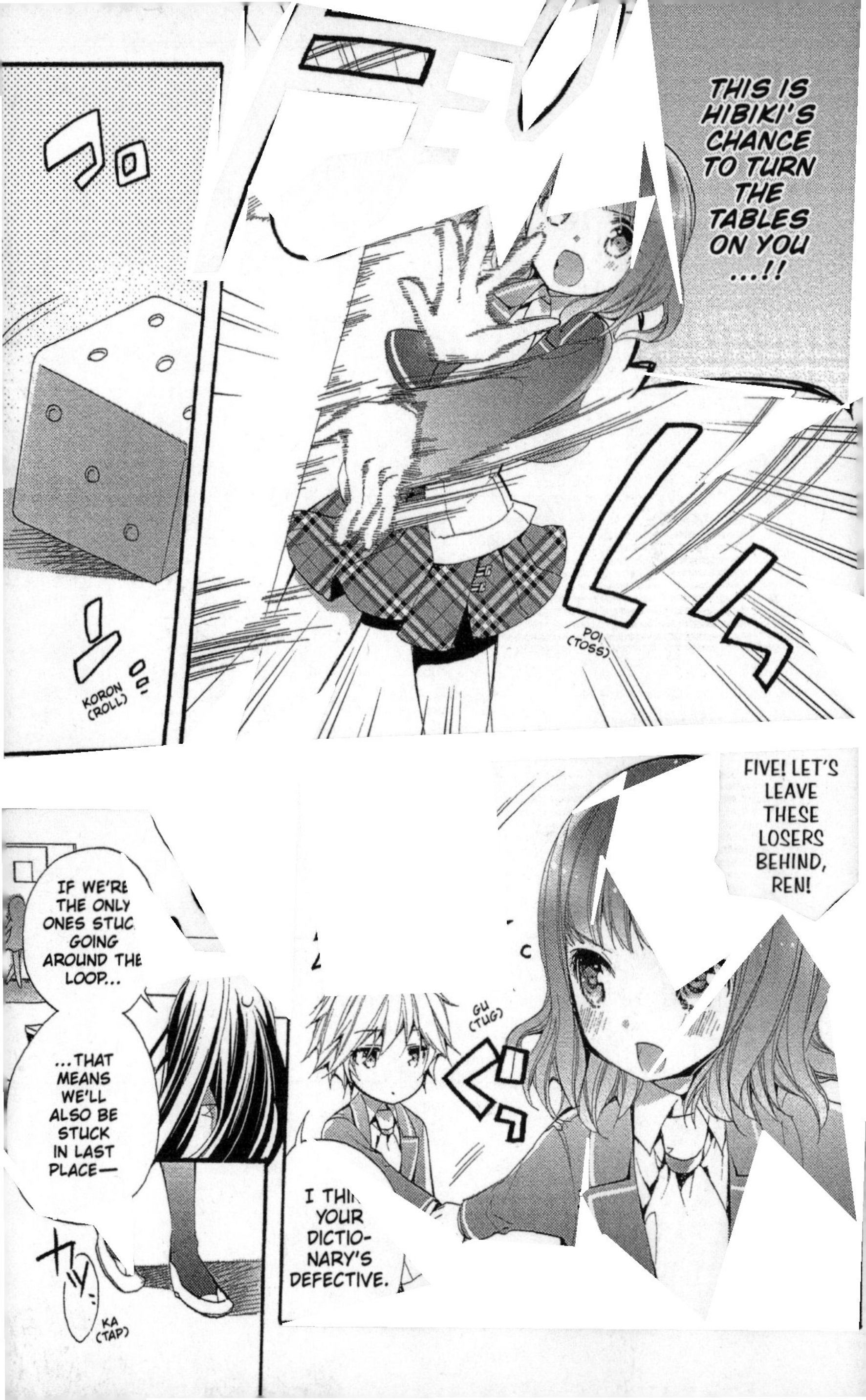
THIS IS HIBIKI'S CHANCE TO TURN THE TABLES ON YOU ...!!
POI (TOSS)
KORON (ROLL)
FIVE! LET'S LEAVE THESE LOSERS BEHIND, REN!
GU (TUG)
I THI YOUR DICTIO-NARY'S DEFECTIVE.
IF WE'RE THE ONLY ONES STUC GOING AROUND THE LOOP...
...THAT MEANS WE'LL ALSO BE STUCK IN LAST PLACE—
KA (TAP)

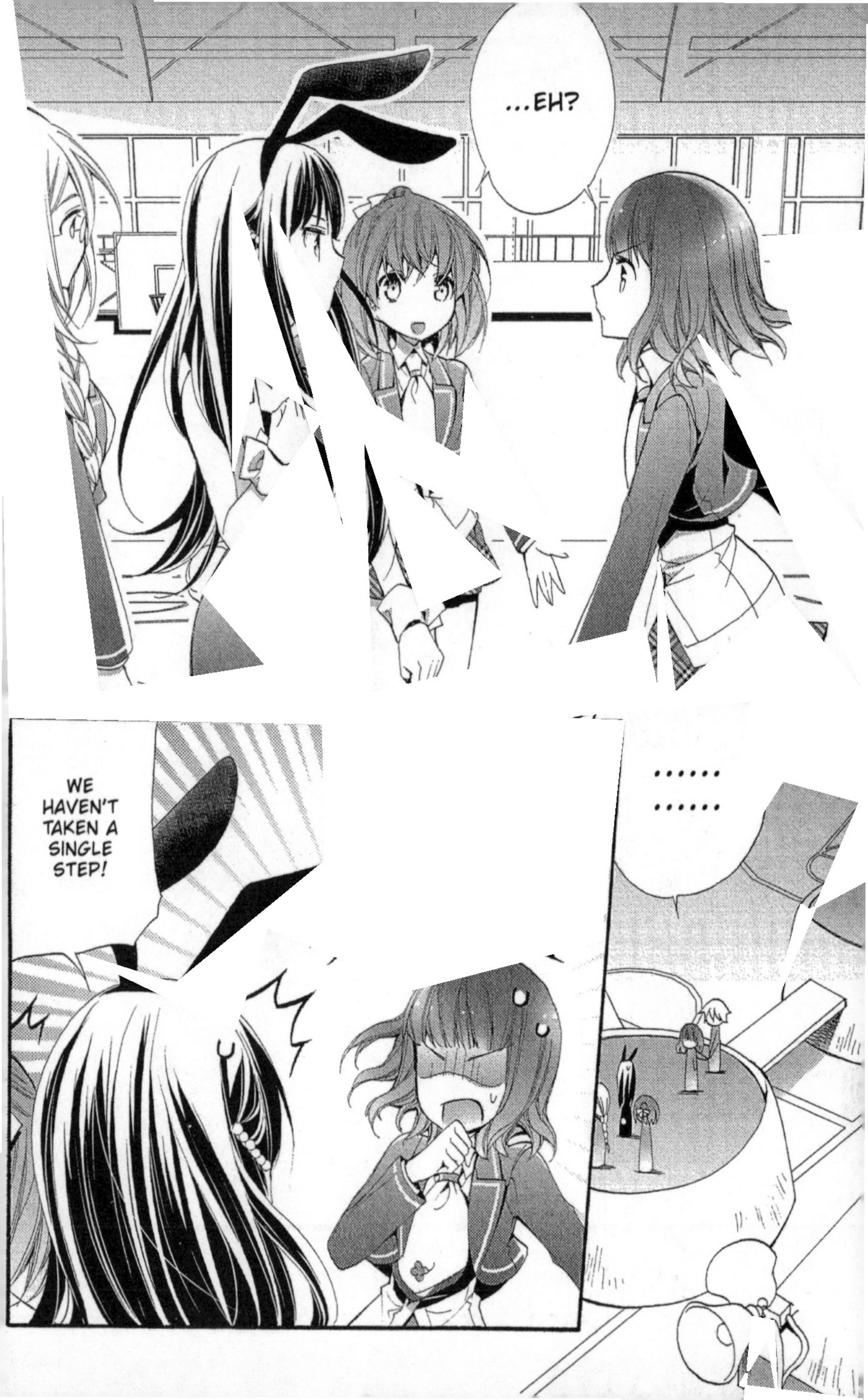
...EH?
......
......
WE HAVEN'T TAKEN A SINGLE STEP!

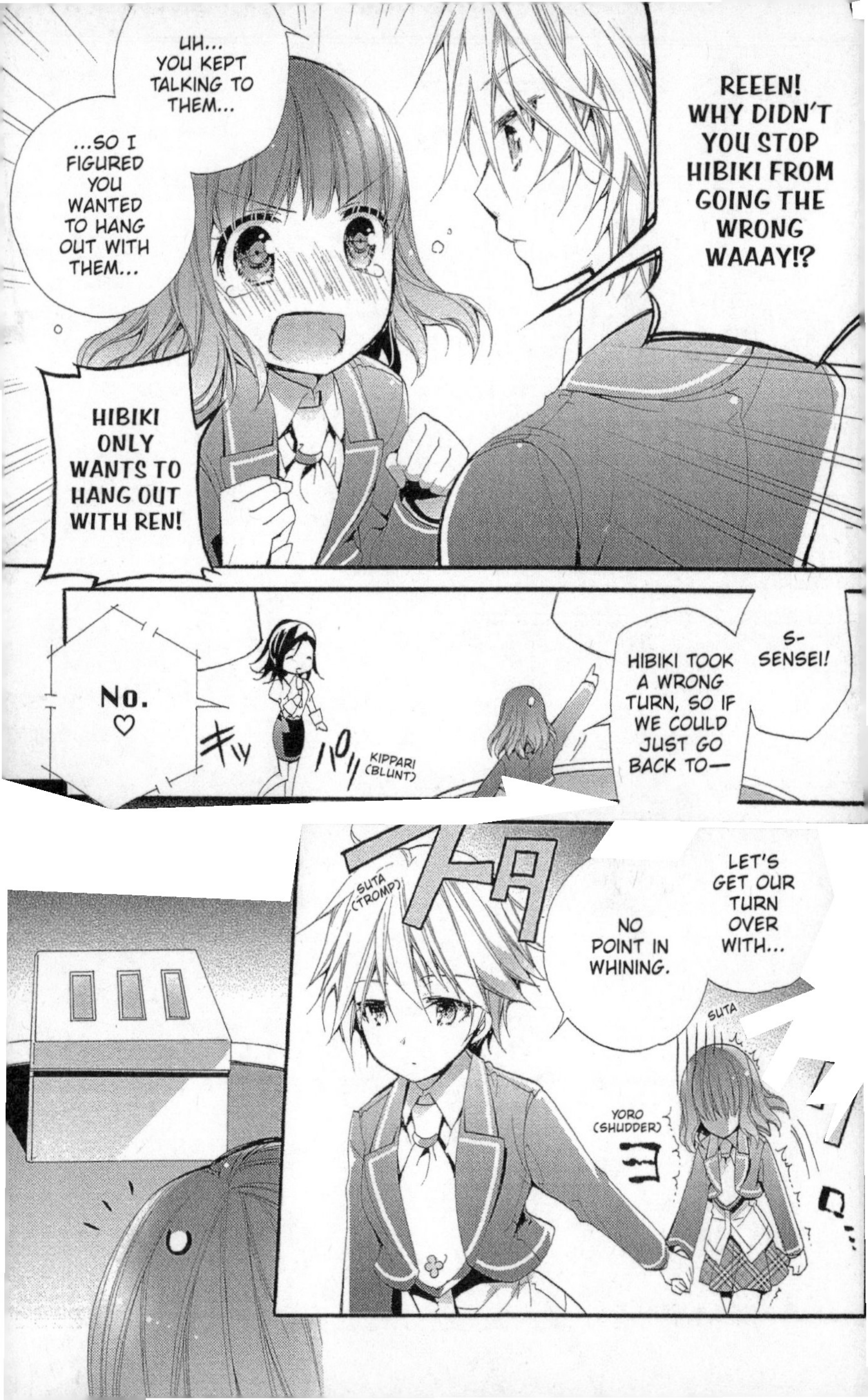
REEEN! WHY DIDN'T YOU STOP HIBIKI FROM GOING THE WRONG WAAAY!?
UH... YOU KEPT TALKING TO THEM...
...SO I FIGURED YOU WANTED TO HANG OUT WITH THEM...
HIBIKI ONLY WANTS TO HANG OUT WITH REN!
S-SENSEI!
HIBIKI TOOK A WRONG TURN, SO IF WE COULD JUST GO BACK TO—
KIPPARI (BLUNT)
No. ♡
SUTA (TROMP)
LET'S GET OUR TURN OVER WITH...
NO POINT IN WHINING.
SUTA
YORO (SHUDDER)

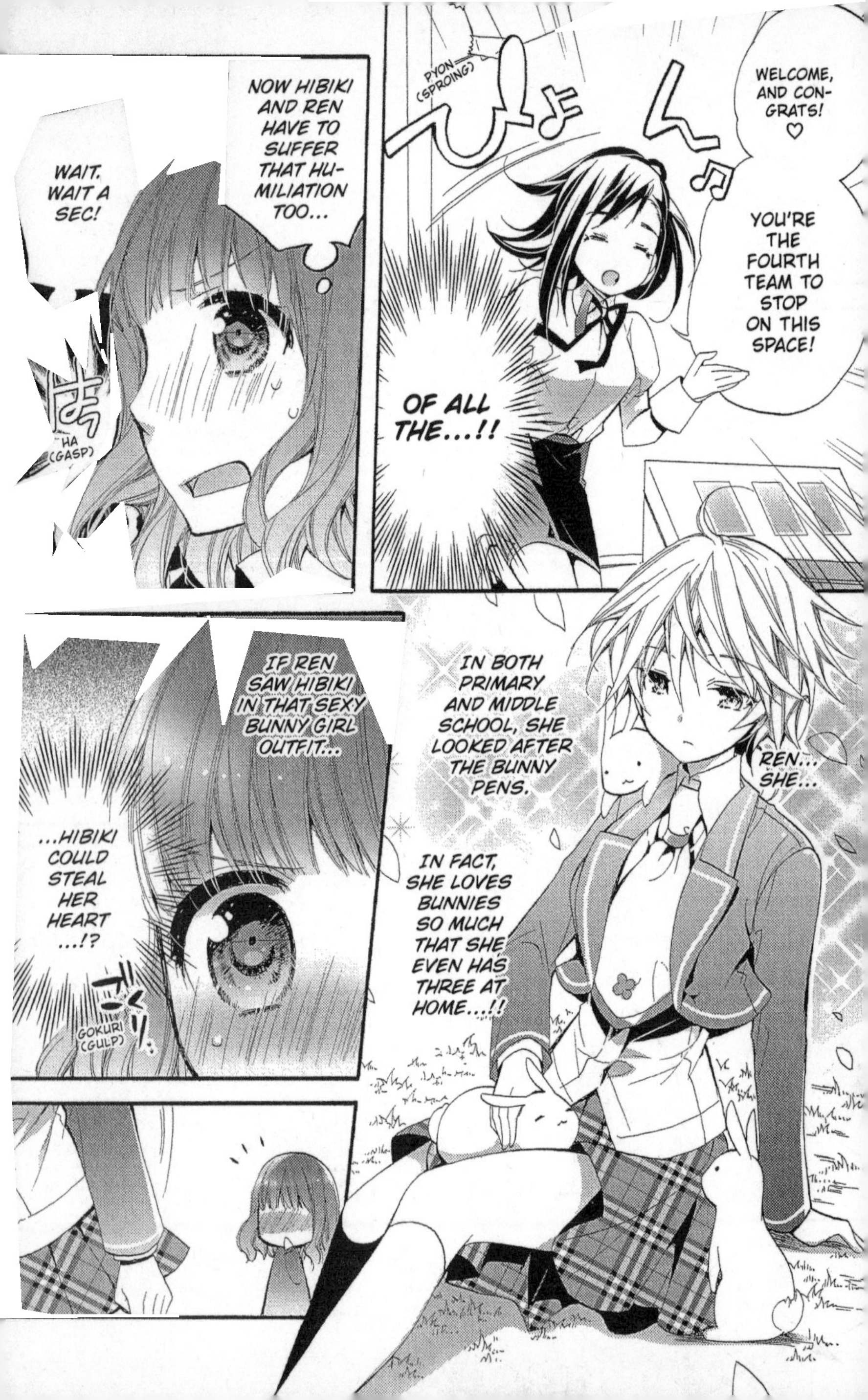
WELCOME, AND CONGRATS! ♡
YOU'RE THE FOURTH TEAM TO STOP ON THIS SPACE!
PYON (SPROING)
OF ALL THE...!!
NOW HIBIKI AND REN HAVE TO SUFFER THAT HUMILIATION TOO...
WAIT. WAIT A SEC!
HA (GASP)
REN... SHE...
IN BOTH PRIMARY AND MIDDLE SCHOOL, SHE LOOKED AFTER THE BUNNY PENS.
IN FACT, SHE LOVES BUNNIES SO MUCH THAT SHE EVEN HAS THREE AT HOME...!!
IF REN SAW HIBIKI IN THAT SEXY BUNNY GIRL OUTFIT...
...HIBIKI COULD STEAL HER HEART...!?
GOKURI (GULP)

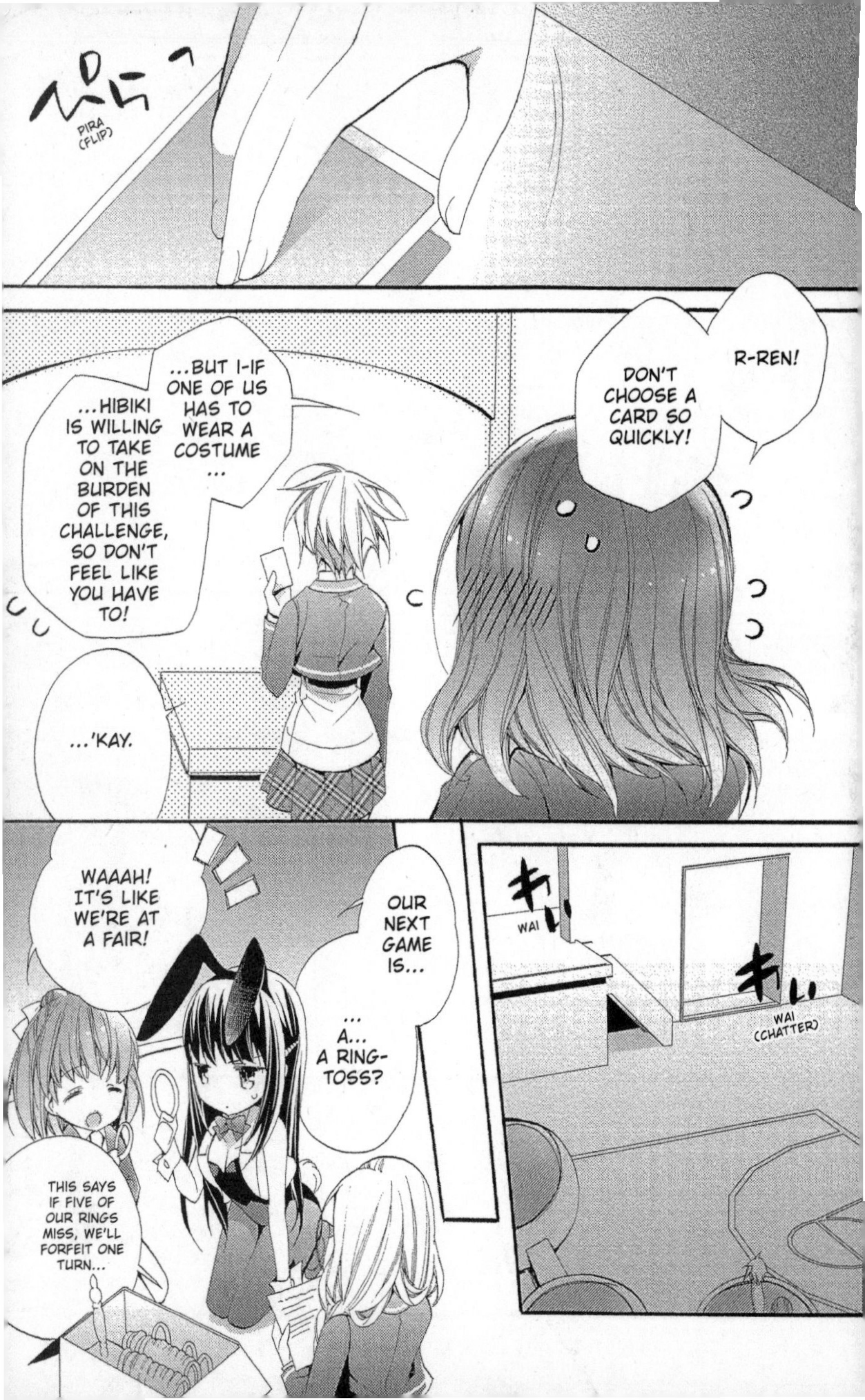
PIRA (FLIP)
R-REN!
DON'T CHOOSE A CARD SO QUICKLY!
...BUT I-IF ONE OF US HAS TO WEAR A COSTUME...
...HIBIKI IS WILLING TO TAKE ON THE BURDEN OF THIS CHALLENGE, SO DON'T FEEL LIKE YOU HAVE TO!
...'KAY.
WAI
WAI (CHATTER)
OUR NEXT GAME IS...
...A... A RING-TOSS?
WAAAH! IT'S LIKE WE'RE AT A FAIR!
THIS SAYS IF FIVE OF OUR RINGS MISS, WE'LL FORFEIT ONE TURN...

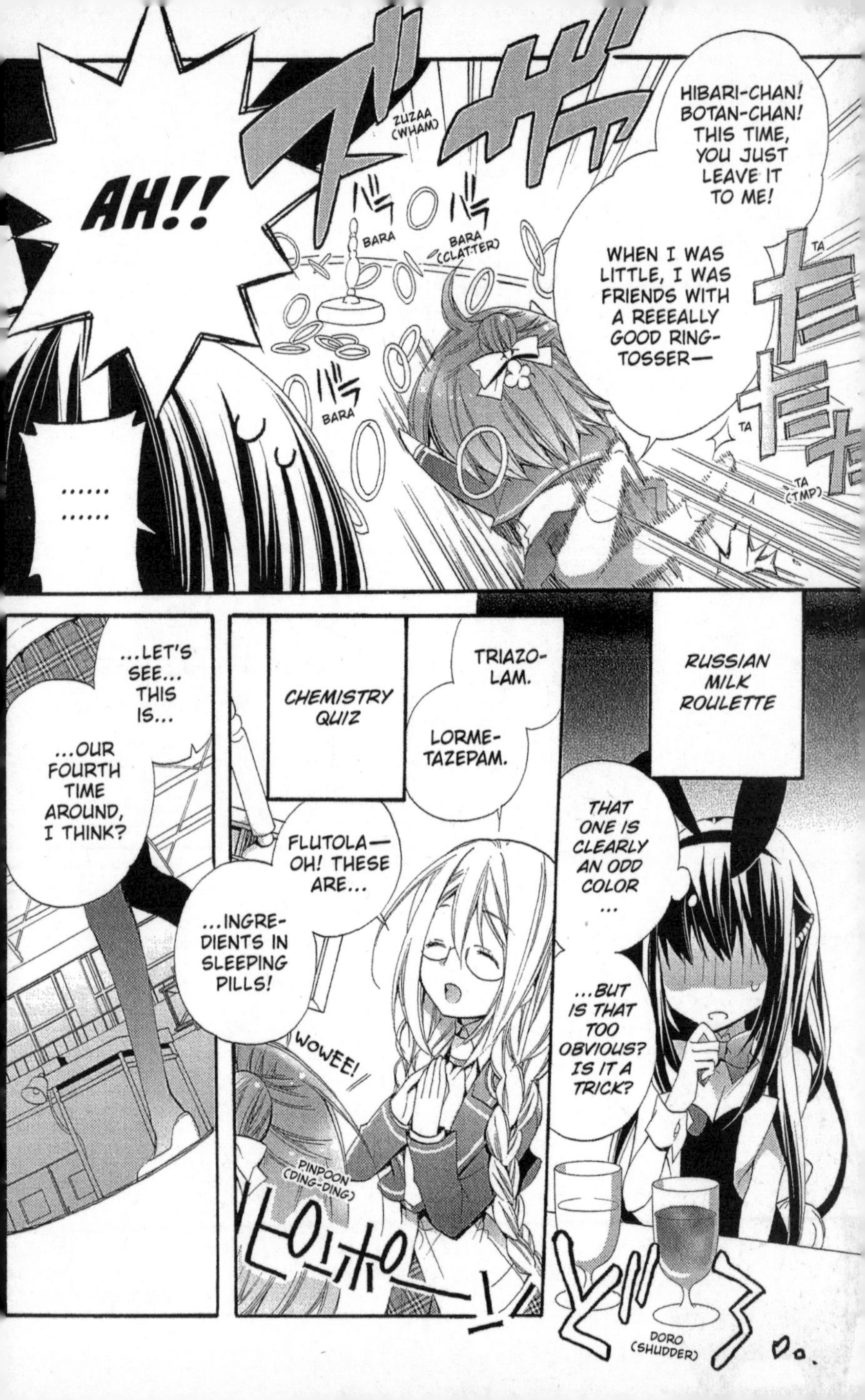
HIBARI-CHAN! BOTAN-CHAN! THIS TIME, YOU JUST LEAVE IT TO ME!
WHEN I WAS LITTLE, I WAS FRIENDS WITH A REEEALLY GOOD RING-TOSSER—
TA
TA
TA (TMP)
ZUZAA (WHAM)
BARA
BARA (CLATTER)
BARA
AH!!
......
......
RUSSIAN MILK ROULETTE
THAT ONE IS CLEARLY AN ODD COLOR...
...BUT IS THAT TOO OBVIOUS? IS IT A TRICK?
DORO (SHUDDER)
CHEMISTRY QUIZ
TRIAZO-LAM.
LORME-TAZEPAM.
FLUTOLA— OH! THESE ARE...
...INGREDIENTS IN SLEEPING PILLS!
WOWEE!
PINPOON (DING-DING)
...LET'S SEE... THIS IS...
...OUR FOURTH TIME AROUND, I THINK?

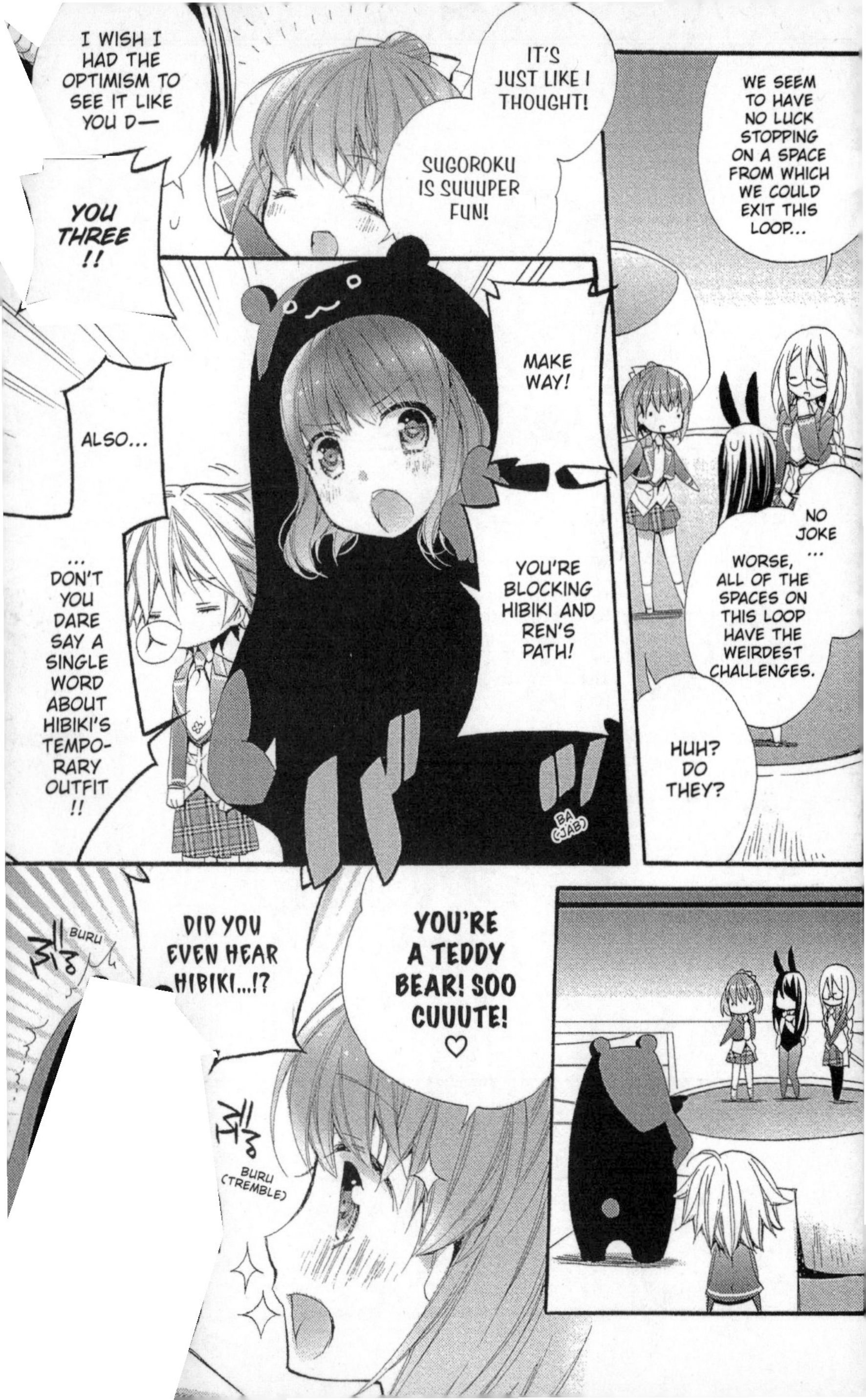

WE SEEM TO HAVE NO LUCK STOPPING ON A SPACE FROM WHICH WE COULD EXIT THIS LOOP...
NO JOKE...
WORSE, ALL OF THE SPACES ON THIS LOOP HAVE THE WEIRDEST CHALLENGES.
HUH? DO THEY?
IT'S JUST LIKE I THOUGHT!
SUGOROKU IS SUUUPER FUN!
I WISH I HAD THE OPTIMISM TO SEE IT LIKE YOU D—
YOU THREE!!
MAKE WAY!
YOU'RE BLOCKING HIBIKI AND REN'S PATH!
BA (JAB)
ALSO...
...DON'T YOU DARE SAY A SINGLE WORD ABOUT HIBIKI'S TEMPORARY OUTFIT!!
YOU'RE A TEDDY BEAR! SOO CUUUTE! ♡
BURU (TREMBLE)
DID YOU EVEN HEAR HIBIKI...!?
BURU

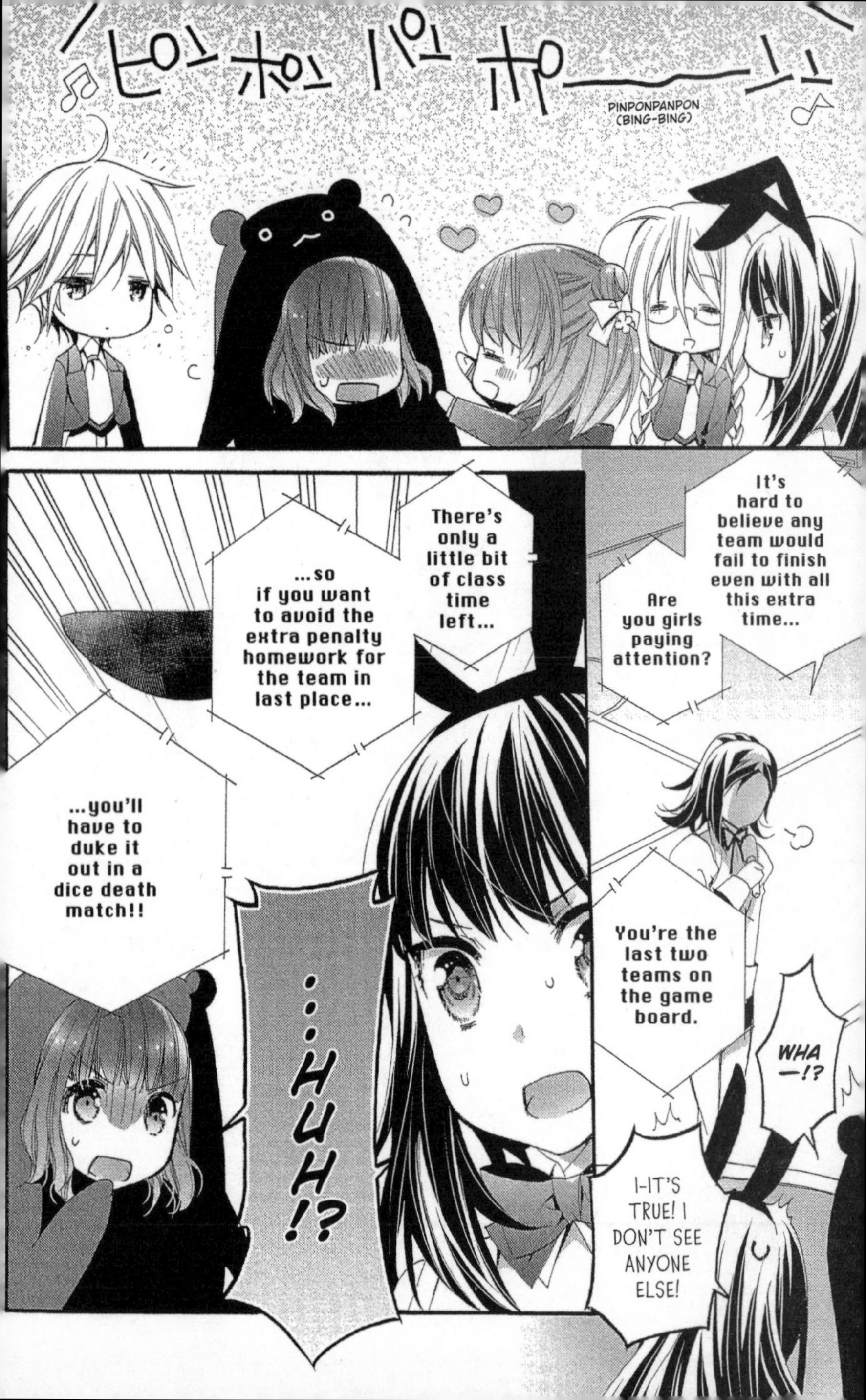
♪ピンポンパンポーーン♪
PINPONPANPON (BING-BING)
It's hard to believe any team would fail to finish even with all this extra time...
Are you girls paying attention?
There's only a little bit of class time left...
...so if you want to avoid the extra penalty homework for the team in last place...
...you'll have to duke it out in a dice death match!!
You're the last two teams on the game board.
WHA—!?
I-IT'S TRUE! I DON'T SEE ANYONE ELSE!
...HUH!?

Anne Happy

unhappy go lucky!

ANNE HANAKOIZUMI

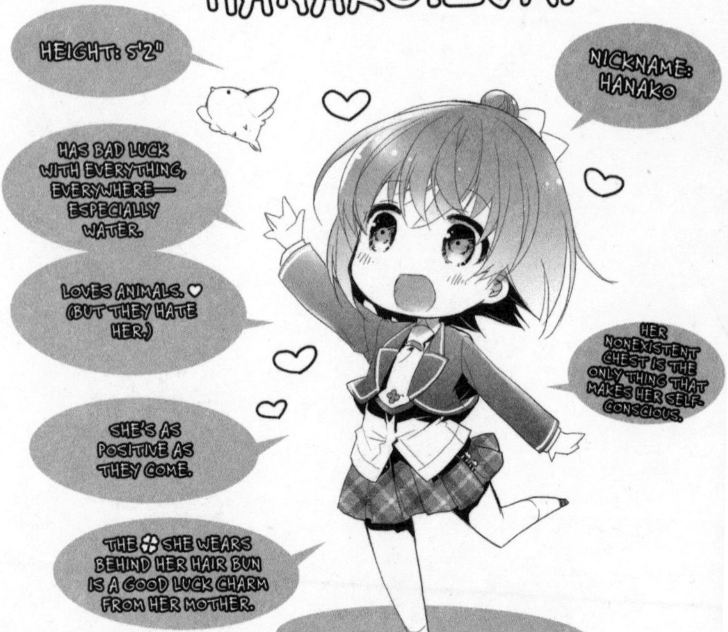
HEIGHT: 5'2"
NICKNAME: HANAKO
HAS BAD LUCK WITH EVERYTHING, EVERYWHERE—ESPECIALLY WATER.
LOVES ANIMALS. ♡ (BUT THEY HATE HER.)
HER NONEXISTENT CHEST IS THE ONLY THING THAT MAKES HER SELF-CONSCIOUS.
SHE'S AS POSITIVE AS THEY COME.
THE 🍀 SHE WEARS BEHIND HER HAIR BUN IS A GOOD LUCK CHARM FROM HER MOTHER.

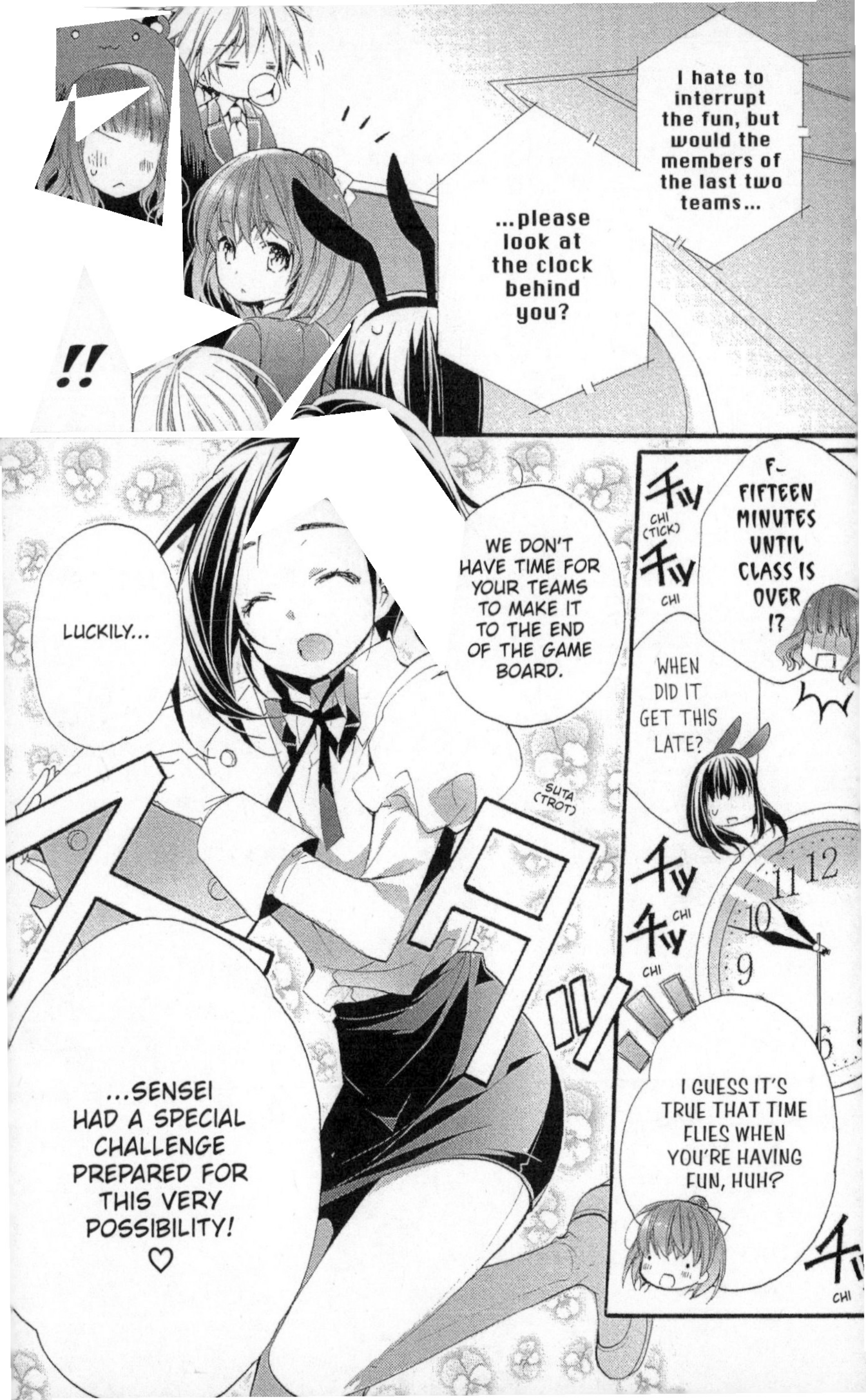
I hate to interrupt the fun, but would the members of the last two teams...
...please look at the clock behind you?
!!
CHI (TICK)
CHI
F- FIFTEEN MINUTES UNTIL CLASS IS OVER !?
WHEN DID IT GET THIS LATE?
CHI
CHI
I GUESS IT'S TRUE THAT TIME FLIES WHEN YOU'RE HAVING FUN, HUH?
CHI
WE DON'T HAVE TIME FOR YOUR TEAMS TO MAKE IT TO THE END OF THE GAME BOARD.
SUTA (TROT)
LUCKILY...
...SENSEI HAD A SPECIAL CHALLENGE PREPARED FOR THIS VERY POSSIBILITY! ♡

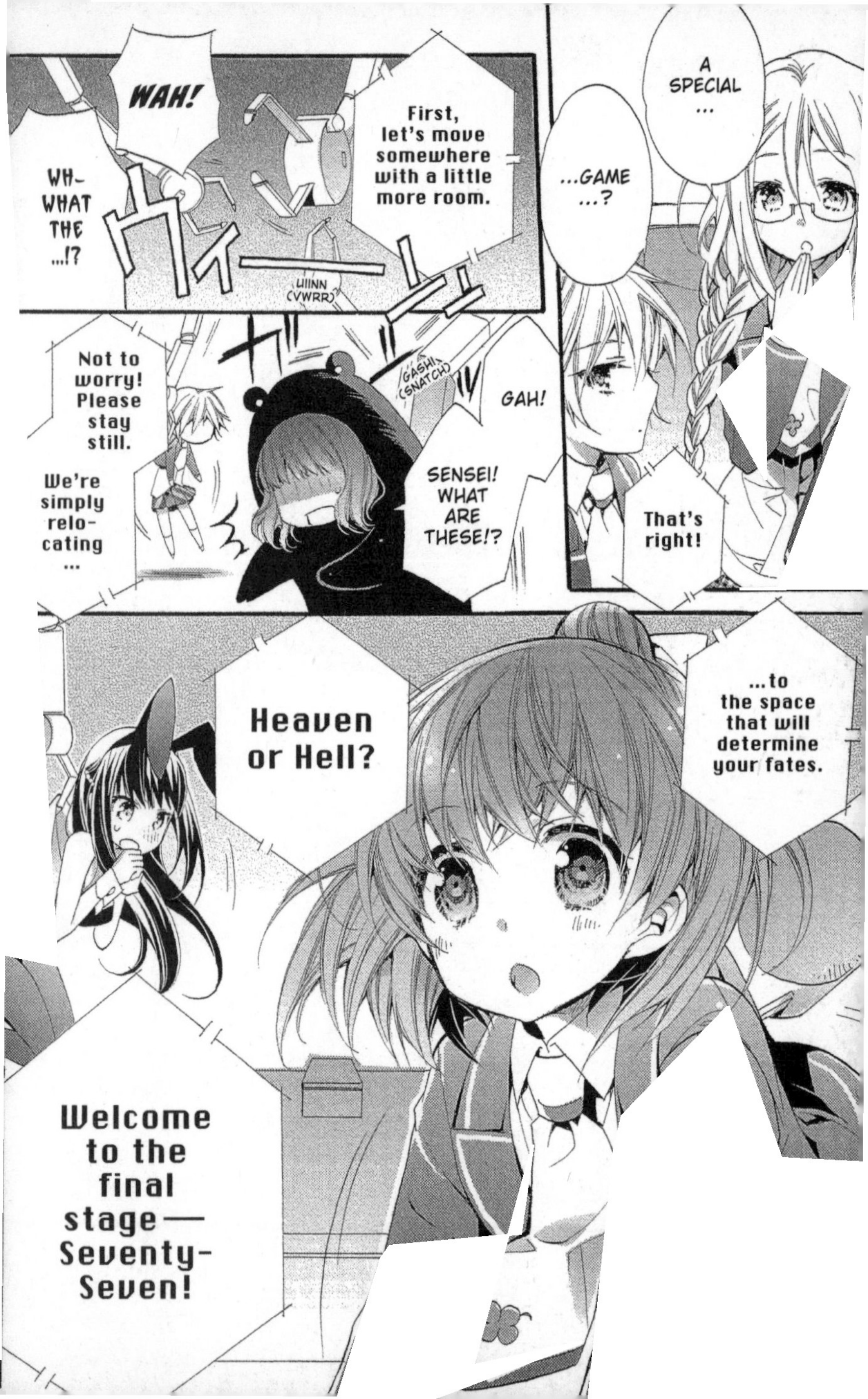
A SPECIAL ...
...GAME ...?
That's right!
First, let's move somewhere with a little more room.
WAH!
WH-WHAT THE ...!?
UIINN (VWRR)
GAH!
SENSEI! WHAT ARE THESE!?
GASHI (SNATCH)
Not to worry! Please stay still.
We're simply relocating ...
...to the space that will determine your fates.
Heaven or Hell?
Welcome to the final stage— Seventy-Seven!

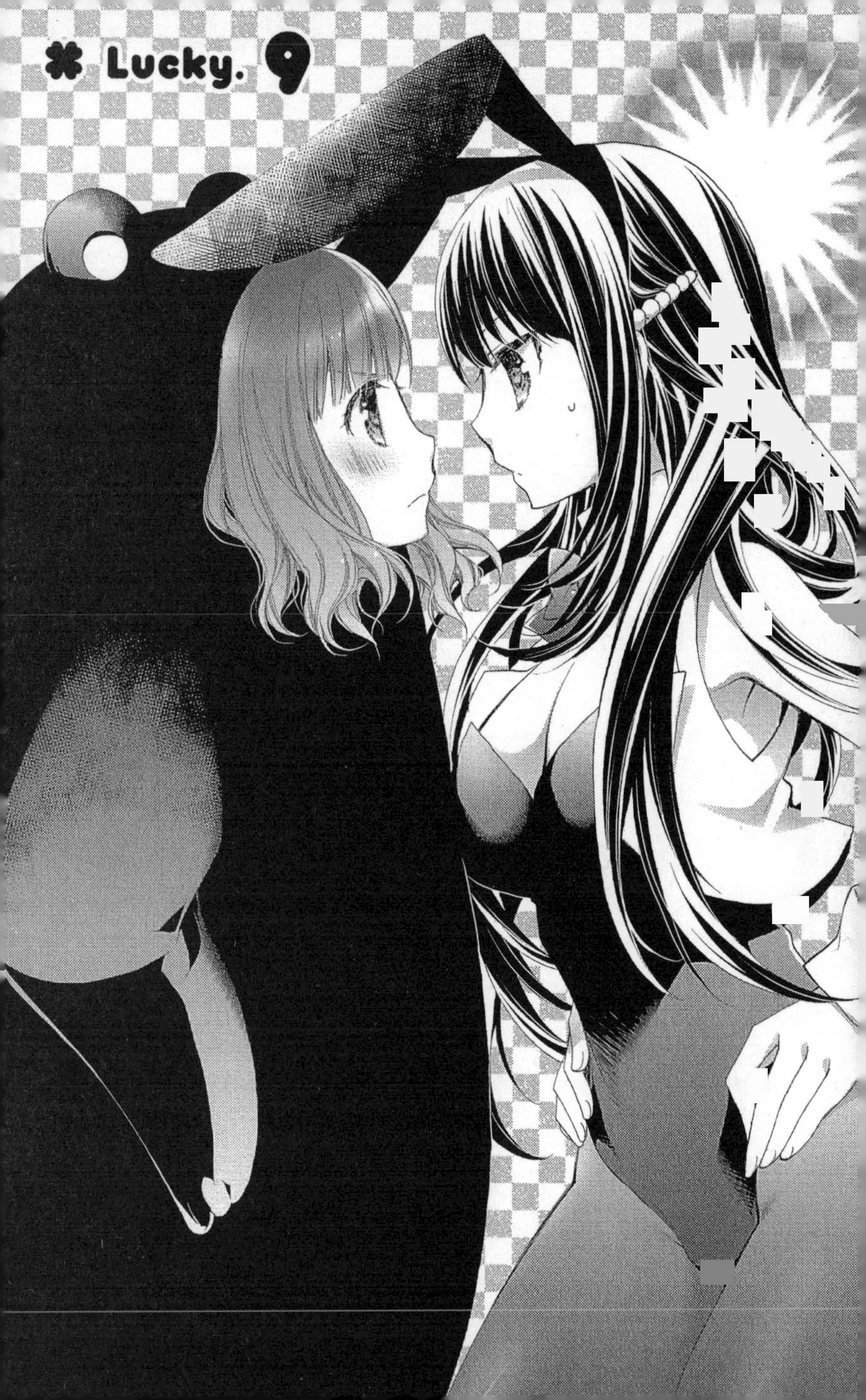
Lucky. 9

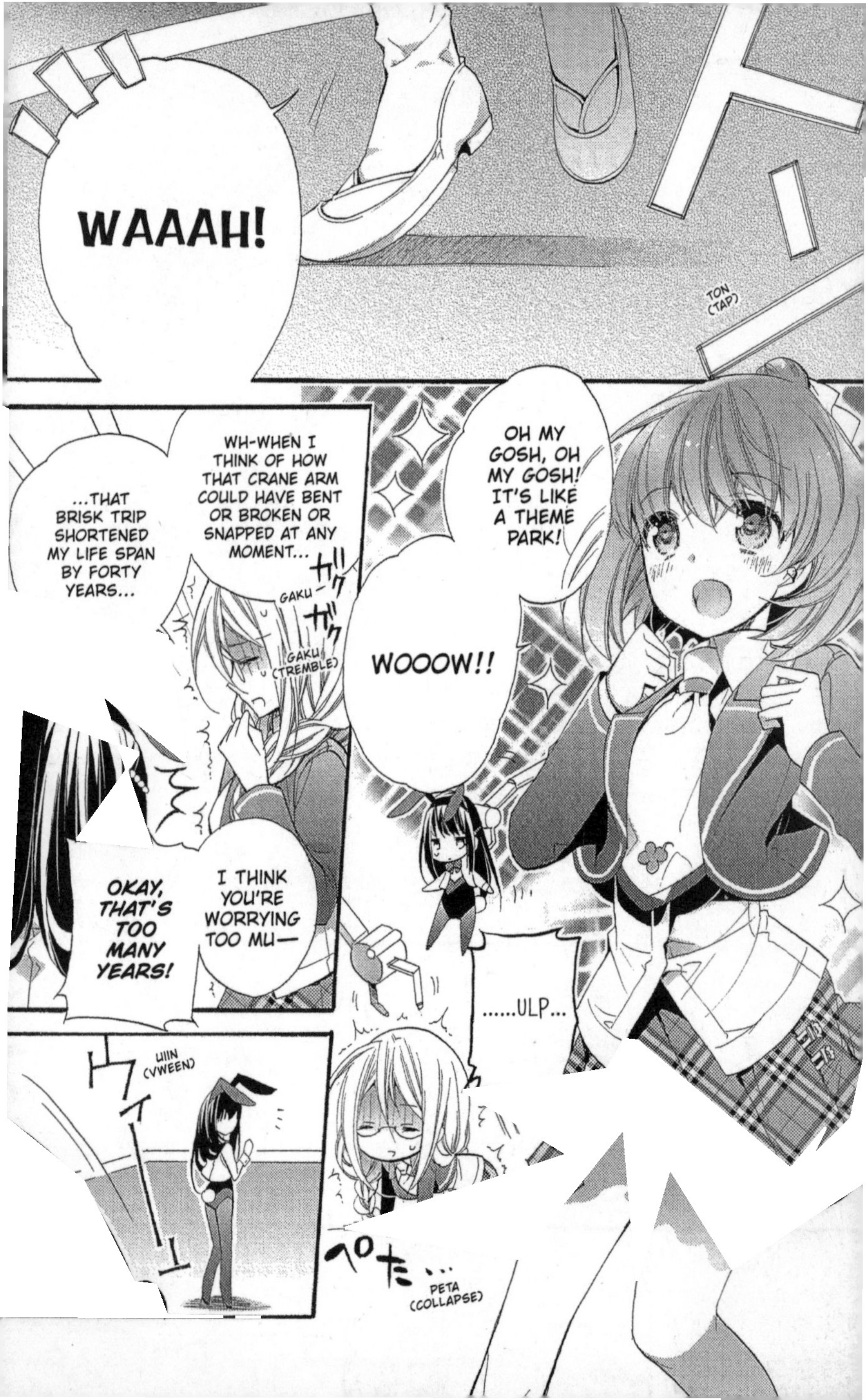
TON (TAP)
WAAAH!
OH MY GOSH, OH MY GOSH! IT'S LIKE A THEME PARK!
WOOOW!!
......ULP...
PETA (COLLAPSE)
WH-WHEN I THINK OF HOW THAT CRANE ARM COULD HAVE BENT OR BROKEN OR SNAPPED AT ANY MOMENT...
...THAT BRISK TRIP SHORTENED MY LIFE SPAN BY FORTY YEARS...
GAKU
GAKU (TREMBLE)
I THINK YOU'RE WORRYING TOO MU—
OKAY, THAT'S TOO MANY YEARS!
UIIN (VWEEN)

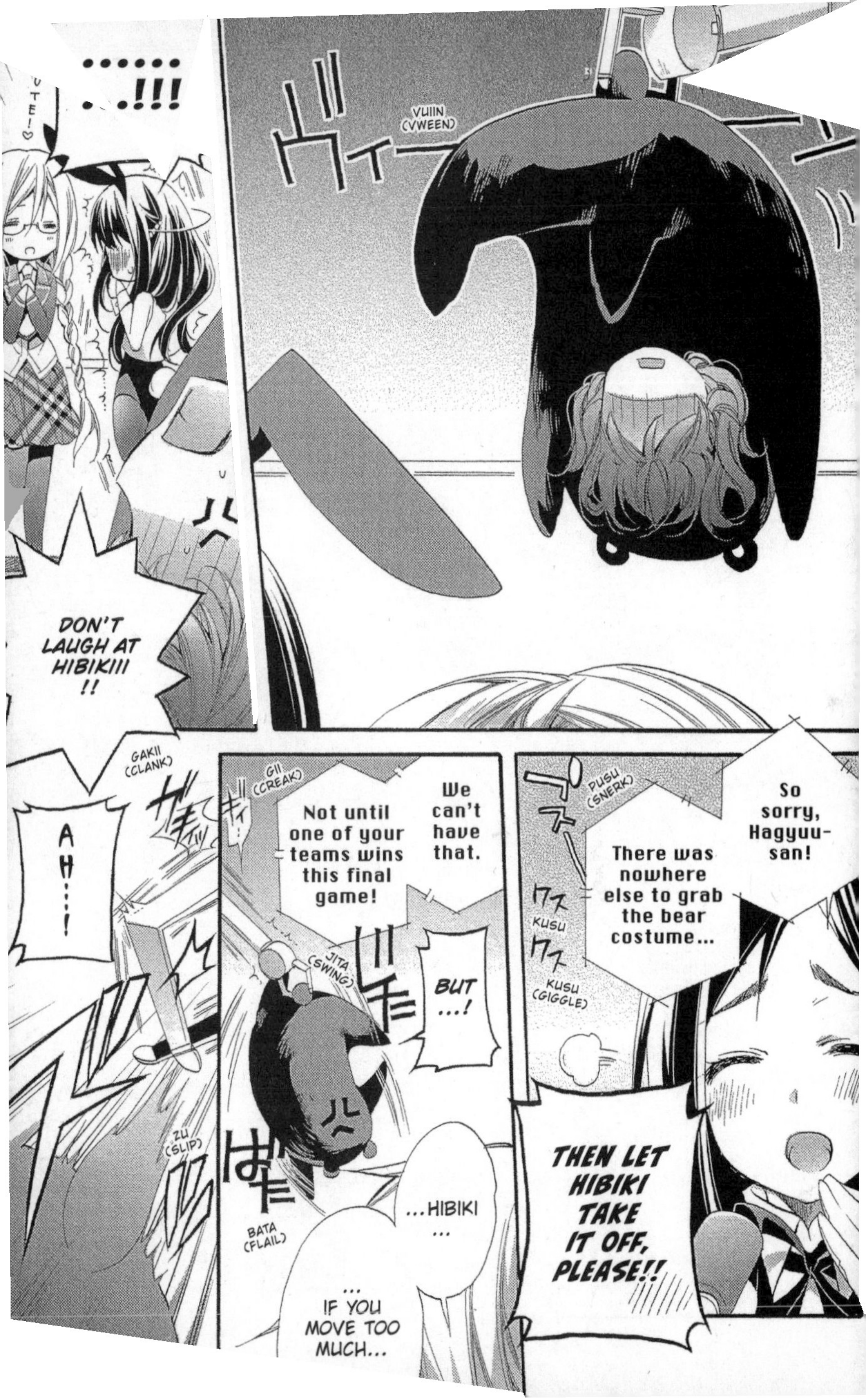
VUIIN (VWEEN)
......
...!!!
DON'T LAUGH AT HIBIKIII !!
So sorry, Hagyuu-san!
There was nowhere else to grab the bear costume...
PUSU (SNERK)
KUSU KUSU (GIGGLE)
THEN LET HIBIKI TAKE IT OFF, PLEASE!!
We can't have that.
Not until one of your teams wins this final game!
GII (CREAK)
JITA (SWING)
BUT ...!
BATA (FLAIL)
...HIBIKI ...
... IF YOU MOVE TOO MUCH...
GAKII (CLANK)
AH...!
ZU (SLIP)

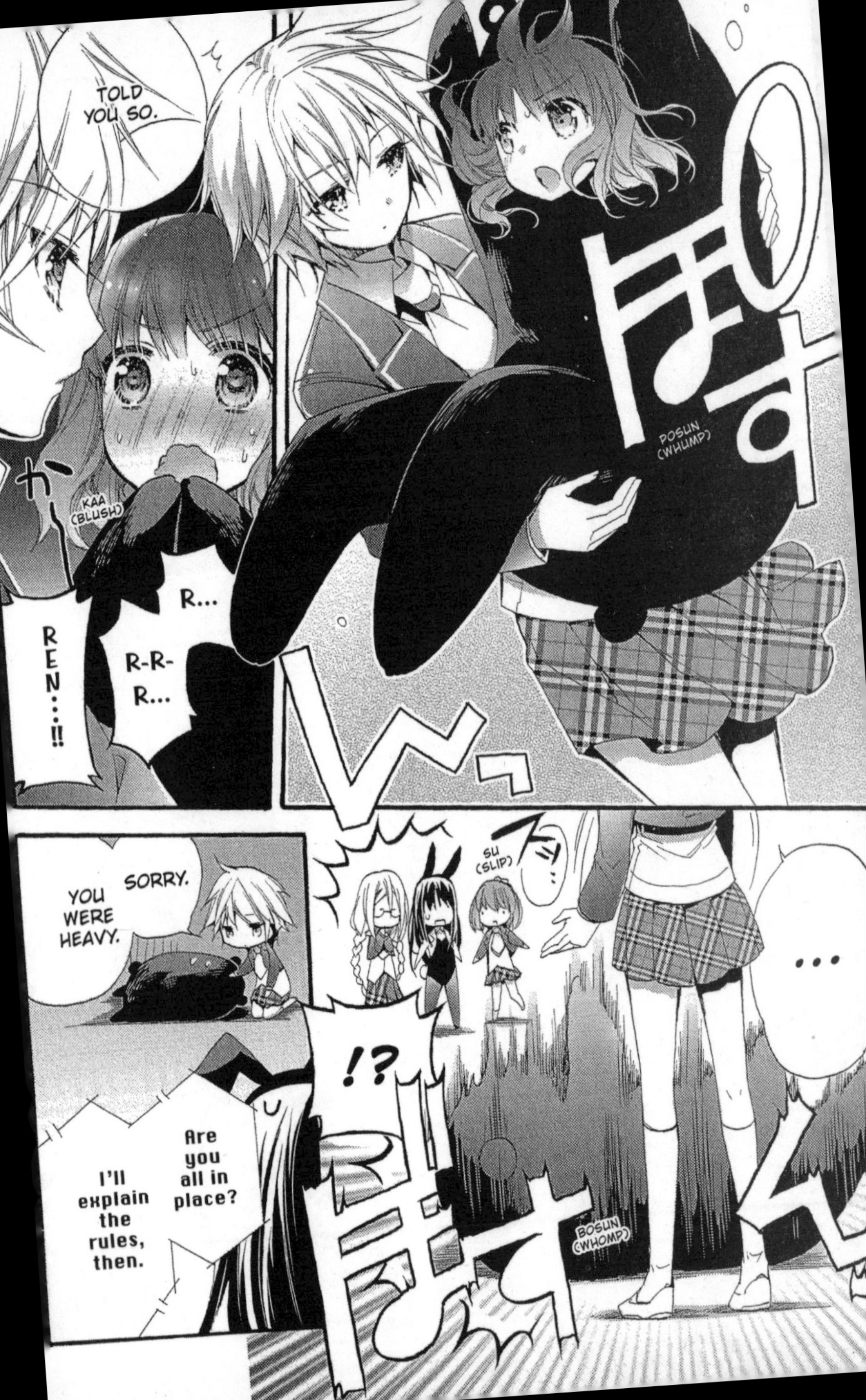
POSUN (WHUMP)
TOLD YOU SO.
KAA (BLUSH)
R...
R-R-R...
REN...!!
...
SU (SLIP)
!?
BOSUN (WHOMP)
SORRY.
YOU WERE HEAVY.
Are you all in place?
I'll explain the rules, then.

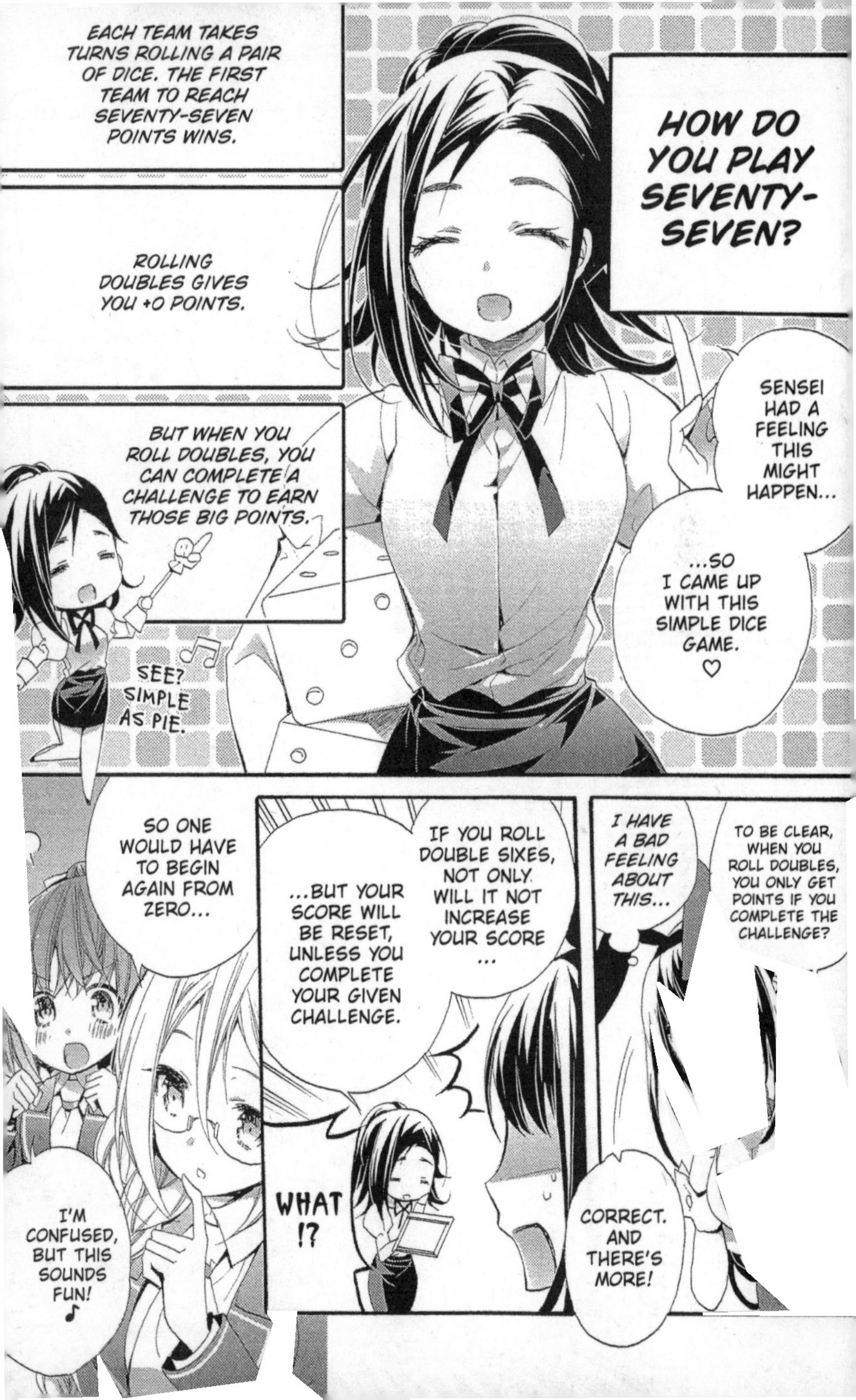
HOW DO YOU PLAY SEVENTY-SEVEN?
SENSEI HAD A FEELING THIS MIGHT HAPPEN...
...SO I CAME UP WITH THIS SIMPLE DICE GAME. ♡
EACH TEAM TAKES TURNS ROLLING A PAIR OF DICE. THE FIRST TEAM TO REACH SEVENTY-SEVEN POINTS WINS.
ROLLING DOUBLES GIVES YOU +0 POINTS.
BUT WHEN YOU ROLL DOUBLES, YOU CAN COMPLETE A CHALLENGE TO EARN THOSE BIG POINTS.
SEE? SIMPLE AS PIE.
TO BE CLEAR, WHEN YOU ROLL DOUBLES, YOU ONLY GET POINTS IF YOU COMPLETE THE CHALLENGE?
I HAVE A BAD FEELING ABOUT THIS...
CORRECT. AND THERE'S MORE!
IF YOU ROLL DOUBLE SIXES, NOT ONLY WILL IT NOT INCREASE YOUR SCORE ...
...BUT YOUR SCORE WILL BE RESET, UNLESS YOU COMPLETE YOUR GIVEN CHALLENGE.
WHAT!?
SO ONE WOULD HAVE TO BEGIN AGAIN FROM ZERO...
I'M CONFUSED, BUT THIS SOUNDS FUN! ♪

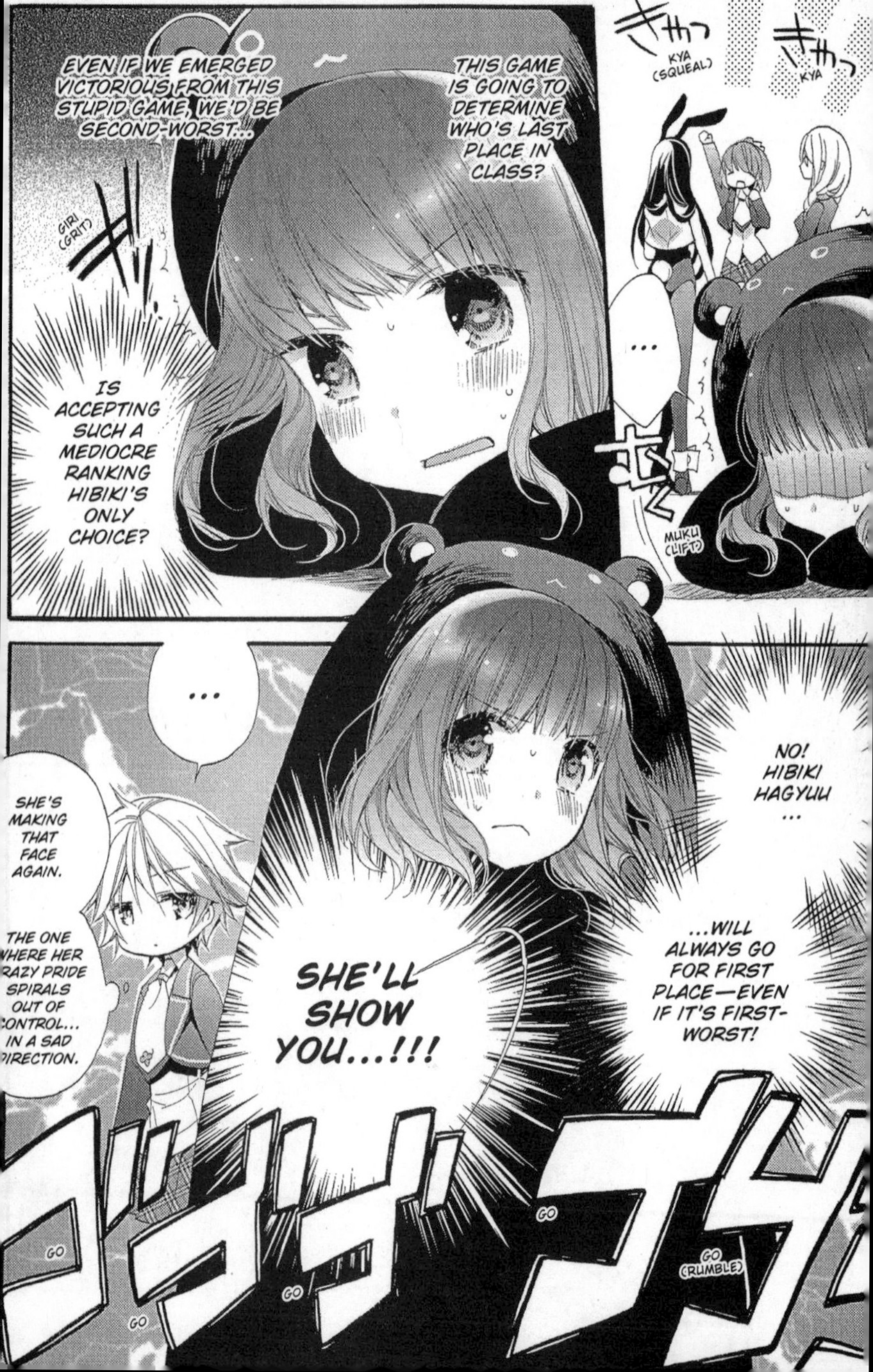

きゃっ
KYA (SQUEAL)
きゃっ
KYA
...
MUKU (LIFT)
THIS GAME IS GOING TO DETERMINE WHO'S LAST PLACE IN CLASS?
EVEN IF WE EMERGED VICTORIOUS FROM THIS STUPID GAME, WE'D BE SECOND-WORST...
GIRI (GRIT)
IS ACCEPTING SUCH A MEDIOCRE RANKING HIBIKI'S ONLY CHOICE?
NO! HIBIKI HAGYUU...
...WILL ALWAYS GO FOR FIRST PLACE—EVEN IF IT'S FIRST-WORST!
SHE'LL SHOW YOU...!!!
...
SHE'S MAKING THAT FACE AGAIN.
THE ONE WHERE HER RAZY PRIDE SPIRALS OUT OF ONTROL... IN A SAD IRECTION.
GO (RUMBLE)
GO
GO
GO
GO

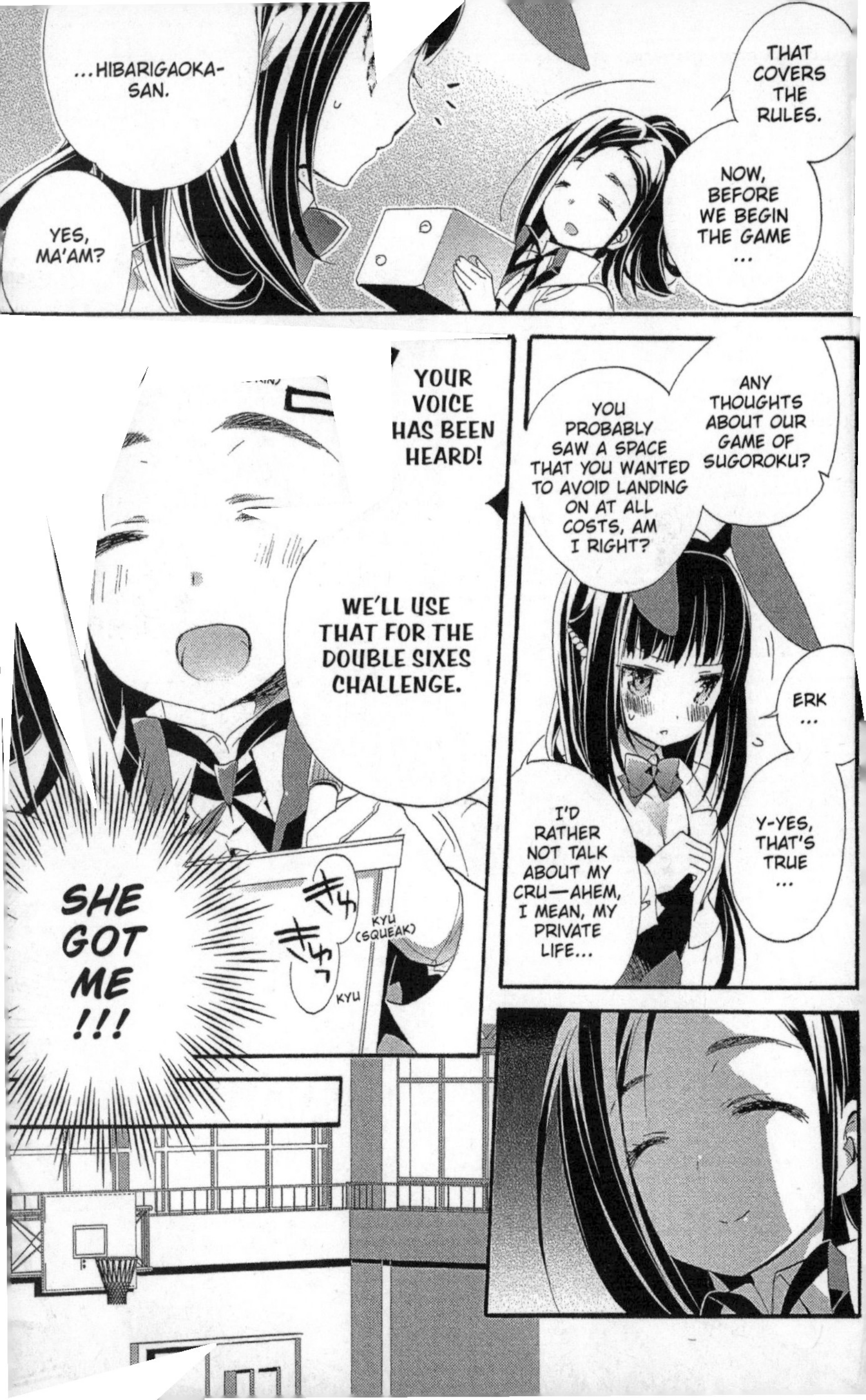
THAT COVERS THE RULES.
NOW, BEFORE WE BEGIN THE GAME ...
...HIBARIGAOKA-SAN.
YES, MA'AM?
ANY THOUGHTS ABOUT OUR GAME OF SUGOROKU?
YOU PROBABLY SAW A SPACE THAT YOU WANTED TO AVOID LANDING ON AT ALL COSTS, AM I RIGHT?
ERK ...
Y-YES, THAT'S TRUE ...
I'D RATHER NOT TALK ABOUT MY CRU—AHEM, I MEAN, MY PRIVATE LIFE...
YOUR VOICE HAS BEEN HEARD!
WE'LL USE THAT FOR THE DOUBLE SIXES CHALLENGE.
きゅ
KYU (SQUEAK)
きゅっ
KYU
SHE GOT ME !!!

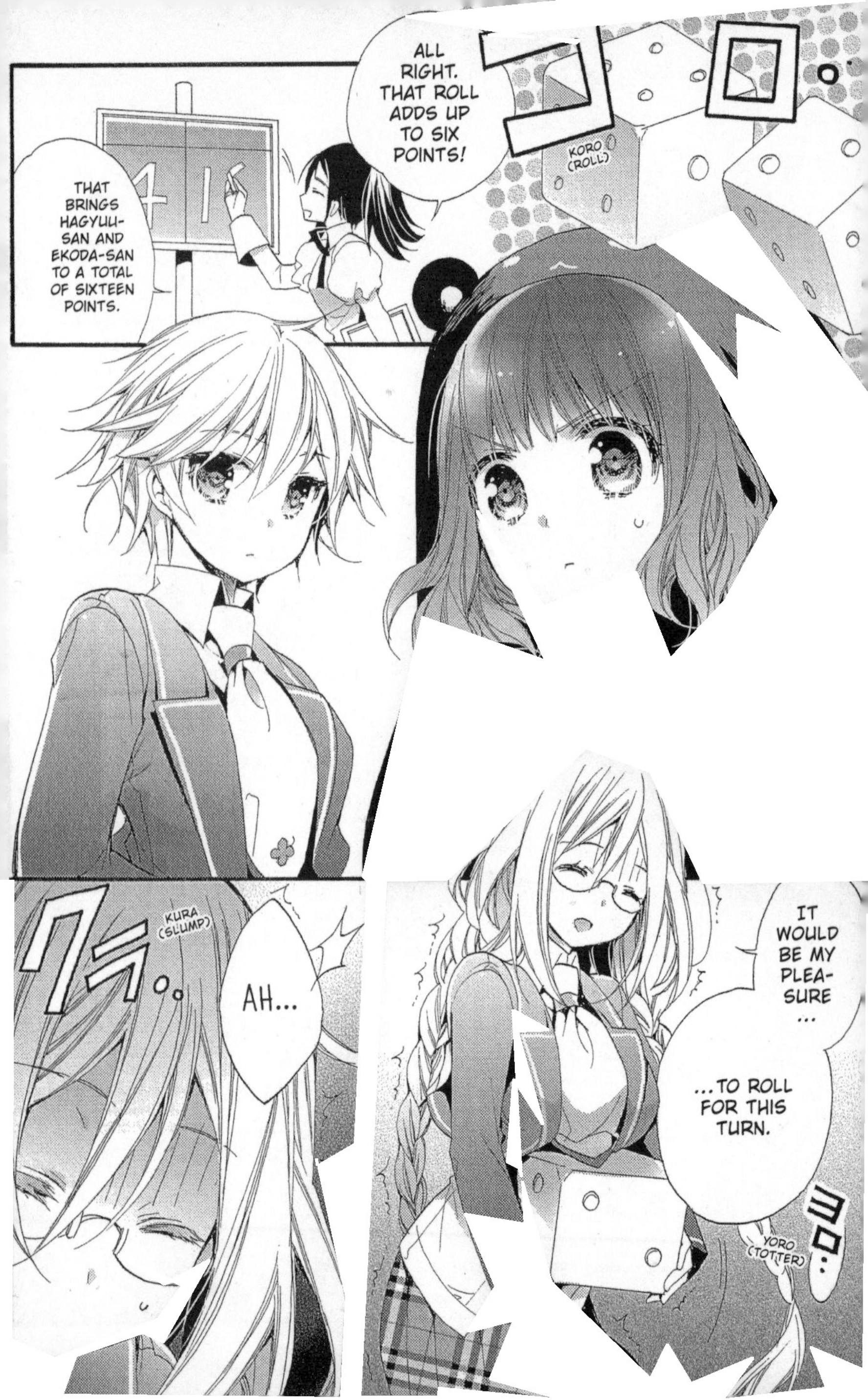
ALL RIGHT. THAT ROLL ADDS UP TO SIX POINTS!
KORO (ROLL)
THAT BRINGS HAGYUU-SAN AND EKODA-SAN TO A TOTAL OF SIXTEEN POINTS.
IT WOULD BE MY PLEASURE...
...TO ROLL FOR THIS TURN.
YORO (TOTTER)
KURA (SLUMP)
AH...

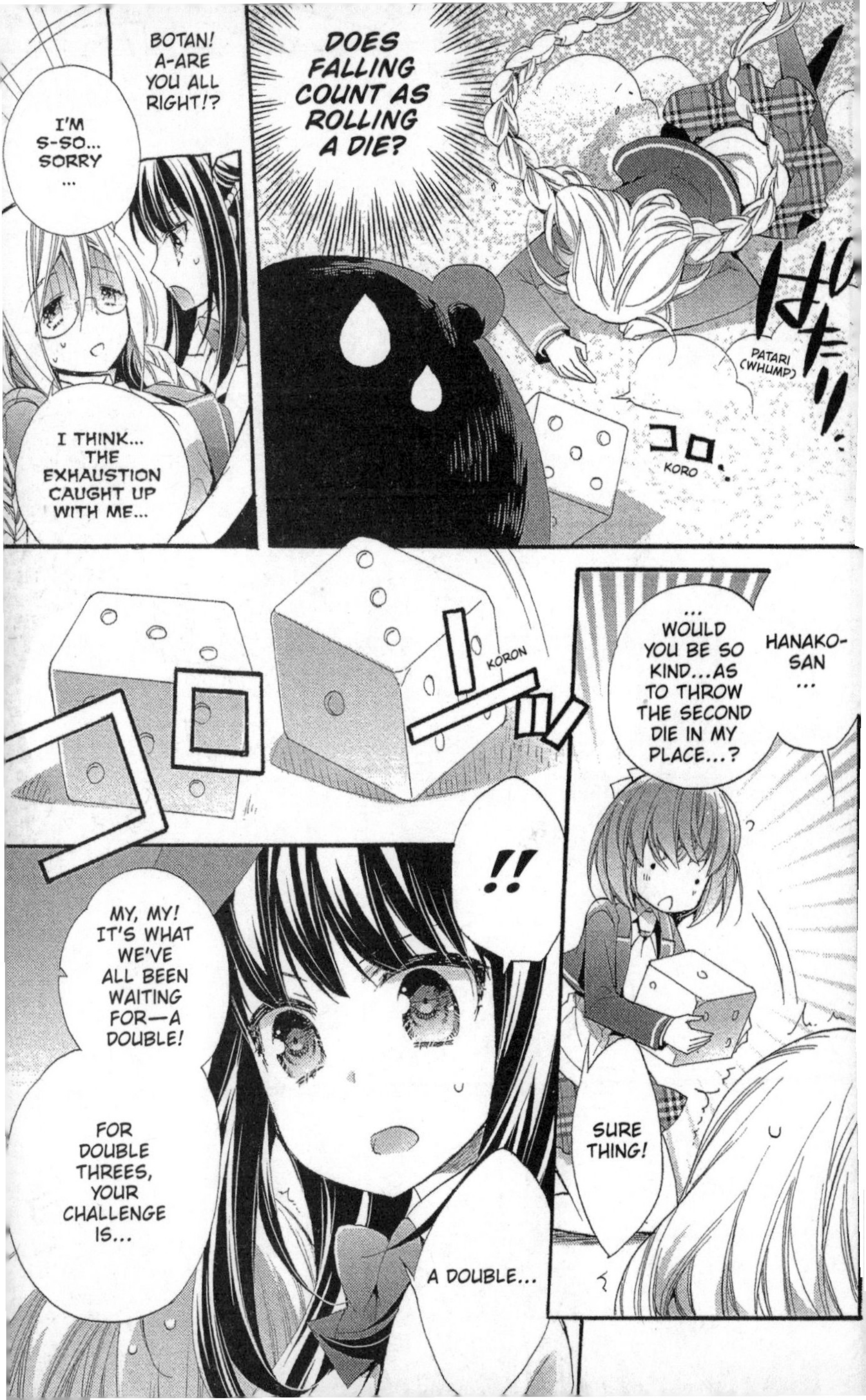
DOES FALLING COUNT AS ROLLING A DIE?
PATARI (WHUMP)
KORO
BOTAN! A-ARE YOU ALL RIGHT!?
I'M S-SO... SORRY...
I THINK... THE EXHAUSTION CAUGHT UP WITH ME...
HANAKO-SAN...
...WOULD YOU BE SO KIND...AS TO THROW THE SECOND DIE IN MY PLACE...?
SURE THING!
KORON
!!
MY, MY! IT'S WHAT WE'VE ALL BEEN WAITING FOR—A DOUBLE!
A DOUBLE...
FOR DOUBLE THREES, YOUR CHALLENGE IS...

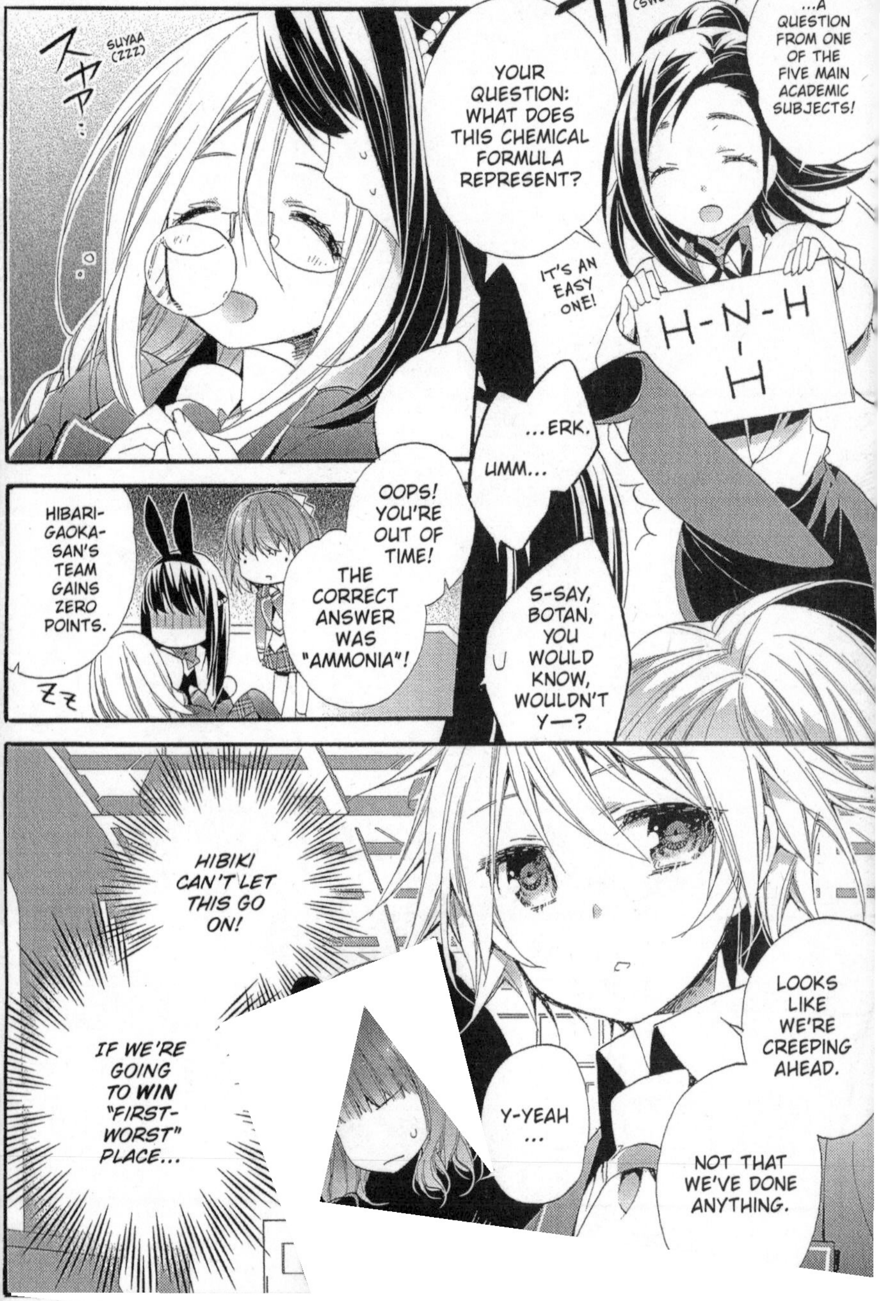
SA (SWOOP)
...A QUESTION FROM ONE OF THE FIVE MAIN ACADEMIC SUBJECTS!
YOUR QUESTION: WHAT DOES THIS CHEMICAL FORMULA REPRESENT?
IT'S AN EASY ONE!
H-N-H
H
...ERK.
UMM...
S-SAY, BOTAN, YOU WOULD KNOW, WOULDN'T Y—?
SUYAA (ZZZ)
OOPS! YOU'RE OUT OF TIME!
THE CORRECT ANSWER WAS "AMMONIA"!
HIBARI-GAOKA-SAN'S TEAM GAINS ZERO POINTS.
LOOKS LIKE WE'RE CREEPING AHEAD.
NOT THAT WE'VE DONE ANYTHING.
Y-YEAH...
HIBIKI CAN'T LET THIS GO ON!
IF WE'RE GOING TO WIN "FIRST-WORST" PLACE...

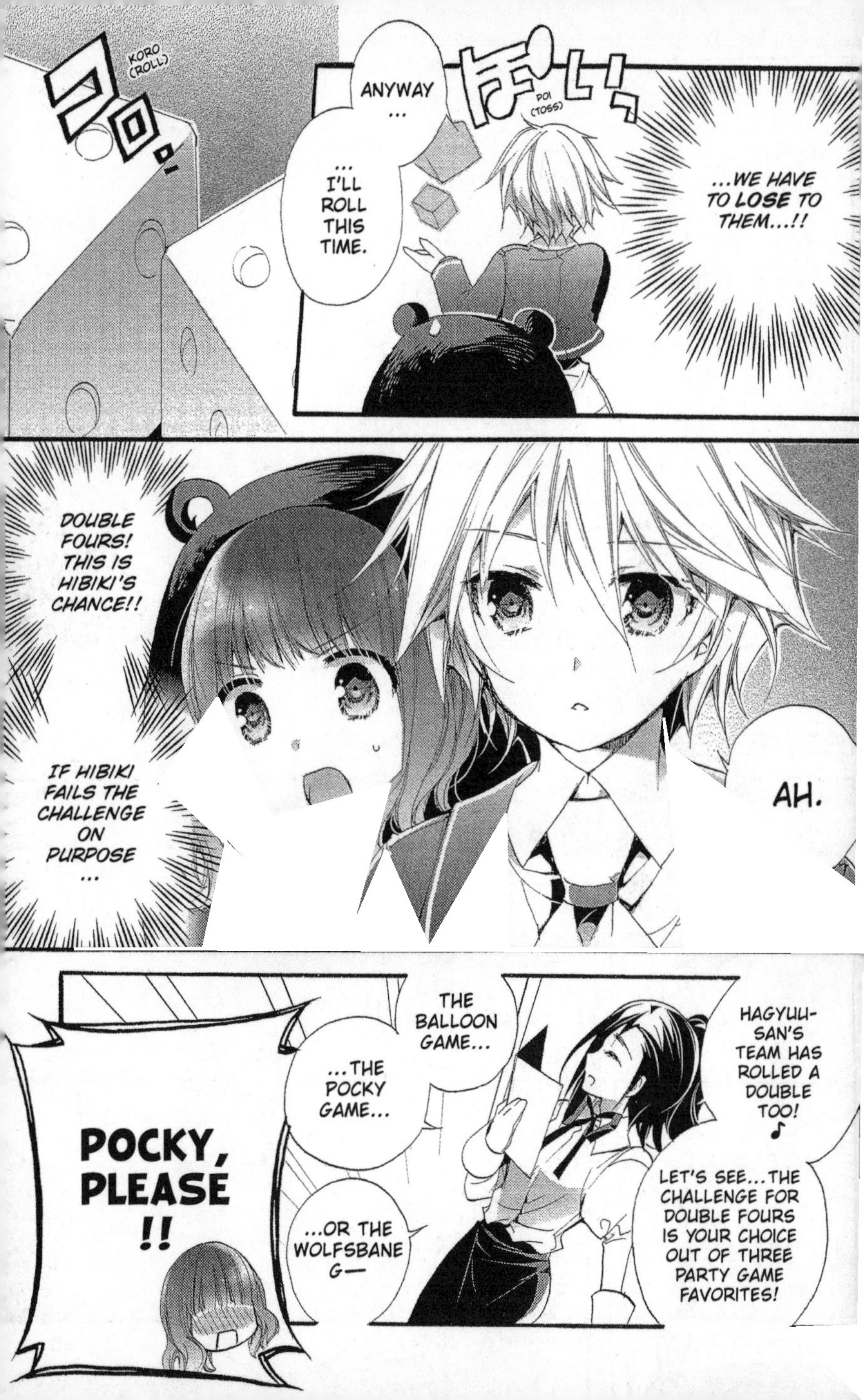
...WE HAVE TO LOSE TO THEM...!!
ANYWAY...
...I'LL ROLL THIS TIME.
POI (TOSS)
KORO (ROLL)
AH.
DOUBLE FOURS! THIS IS HIBIKI'S CHANCE!!
IF HIBIKI FAILS THE CHALLENGE ON PURPOSE...
HAGYUU-SAN'S TEAM HAS ROLLED A DOUBLE TOO! ♪
LET'S SEE...THE CHALLENGE FOR DOUBLE FOURS IS YOUR CHOICE OUT OF THREE PARTY GAME FAVORITES!
THE BALLOON GAME...
...THE POCKY GAME...
...OR THE WOLFSBANE G—
POCKY, PLEASE!!

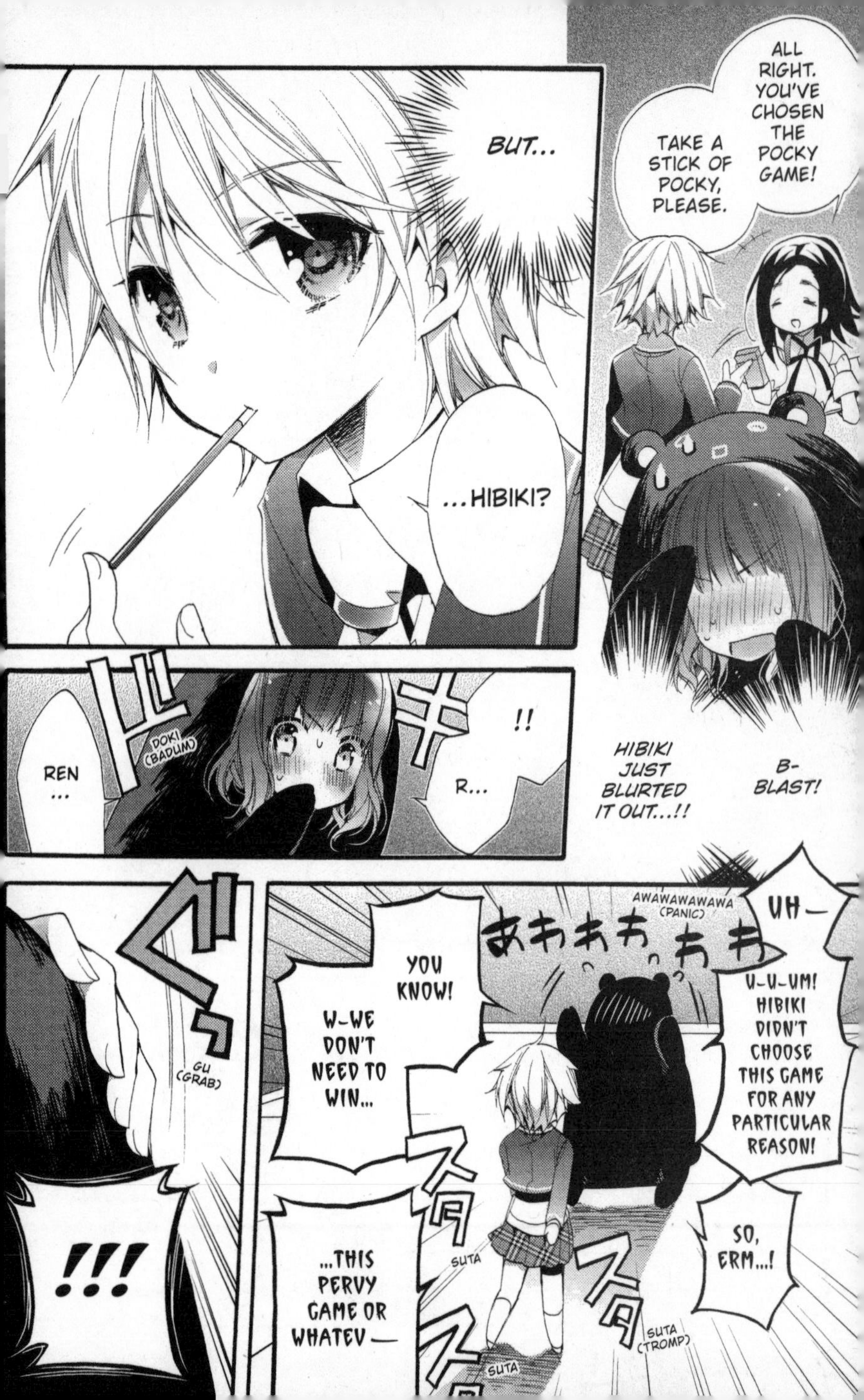

ALL RIGHT. YOU'VE CHOSEN THE POCKY GAME!
TAKE A STICK OF POCKY, PLEASE.
B-BLAST!
HIBIKI JUST BLURTED IT OUT...!!
BUT...
...HIBIKI?
!!
R...
DOKI (BADUM)
REN ...
UH—
AWAWAWAWAWA (PANIC)
U-U-UM! HIBIKI DIDN'T CHOOSE THIS GAME FOR ANY PARTICULAR REASON!
YOU KNOW!
W-WE DON'T NEED TO WIN...
SO, ERM...!
SUTA (TROMP)
SUTA
SUTA
...THIS PERVY GAME OR WHATEV—
GU (GRAB)
!!!

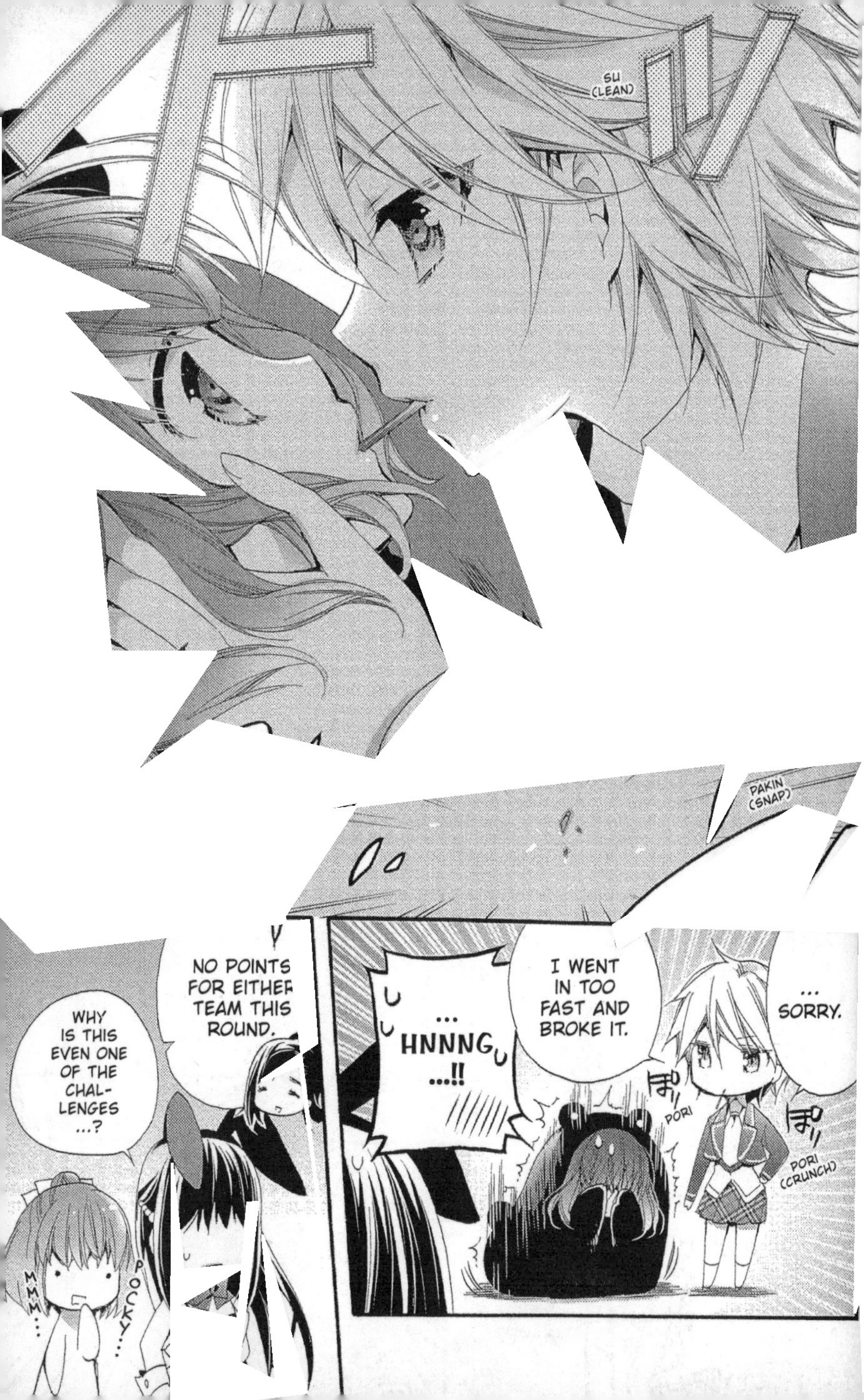
SU (CLEAN)
PAKIN (SNAP)
... SORRY.
I WENT IN TOO FAST AND BROKE IT.
... HNNNG ...!!
ぽり
PORI
ぽり
PORI (CRUNCH)
NO POINTS FOR EITHER TEAM THIS ROUND.
WHY IS THIS EVEN ONE OF THE CHAL-LENGES ...?
POCKY...
M-MM...

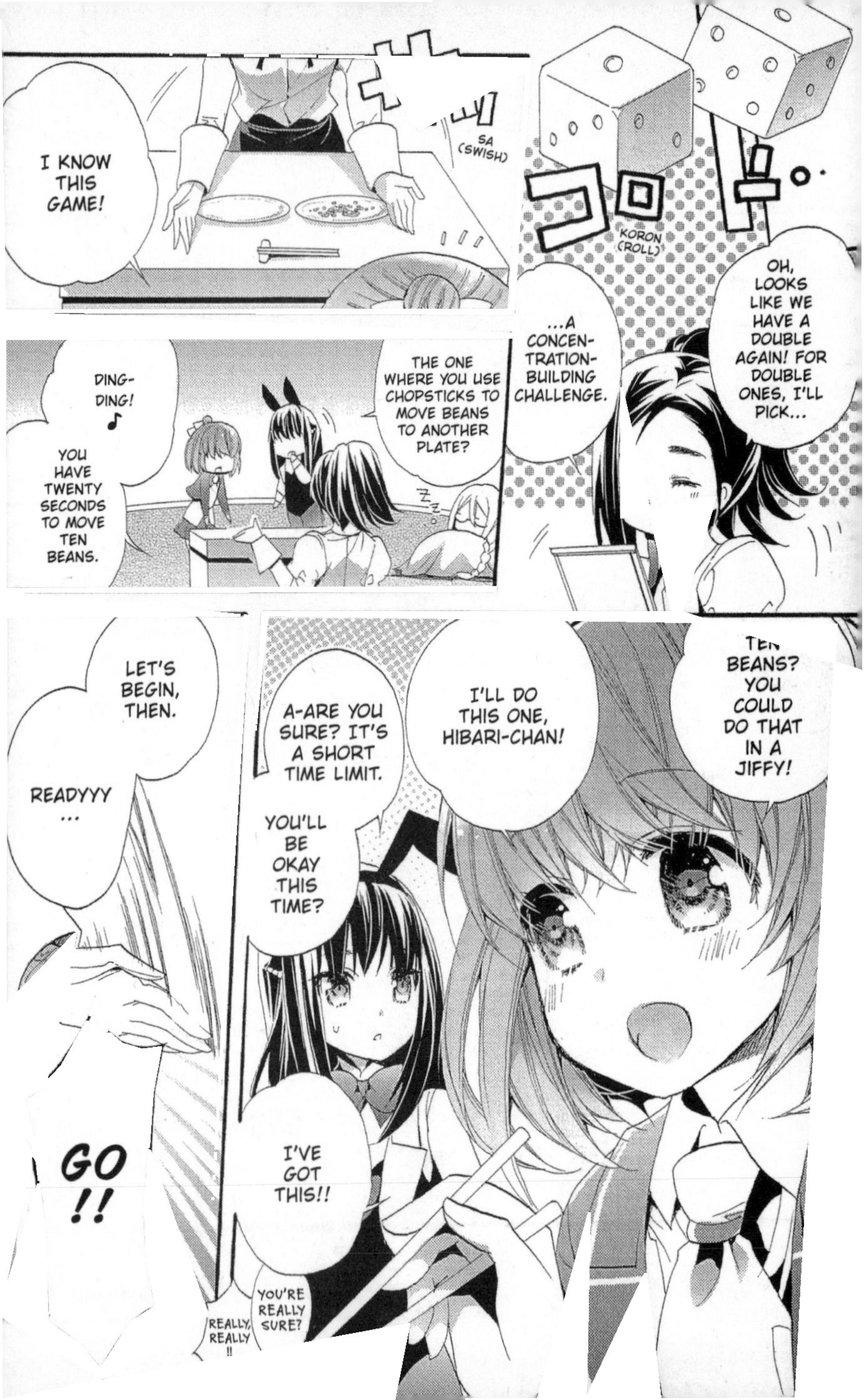
KORON (ROLL)
OH, LOOKS LIKE WE HAVE A DOUBLE AGAIN! FOR DOUBLE ONES, I'LL PICK...
...A CONCEN-TRATION-BUILDING CHALLENGE.
SA (SWISH)
I KNOW THIS GAME!
THE ONE WHERE YOU USE CHOPSTICKS TO MOVE BEANS TO ANOTHER PLATE?
DING-DING! ♪
YOU HAVE TWENTY SECONDS TO MOVE TEN BEANS.
TEN BEANS? YOU COULD DO THAT IN A JIFFY!
I'LL DO THIS ONE, HIBARI-CHAN!
A-ARE YOU SURE? IT'S A SHORT TIME LIMIT.
YOU'LL BE OKAY THIS TIME?
I'VE GOT THIS!!
YOU'RE REALLY SURE?
REALLY, REALLY !!
LET'S BEGIN, THEN.
READYYY...
GO!!

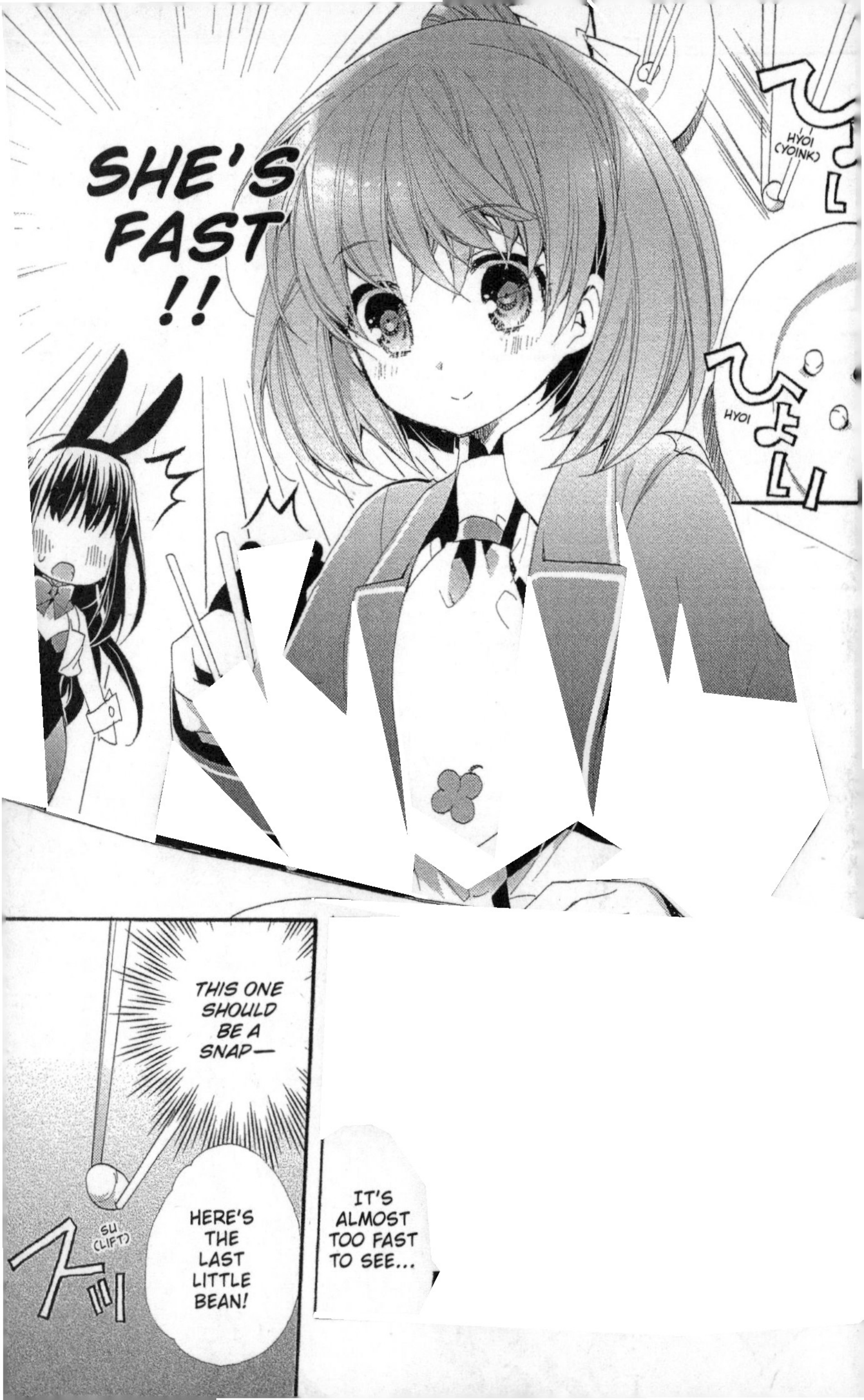
HYOI (YOINK)
HYOI
SHE'S FAST!!
IT'S ALMOST TOO FAST TO SEE...
THIS ONE SHOULD BE A SNAP—
HERE'S THE LAST LITTLE BEAN!
SU (LIFT)

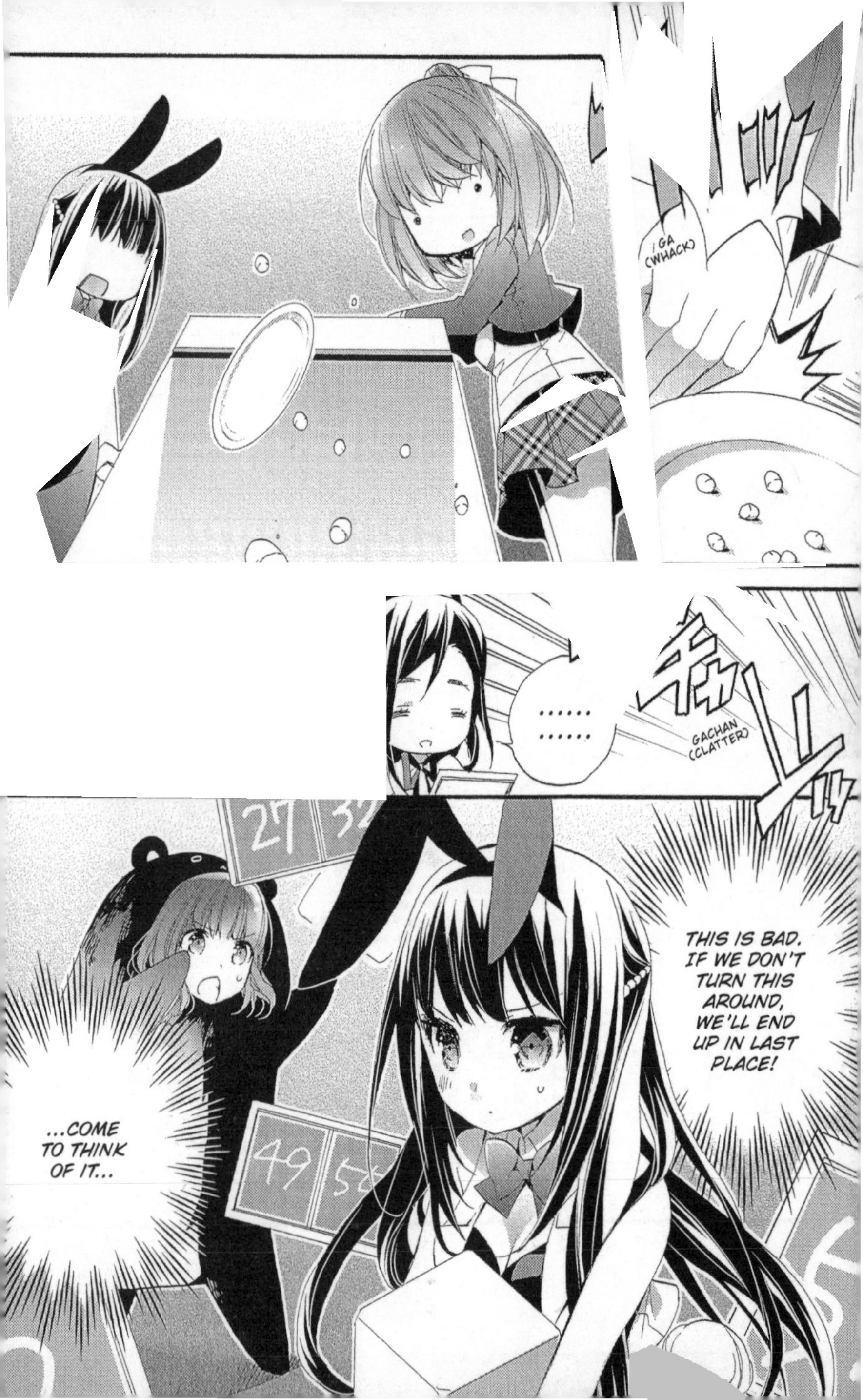
GA (WHACK)
......
......
GACHAN (CLATTER)
THIS IS BAD. IF WE DON'T TURN THIS AROUND, WE'LL END UP IN LAST PLACE!
...COME TO THINK OF IT...

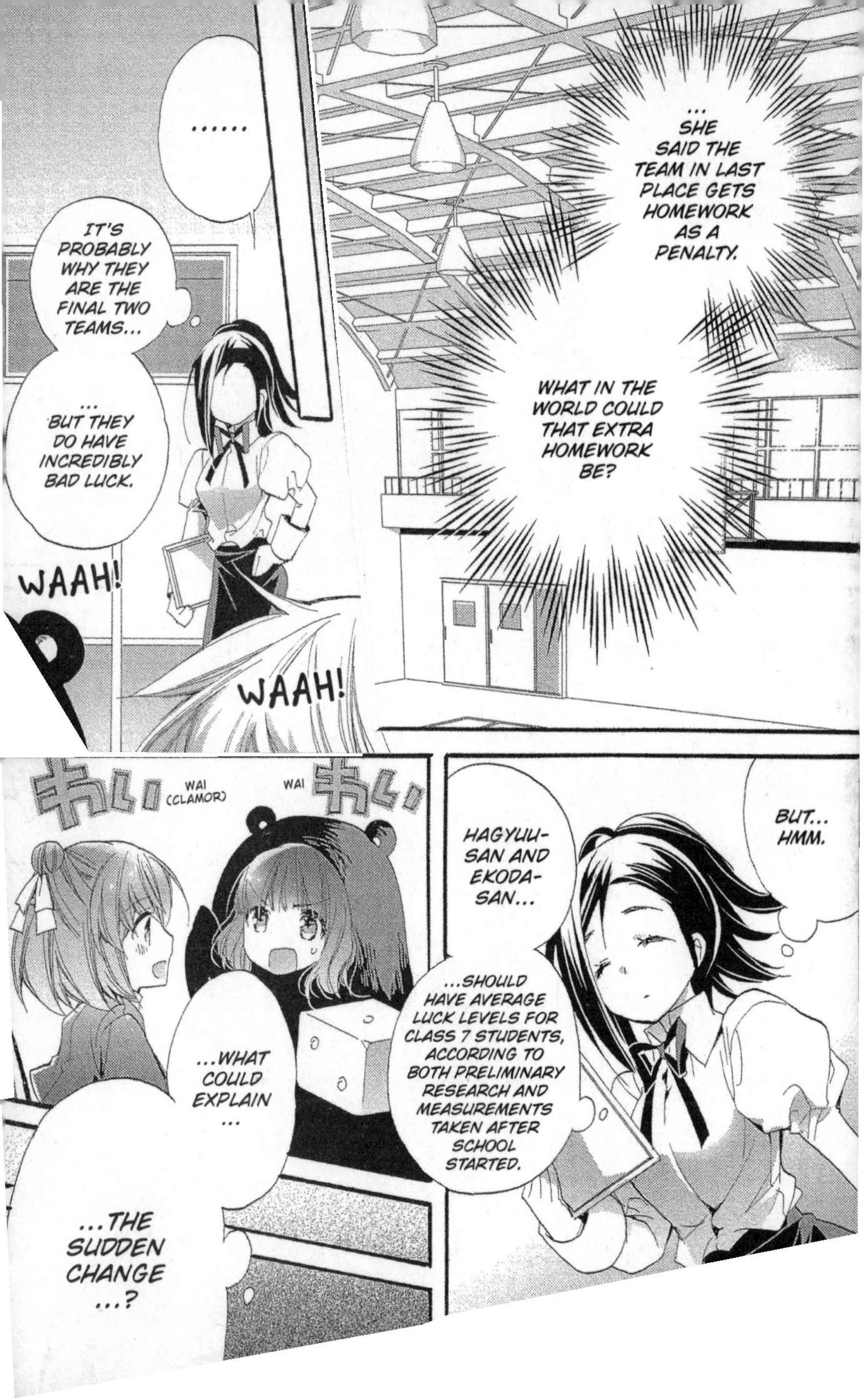
... SHE SAID THE TEAM IN LAST PLACE GETS HOMEWORK AS A PENALTY.
WHAT IN THE WORLD COULD THAT EXTRA HOMEWORK BE?
......
IT'S PROBABLY WHY THEY ARE THE FINAL TWO TEAMS...
... BUT THEY DO HAVE INCREDIBLY BAD LUCK.
WAAH!
WAAH!
BUT... HMM.
HAGYUU-SAN AND EKODA-SAN...
...SHOULD HAVE AVERAGE LUCK LEVELS FOR CLASS 7 STUDENTS, ACCORDING TO BOTH PRELIMINARY RESEARCH AND MEASUREMENTS TAKEN AFTER SCHOOL STARTED.
WAI
WAI (CLAMOR)
...WHAT COULD EXPLAIN ...
...THE SUDDEN CHANGE ...?

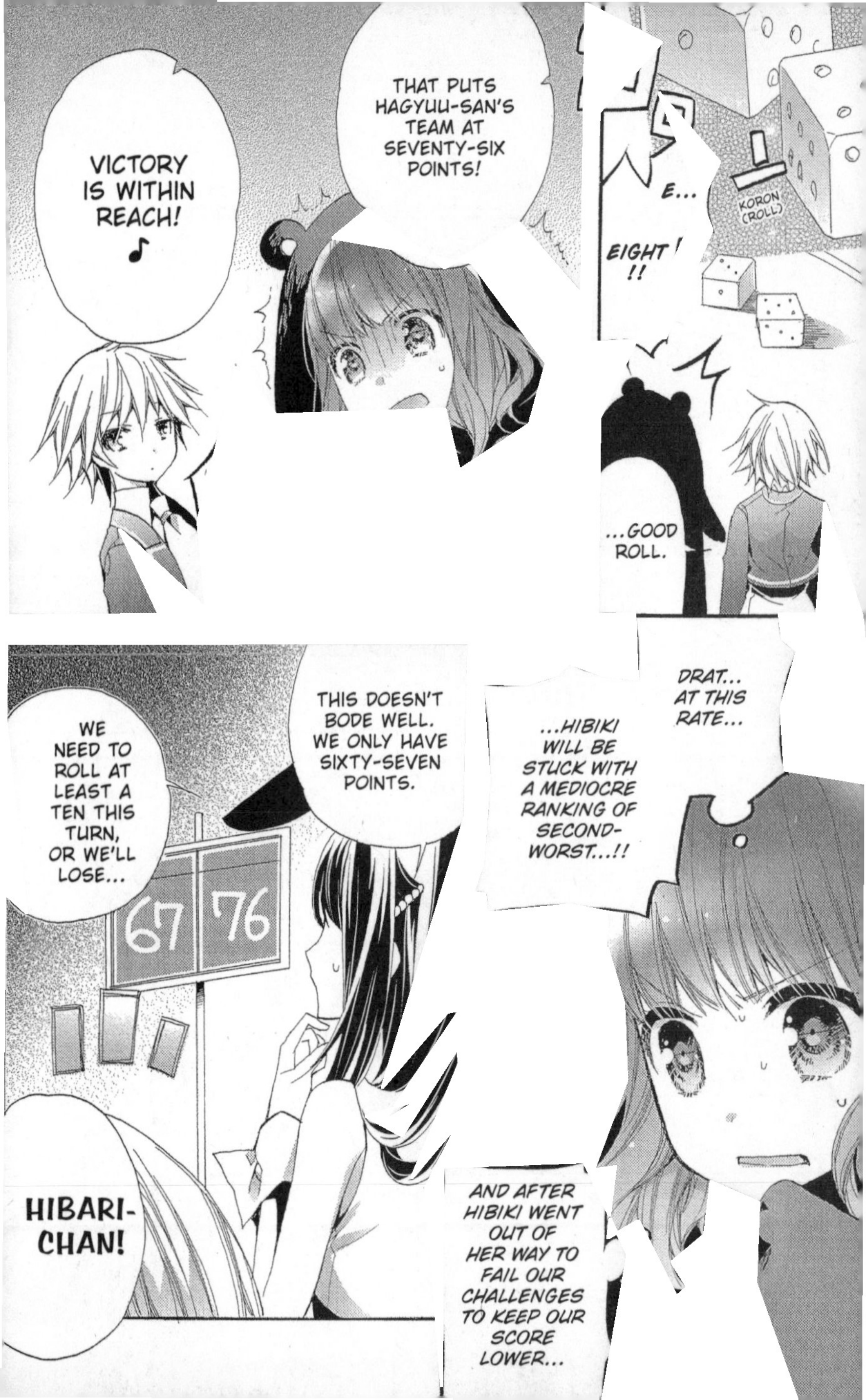
E...
EIGHT!!
KORON (ROLL)
...GOOD ROLL.
THAT PUTS HAGYUU-SAN'S TEAM AT SEVENTY-SIX POINTS!
VICTORY IS WITHIN REACH! ♪
DRAT... AT THIS RATE...
...HIBIKI WILL BE STUCK WITH A MEDIOCRE RANKING OF SECOND-WORST...!!
AND AFTER HIBIKI WENT OUT OF HER WAY TO FAIL OUR CHALLENGES TO KEEP OUR SCORE LOWER...
THIS DOESN'T BODE WELL. WE ONLY HAVE SIXTY-SEVEN POINTS.
WE NEED TO ROLL AT LEAST A TEN THIS TURN, OR WE'LL LOSE...
67
76
HIBARI-CHAN!

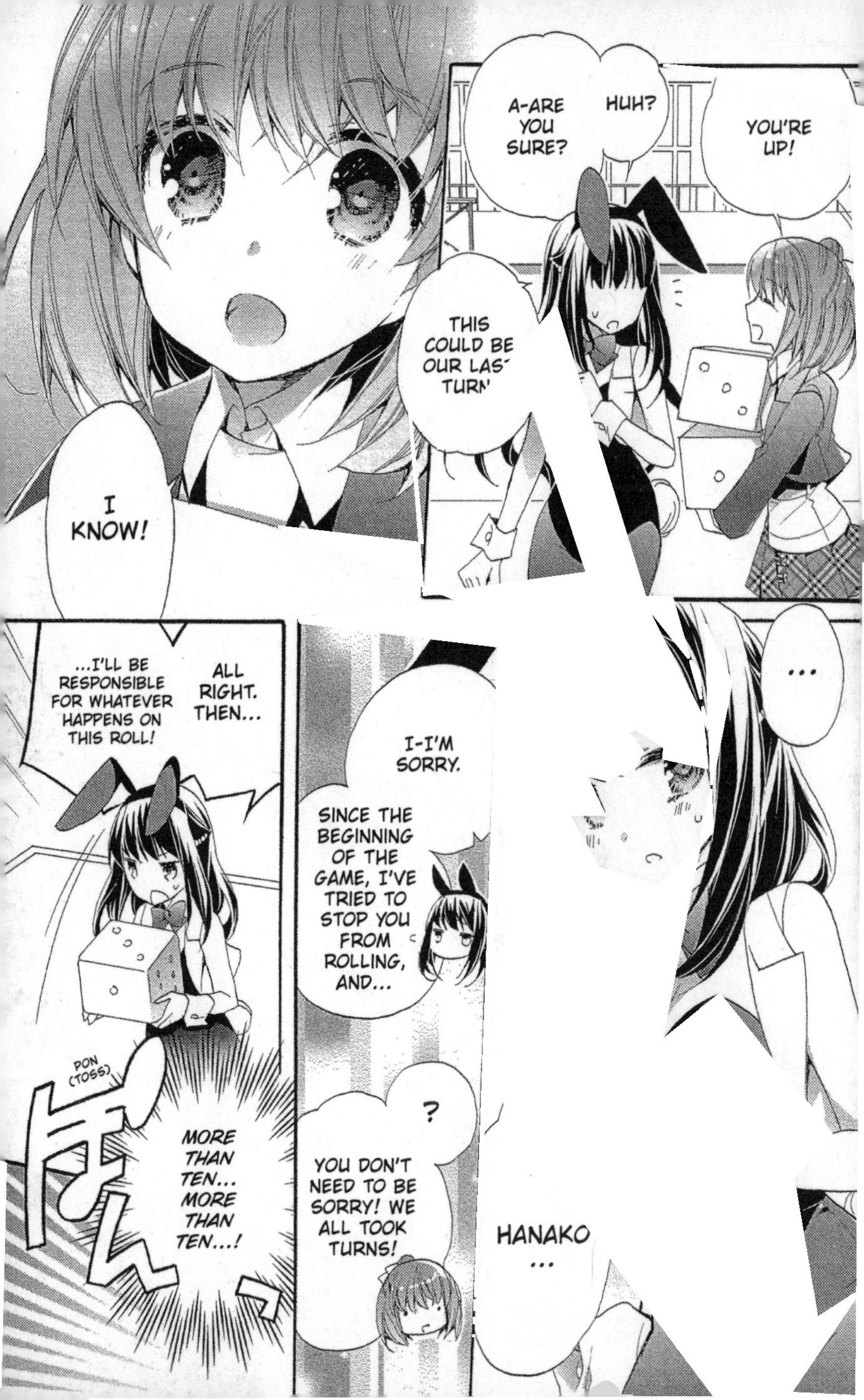
YOU'RE UP!
HUH?
A-ARE YOU SURE?
THIS COULD BE OUR LAS TURN
I KNOW!
...
HANAKO ...
I-I'M SORRY.
SINCE THE BEGINNING OF THE GAME, I'VE TRIED TO STOP YOU FROM ROLLING, AND...
?
YOU DON'T NEED TO BE SORRY! WE ALL TOOK TURNS!
ALL RIGHT. THEN...
...I'LL BE RESPONSIBLE FOR WHATEVER HAPPENS ON THIS ROLL!
PON (TOSS)
ぽんっ
MORE THAN TEN... MORE THAN TEN...!

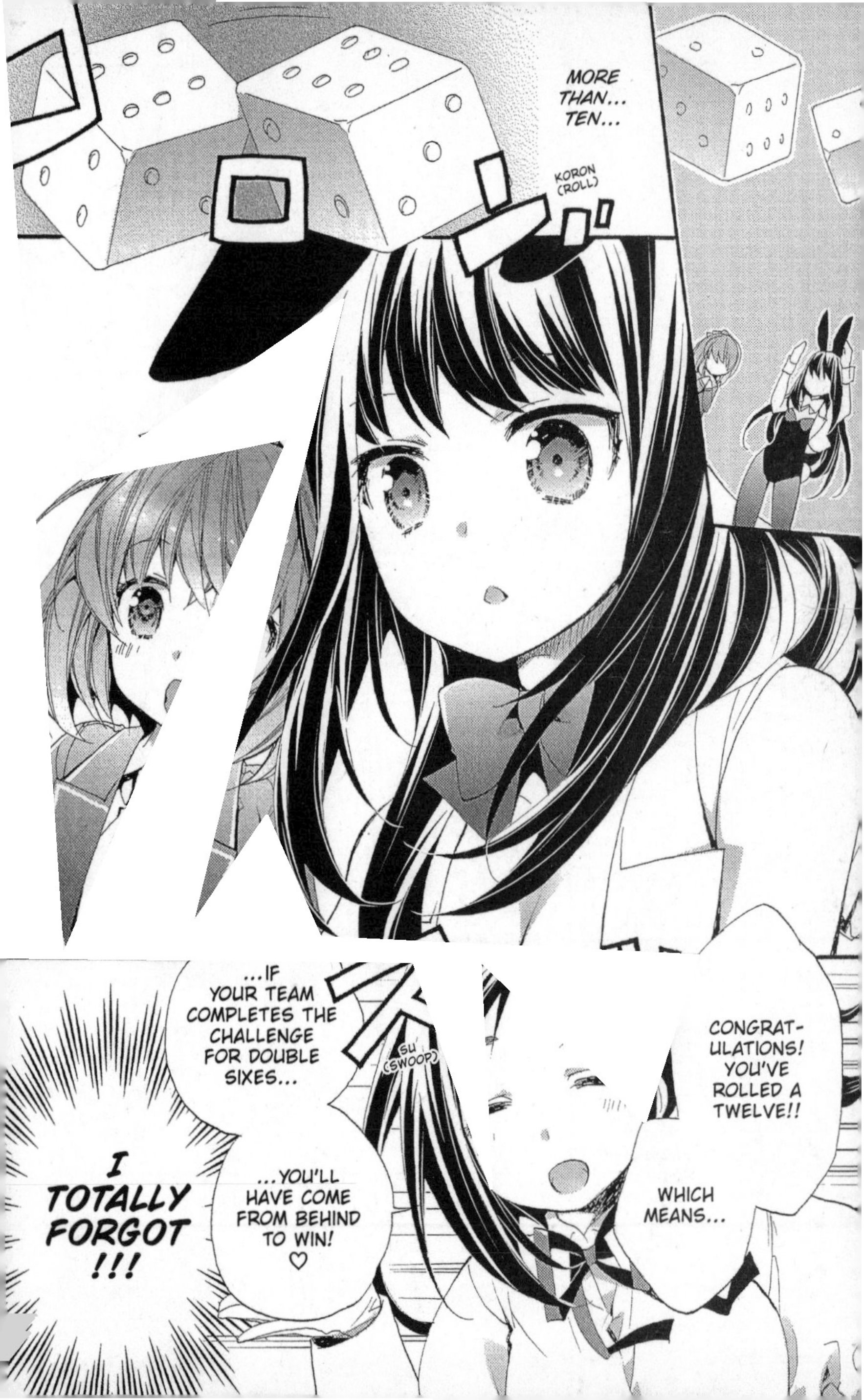
MORE THAN... TEN...
KORON (ROLL)
CONGRAT-ULATIONS! YOU'VE ROLLED A TWELVE!!
WHICH MEANS...
SU (SWOOP)
...IF YOUR TEAM COMPLETES THE CHALLENGE FOR DOUBLE SIXES...
...YOU'LL HAVE COME FROM BEHIND TO WIN! ♡
I TOTALLY FORGOT!!!

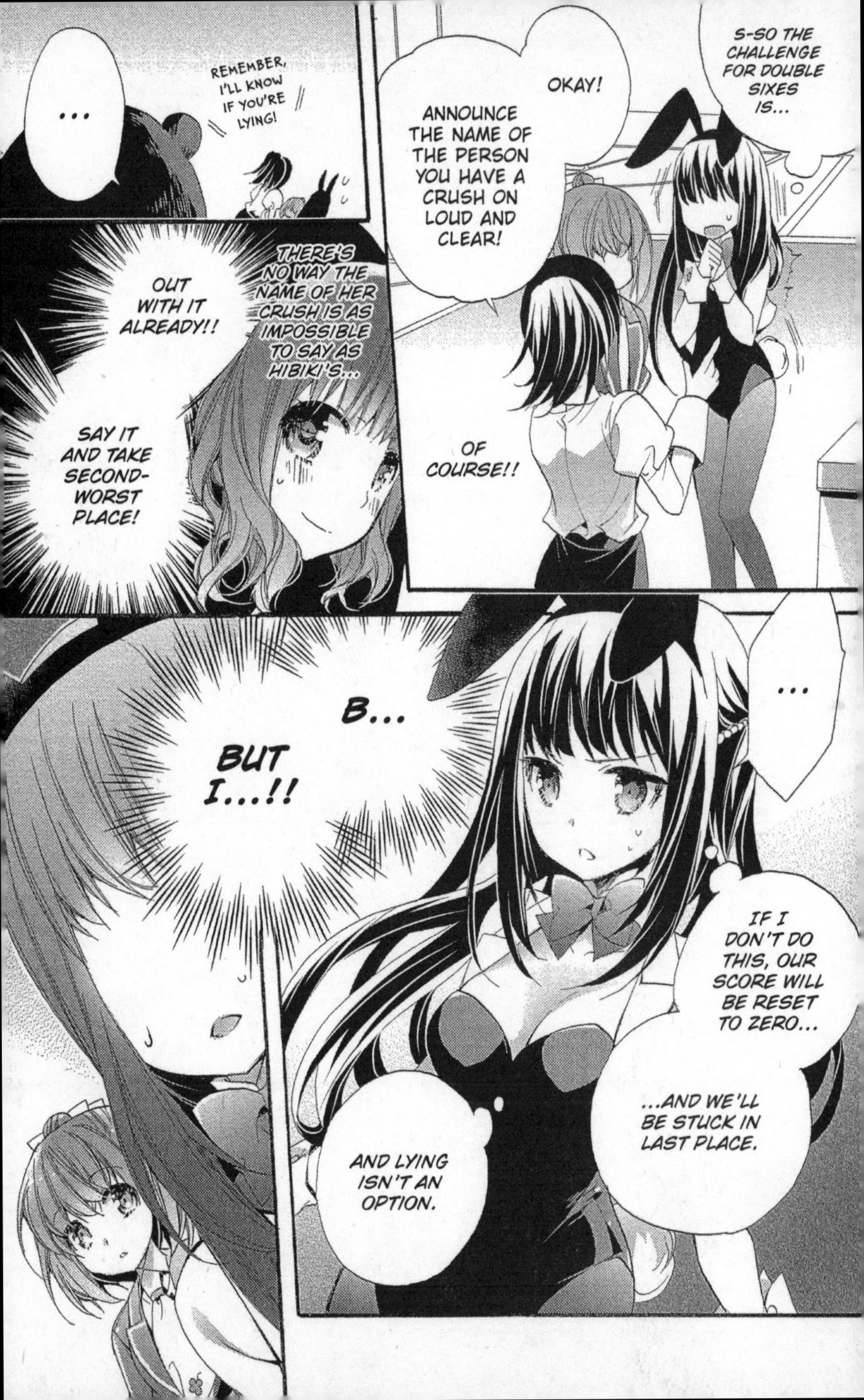
S-SO THE CHALLENGE FOR DOUBLE SIXES IS...
OKAY!
ANNOUNCE THE NAME OF THE PERSON YOU HAVE A CRUSH ON LOUD AND CLEAR!
OF COURSE!!
REMEMBER, I'LL KNOW IF YOU'RE LYING!
...
THERE'S NO WAY THE NAME OF HER CRUSH IS AS IMPOSSIBLE TO SAY AS HIBIKI'S...
OUT WITH IT ALREADY!!
SAY IT AND TAKE SECOND-WORST PLACE!
...
B...
BUT I...!!
IF I DON'T DO THIS, OUR SCORE WILL BE RESET TO ZERO...
...AND WE'LL BE STUCK IN LAST PLACE.
AND LYING ISN'T AN OPTION.

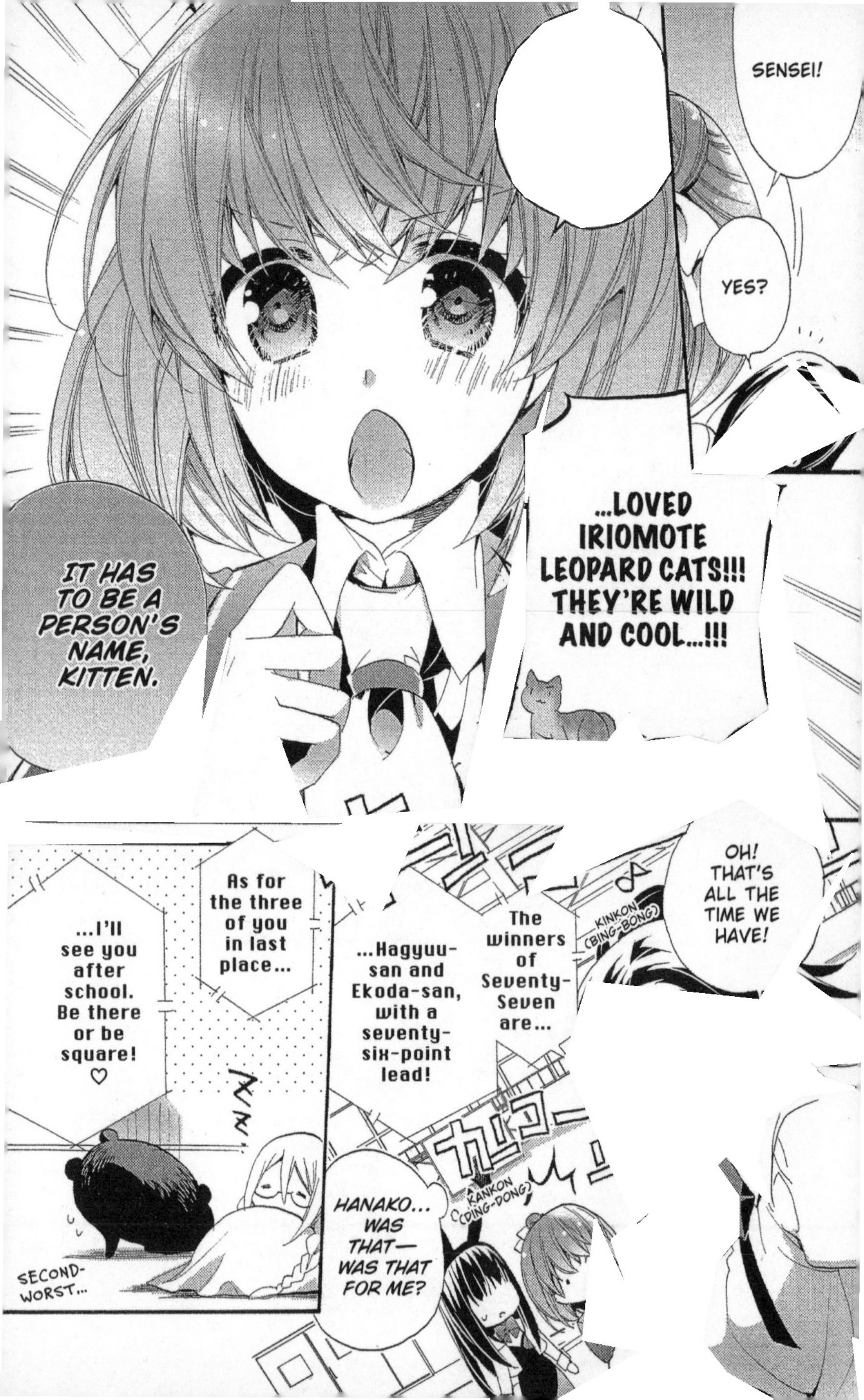
SENSEI!
YES?
...LOVED IRIOMOTE LEOPARD CATS!!! THEY'RE WILD AND COOL...!!!
IT HAS TO BE A PERSON'S NAME, KITTEN.
OH! THAT'S ALL THE TIME WE HAVE!
KINKON (BING-BONG)
The winners of Seventy-Seven are...
...Hagyuu-san and Ekoda-san, with a seventy-six-point lead!
KANKON (DING-DONG)
HANAKO... WAS THAT— WAS THAT FOR ME?
As for the three of you in last place...
...I'll see you after school. Be there or be square! ♡
SECOND-WORST...

Anne Happy

unhappy go lucky!

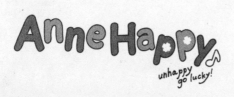

RURI HIBARIGAOKA

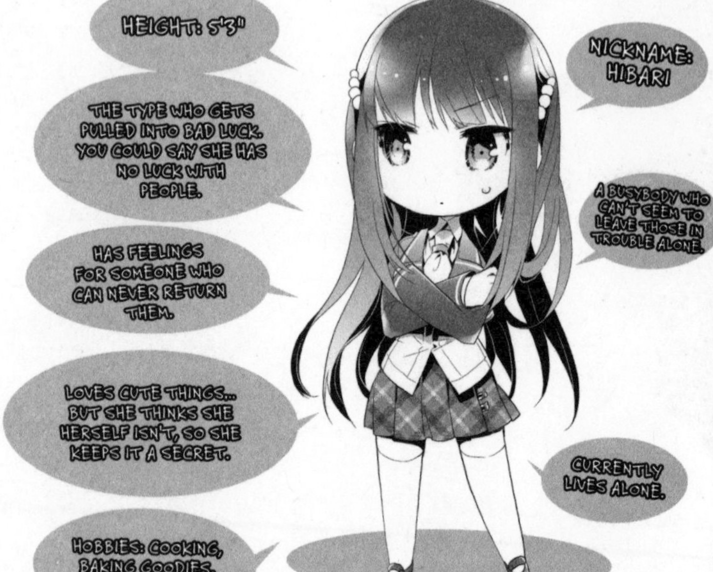
NICKNAME: HIBARI
HEIGHT: 5'3"
THE TYPE WHO GETS PULLED INTO BAD LUCK. YOU COULD SAY SHE HAS NO LUCK WITH PEOPLE.
A BUSYBODY WHO CAN'T SEEM TO LEAVE THOSE IN TROUBLE ALONE.
HAS FEELINGS FOR SOMEONE WHO CAN NEVER RETURN THEM.
LOVES CUTE THINGS... BUT SHE THINKS SHE HERSELF ISN'T, SO SHE KEEPS IT A SECRET.
CURRENTLY LIVES ALONE.
HOBBIES: COOKING, BAKING GOODIES, ETC.

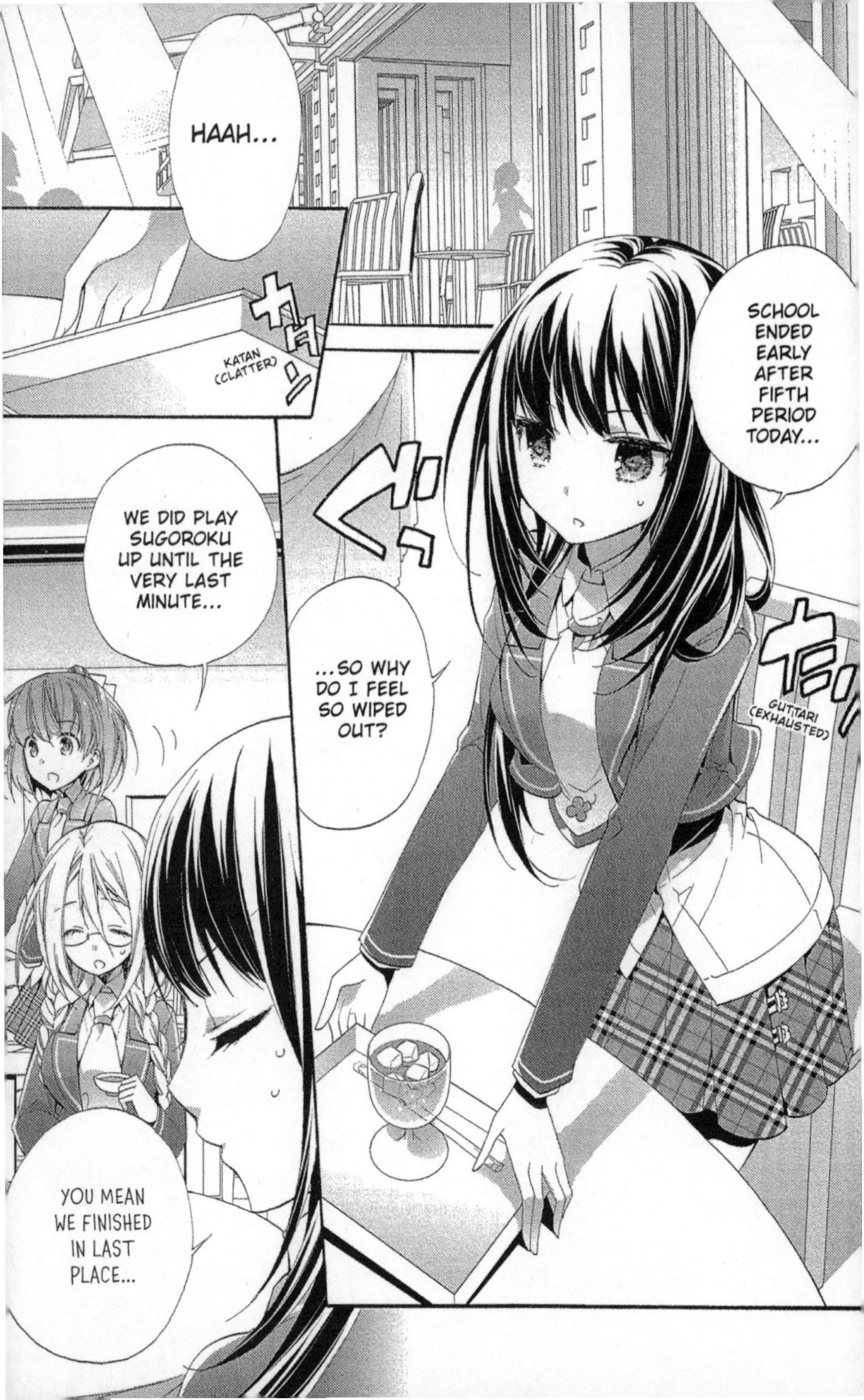
HAAH...
KATAN (CLATTER)
SCHOOL ENDED EARLY AFTER FIFTH PERIOD TODAY...
GUTTARI (EXHAUSTED)
WE DID PLAY SUGOROKU UP UNTIL THE VERY LAST MINUTE...
...SO WHY DO I FEEL SO WIPED OUT?
YOU MEAN WE FINISHED IN LAST PLACE...

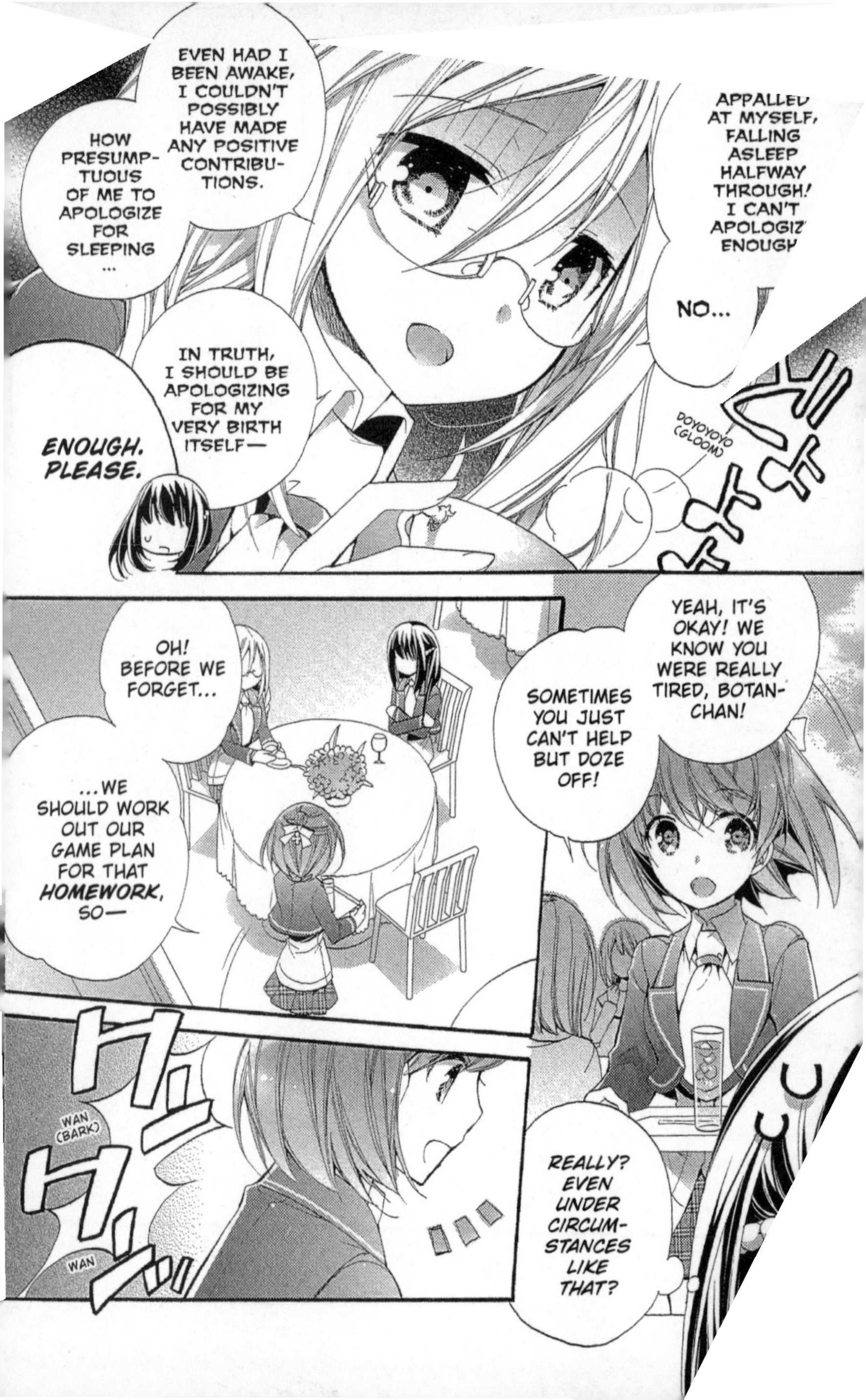
APPALLED AT MYSELF, FALLING ASLEEP HALFWAY THROUGH! I CAN'T APOLOGIZ ENOUGH
NO...
EVEN HAD I BEEN AWAKE, I COULDN'T POSSIBLY HAVE MADE ANY POSITIVE CONTRIBU-TIONS.
HOW PRESUMP-TUOUS OF ME TO APOLOGIZE FOR SLEEPING ...
IN TRUTH, I SHOULD BE APOLOGIZING FOR MY VERY BIRTH ITSELF—
DOYOYOYO (GLOOM)
ENOUGH. PLEASE.
YEAH, IT'S OKAY! WE KNOW YOU WERE REALLY TIRED, BOTAN-CHAN!
SOMETIMES YOU JUST CAN'T HELP BUT DOZE OFF!
REALLY? EVEN UNDER CIRCUM-STANCES LIKE THAT?
OH! BEFORE WE FORGET...
...WE SHOULD WORK OUT OUR GAME PLAN FOR THAT *HOMEWORK*, SO—
WAN (BARK)
WAN

Lucky. 10

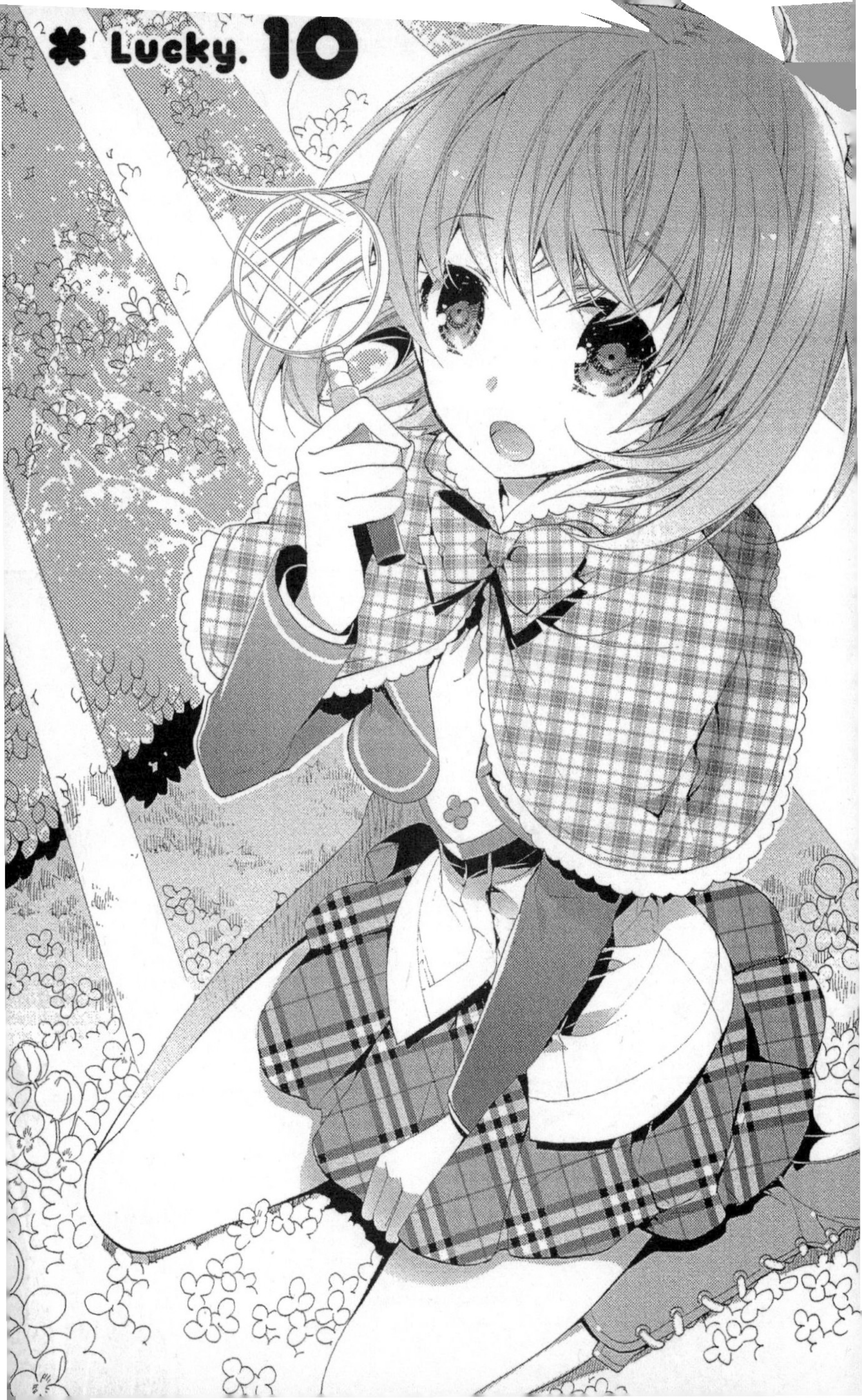

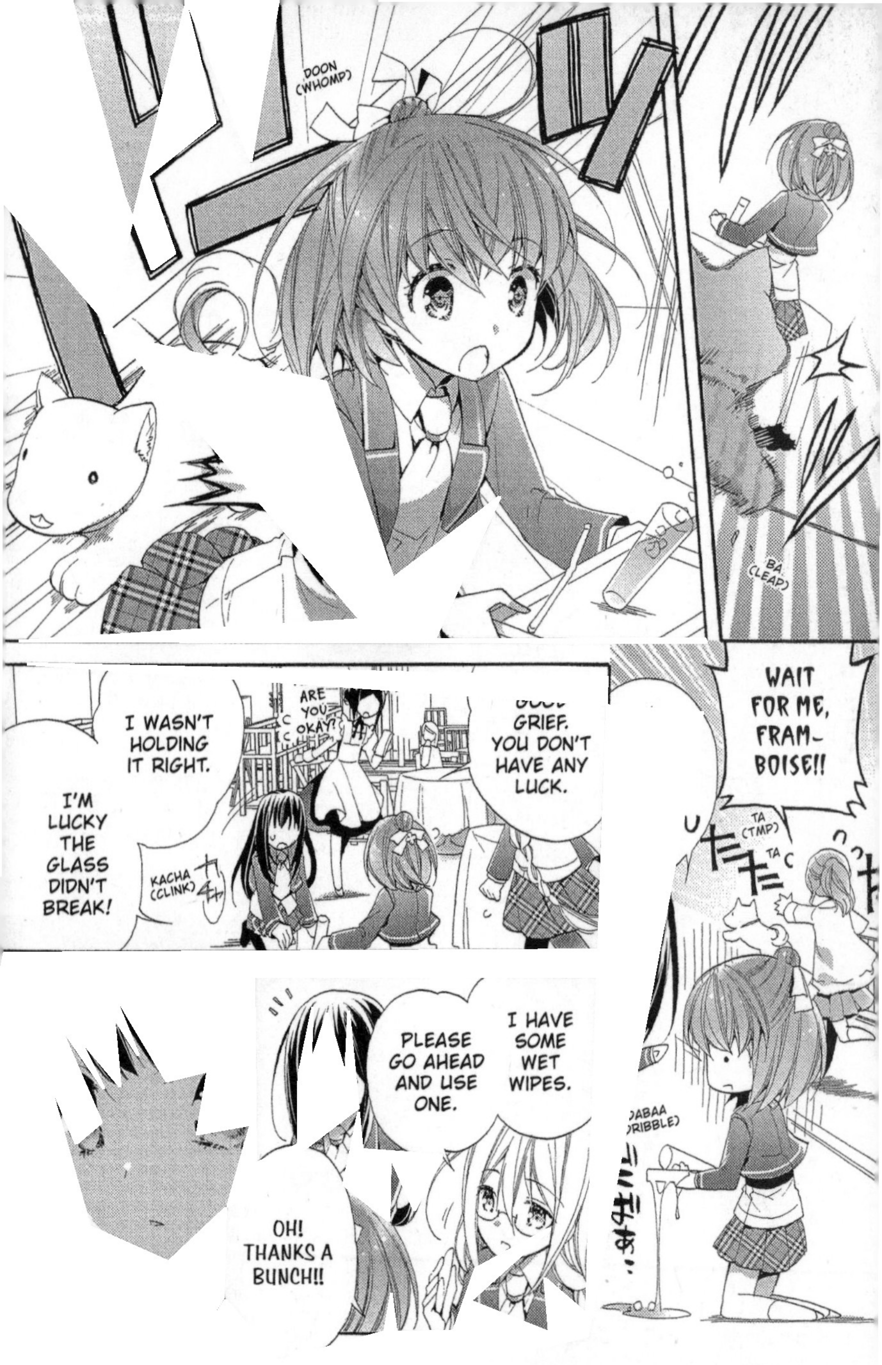
BA (LEAP)
DOON (WHOMP)
WAIT FOR ME, FRAMBOISE!!
TA (TMP)
TA
DABAA (DRIBBLE)
GOOD GRIEF. YOU DON'T HAVE ANY LUCK.
ARE YOU OKAY?
I WASN'T HOLDING IT RIGHT.
I'M LUCKY THE GLASS DIDN'T BREAK!
KACHA (CLINK)
I HAVE SOME WET WIPES.
PLEASE GO AHEAD AND USE ONE.
OH! THANKS A BUNCH!!

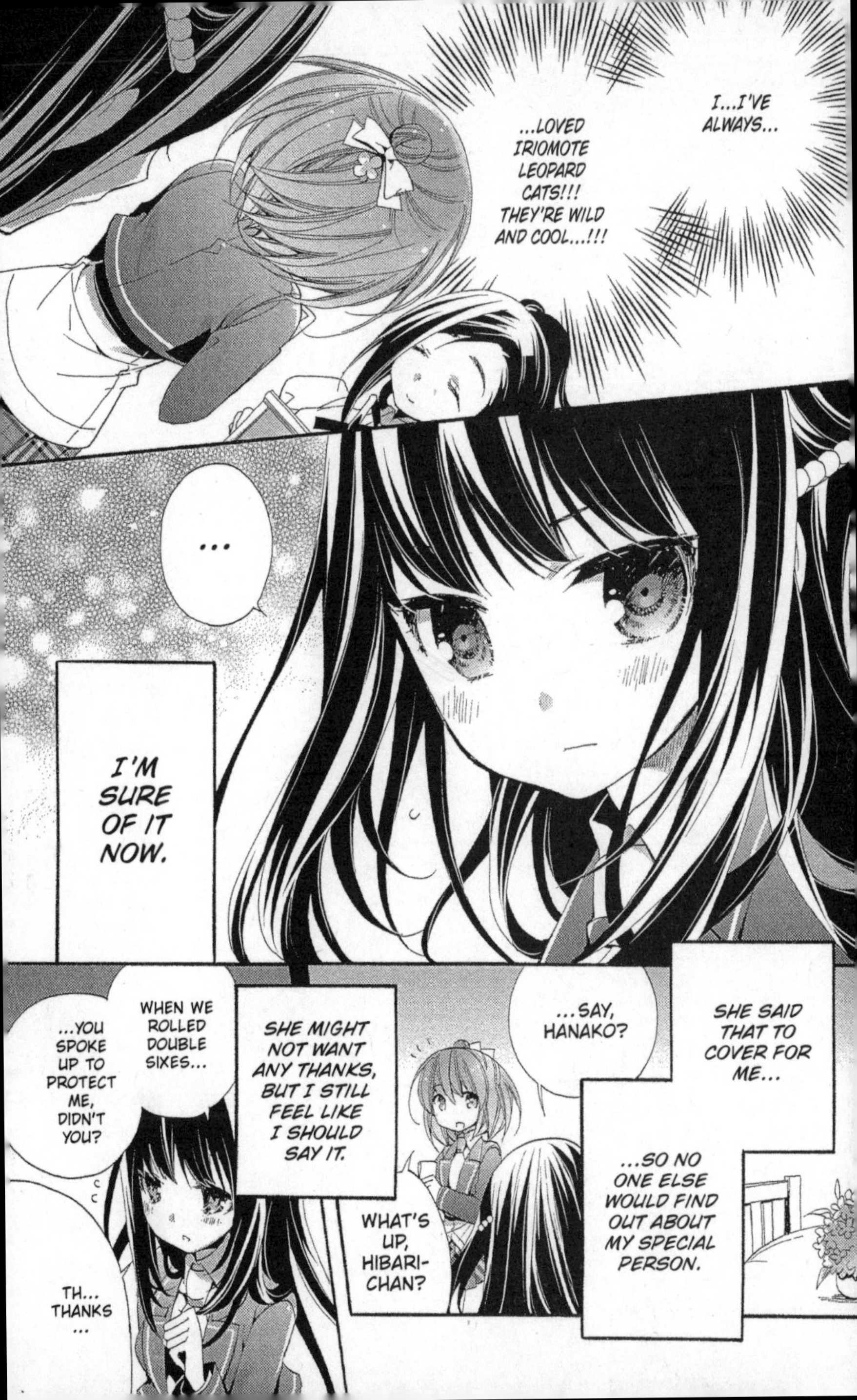
I...I'VE ALWAYS...
...LOVED IRIOMOTE LEOPARD CATS!!! THEY'RE WILD AND COOL...!!!
...
I'M SURE OF IT NOW.
SHE SAID THAT TO COVER FOR ME...
...SO NO ONE ELSE WOULD FIND OUT ABOUT MY SPECIAL PERSON.
...SAY, HANAKO?
WHAT'S UP, HIBARI-CHAN?
SHE MIGHT NOT WANT ANY THANKS, BUT I STILL FEEL LIKE I SHOULD SAY IT.
WHEN WE ROLLED DOUBLE SIXES...
...YOU SPOKE UP TO PROTECT ME, DIDN'T YOU?
TH... THANKS ...

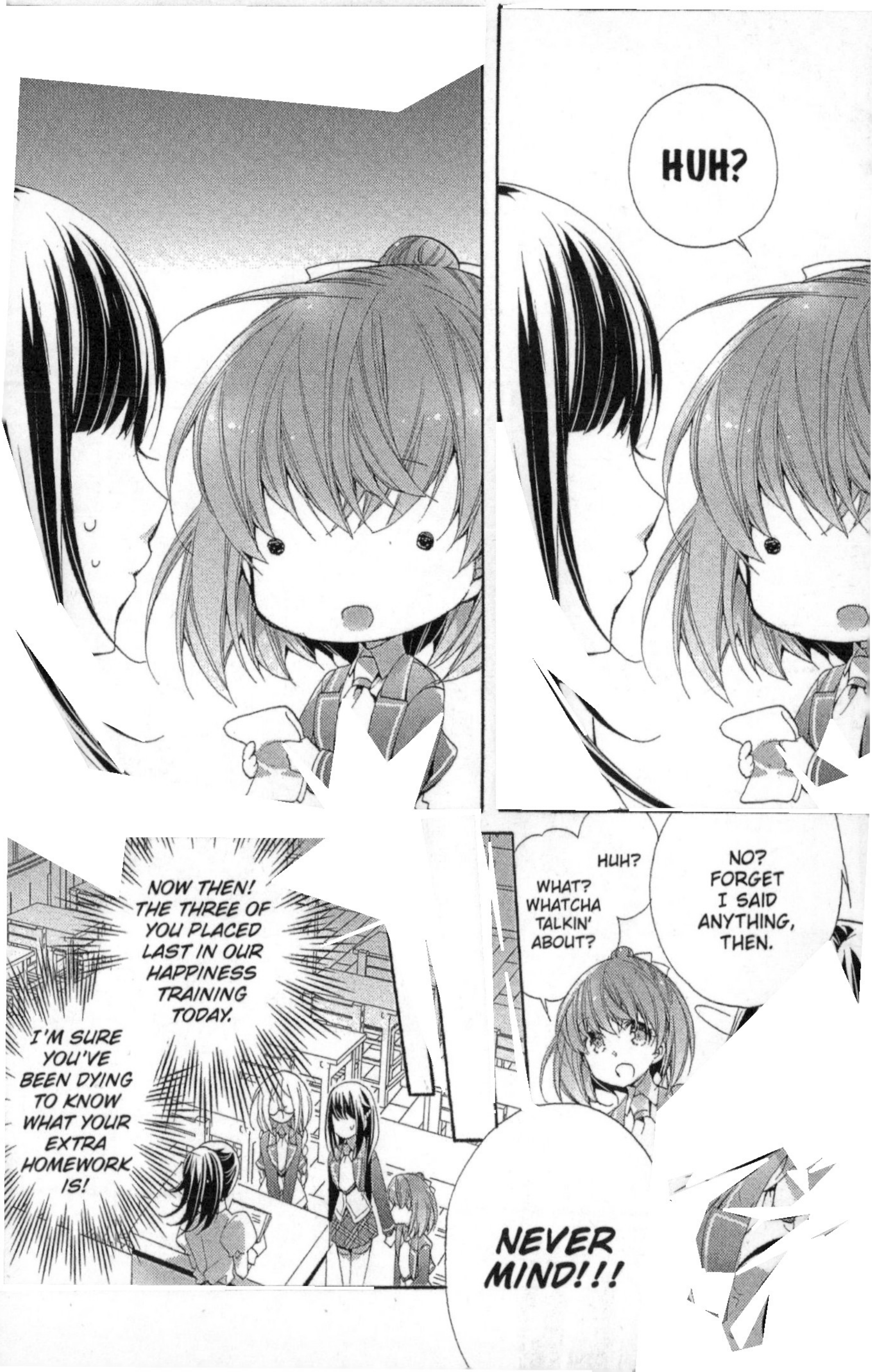
HUH?
NO? FORGET I SAID ANYTHING, THEN.
HUH? WHAT? WHATCHA TALKIN' ABOUT?
NEVER MIND!!!
NOW THEN! THE THREE OF YOU PLACED LAST IN OUR HAPPINESS TRAINING TODAY.
I'M SURE YOU'VE BEEN DYING TO KNOW WHAT YOUR EXTRA HOMEWORK IS!

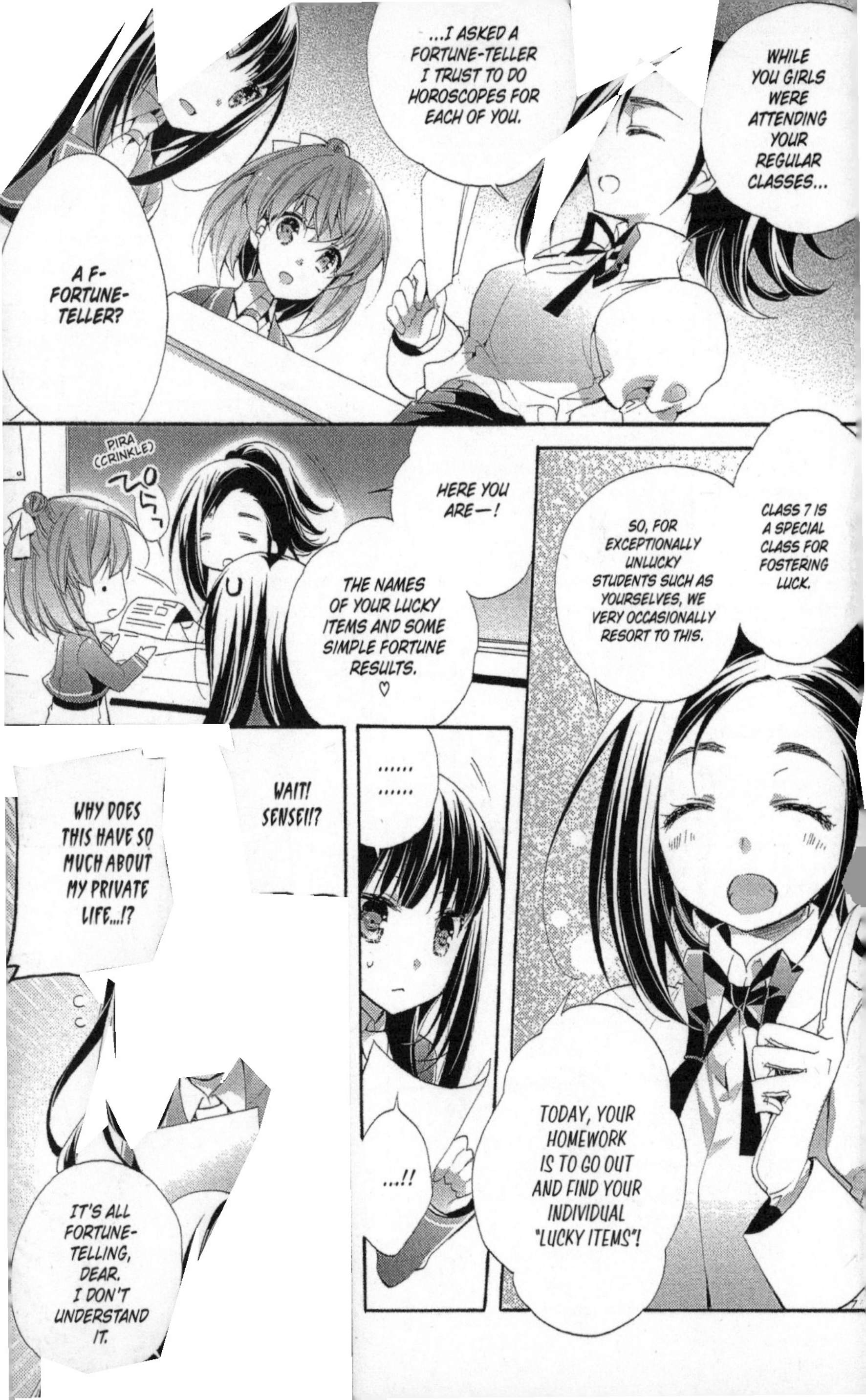
WHILE YOU GIRLS WERE ATTENDING YOUR REGULAR CLASSES...
...I ASKED A FORTUNE-TELLER I TRUST TO DO HOROSCOPES FOR EACH OF YOU.
A F-FORTUNE-TELLER?
CLASS 7 IS A SPECIAL CLASS FOR FOSTERING LUCK.
SO, FOR EXCEPTIONALLY UNLUCKY STUDENTS SUCH AS YOURSELVES, WE VERY OCCASIONALLY RESORT TO THIS.
TODAY, YOUR HOMEWORK IS TO GO OUT AND FIND YOUR INDIVIDUAL "LUCKY ITEMS"!
HERE YOU ARE—!
THE NAMES OF YOUR LUCKY ITEMS AND SOME SIMPLE FORTUNE RESULTS. ♡
PIRA (CRINKLE)
......
......
...!!
WAIT! SENSEI!?
WHY DOES THIS HAVE SO MUCH ABOUT MY PRIVATE LIFE...!?
IT'S ALL FORTUNE-TELLING, DEAR. I DON'T UNDERSTAND IT.

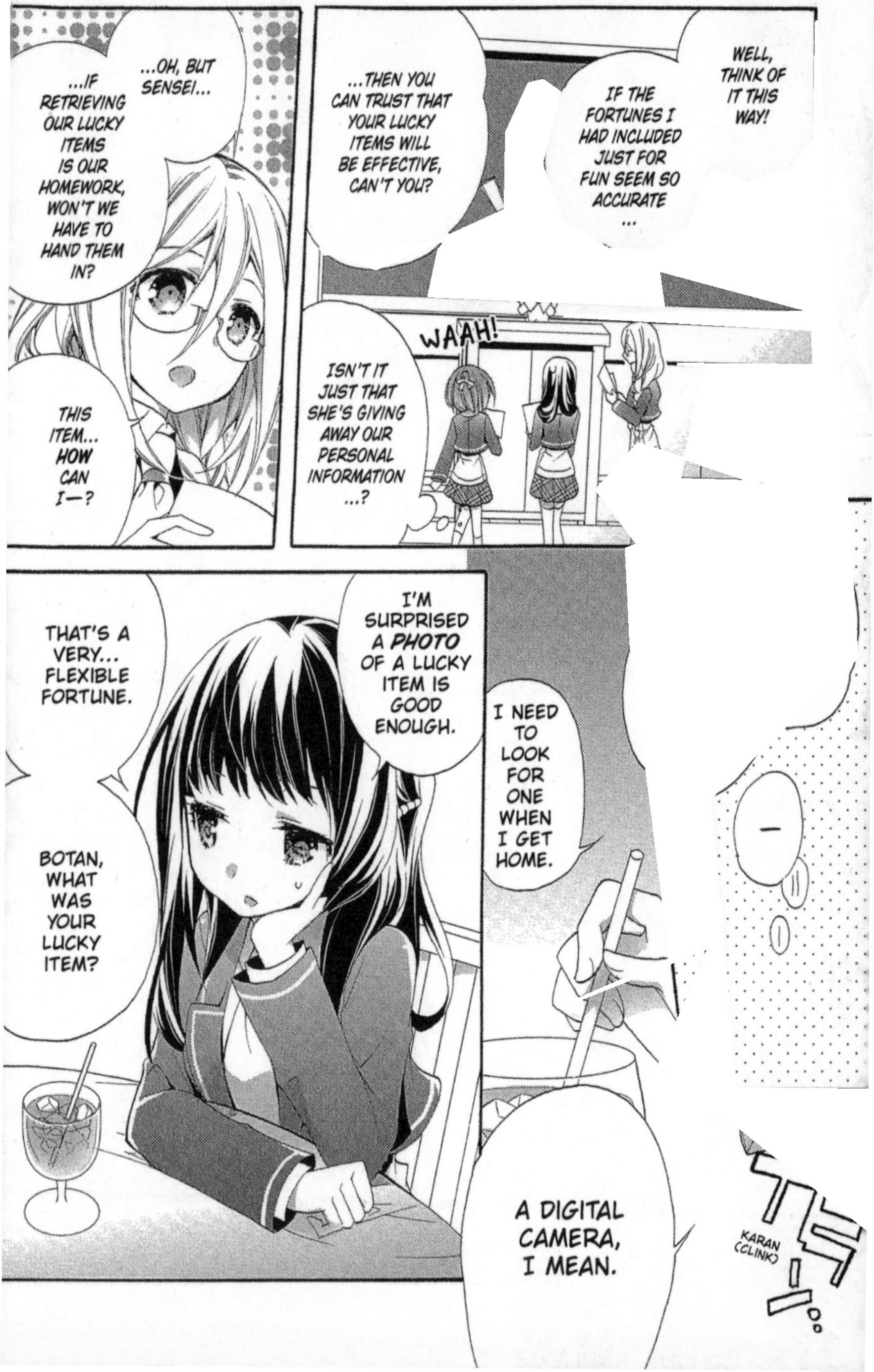
WELL, THINK OF IT THIS WAY!
IF THE FORTUNES I HAD INCLUDED JUST FOR FUN SEEM SO ACCURATE ...
...THEN YOU CAN TRUST THAT YOUR LUCKY ITEMS WILL BE EFFECTIVE, CAN'T YOU?
WAAH!
ISN'T IT JUST THAT SHE'S GIVING AWAY OUR PERSONAL INFORMATION ...?
...OH, BUT SENSEI...
...IF RETRIEVING OUR LUCKY ITEMS IS OUR HOMEWORK, WON'T WE HAVE TO HAND THEM IN?
THIS ITEM... HOW CAN I—?
I NEED TO LOOK FOR ONE WHEN I GET HOME.
KARAN (CLINK)
A DIGITAL CAMERA, I MEAN.
I'M SURPRISED A PHOTO OF A LUCKY ITEM IS GOOD ENOUGH.
THAT'S A VERY... FLEXIBLE FORTUNE.
BOTAN, WHAT WAS YOUR LUCKY ITEM?

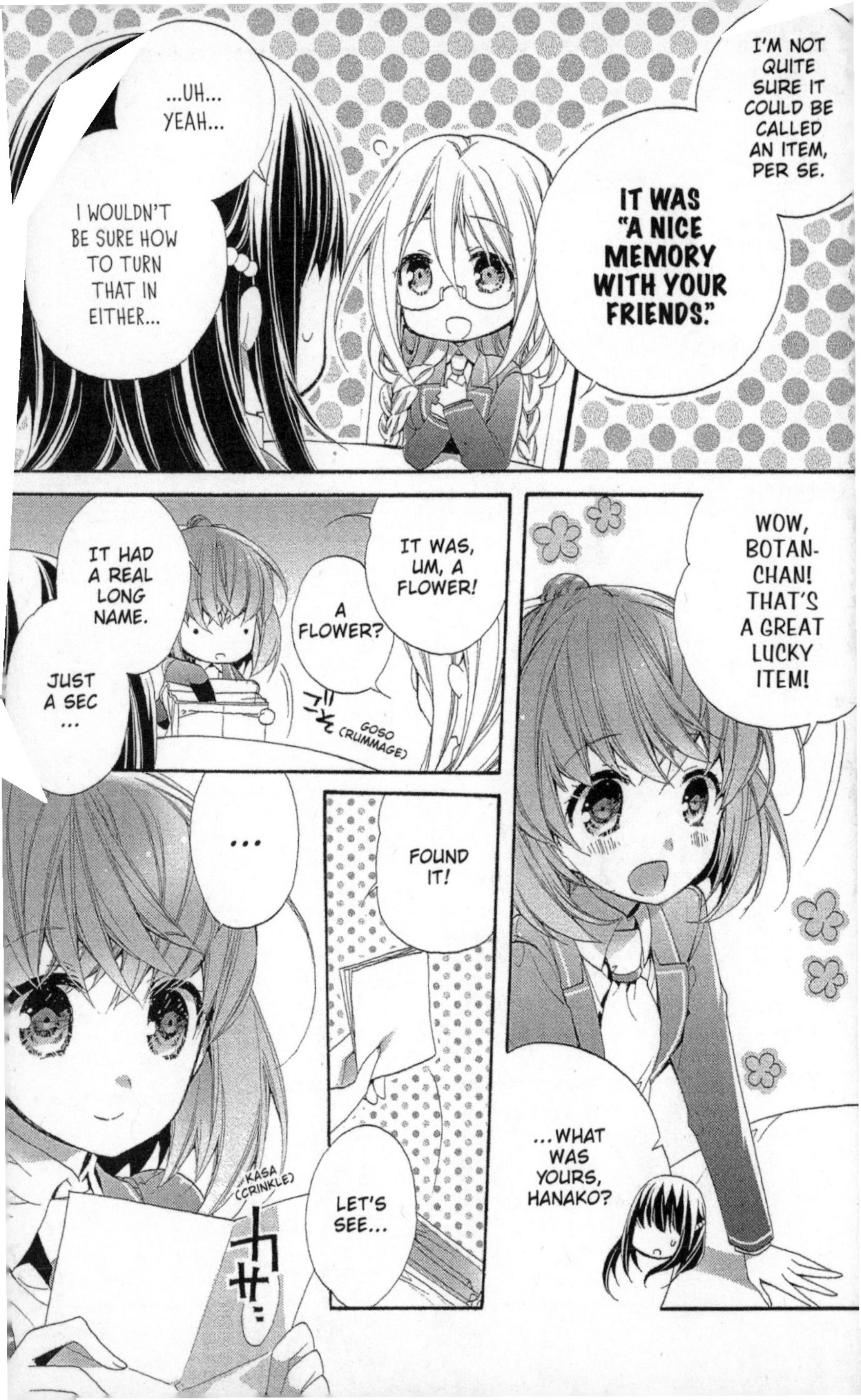
I'M NOT QUITE SURE IT COULD BE CALLED AN ITEM, PER SE.
IT WAS "A NICE MEMORY WITH YOUR FRIENDS."
...UH... YEAH...
I WOULDN'T BE SURE HOW TO TURN THAT IN EITHER...
WOW, BOTAN-CHAN! THAT'S A GREAT LUCKY ITEM!
...WHAT WAS YOURS, HANAKO?
IT WAS, UM, A FLOWER!
A FLOWER?
GOSO (RUMMAGE)
IT HAD A REAL LONG NAME.
JUST A SEC...
FOUND IT!
LET'S SEE...
...
KASA (CRINKLE)

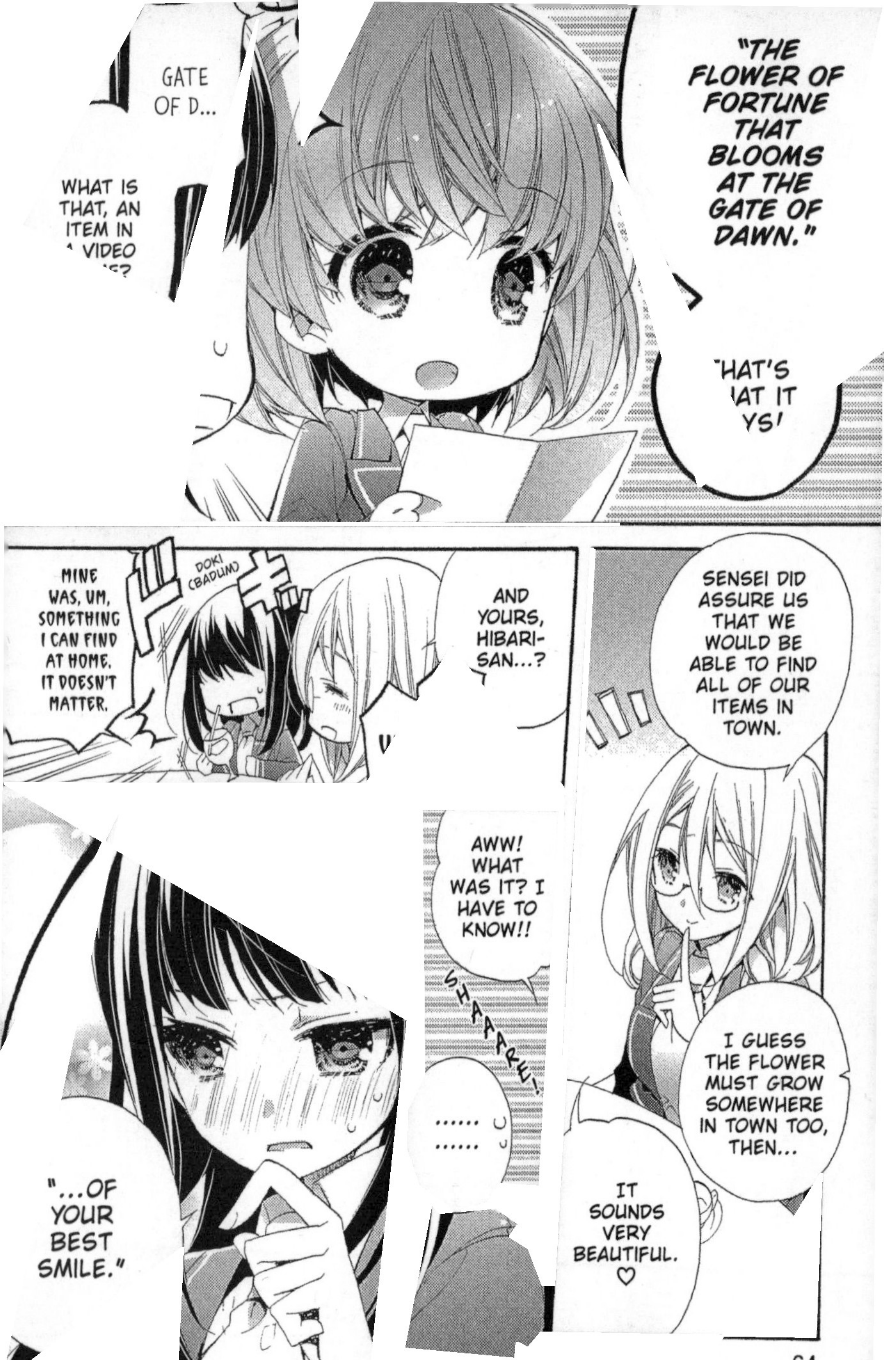
"THE FLOWER OF FORTUNE THAT BLOOMS AT THE GATE OF DAWN."
HAT'S AT IT YS!
GATE OF D...
WHAT IS THAT, AN ITEM IN VIDEO
SENSEI DID ASSURE US THAT WE WOULD BE ABLE TO FIND ALL OF OUR ITEMS IN TOWN.
I GUESS THE FLOWER MUST GROW SOMEWHERE IN TOWN TOO, THEN...
IT SOUNDS VERY BEAUTIFUL. ♡
AND YOURS, HIBARI-SAN...?
DOKI (BADUM)
MINE WAS, UM, SOMETHING I CAN FIND AT HOME. IT DOESN'T MATTER.
AWW! WHAT WAS IT? I HAVE TO KNOW!!
SHAAARE!
....
"...OF YOUR BEST SMILE."

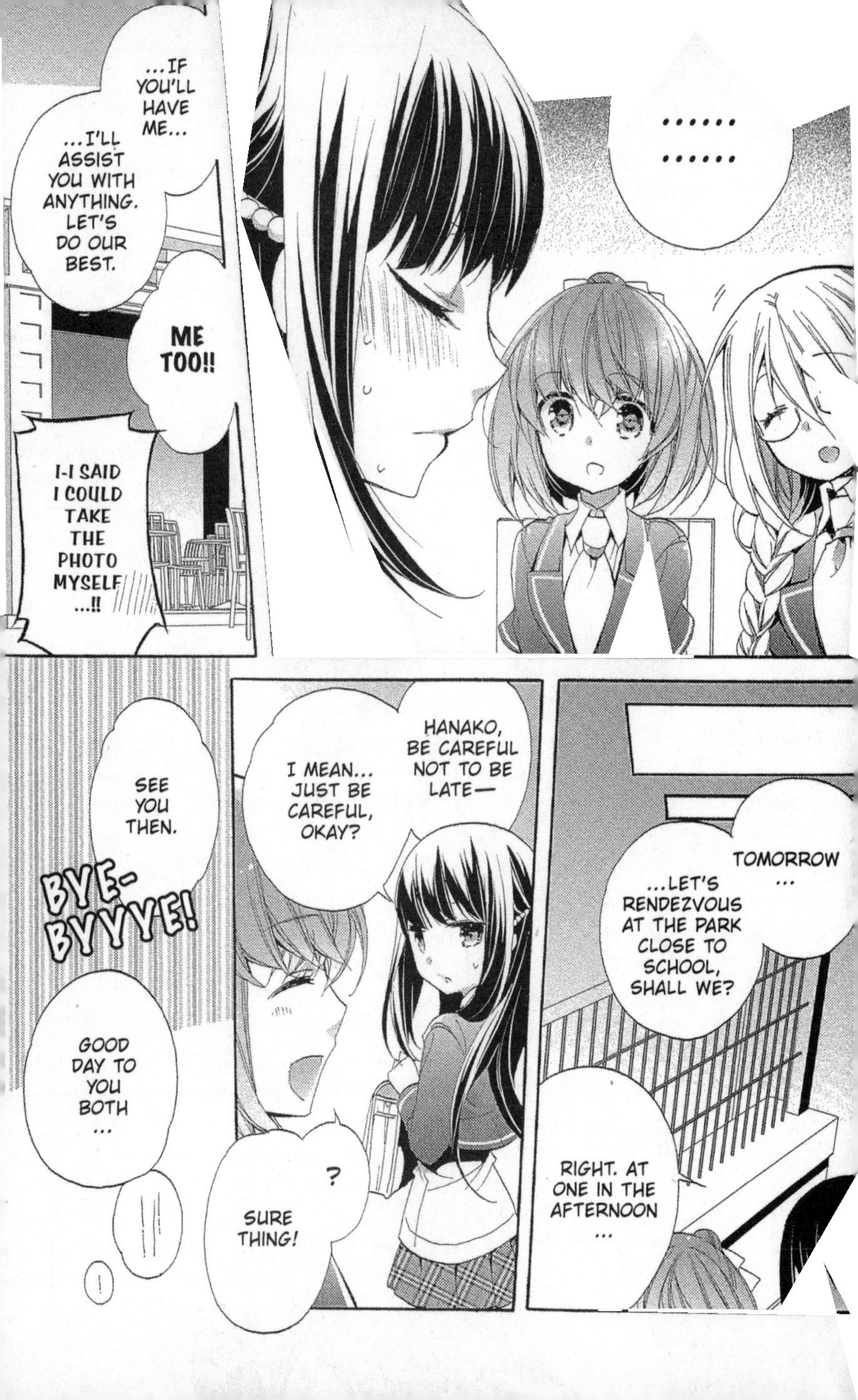
......
......
...IF YOU'LL HAVE ME...
...I'LL ASSIST YOU WITH ANYTHING. LET'S DO OUR BEST.
ME TOO!!
I-I SAID I COULD TAKE THE PHOTO MYSELF ...!!
TOMORROW ...
...LET'S RENDEZVOUS AT THE PARK CLOSE TO SCHOOL, SHALL WE?
RIGHT. AT ONE IN THE AFTERNOON ...
HANAKO, BE CAREFUL NOT TO BE LATE—
I MEAN... JUST BE CAREFUL, OKAY?
?
SURE THING!
SEE YOU THEN.
BYE-BYYYE!
GOOD DAY TO YOU BOTH ...
!

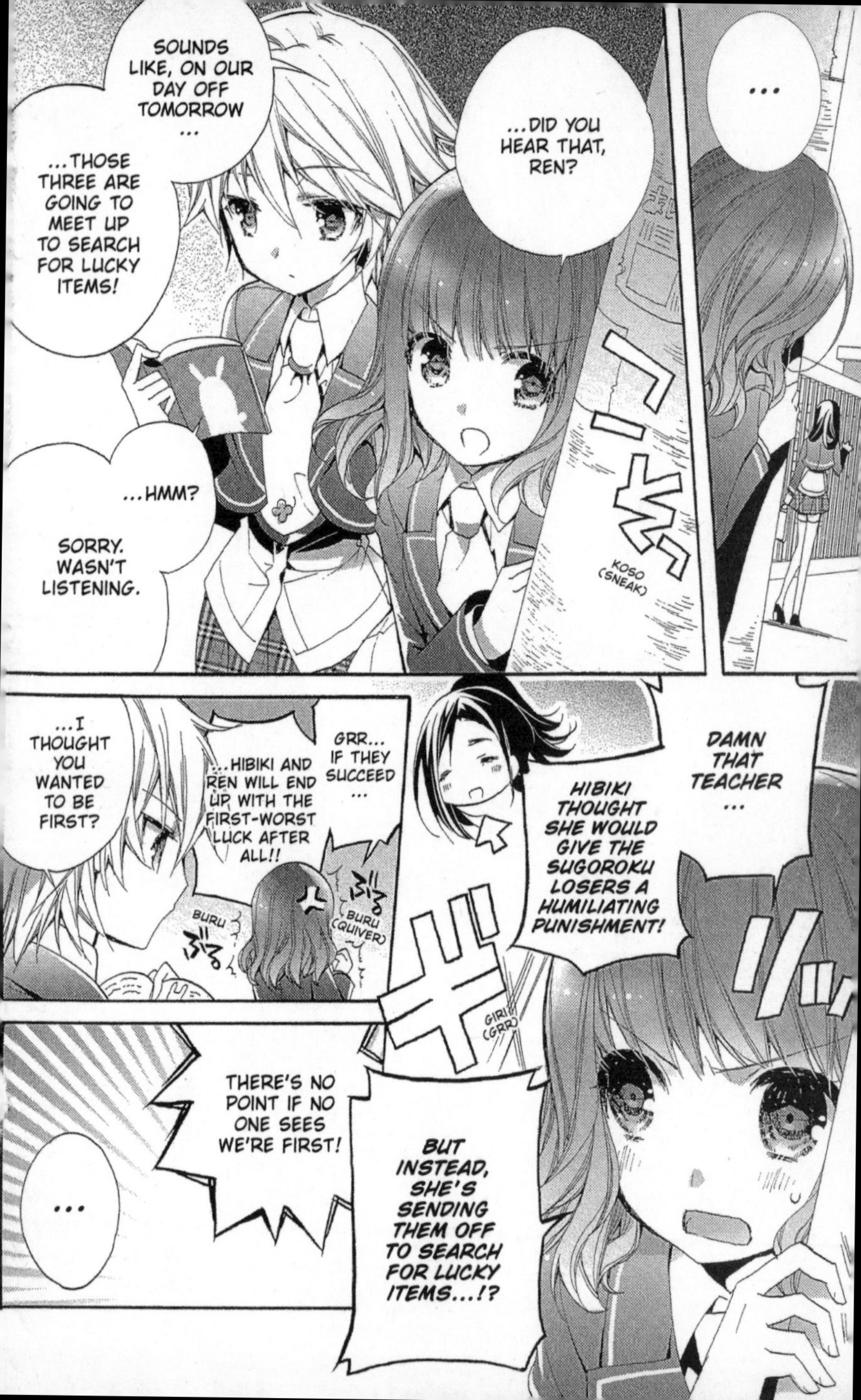
...
...DID YOU HEAR THAT, REN?
SOUNDS LIKE, ON OUR DAY OFF TOMORROW ...
...THOSE THREE ARE GOING TO MEET UP TO SEARCH FOR LUCKY ITEMS!
KOSO (SNEAK)
...HMM?
SORRY. WASN'T LISTENING.
DAMN THAT TEACHER ...
HIBIKI THOUGHT SHE WOULD GIVE THE SUGOROKU LOSERS A HUMILIATING PUNISHMENT!
BUT INSTEAD, SHE'S SENDING THEM OFF TO SEARCH FOR LUCKY ITEMS...!?
GIRI (GRR)
GRR... IF THEY SUCCEED ...
...HIBIKI AND REN WILL END UP WITH THE FIRST-WORST LUCK AFTER ALL!!
BURU (QUIVER)
BURU
...I THOUGHT YOU WANTED TO BE FIRST?
THERE'S NO POINT IF NO ONE SEES WE'RE FIRST!
...

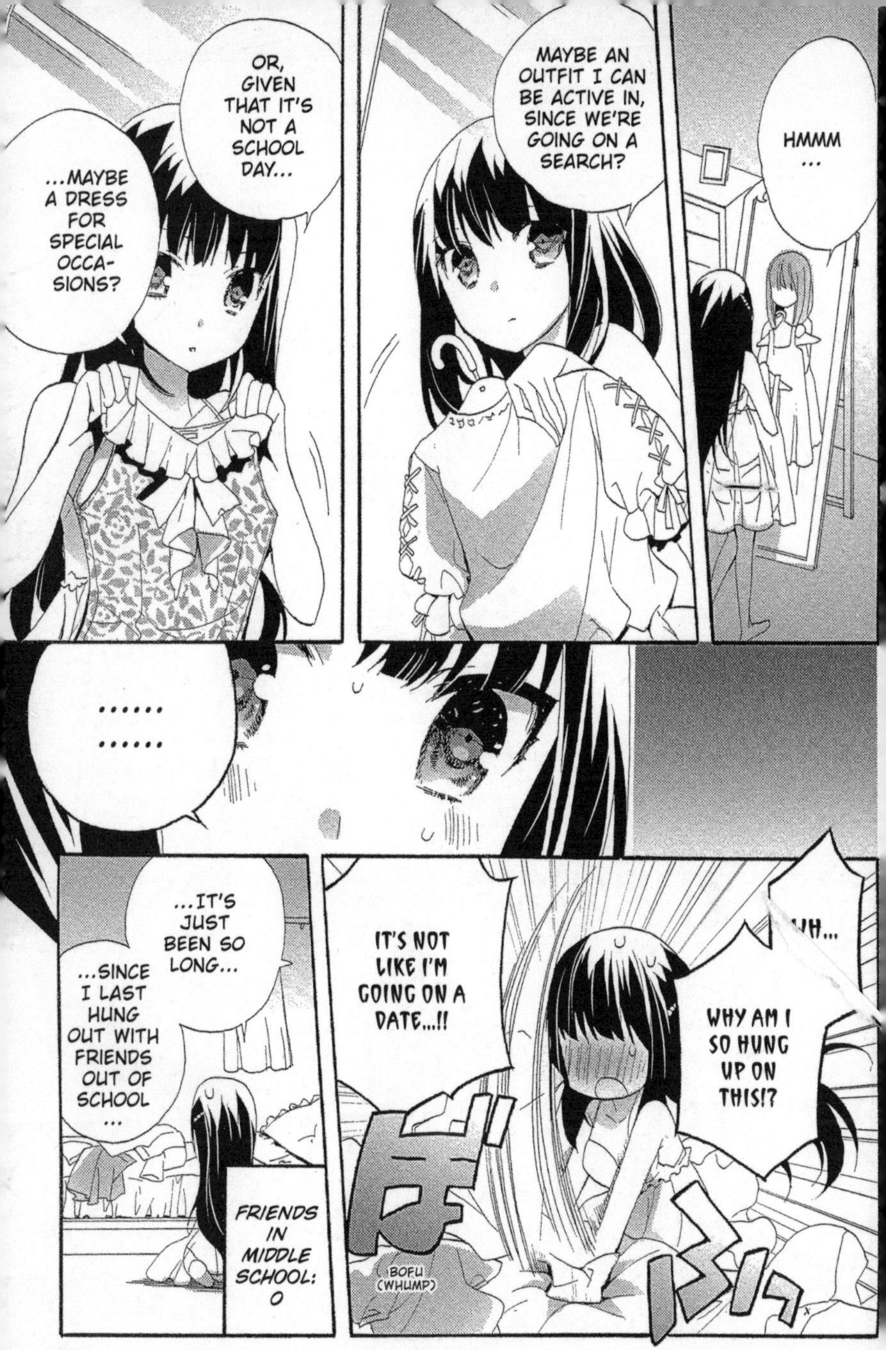
HMMM ...
MAYBE AN OUTFIT I CAN BE ACTIVE IN, SINCE WE'RE GOING ON A SEARCH?
OR, GIVEN THAT IT'S NOT A SCHOOL DAY...
...MAYBE A DRESS FOR SPECIAL OCCASIONS?
....
UH...
WHY AM I SO HUNG UP ON THIS!?
IT'S NOT LIKE I'M GOING ON A DATE...!!
BOFU (WHUMP)
...IT'S JUST BEEN SO LONG...
...SINCE I LAST HUNG OUT WITH FRIENDS OUT OF SCHOOL ...
FRIENDS IN MIDDLE SCHOOL: 0

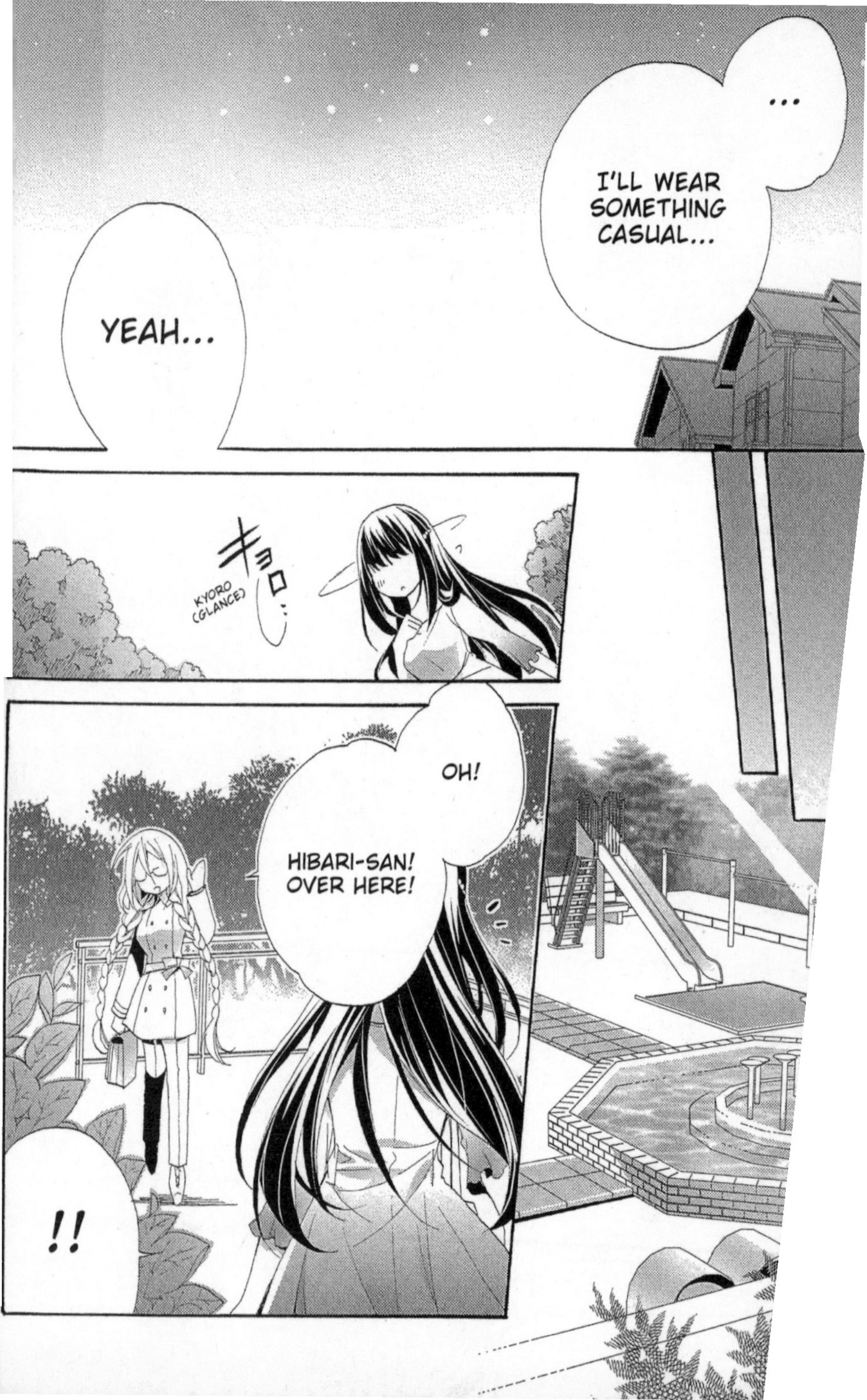
...
I'LL WEAR SOMETHING CASUAL...
YEAH...
キョロ
KYORO (GLANCE)
OH!
HIBARI-SAN! OVER HERE!
!!

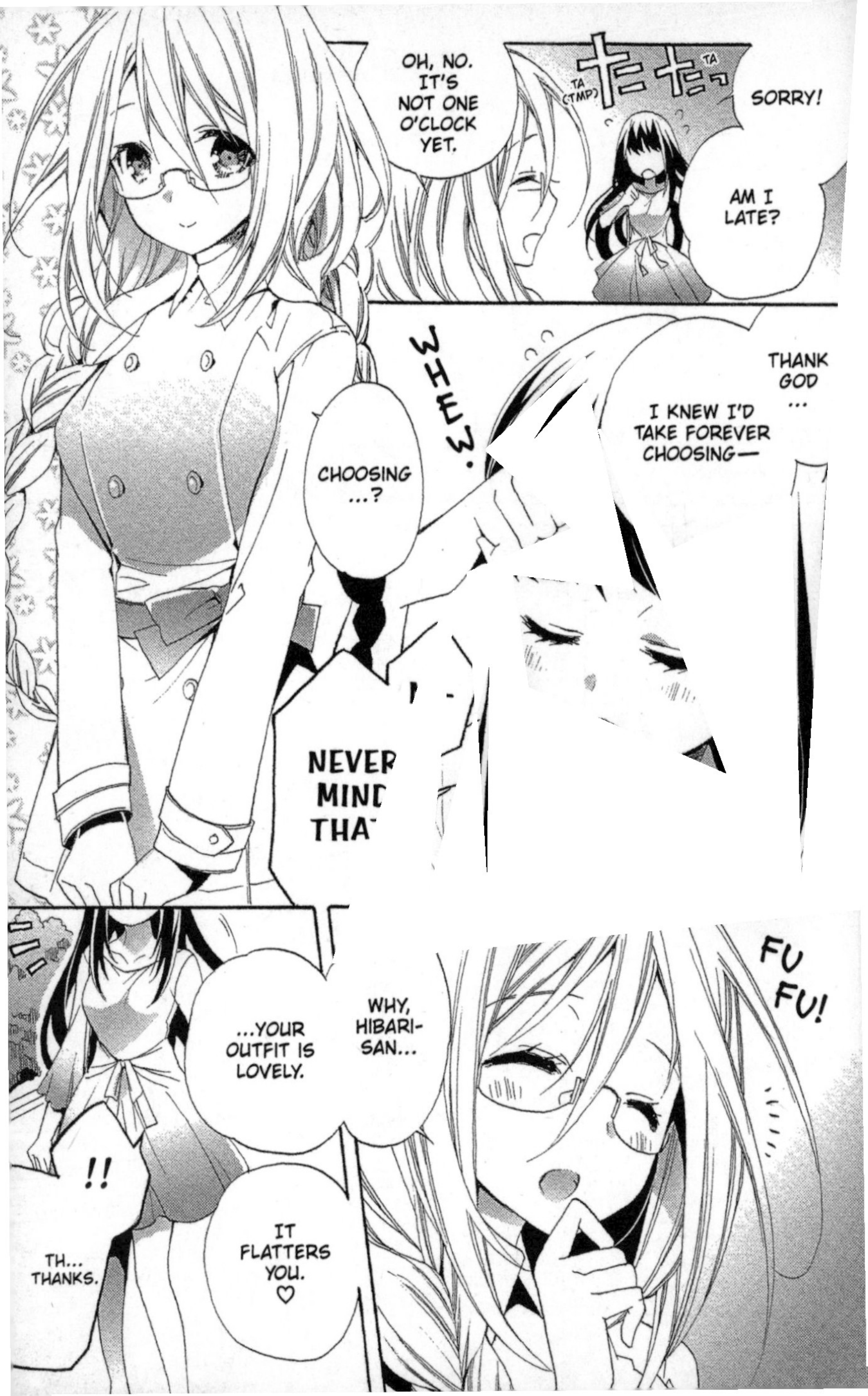
TA TA (TMP)
SORRY!
AM I LATE?
OH, NO. IT'S NOT ONE O'CLOCK YET.
THANK GOD...
I KNEW I'D TAKE FOREVER CHOOSING—
WHEW.
CHOOSING ...?
NEVER MIND THAT
FU FU!
WHY, HIBARI-SAN...
...YOUR OUTFIT IS LOVELY.
IT FLATTERS YOU. ♡
!!
TH... THANKS.

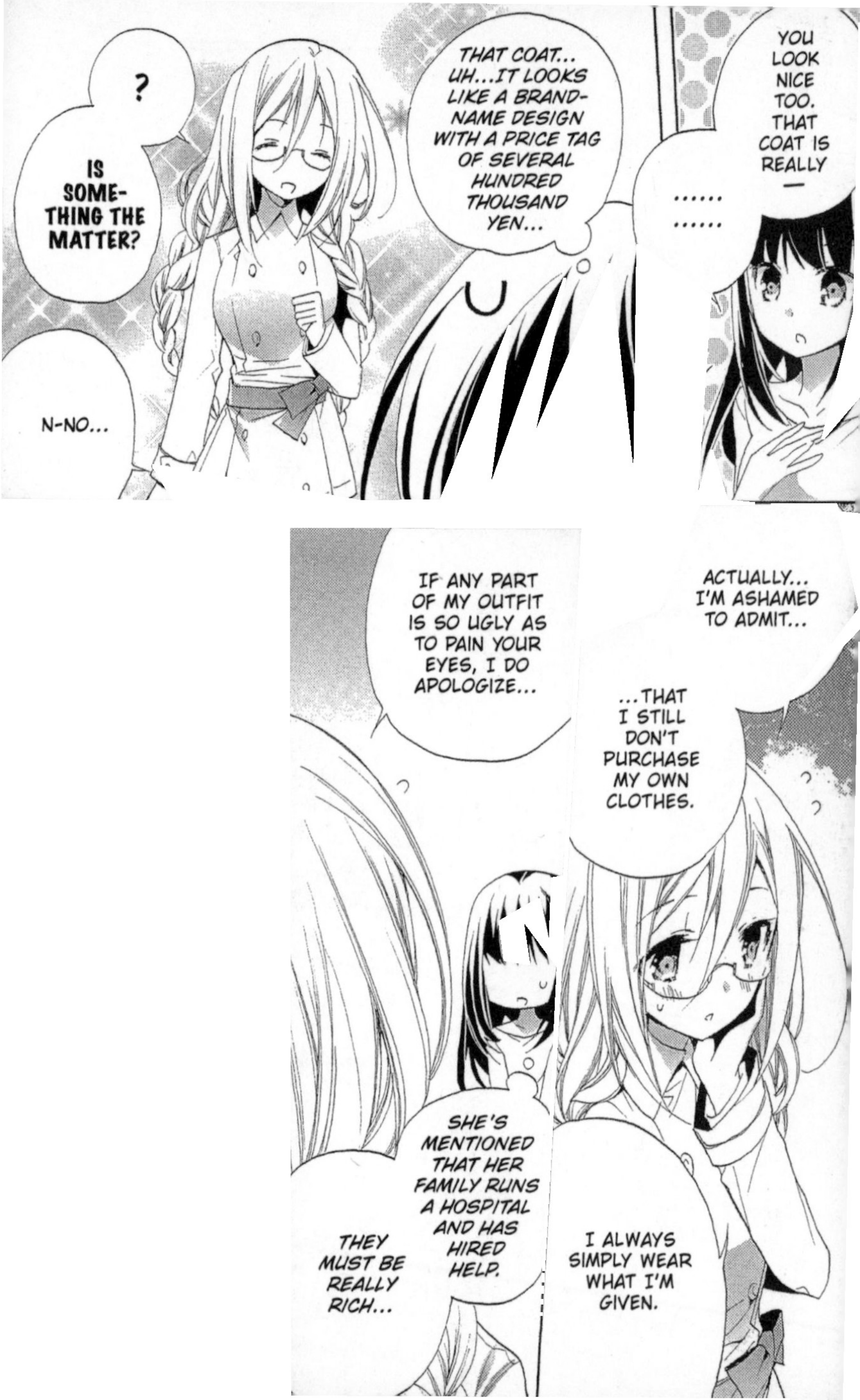
YOU LOOK NICE TOO. THAT COAT IS REALLY—
......
......
THAT COAT... UH...IT LOOKS LIKE A BRAND-NAME DESIGN WITH A PRICE TAG OF SEVERAL HUNDRED THOUSAND YEN...
?
IS SOMETHING THE MATTER?
N-NO...
IF ANY PART OF MY OUTFIT IS SO UGLY AS TO PAIN YOUR EYES, I DO APOLOGIZE...
ACTUALLY... I'M ASHAMED TO ADMIT...
...THAT I STILL DON'T PURCHASE MY OWN CLOTHES.
I ALWAYS SIMPLY WEAR WHAT I'M GIVEN.
SHE'S MENTIONED THAT HER FAMILY RUNS A HOSPITAL AND HAS HIRED HELP.
THEY MUST BE REALLY RICH...

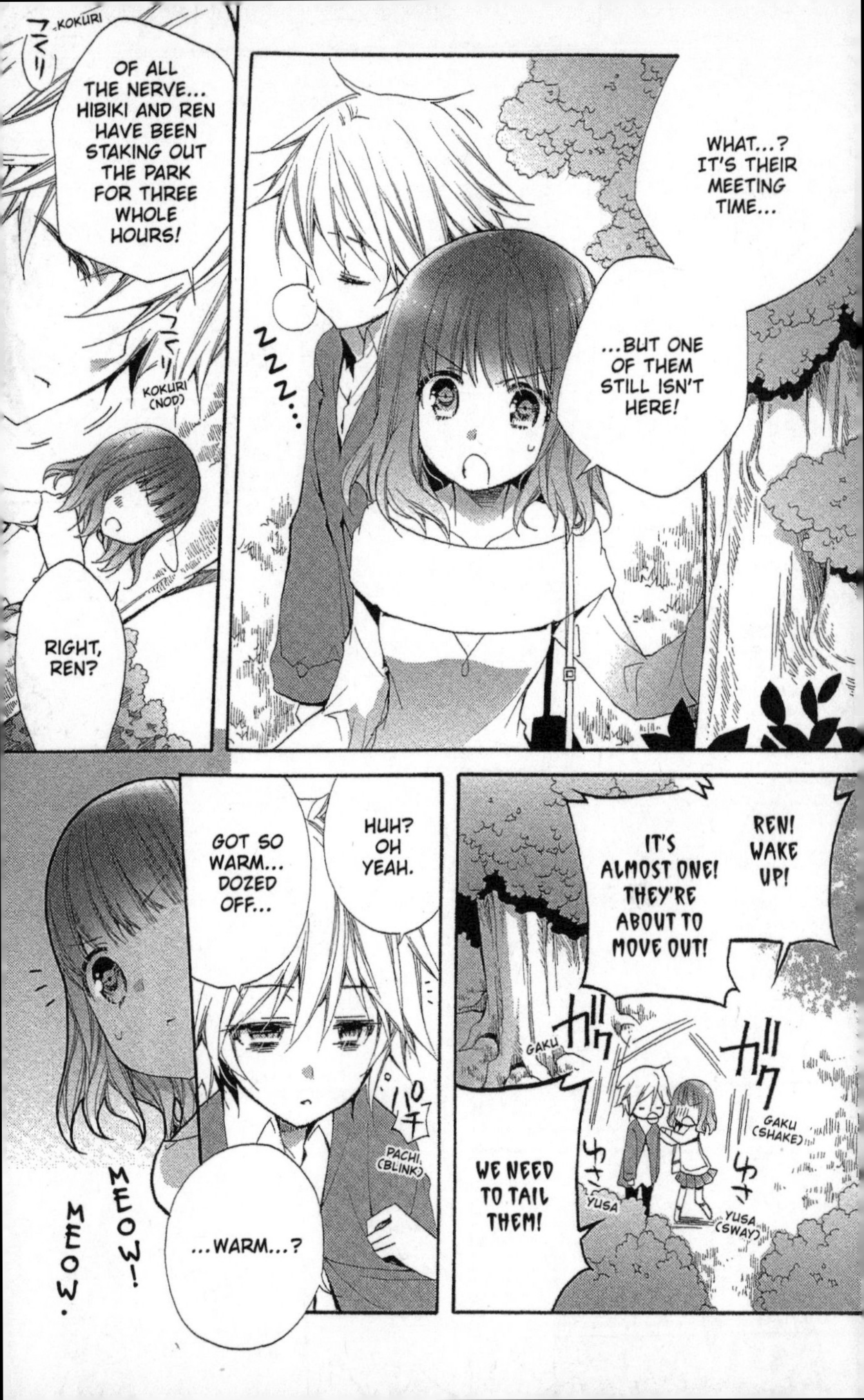
WHAT...? IT'S THEIR MEETING TIME...
...BUT ONE OF THEM STILL ISN'T HERE!
ZZZ...
KOKURI
OF ALL THE NERVE... HIBIKI AND REN HAVE BEEN STAKING OUT THE PARK FOR THREE WHOLE HOURS!
KOKURI (NOD)
RIGHT, REN?
REN! WAKE UP!
IT'S ALMOST ONE! THEY'RE ABOUT TO MOVE OUT!
GAKU
GAKU (SHAKE)
WE NEED TO TAIL THEM!
YUSA
YUSA (SWAY)
HUH? OH YEAH.
GOT SO WARM... DOZED OFF...
PACHI (BLINK)
...WARM...?
MEOW!
MEOW.

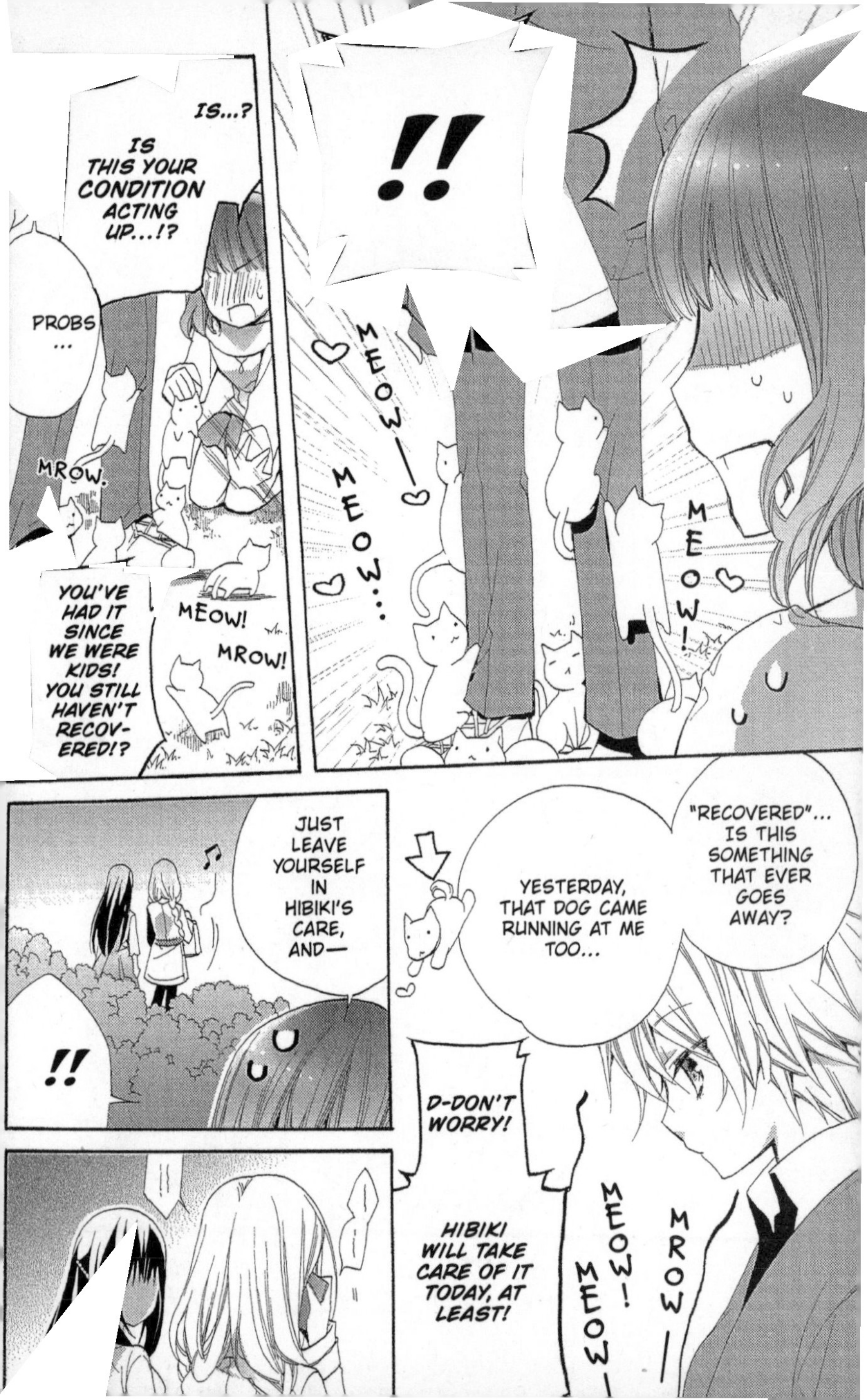
!!
MEOW—
MEOW...
MEOW!
IS...?
IS THIS YOUR CONDITION ACTING UP...!?
PROBS...
MROW.
YOU'VE HAD IT SINCE WE WERE KIDS! YOU STILL HAVEN'T RECOVERED!?
MEOW!
MROW!
"RECOVERED"... IS THIS SOMETHING THAT EVER GOES AWAY?
YESTERDAY, THAT DOG CAME RUNNING AT ME TOO...
D-DON'T WORRY!
HIBIKI WILL TAKE CARE OF IT TODAY, AT LEAST!
MROW—
MEOW!
MEOW—
JUST LEAVE YOURSELF IN HIBIKI'S CARE, AND—
!!

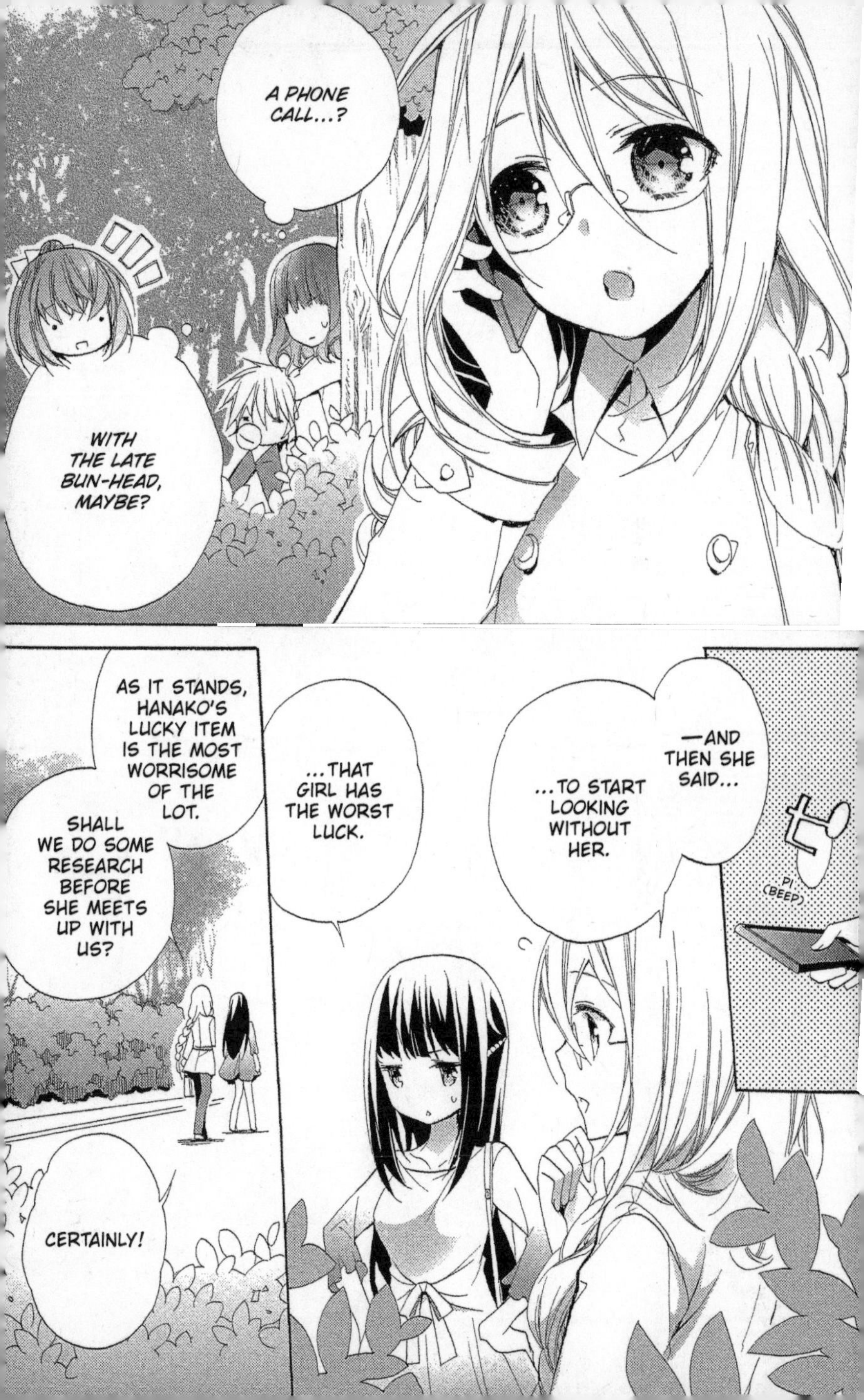
A PHONE CALL...?
WITH THE LATE BUN-HEAD, MAYBE?
—AND THEN SHE SAID...
PI (BEEP)
...TO START LOOKING WITHOUT HER.
...THAT GIRL HAS THE WORST LUCK.
AS IT STANDS, HANAKO'S LUCKY ITEM IS THE MOST WORRISOME OF THE LOT.
SHALL WE DO SOME RESEARCH BEFORE SHE MEETS UP WITH US?
CERTAINLY!

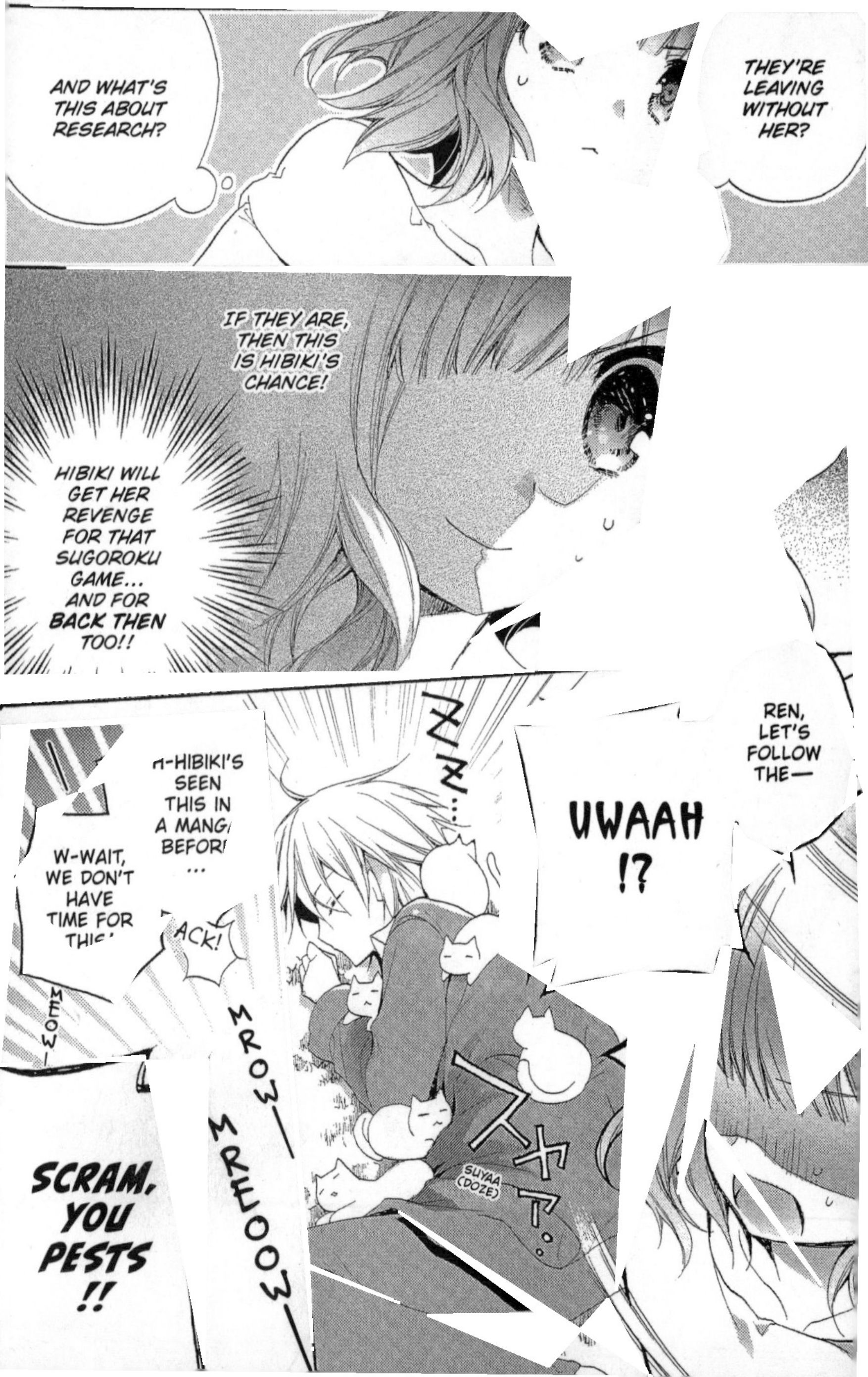
THEY'RE LEAVING WITHOUT HER?
AND WHAT'S THIS ABOUT RESEARCH?
IF THEY ARE, THEN THIS IS HIBIKI'S CHANCE!
HIBIKI WILL GET HER REVENGE FOR THAT SUGOROKU GAME... AND FOR BACK THEN TOO!!
REN, LET'S FOLLOW THE—
UWAAH !?
ZZZ...
SUYAA (DOZE)
MROW—
MREOOW—
-HIBIKI'S SEEN THIS IN A MANG BEFOR ...
W-WAIT, WE DON'T HAVE TIME FOR
ACK!
MEOW—
SCRAM, YOU PESTS!!

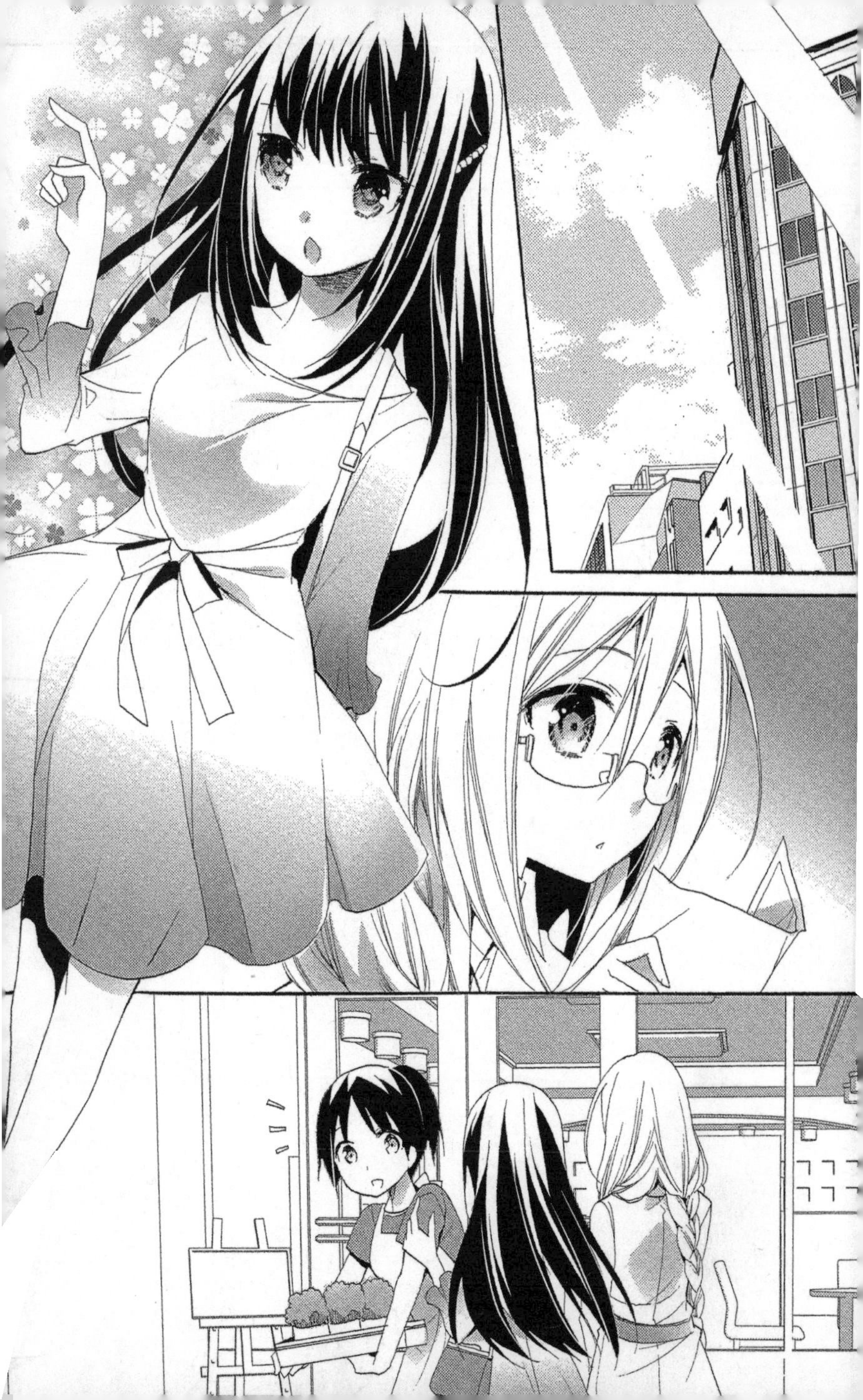

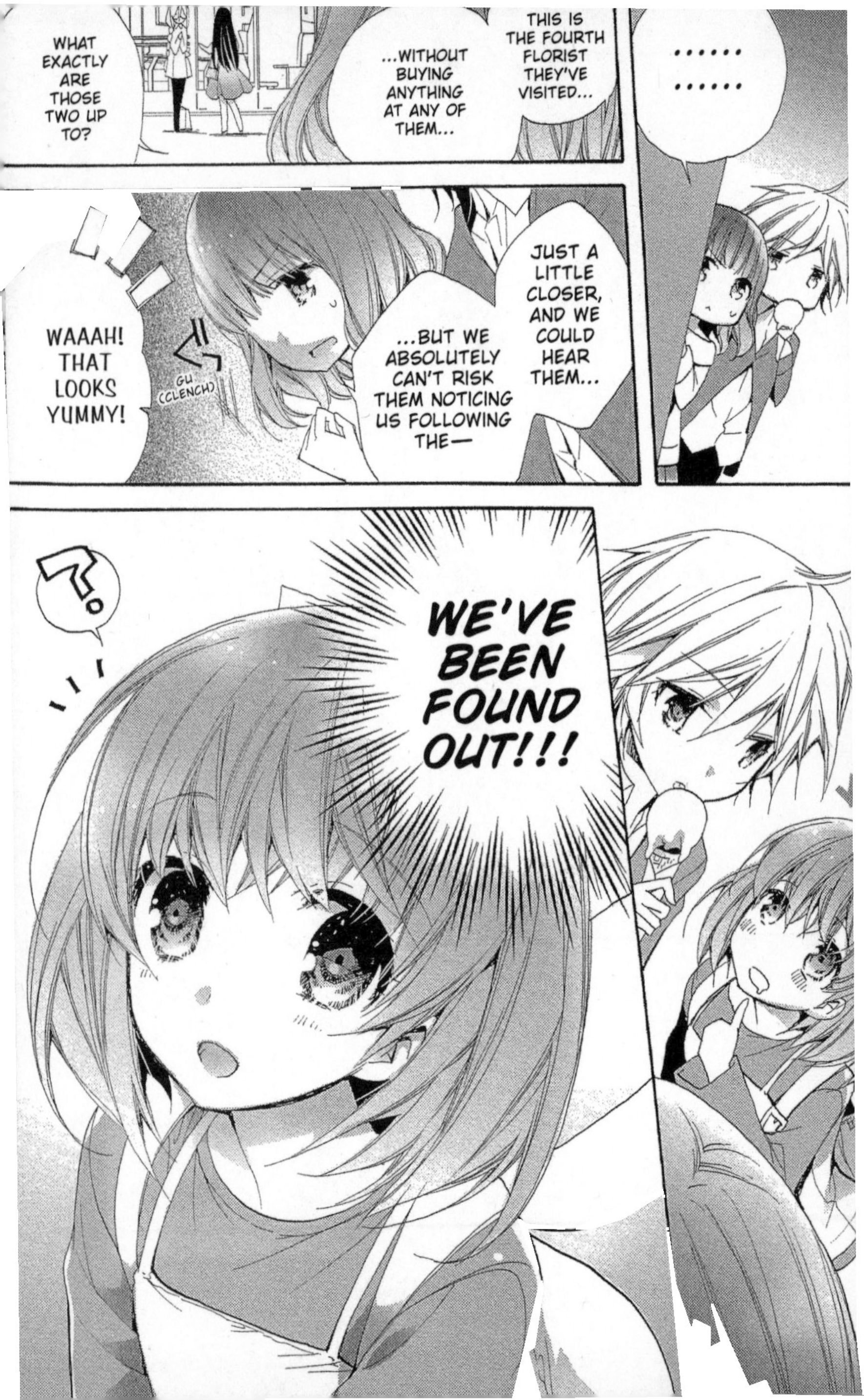
......
......
THIS IS THE FOURTH FLORIST THEY'VE VISITED...
...WITHOUT BUYING ANYTHING AT ANY OF THEM...
WHAT EXACTLY ARE THOSE TWO UP TO?
JUST A LITTLE CLOSER, AND WE COULD HEAR THEM...
...BUT WE ABSOLUTELY CAN'T RISK THEM NOTICING US FOLLOWING THE—
GU (CLENCH)
WAAAH! THAT LOOKS YUMMY!
WE'VE BEEN FOUND OUT!!!
?

Anne Happy

unhappy go lucky!

BOTAN KUMEGAWA

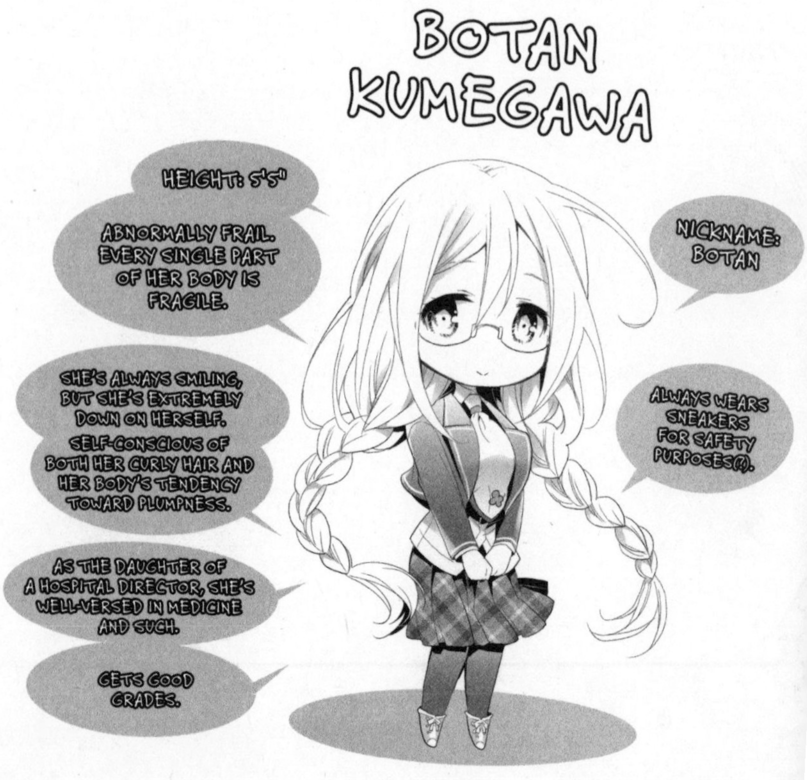
HEIGHT: 5'5"
ABNORMALLY FRAIL. EVERY SINGLE PART OF HER BODY IS FRAGILE.
NICKNAME: BOTAN
SHE'S ALWAYS SMILING, BUT SHE'S EXTREMELY DOWN ON HERSELF.
SELF-CONSCIOUS OF BOTH HER CURLY HAIR AND HER BODY'S TENDENCY TOWARD PLUMPNESS.
ALWAYS WEARS SNEAKERS FOR SAFETY PURPOSES(?).
AS THE DAUGHTER OF A HOSPITAL DIRECTOR, SHE'S WELL-VERSED IN MEDICINE AND SUCH.
GETS GOOD GRADES.

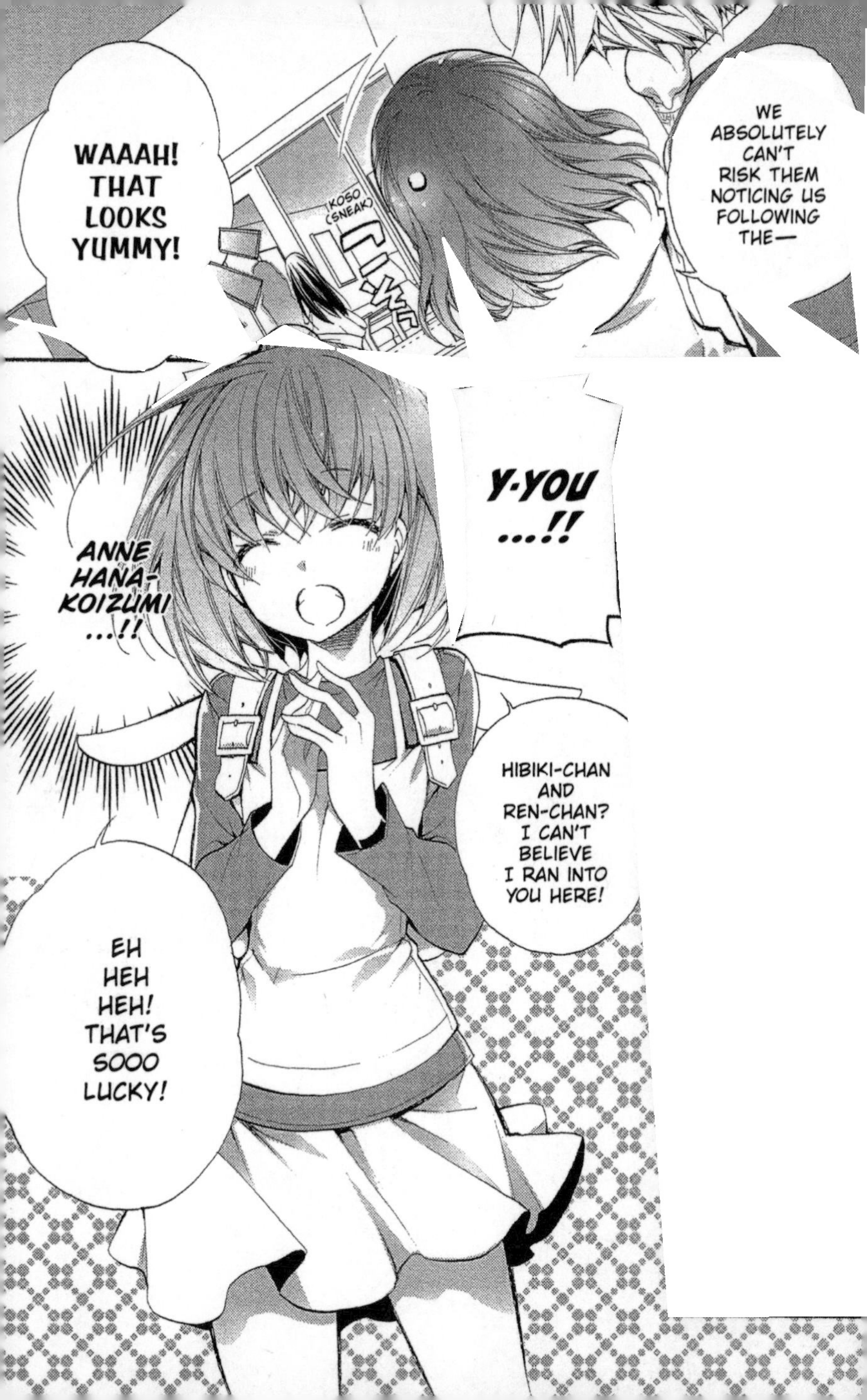
WE ABSOLUTELY CAN'T RISK THEM NOTICING US FOLLOWING THE—
KOSO (SNEAK)
WAAAH! THAT LOOKS YUMMY!
Y-YOU ...!!
ANNE HANA-KOIZUMI ...!!
HIBIKI-CHAN AND REN-CHAN? I CAN'T BELIEVE I RAN INTO YOU HERE!
EH HEH HEH! THAT'S SOOO LUCKY!

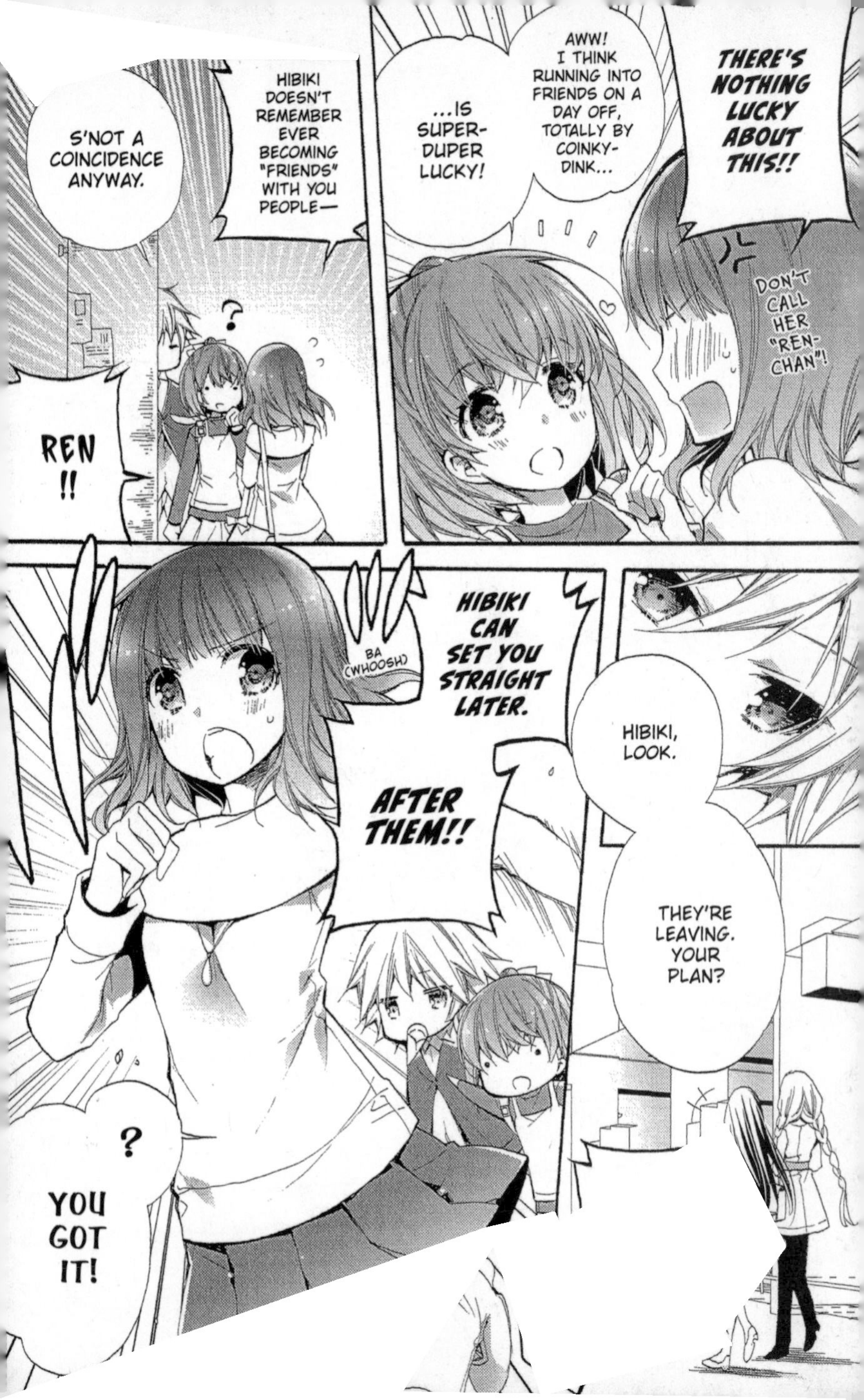

AWW! I THINK RUNNING INTO FRIENDS ON A DAY OFF, TOTALLY BY COINKY-DINK...
...IS SUPER-DUPER LUCKY!
THERE'S NOTHING LUCKY ABOUT THIS!!
DON'T CALL HER "REN-CHAN"!
HIBIKI DOESN'T REMEMBER EVER BECOMING "FRIENDS" WITH YOU PEOPLE—
S'NOT A COINCIDENCE ANYWAY.
REN!!
HIBIKI, LOOK.
THEY'RE LEAVING. YOUR PLAN?
HIBIKI CAN SET YOU STRAIGHT LATER.
BA (WHOOSH)
AFTER THEM!!
?
YOU GOT IT!

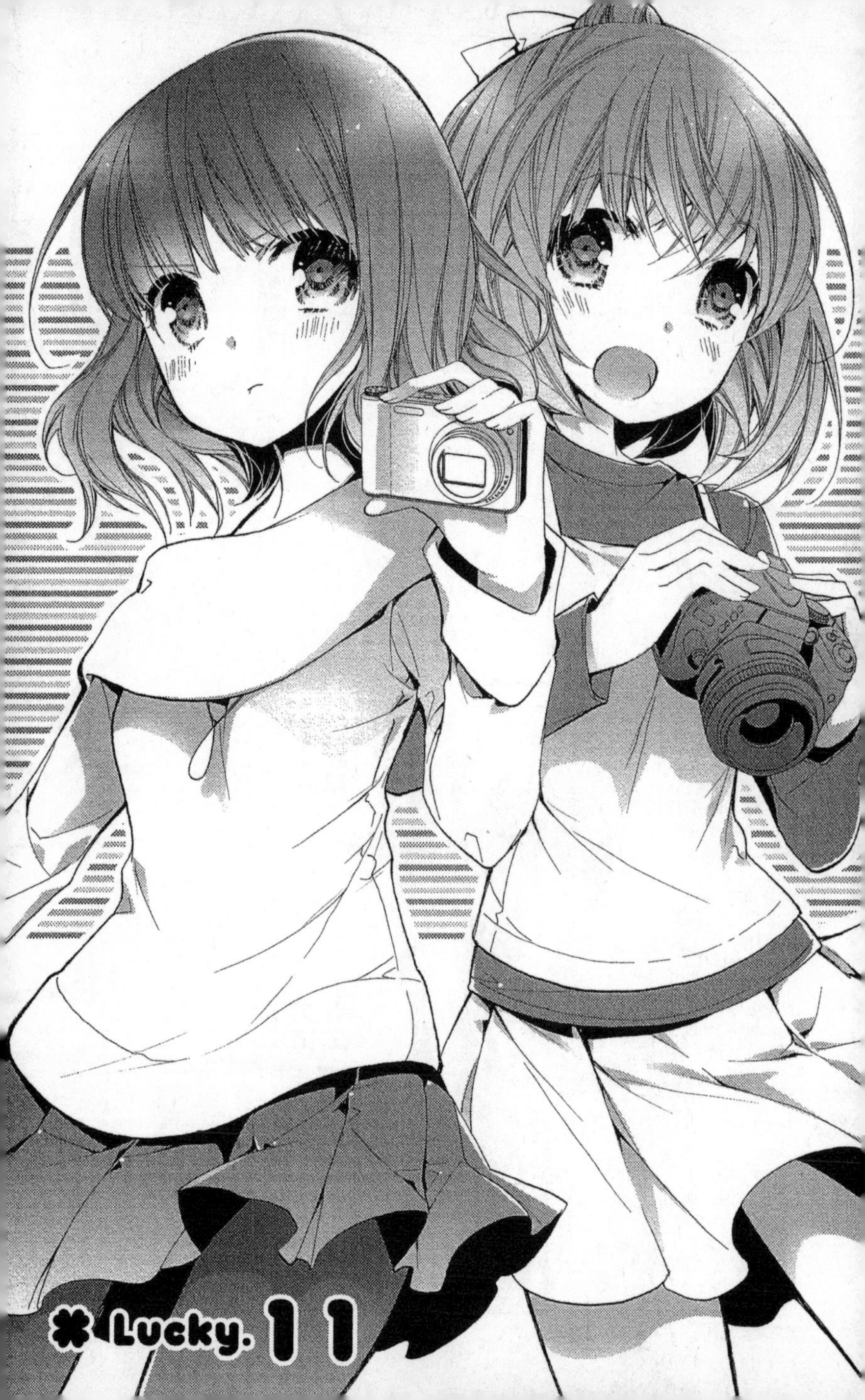
Lucky. 11

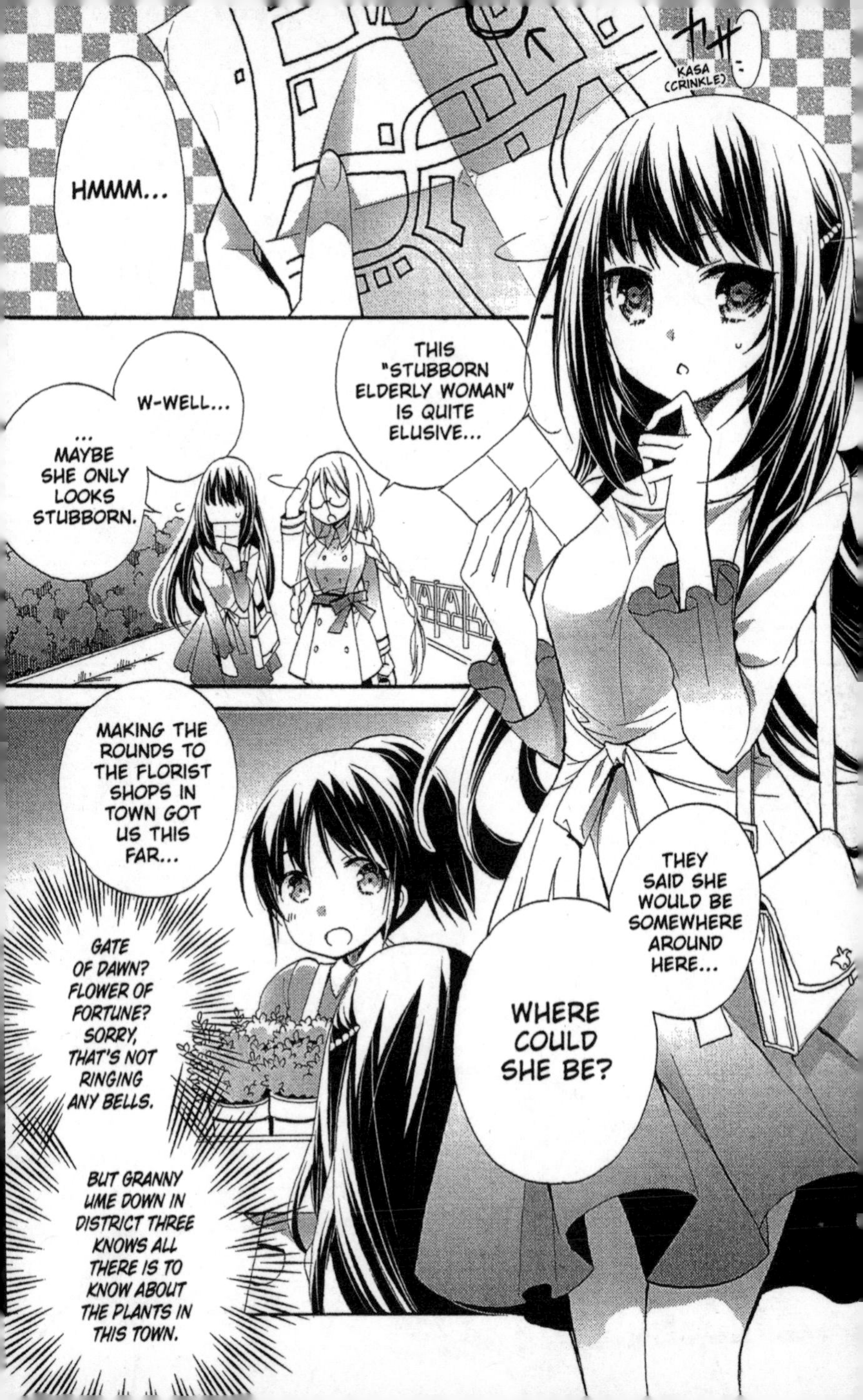
カサ
KASA (CRINKLE)
HMMM...
THIS "STUBBORN ELDERLY WOMAN" IS QUITE ELUSIVE...
W-WELL...
... MAYBE SHE ONLY LOOKS STUBBORN.
MAKING THE ROUNDS TO THE FLORIST SHOPS IN TOWN GOT US THIS FAR...
THEY SAID SHE WOULD BE SOMEWHERE AROUND HERE...
WHERE COULD SHE BE?
GATE OF DAWN? FLOWER OF FORTUNE? SORRY, THAT'S NOT RINGING ANY BELLS.
BUT GRANNY UME DOWN IN DISTRICT THREE KNOWS ALL THERE IS TO KNOW ABOUT THE PLANTS IN THIS TOWN.

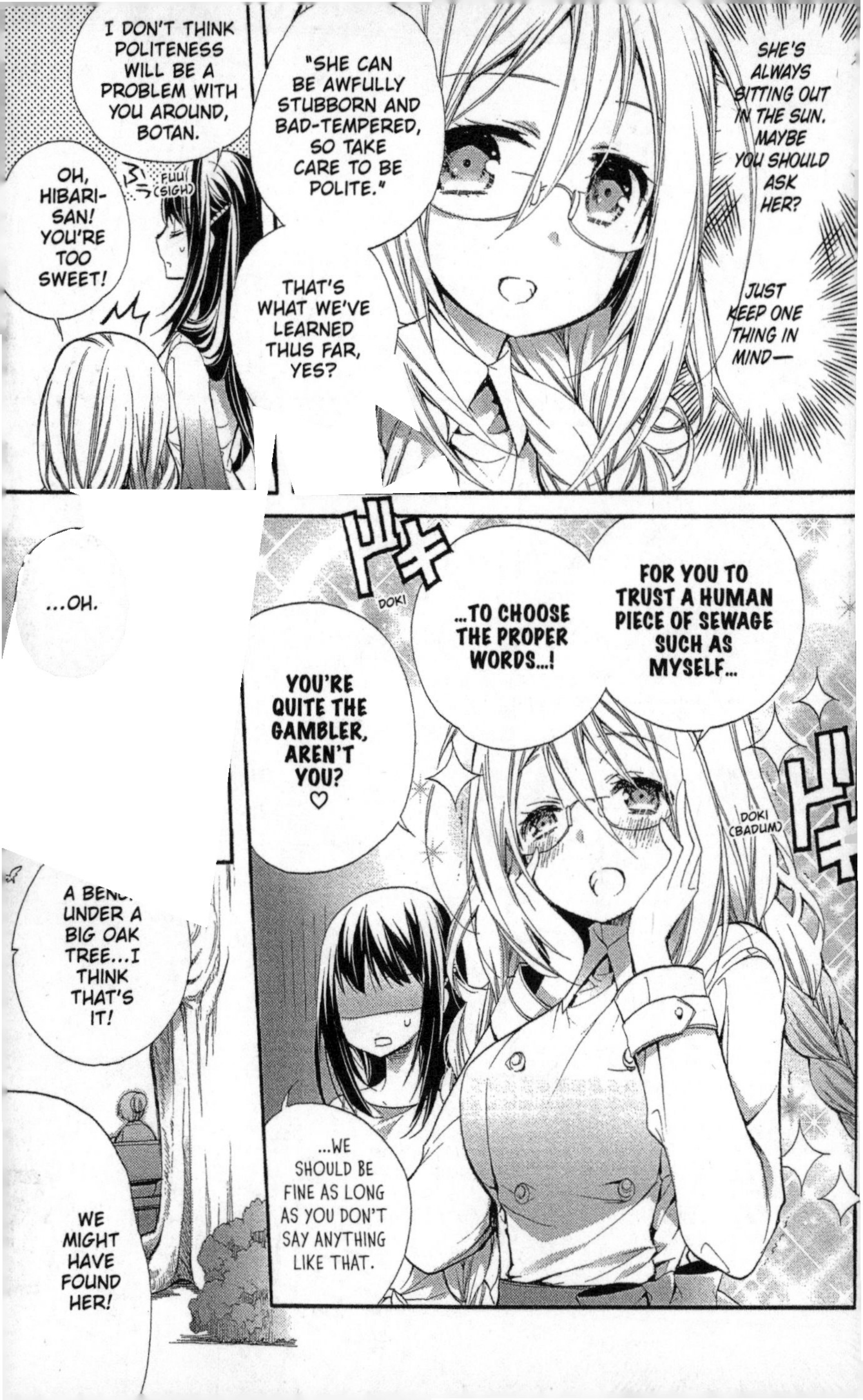
SHE'S ALWAYS SITTING OUT IN THE SUN. MAYBE YOU SHOULD ASK HER?
JUST KEEP ONE THING IN MIND—
"SHE CAN BE AWFULLY STUBBORN AND BAD-TEMPERED, SO TAKE CARE TO BE POLITE."
THAT'S WHAT WE'VE LEARNED THUS FAR, YES?
I DON'T THINK POLITENESS WILL BE A PROBLEM WITH YOU AROUND, BOTAN.
FUU (SIGH)
OH, HIBARI-SAN! YOU'RE TOO SWEET!
DOKI
FOR YOU TO TRUST A HUMAN PIECE OF SEWAGE SUCH AS MYSELF...
...TO CHOOSE THE PROPER WORDS...!
DOKI (BADUM)
YOU'RE QUITE THE GAMBLER, AREN'T YOU? ♡
...WE SHOULD BE FINE AS LONG AS YOU DON'T SAY ANYTHING LIKE THAT.
...OH.
A BENC UNDER A BIG OAK TREE...I THINK THAT'S IT!
WE MIGHT HAVE FOUND HER!

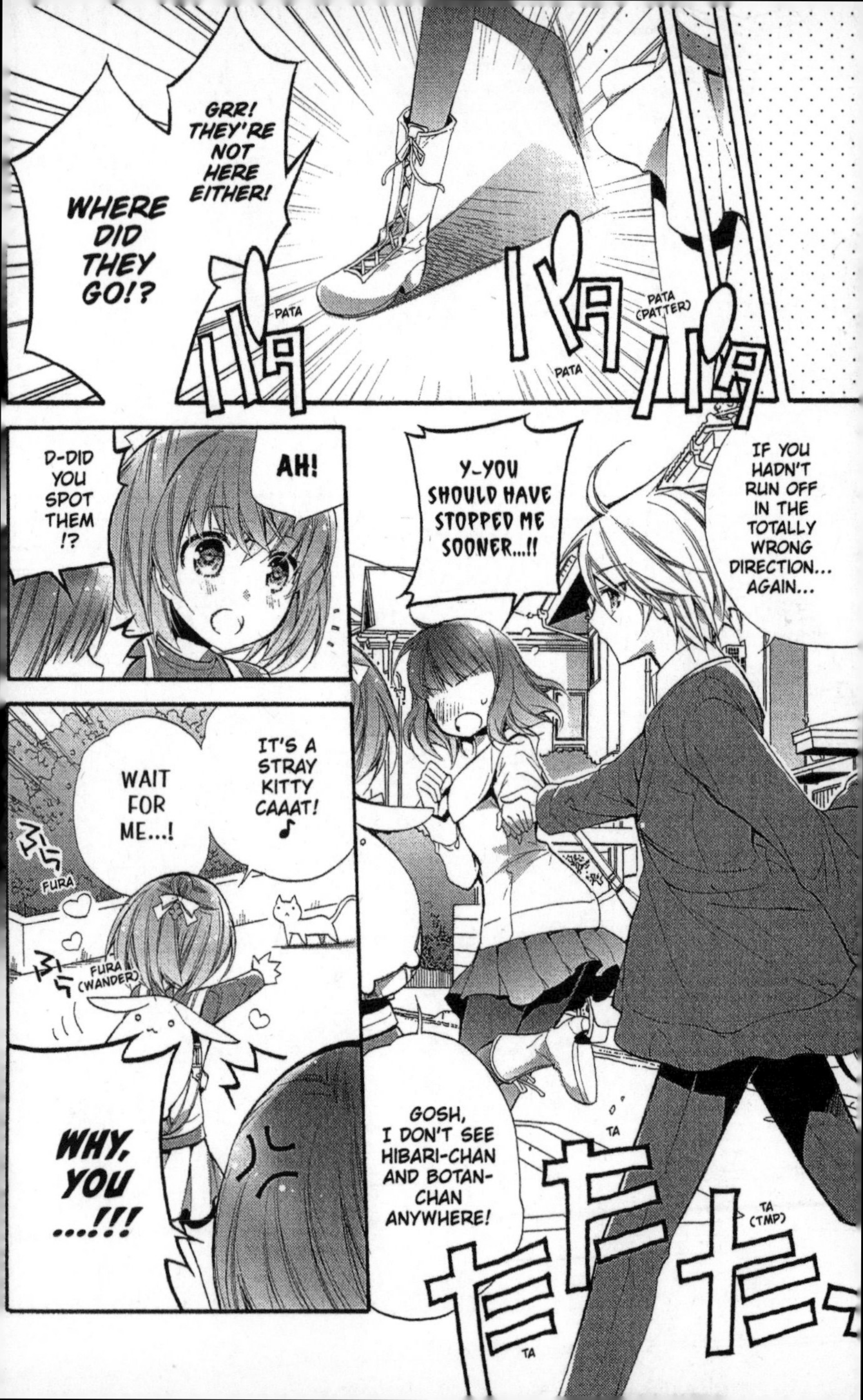
PATA (PATTER)
PATA
GRR! THEY'RE NOT HERE EITHER!
PATA
WHERE DID THEY GO!?
IF YOU HADN'T RUN OFF IN THE TOTALLY WRONG DIRECTION... AGAIN...
Y-YOU SHOULD HAVE STOPPED ME SOONER...!!
TA
TA (TMP)
TA
GOSH, I DON'T SEE HIBARI-CHAN AND BOTAN-CHAN ANYWHERE!
AH!
D-DID YOU SPOT THEM!?
IT'S A STRAY KITTY CAAAT! ♪
WAIT FOR ME...!
FURA
FURA (WANDER)
WHY, YOU...!!!

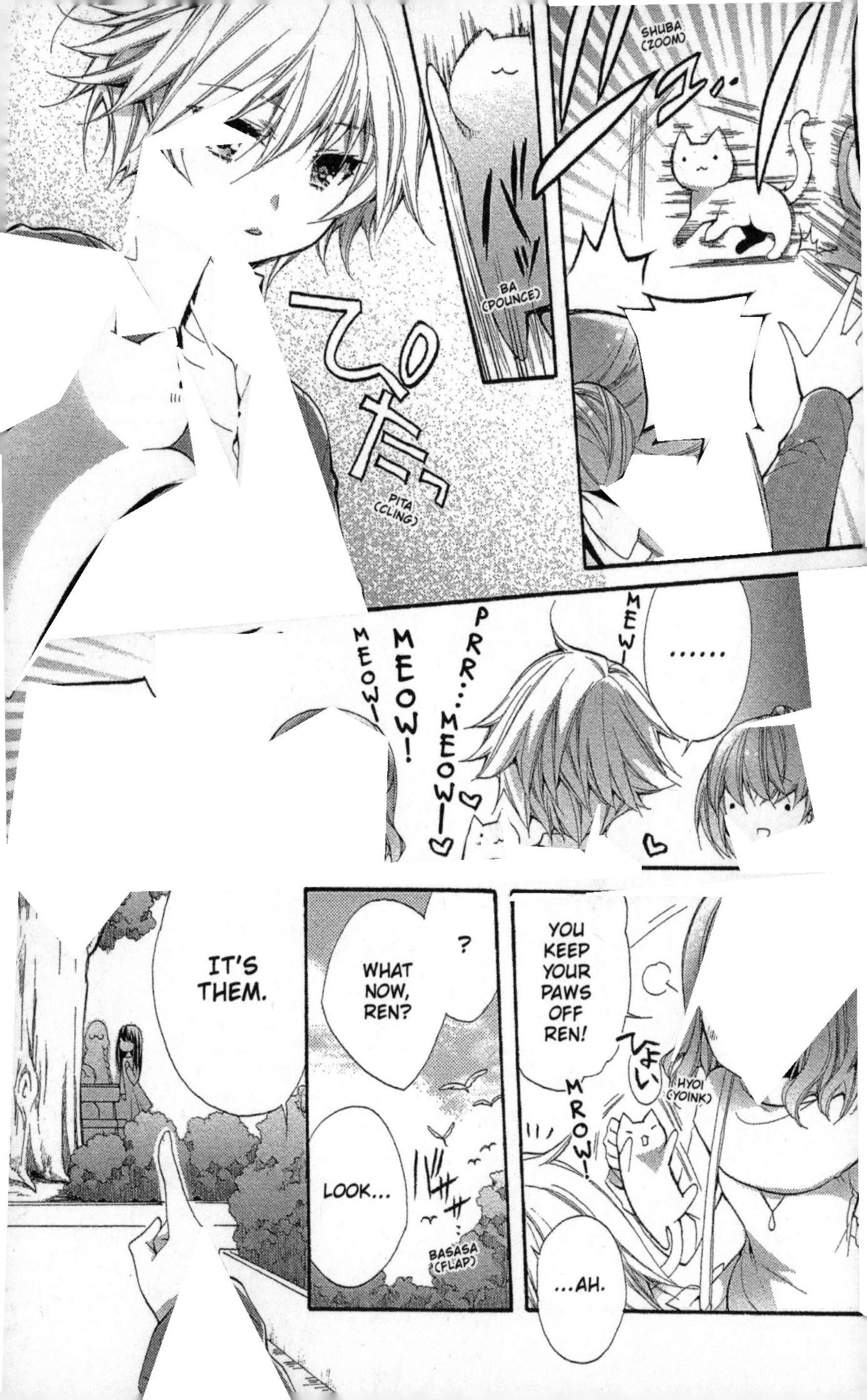
SHUBA (ZOOM)
BA (POUNCE)
PITA (CLING)
MEW!
......
PRR... MEOW! ♥
MEOW!
MEOW!
YOU KEEP YOUR PAWS OFF REN!
HYOI (YOINK)
MROW!
...AH.
?
WHAT NOW, REN?
LOOK...
BASASA (FLAP)
IT'S THEM.

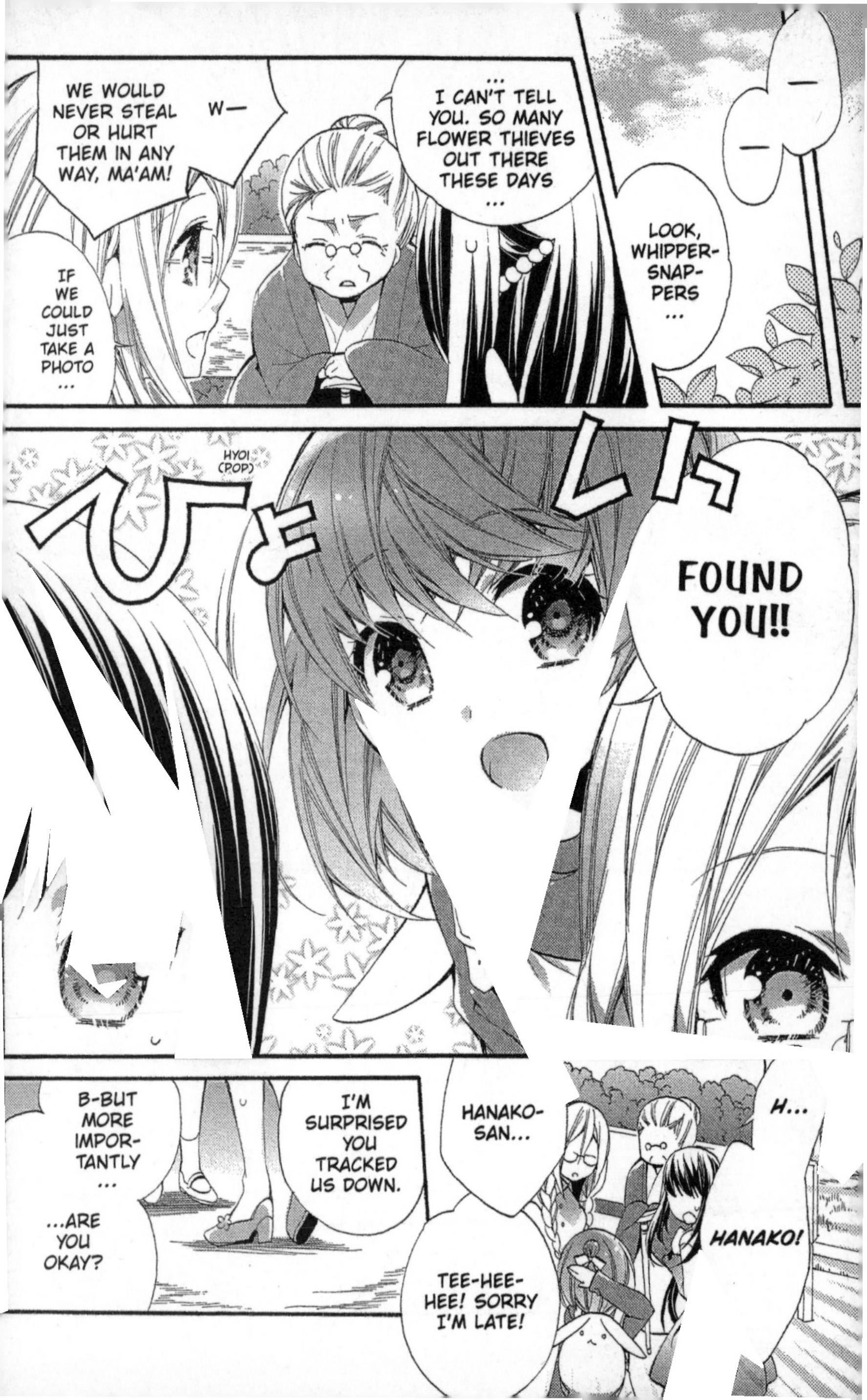
—
—
LOOK, WHIPPER-SNAPPERS ...
... I CAN'T TELL YOU. SO MANY FLOWER THIEVES OUT THERE THESE DAYS ...
W—
WE WOULD NEVER STEAL OR HURT THEM IN ANY WAY, MA'AM!
IF WE COULD JUST TAKE A PHOTO ...
FOUND YOU!!
HYOI (POP)
H...
HANAKO!
HANAKO-SAN...
TEE-HEE-HEE! SORRY I'M LATE!
I'M SURPRISED YOU TRACKED US DOWN.
B-BUT MORE IMPORTANTLY ...
...ARE YOU OKAY?

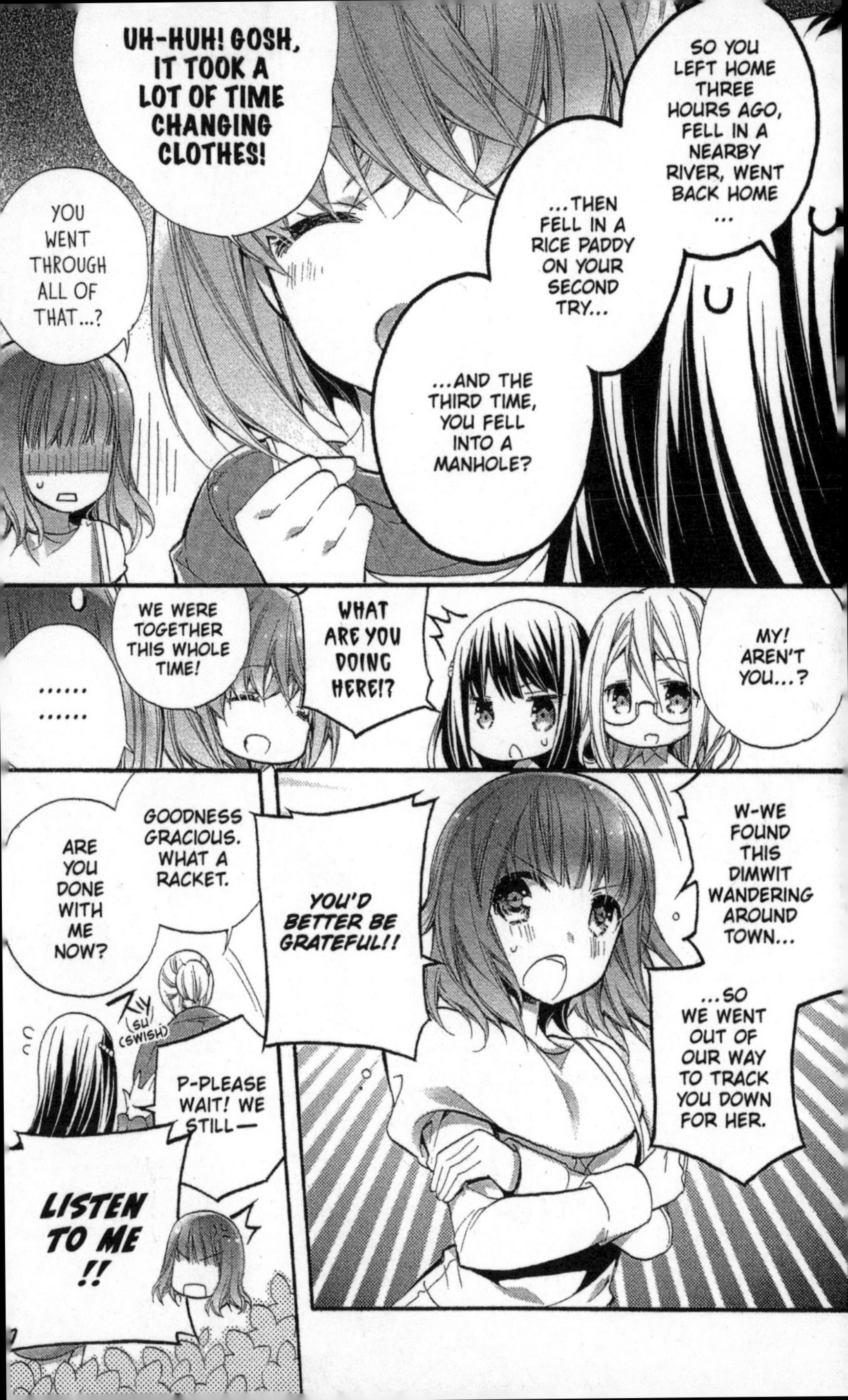
SO YOU LEFT HOME THREE HOURS AGO, FELL IN A NEARBY RIVER, WENT BACK HOME ...
...THEN FELL IN A RICE PADDY ON YOUR SECOND TRY...
...AND THE THIRD TIME, YOU FELL INTO A MANHOLE?
UH-HUH! GOSH, IT TOOK A LOT OF TIME CHANGING CLOTHES!
YOU WENT THROUGH ALL OF THAT...?
MY! AREN'T YOU...?
WHAT ARE YOU DOING HERE!?
WE WERE TOGETHER THIS WHOLE TIME!
....
W-WE FOUND THIS DIMWIT WANDERING AROUND TOWN...
...SO WE WENT OUT OF OUR WAY TO TRACK YOU DOWN FOR HER.
YOU'D BETTER BE GRATEFUL!!
GOODNESS GRACIOUS. WHAT A RACKET.
ARE YOU DONE WITH ME NOW?
SU (SWISH)
P-PLEASE WAIT! WE STILL—
LISTEN TO ME !!

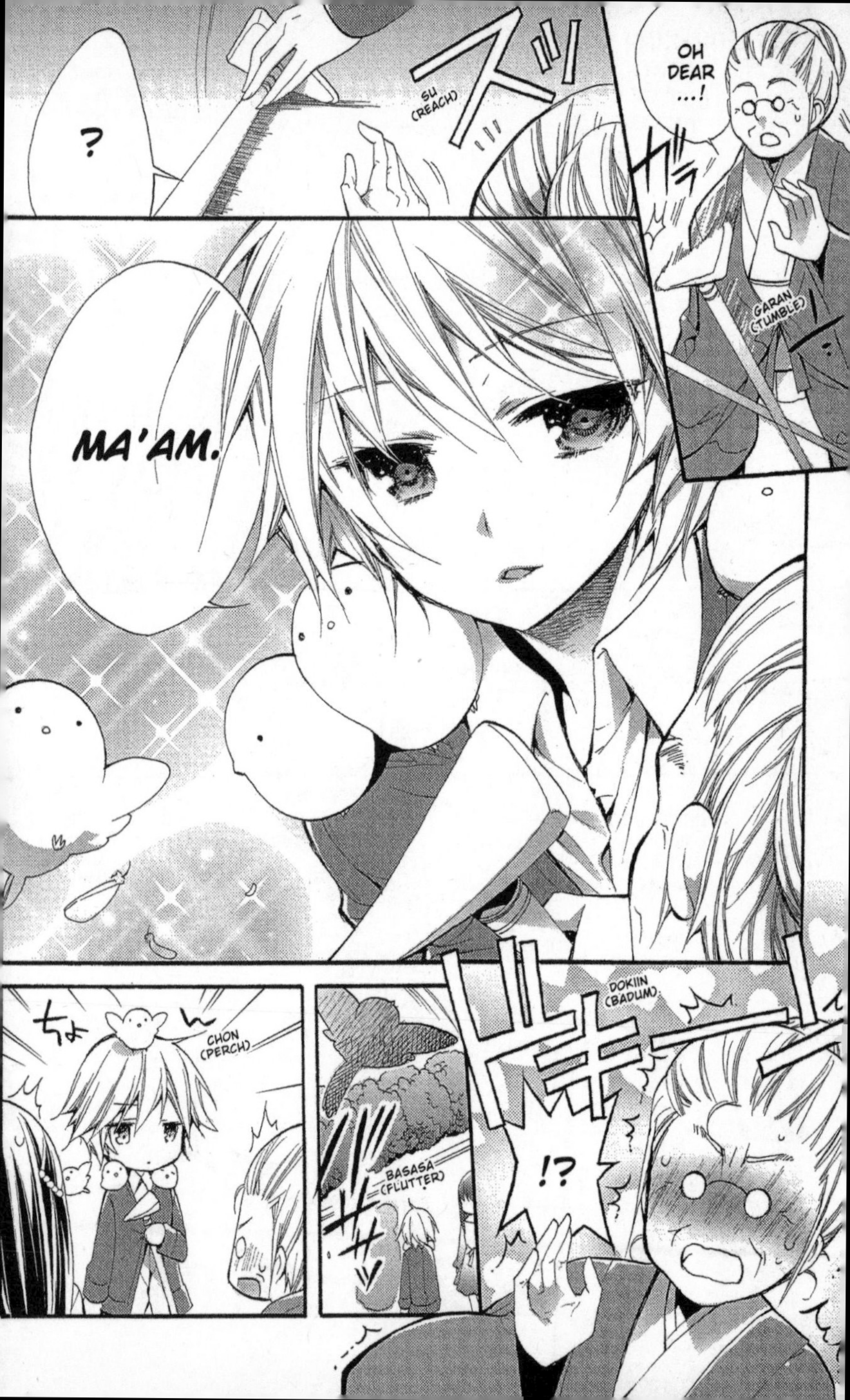
OH DEAR ....!
ガラ
GARAN (TUMBLE)
スッ
SU (REACH)
?
MA'AM.
DOKIIN (BADUM)
!?
BASASA (FLUTTER)
ちょん
CHON (PERCH)

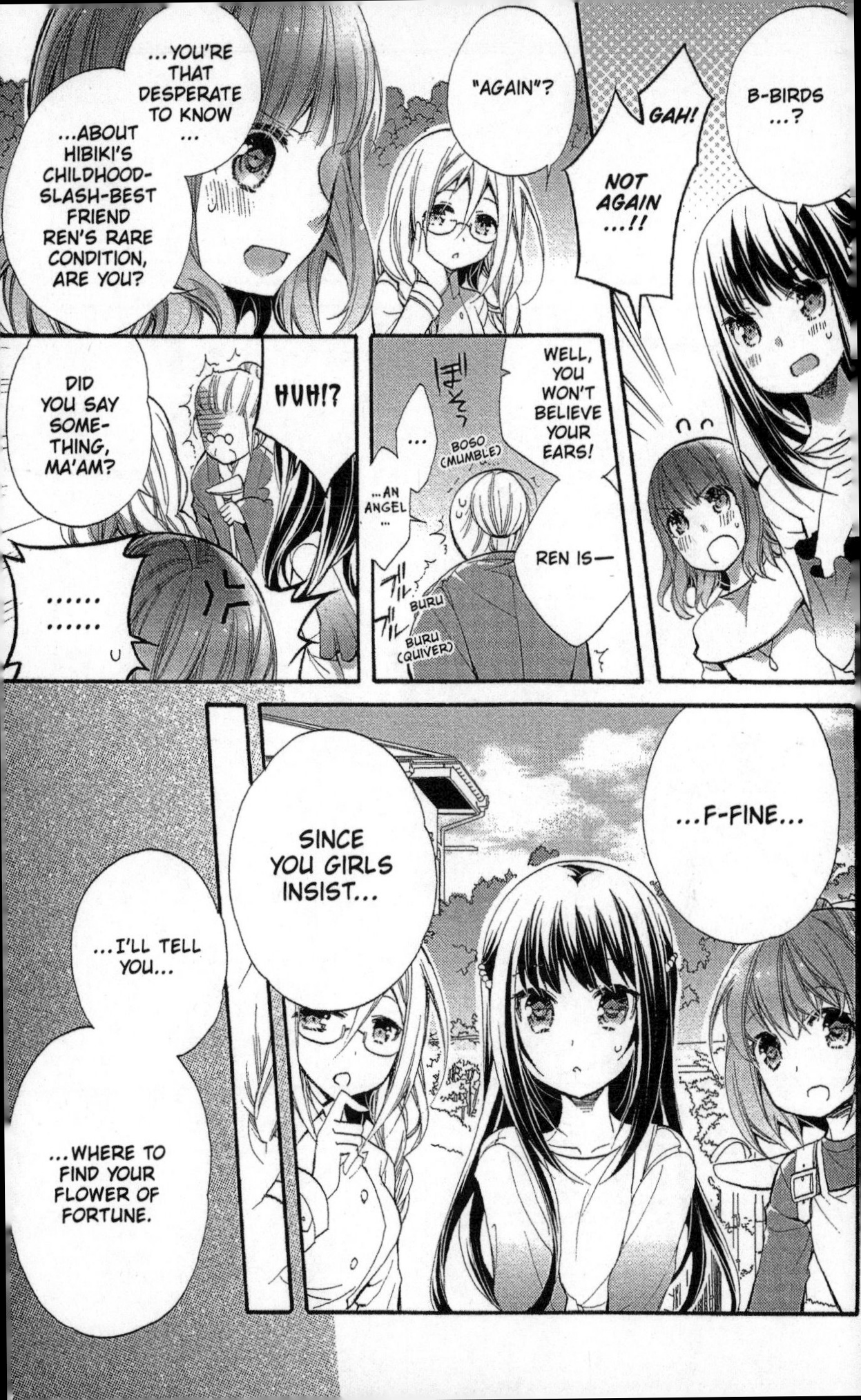
B-BIRDS ...?
GAH!
NOT AGAIN ...!!
"AGAIN"?
...YOU'RE THAT DESPERATE TO KNOW ...
...ABOUT HIBIKI'S CHILDHOOD-SLASH-BEST FRIEND REN'S RARE CONDITION, ARE YOU?
WELL, YOU WON'T BELIEVE YOUR EARS!
REN IS—
BOSO (MUMBLE)
...
...AN ANGEL ...
BURU BURU (QUIVER)
HUH!?
DID YOU SAY SOME-THING, MA'AM?
....
...F-FINE...
SINCE YOU GIRLS INSIST...
...I'LL TELL YOU...
...WHERE TO FIND YOUR FLOWER OF FORTUNE.

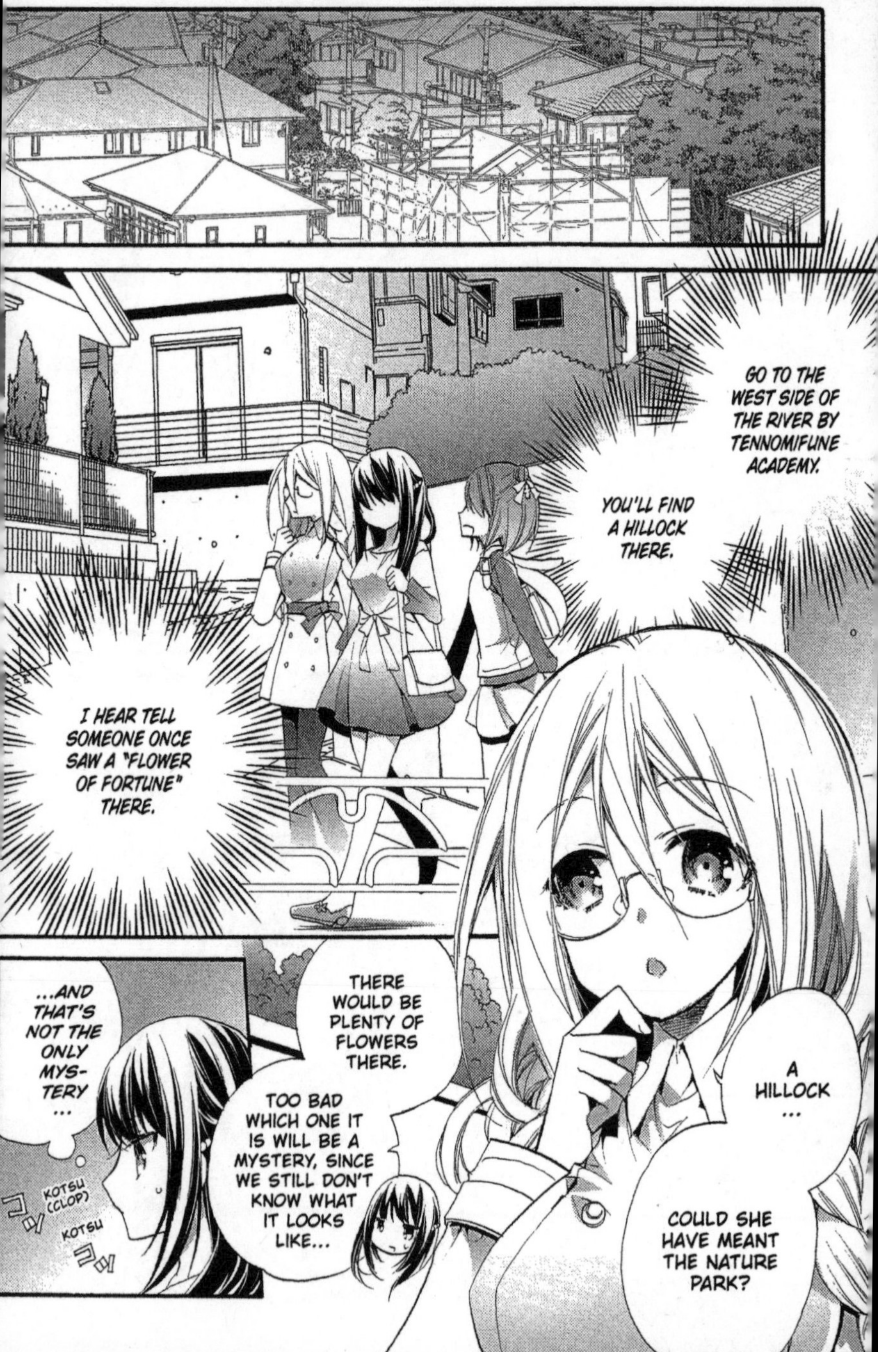
GO TO THE WEST SIDE OF THE RIVER BY TENNOMIFUNE ACADEMY.
YOU'LL FIND A HILLOCK THERE.
I HEAR TELL SOMEONE ONCE SAW A "FLOWER OF FORTUNE" THERE.
A HILLOCK...
COULD SHE HAVE MEANT THE NATURE PARK?
THERE WOULD BE PLENTY OF FLOWERS THERE.
TOO BAD WHICH ONE IT IS WILL BE A MYSTERY, SINCE WE STILL DON'T KNOW WHAT IT LOOKS LIKE...
...AND THAT'S NOT THE ONLY MYSTERY...
KOTSU (CLOP)
KOTSU

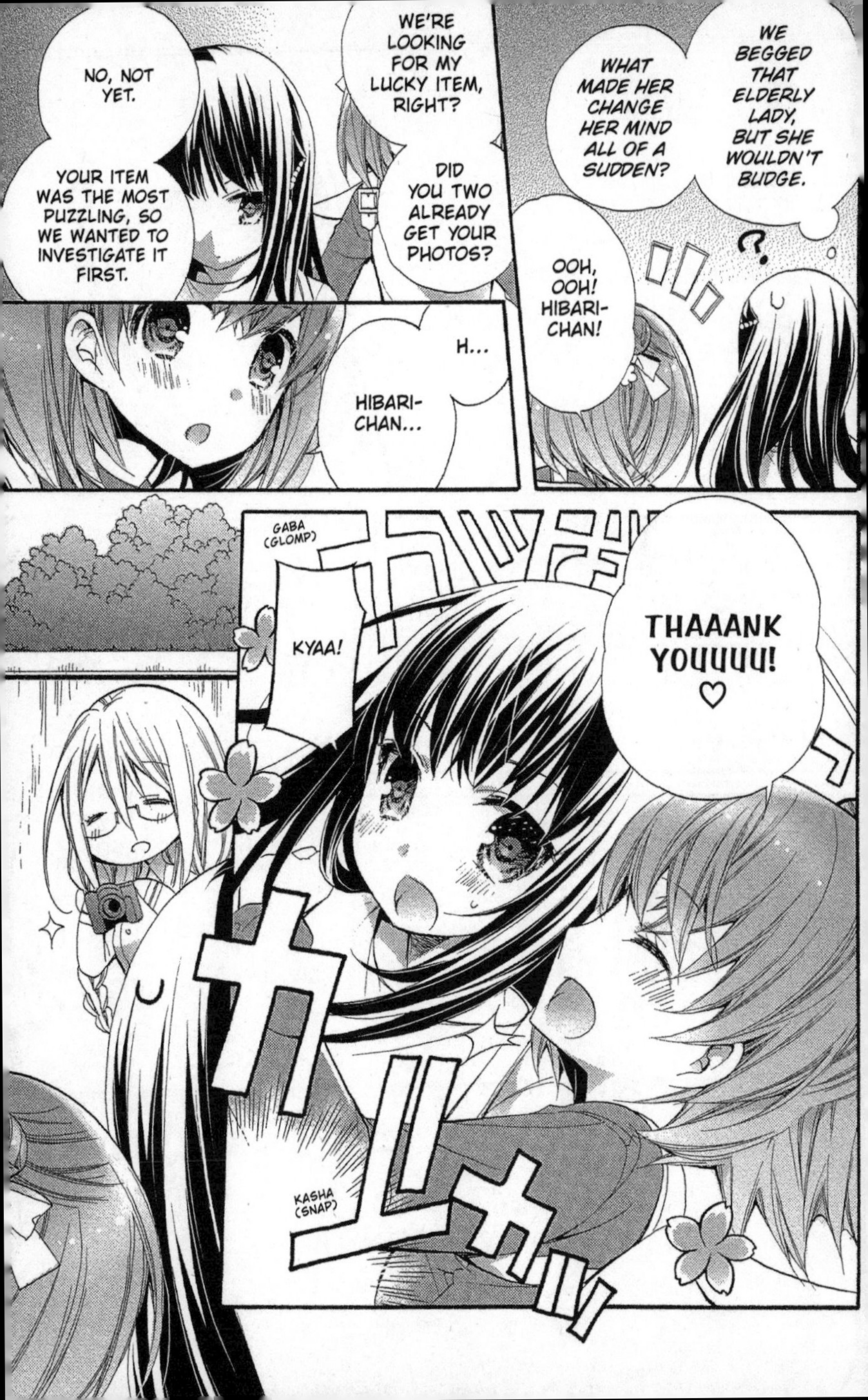
WE BEGGED THAT ELDERLY LADY, BUT SHE WOULDN'T BUDGE.
WHAT MADE HER CHANGE HER MIND ALL OF A SUDDEN?
WE'RE LOOKING FOR MY LUCKY ITEM, RIGHT?
DID YOU TWO ALREADY GET YOUR PHOTOS?
NO, NOT YET.
YOUR ITEM WAS THE MOST PUZZLING, SO WE WANTED TO INVESTIGATE IT FIRST.
OOH, OOH! HIBARI-CHAN!
H...
HIBARI-CHAN...
THAAANK YOUUUU! ♡
GABA (GLOMP)
KYAA!
KASHA (SNAP)

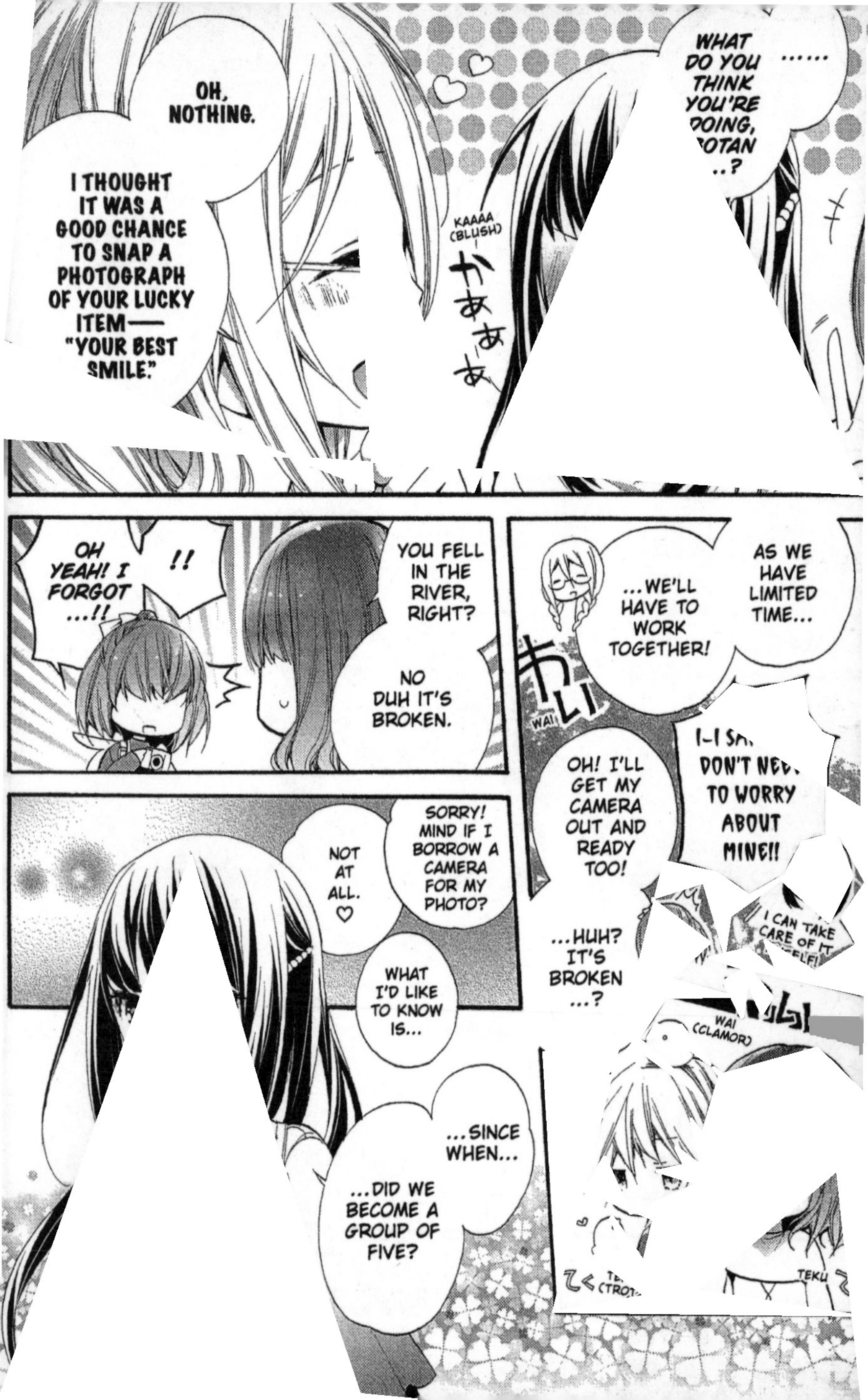

WHAT DO YOU THINK YOU'RE DOING, ...OTAN ...?
......
KAAAA (BLUSH)
かあああ
OH, NOTHING.
I THOUGHT IT WAS A GOOD CHANCE TO SNAP A PHOTOGRAPH OF YOUR LUCKY ITEM— "YOUR BEST SMILE."
AS WE HAVE LIMITED TIME...
...WE'LL HAVE TO WORK TOGETHER!
わい
WAI
I-I SA... DON'T NEE... TO WORRY ABOUT MINE!!
OH! I'LL GET MY CAMERA OUT AND READY TOO!
I CAN TAKE CARE OF IT ...ELF!
...HUH? IT'S BROKEN ...?
WAI (CLAMOR)
TEKU
TE... (TROT...
YOU FELL IN THE RIVER, RIGHT?
!!
OH YEAH! I FORGOT ...!!
NO DUH IT'S BROKEN.
SORRY! MIND IF I BORROW A CAMERA FOR MY PHOTO?
NOT AT ALL. ♡
WHAT I'D LIKE TO KNOW IS...
...SINCE WHEN...
...DID WE BECOME A GROUP OF FIVE?

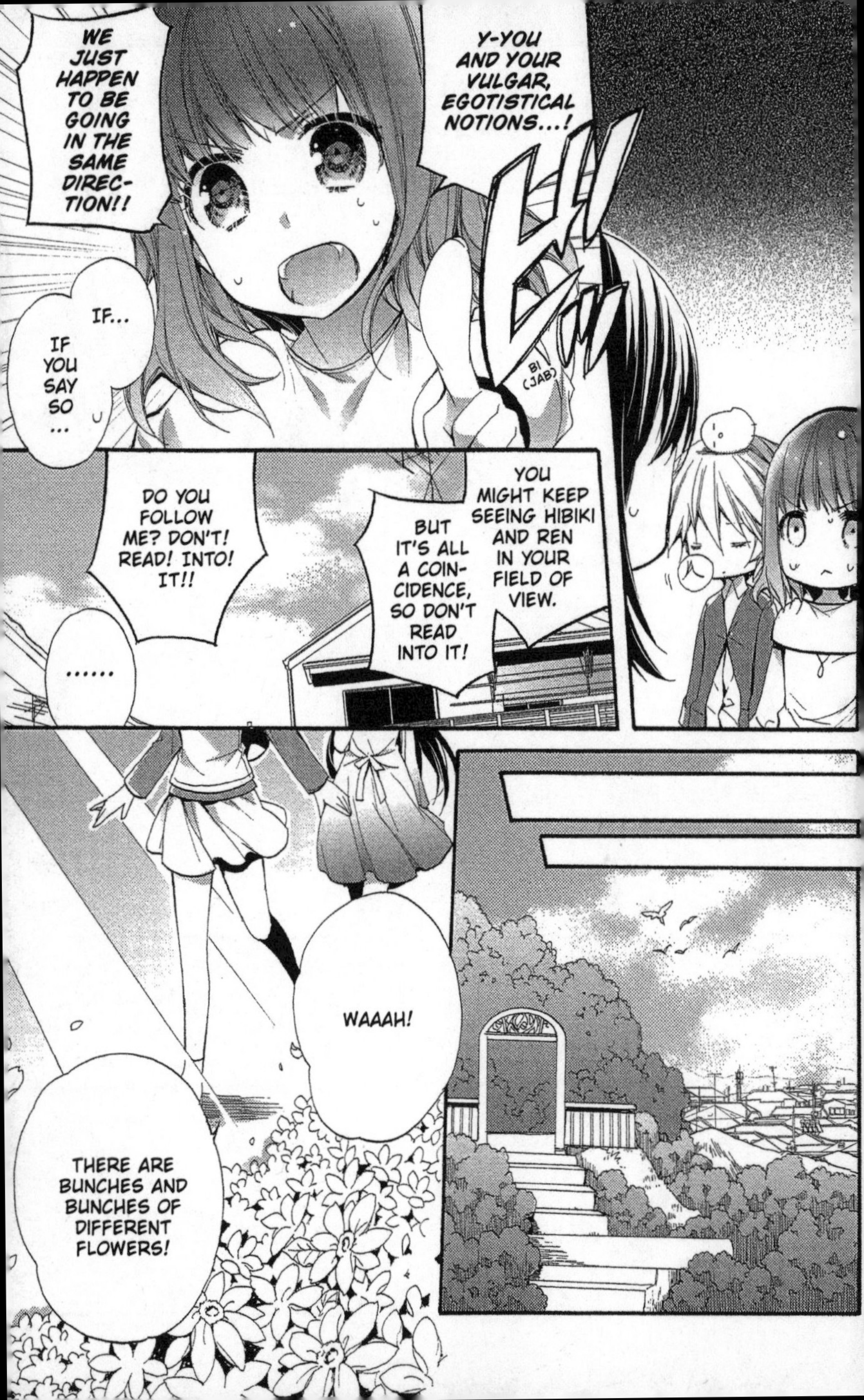
Y-YOU AND YOUR VULGAR, EGOTISTICAL NOTIONS...!
WE JUST HAPPEN TO BE GOING IN THE SAME DIRECTION!!
BI (JAB)
IF... IF YOU SAY SO...
YOU MIGHT KEEP SEEING HIBIKI AND REN IN YOUR FIELD OF VIEW.
BUT IT'S ALL A COINCIDENCE, SO DON'T READ INTO IT!
DO YOU FOLLOW ME? DON'T! READ! INTO! IT!!
......
WAAAH!
THERE ARE BUNCHES AND BUNCHES OF DIFFERENT FLOWERS!

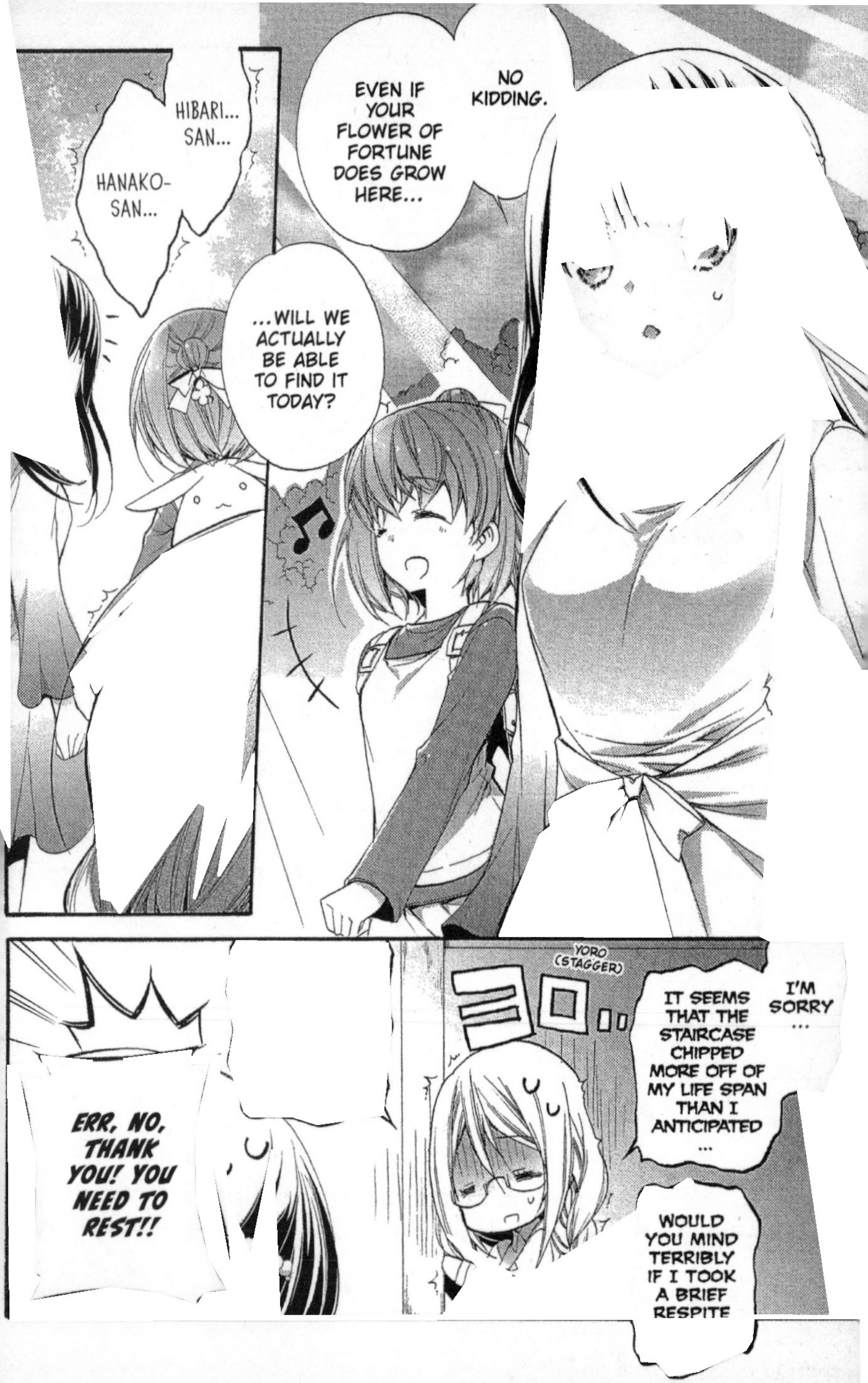
NO KIDDING.
EVEN IF YOUR FLOWER OF FORTUNE DOES GROW HERE...
...WILL WE ACTUALLY BE ABLE TO FIND IT TODAY?
HIBARI... SAN...
HANAKO-SAN...
I'M SORRY...
IT SEEMS THAT THE STAIRCASE CHIPPED MORE OFF OF MY LIFE SPAN THAN I ANTICIPATED...
YORO (STAGGER)
WOULD YOU MIND TERRIBLY IF I TOOK A BRIEF RESPITE
ERR, NO, THANK YOU! YOU NEED TO REST!!

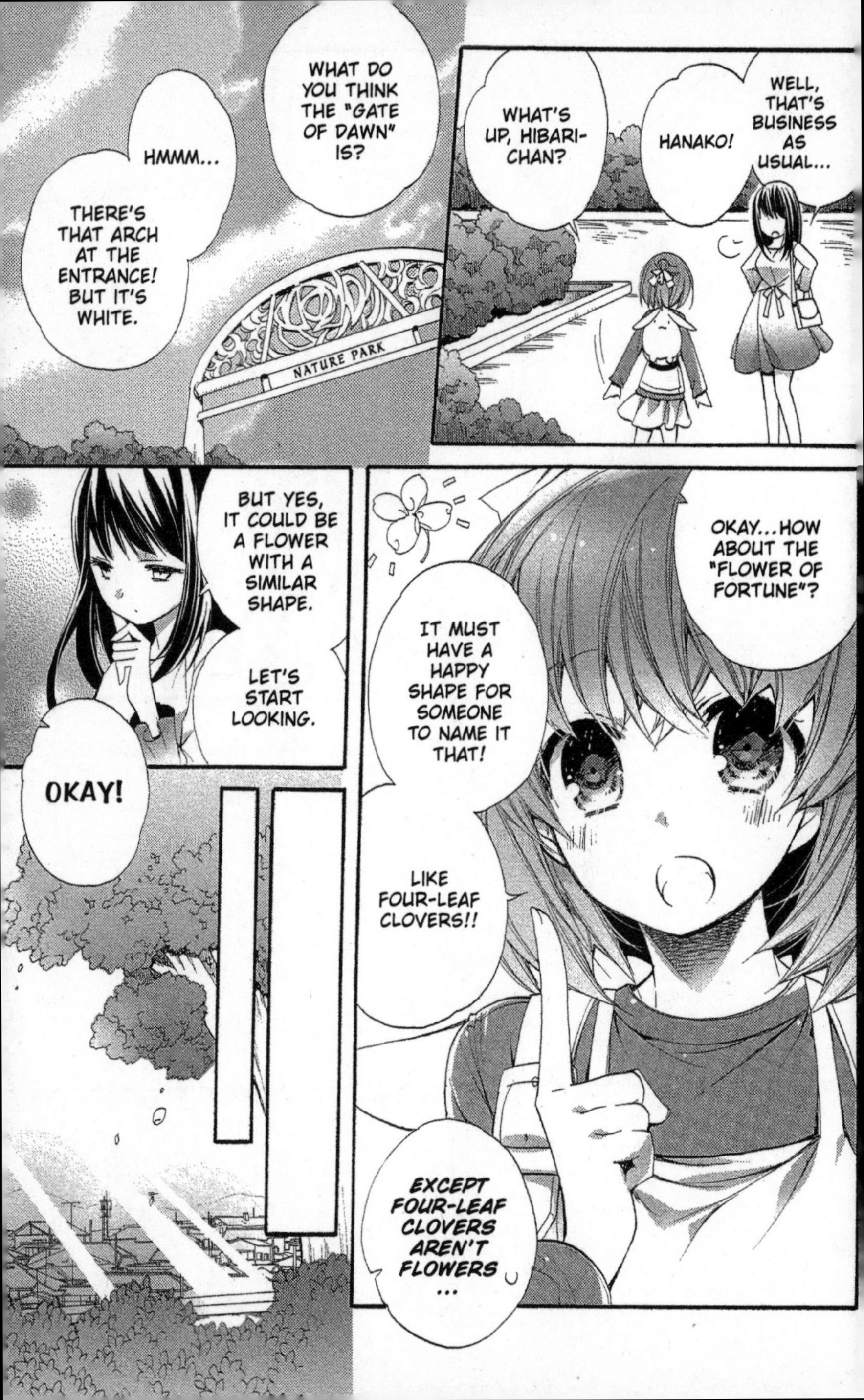
WELL, THAT'S BUSINESS AS USUAL...
HANAKO!
WHAT'S UP, HIBARI-CHAN?
WHAT DO YOU THINK THE "GATE OF DAWN" IS?
HMMM...
THERE'S THAT ARCH AT THE ENTRANCE! BUT IT'S WHITE.
NATURE PARK
OKAY...HOW ABOUT THE "FLOWER OF FORTUNE"?
IT MUST HAVE A HAPPY SHAPE FOR SOMEONE TO NAME IT THAT!
LIKE FOUR-LEAF CLOVERS!!
EXCEPT FOUR-LEAF CLOVERS AREN'T FLOWERS...
BUT YES, IT COULD BE A FLOWER WITH A SIMILAR SHAPE.
LET'S START LOOKING.
OKAY!

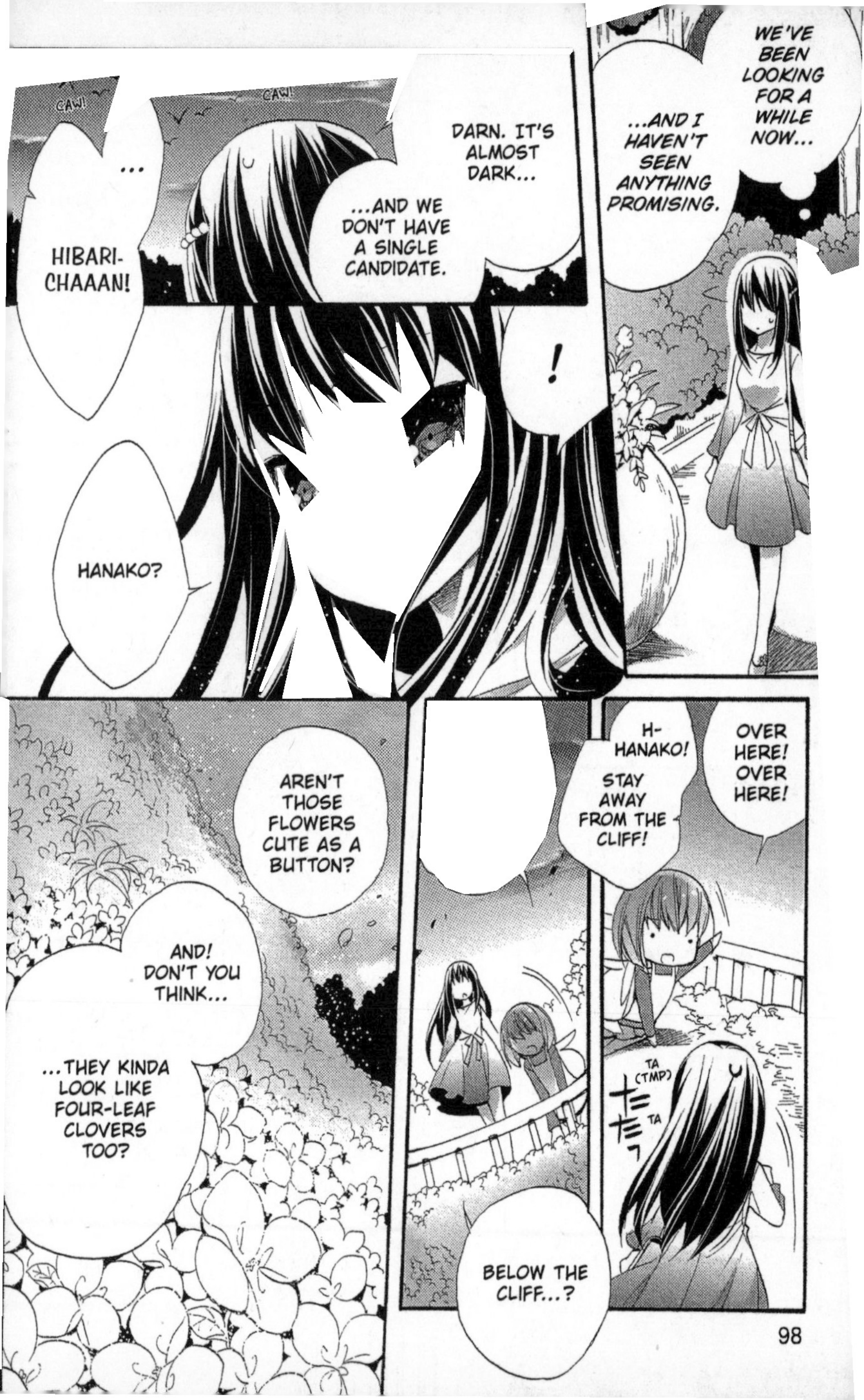
WE'VE BEEN LOOKING FOR A WHILE NOW...
...AND I HAVEN'T SEEN ANYTHING PROMISING.
CAW!
CAW!
DARN. IT'S ALMOST DARK...
...AND WE DON'T HAVE A SINGLE CANDIDATE.
...
HIBARI-CHAAAN!
!
HANAKO?
OVER HERE! OVER HERE!
H-HANAKO!
STAY AWAY FROM THE CLIFF!
TA (TMP)
TA
BELOW THE CLIFF...?
AREN'T THOSE FLOWERS CUTE AS A BUTTON?
AND! DON'T YOU THINK...
...THEY KINDA LOOK LIKE FOUR-LEAF CLOVERS TOO?

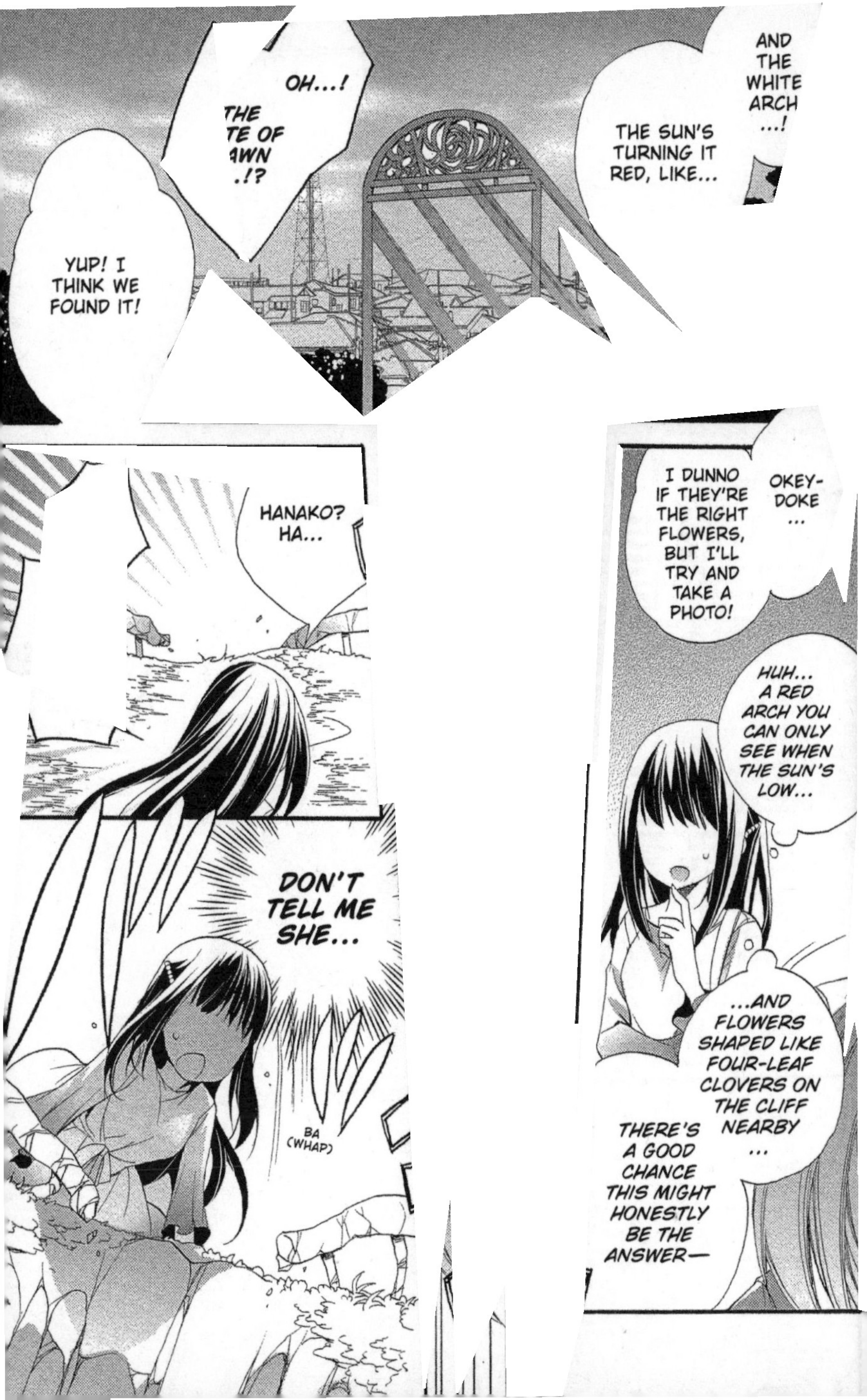
AND THE WHITE ARCH...!
THE SUN'S TURNING IT RED, LIKE...
OH...!
YUP! I THINK WE FOUND IT!
OKEY-DOKE...
I DUNNO IF THEY'RE THE RIGHT FLOWERS, BUT I'LL TRY AND TAKE A PHOTO!
HUH... A RED ARCH YOU CAN ONLY SEE WHEN THE SUN'S LOW...
...AND FLOWERS SHAPED LIKE FOUR-LEAF CLOVERS ON THE CLIFF NEARBY...
THERE'S A GOOD CHANCE THIS MIGHT HONESTLY BE THE ANSWER—
HANAKO? HA...
DON'T TELL ME SHE...
BA (WHAP)

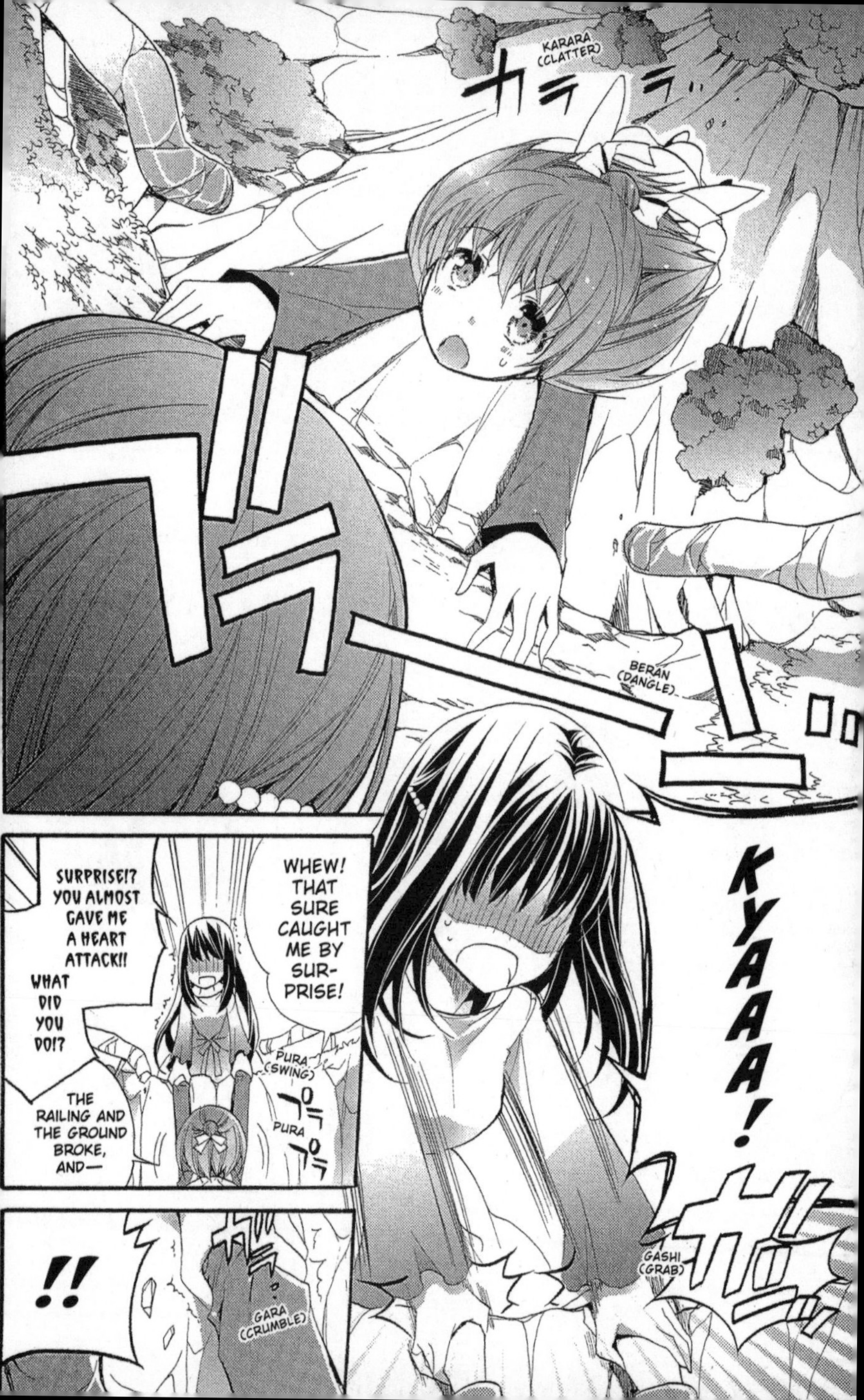
KARARA (CLATTER)
BERAN (DANGLE)
KYAAAA!
GASHI (GRAB)
WHEW! THAT SURE CAUGHT ME BY SUR-PRISE!
SURPRISE!? YOU ALMOST GAVE ME A HEART ATTACK!!
WHAT DID YOU DO!?
PURA (SWING)
PURA
THE RAILING AND THE GROUND BROKE, AND—
!!
GARA (CRUMBLE)

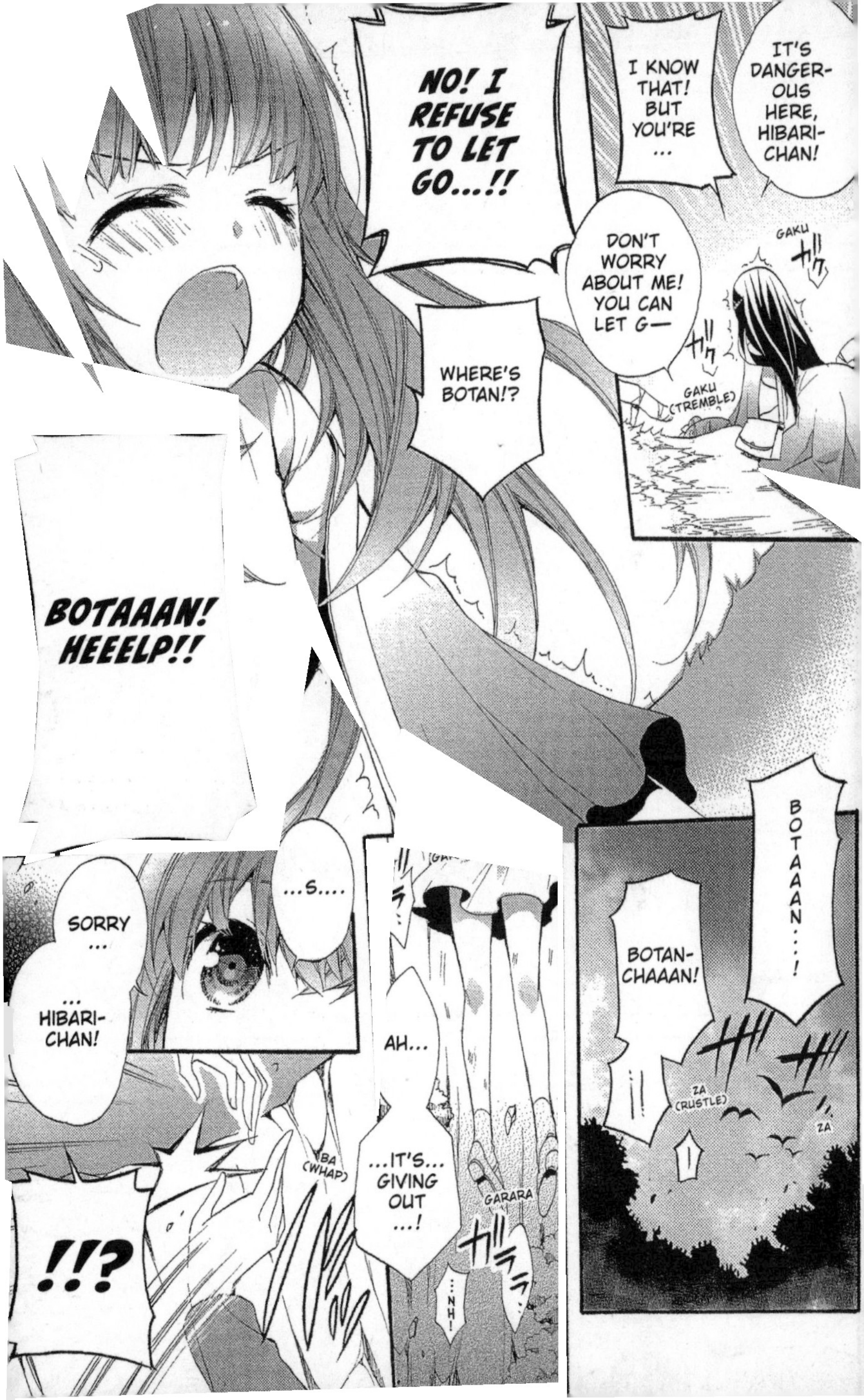

IT'S DANGER-OUS HERE, HIBARI-CHAN!
I KNOW THAT! BUT YOU'RE ...
DON'T WORRY ABOUT ME! YOU CAN LET G—
GAKU
GAKU (TREMBLE)
NO! I REFUSE TO LET GO...!!
WHERE'S BOTAN!?
BOTAAAN! HEEELP!!
BOTAAAN...!
BOTAN-CHAAAN!
!!
ZA (RUSTLE)
ZA
!
AH...
...IT'S... GIVING OUT ...!
GARARA
...NH!
...S....
SORRY ...
... HIBARI-CHAN!
BA (WHAP)
!!?

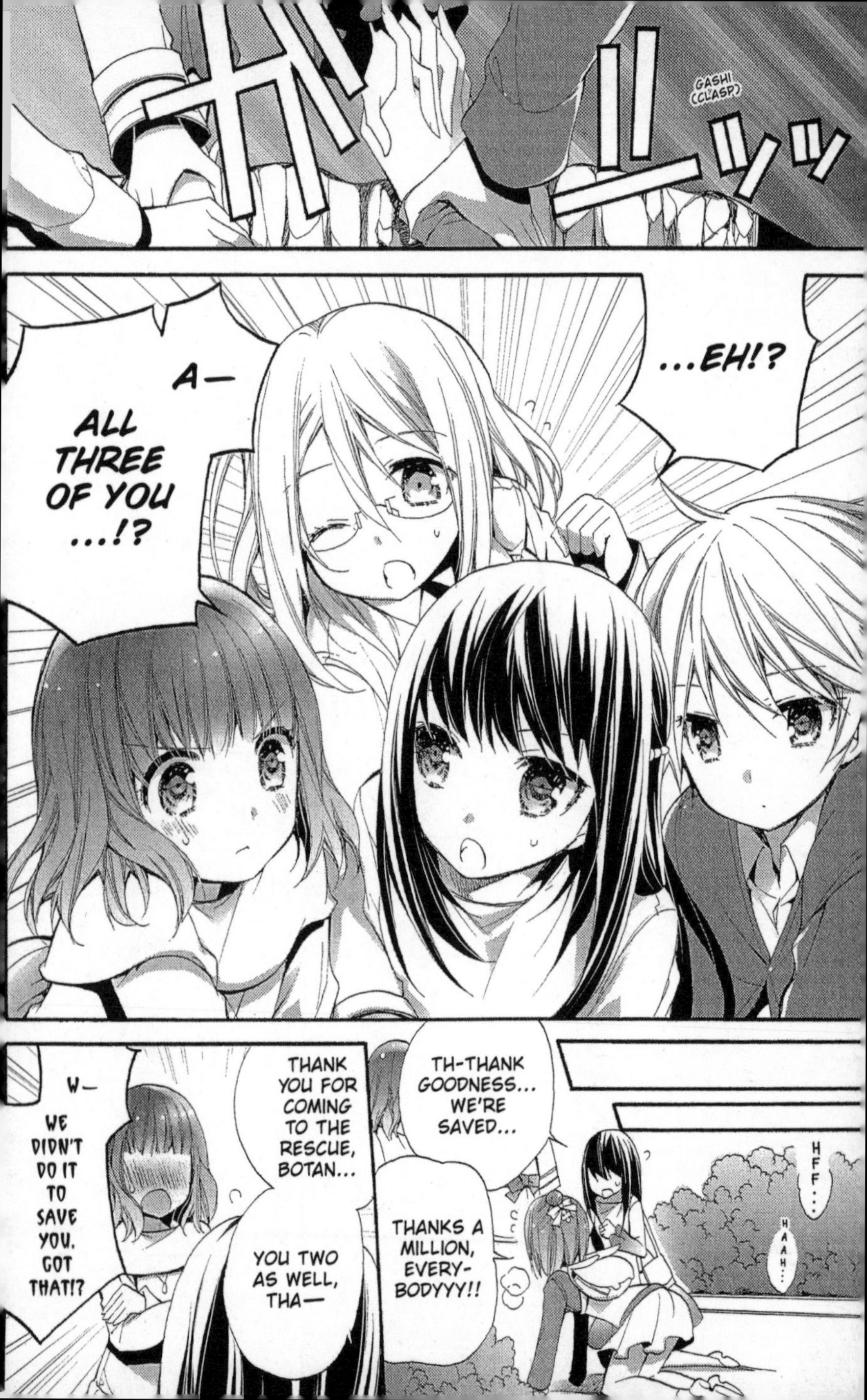
GASHI (CLASP)
...EH!?
A—
ALL THREE OF YOU ...!?
HFF...
HAAH...
TH-THANK GOODNESS... WE'RE SAVED...
THANKS A MILLION, EVERY-BODYYY!!
THANK YOU FOR COMING TO THE RESCUE, BOTAN...
YOU TWO AS WELL, THA—
W—
WE DIDN'T DO IT TO SAVE YOU. GOT THAT!?

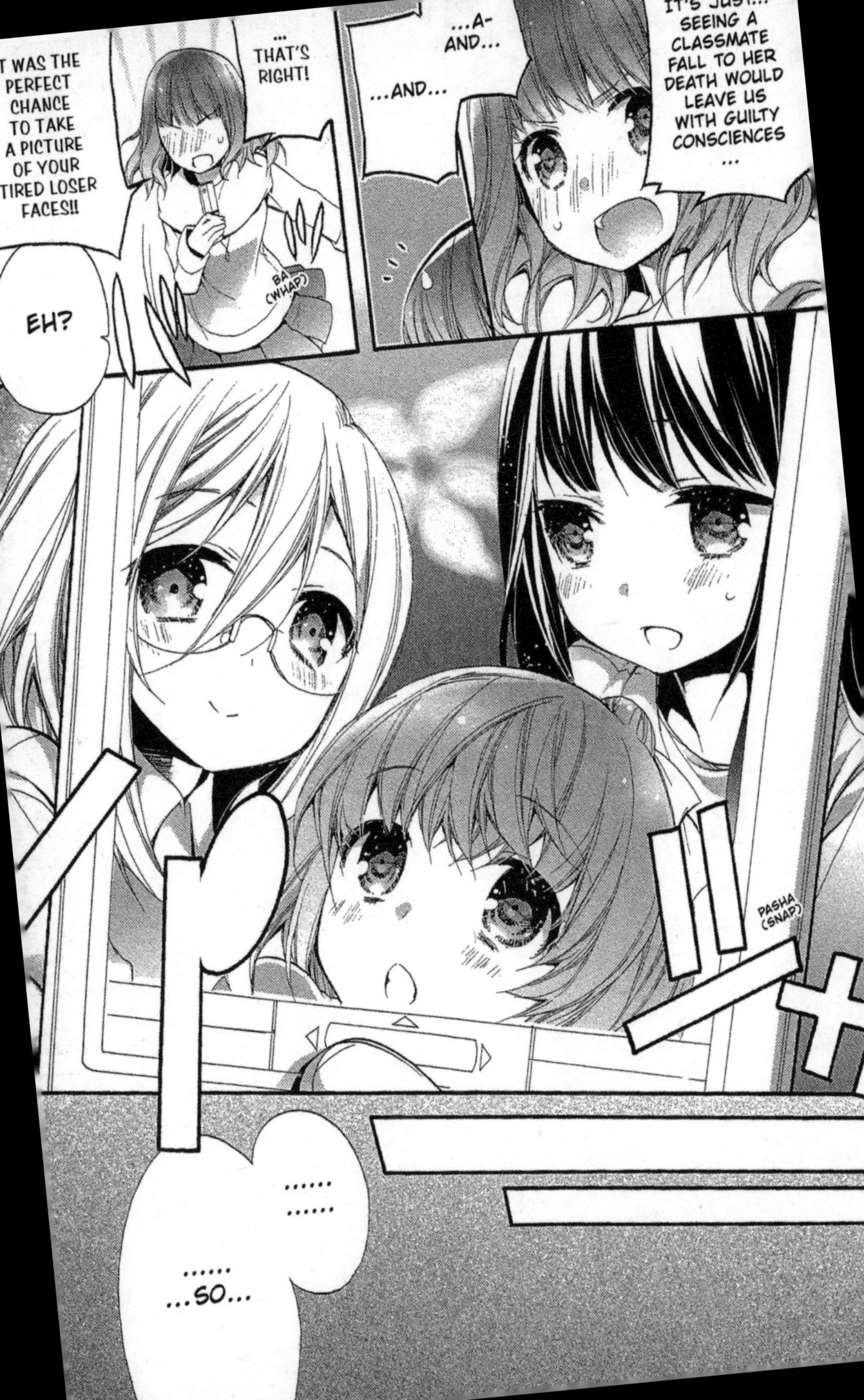

IT'S JUST... SEEING A CLASSMATE FALL TO HER DEATH WOULD LEAVE US WITH GUILTY CONSCIENCES ...
...A- AND...
...AND...
... THAT'S RIGHT!
T WAS THE PERFECT CHANCE TO TAKE A PICTURE OF YOUR TIRED LOSER FACES!!
BA (WHAP)
EH?
PASHA (SNAP)
....
....SO...

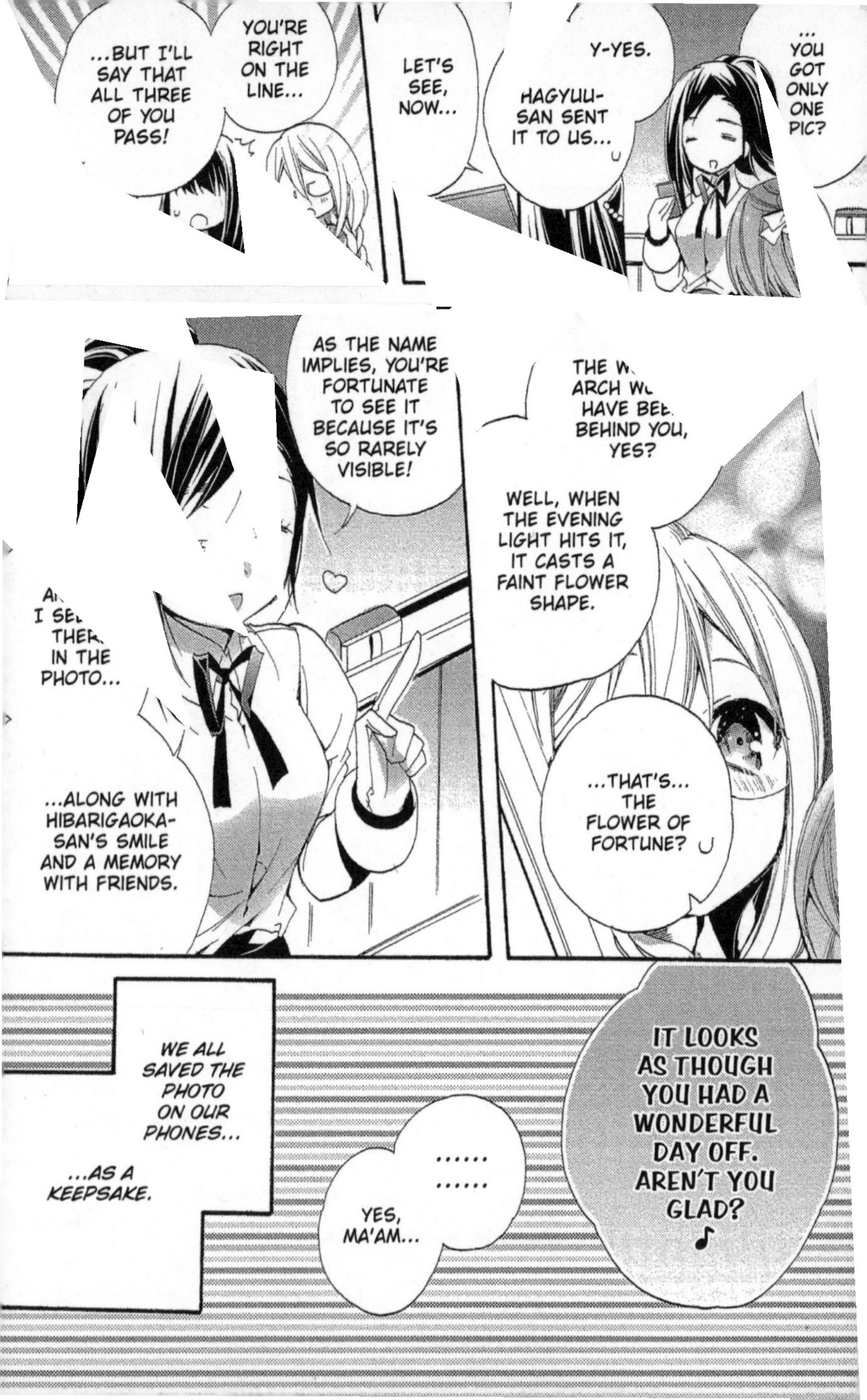
...YOU GOT ONLY ONE PIC?
Y-YES.
HAGYUU-SAN SENT IT TO US...
LET'S SEE, NOW...
YOU'RE RIGHT ON THE LINE...
...BUT I'LL SAY THAT ALL THREE OF YOU PASS!
BEHIND YOU, YES?
WELL, WHEN THE EVENING LIGHT HITS IT, IT CASTS A FAINT FLOWER SHAPE.
...THAT'S... THE FLOWER OF FORTUNE?
AS THE NAME IMPLIES, YOU'RE FORTUNATE TO SEE IT BECAUSE IT'S SO RARELY VISIBLE!
IN THE PHOTO...
...ALONG WITH HIBARIGAOKA-SAN'S SMILE AND A MEMORY WITH FRIENDS.
IT LOOKS AS THOUGH YOU HAD A WONDERFUL DAY OFF. AREN'T YOU GLAD? ♪
....
YES, MA'AM...
WE ALL SAVED THE PHOTO ON OUR PHONES...
...AS A KEEPSAKE.

Anne Happy

unhappy go lucky!

HIBIKI HAGYUU

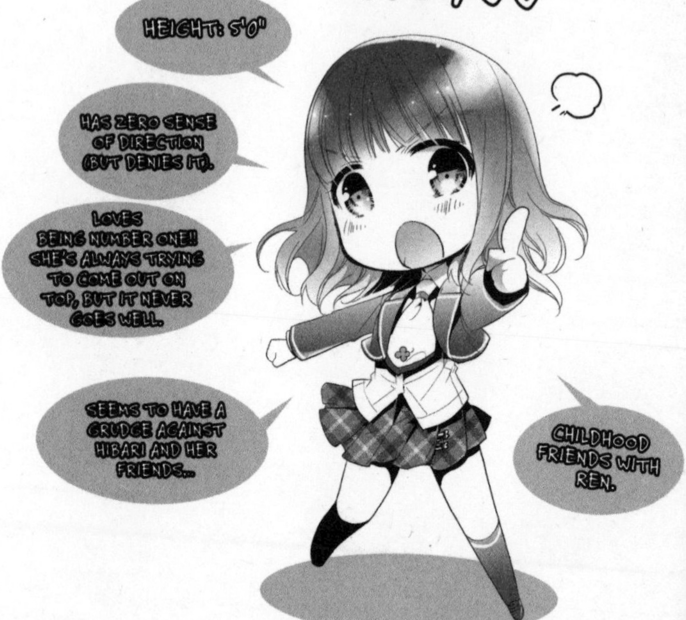
HEIGHT: 5'0"
HAS ZERO SENSE OF DIRECTION (BUT DENIES IT).
LOVES BEING NUMBER ONE!! SHE'S ALWAYS TRYING TO COME OUT ON TOP, BUT IT NEVER GOES WELL.
SEEMS TO HAVE A GRUDGE AGAINST HIBARI AND HER FRIENDS...
CHILDHOOD FRIENDS WITH REN.

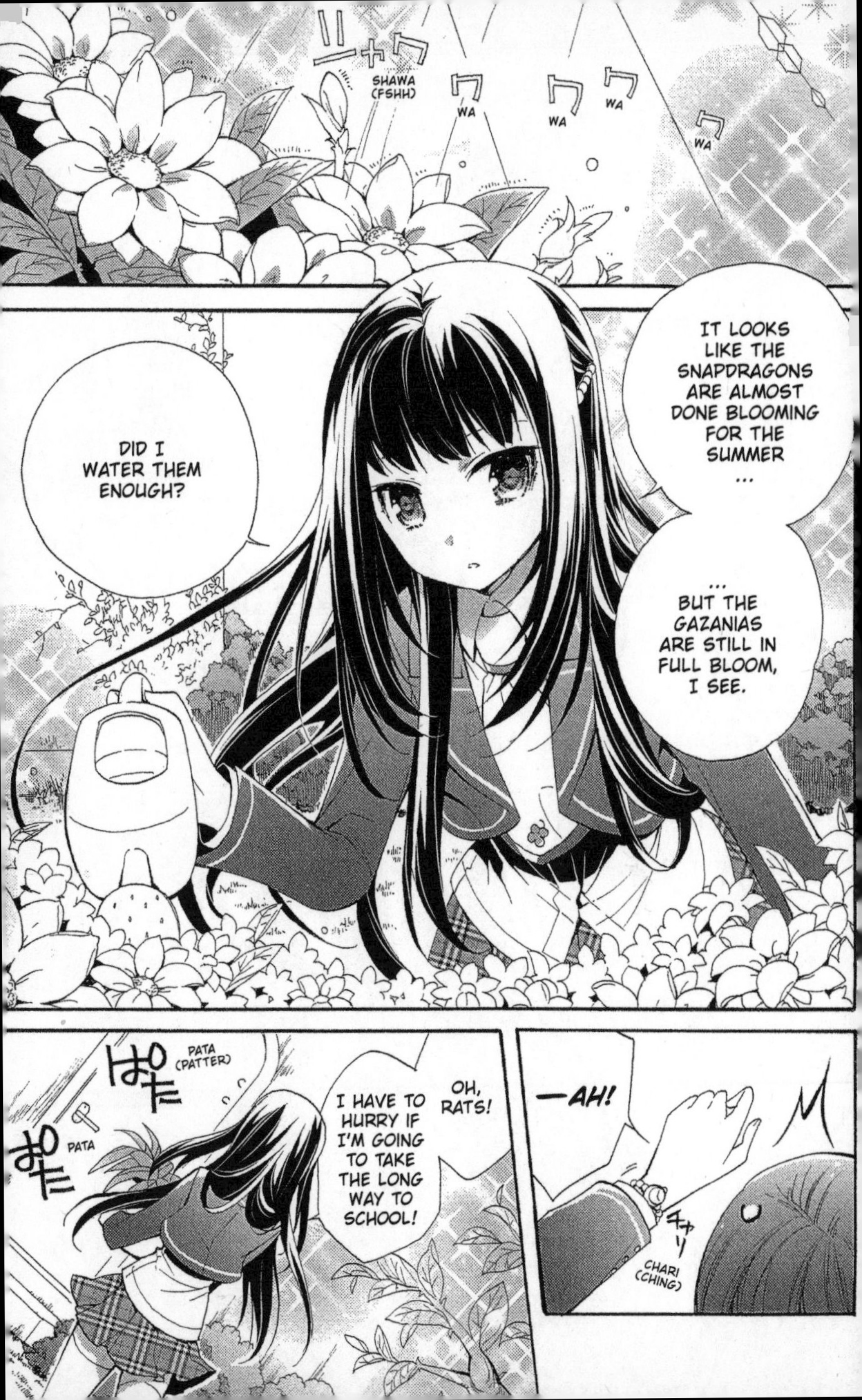
SHAWA (FSHH)
WA
WA
WA
WA
IT LOOKS LIKE THE SNAPDRAGONS ARE ALMOST DONE BLOOMING FOR THE SUMMER ...
... BUT THE GAZANIAS ARE STILL IN FULL BLOOM, I SEE.
DID I WATER THEM ENOUGH?
—AH!
CHARI (CHING)
OH, RATS!
I HAVE TO HURRY IF I'M GOING TO TAKE THE LONG WAY TO SCHOOL!
PATA (PATTER)
PATA

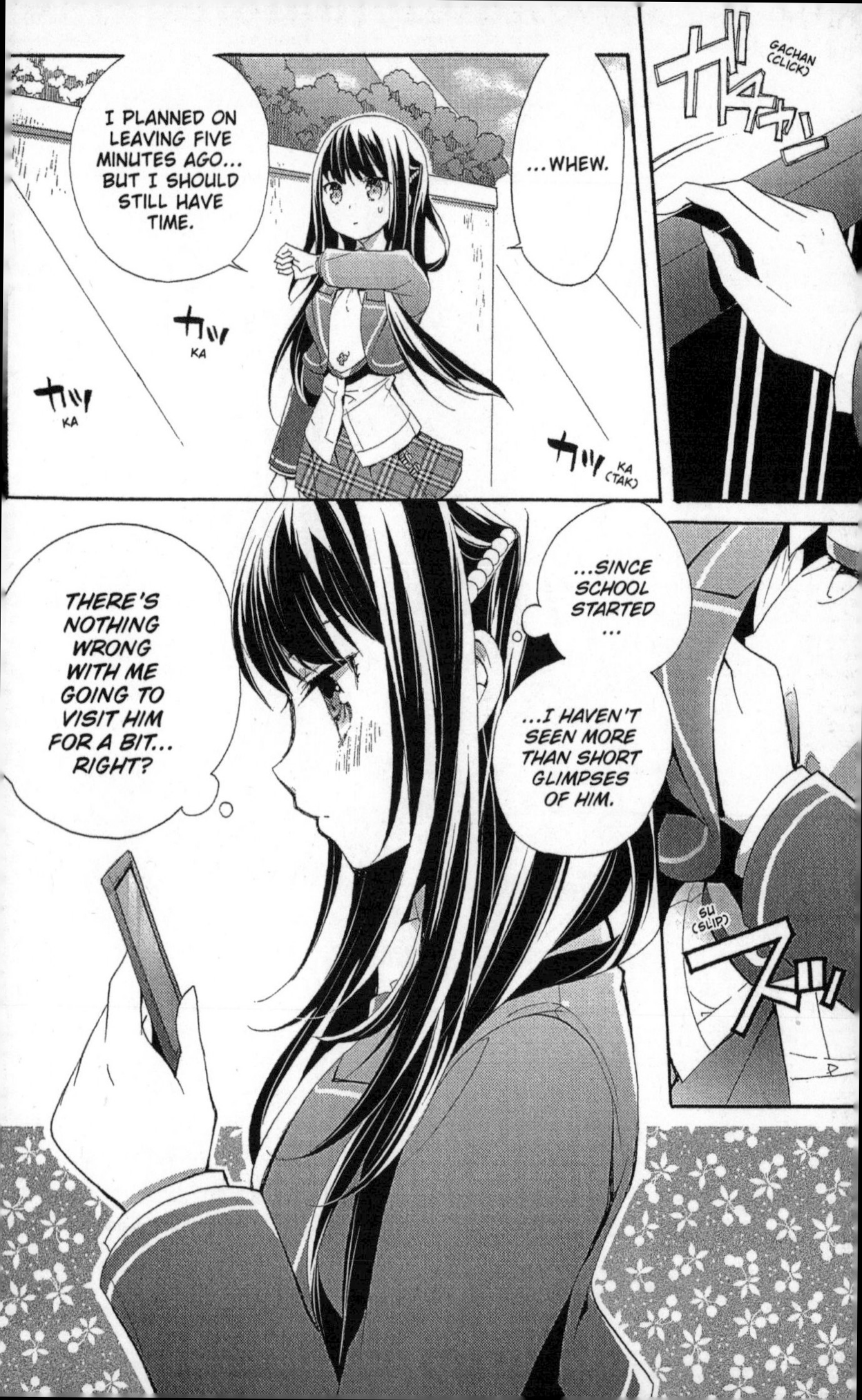
GACHAN (CLICK)
...WHEW.
I PLANNED ON LEAVING FIVE MINUTES AGO... BUT I SHOULD STILL HAVE TIME.
KA (TAK)
KA
KA
SU (SLIP)
...SINCE SCHOOL STARTED...
...I HAVEN'T SEEN MORE THAN SHORT GLIMPSES OF HIM.
THERE'S NOTHING WRONG WITH ME GOING TO VISIT HIM FOR A BIT... RIGHT?

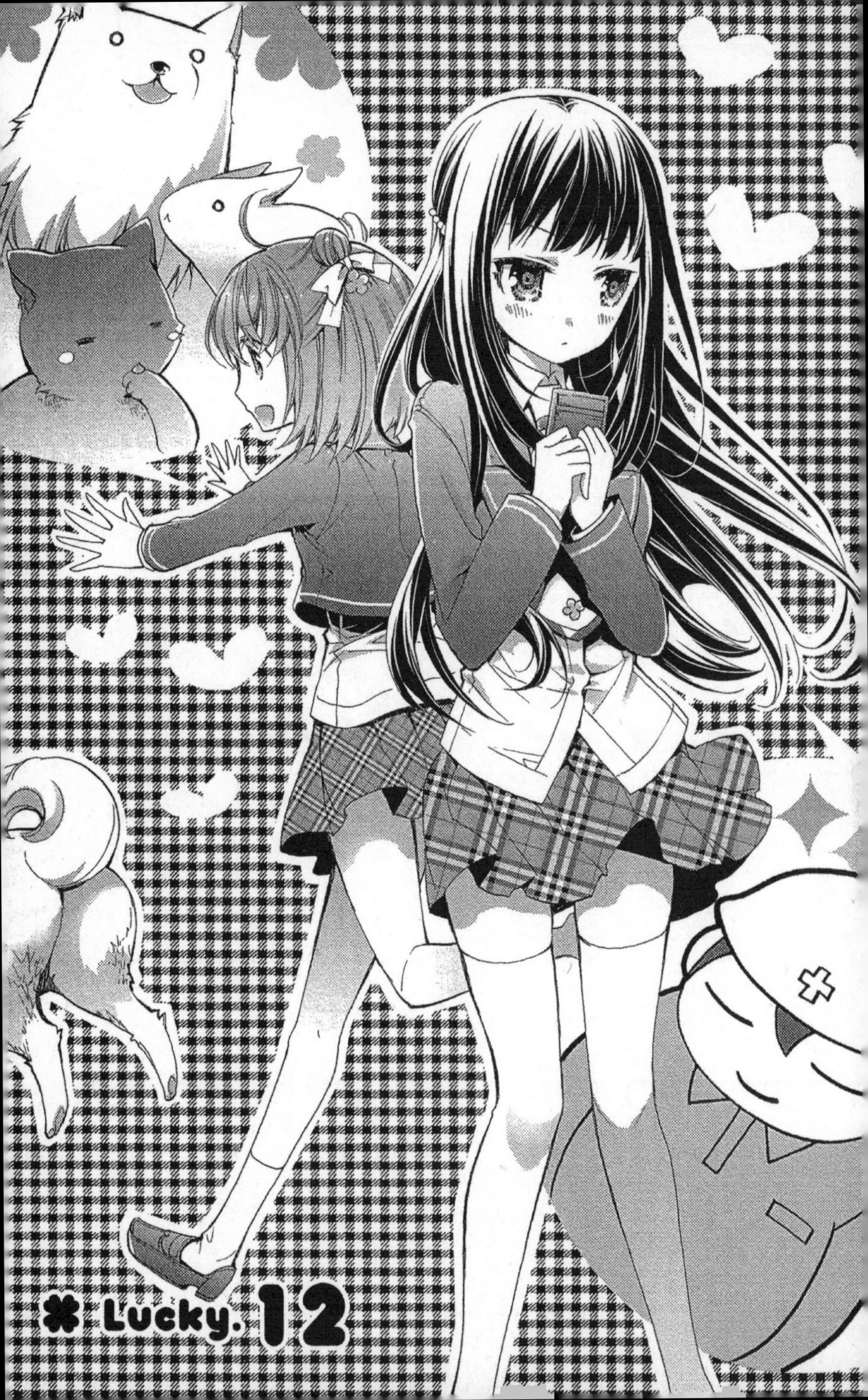
Lucky. 12

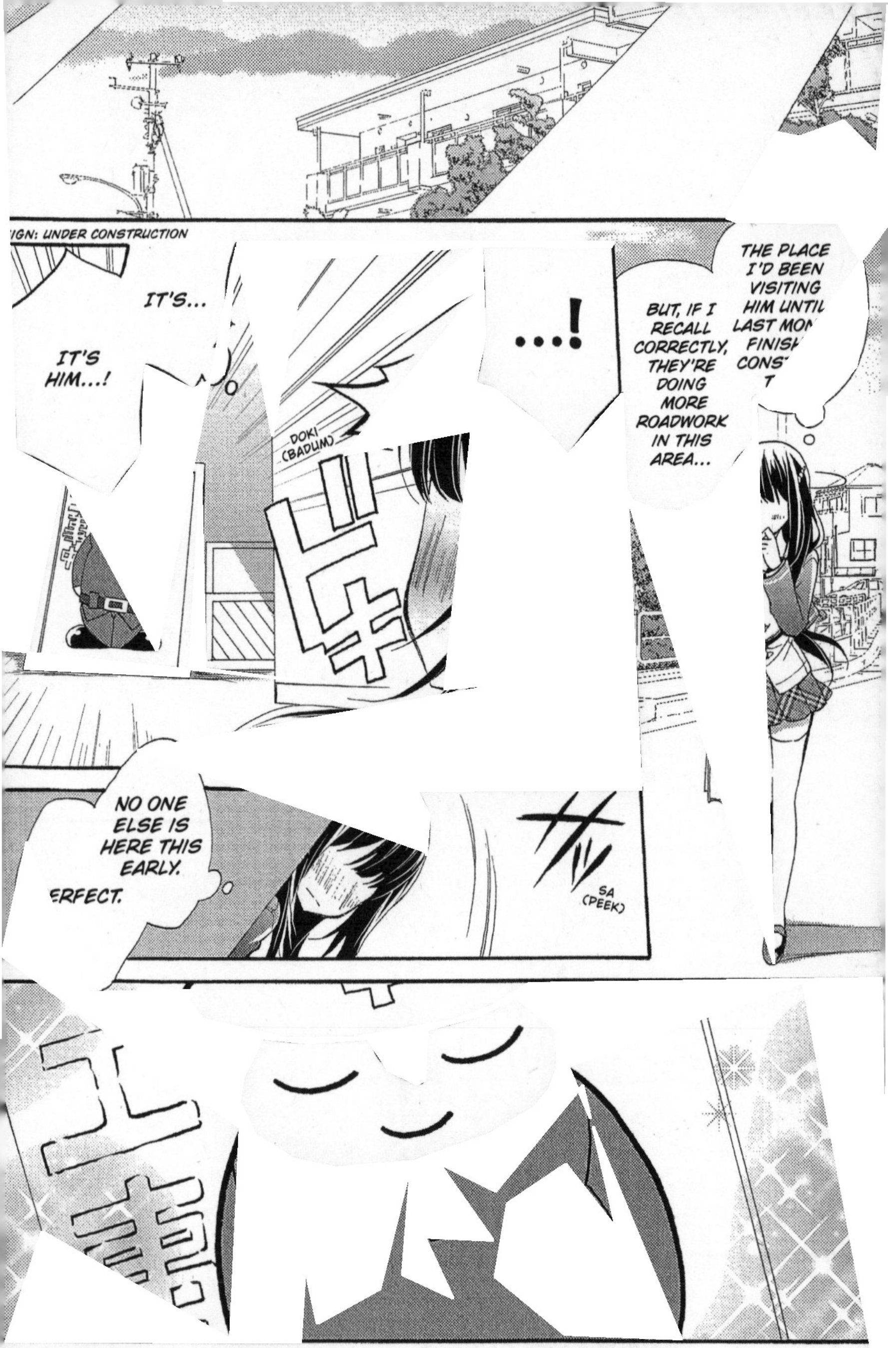
IGN: UNDER CONSTRUCTION
THE PLACE I'D BEEN VISITING HIM UNTIL LAST MON FINISH CONST
BUT, IF I RECALL CORRECTLY, THEY'RE DOING MORE ROADWORK IN THIS AREA...
...!
DOKI (BADUM)
IT'S...
IT'S HIM...!
SA (PEEK)
NO ONE ELSE IS HERE THIS EARLY.
ERFECT.

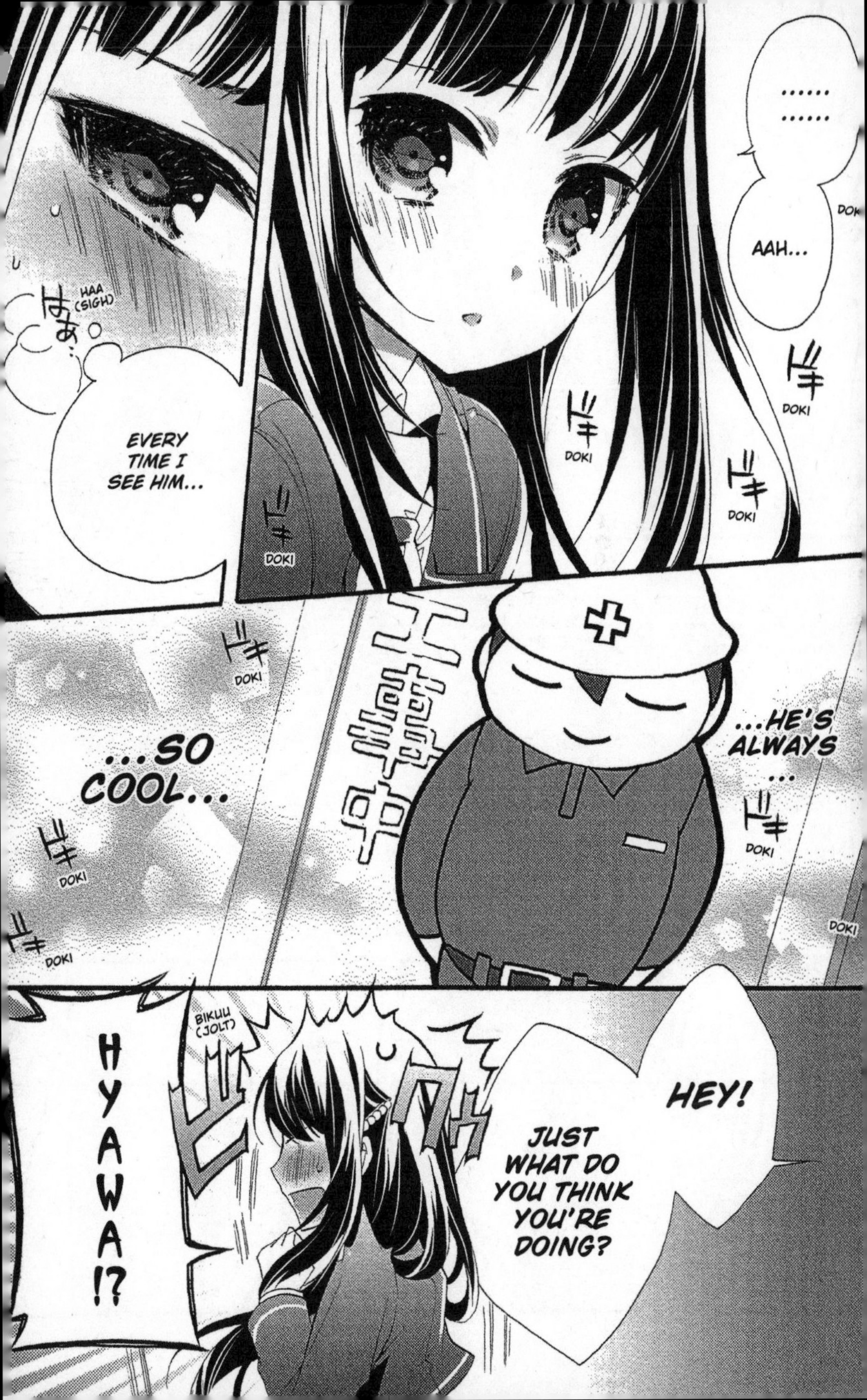

......
......
AAH...
DOKI
ドキ
DOKI
ドキ
DOKI
ドキ
DOKI
ドキ
DOKI
はぁ…
HAA (SIGH)
EVERY TIME I SEE HIM...
...HE'S ALWAYS...
ドキ
DOKI
DOKI
工事中
ドキ
DOKI
...SO COOL...
ドキ
DOKI
ドキ
DOKI
HEY!
JUST WHAT DO YOU THINK YOU'RE DOING?
BIKUU (JOLT)
HYAWA!?

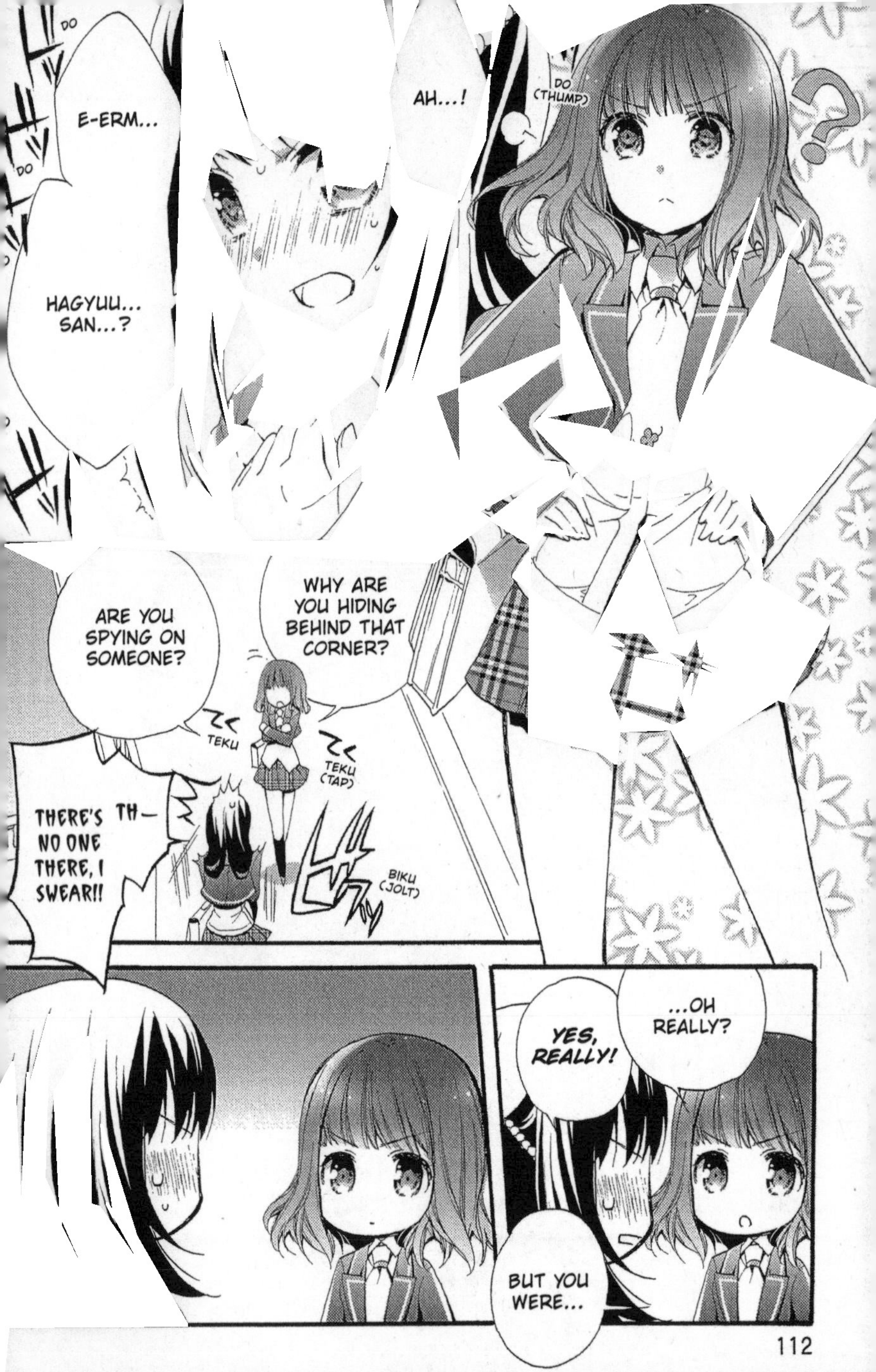
DO (THUMP)
AH...!
DO
E-ERM...
DO
HAGYUU... SAN...?
WHY ARE YOU HIDING BEHIND THAT CORNER?
TEKU (TAP)
TEKU
ARE YOU SPYING ON SOMEONE?
BIKU (JOLT)
TH—
THERE'S NO ONE THERE, I SWEAR!!
...OH REALLY?
YES, REALLY!
BUT YOU WERE...

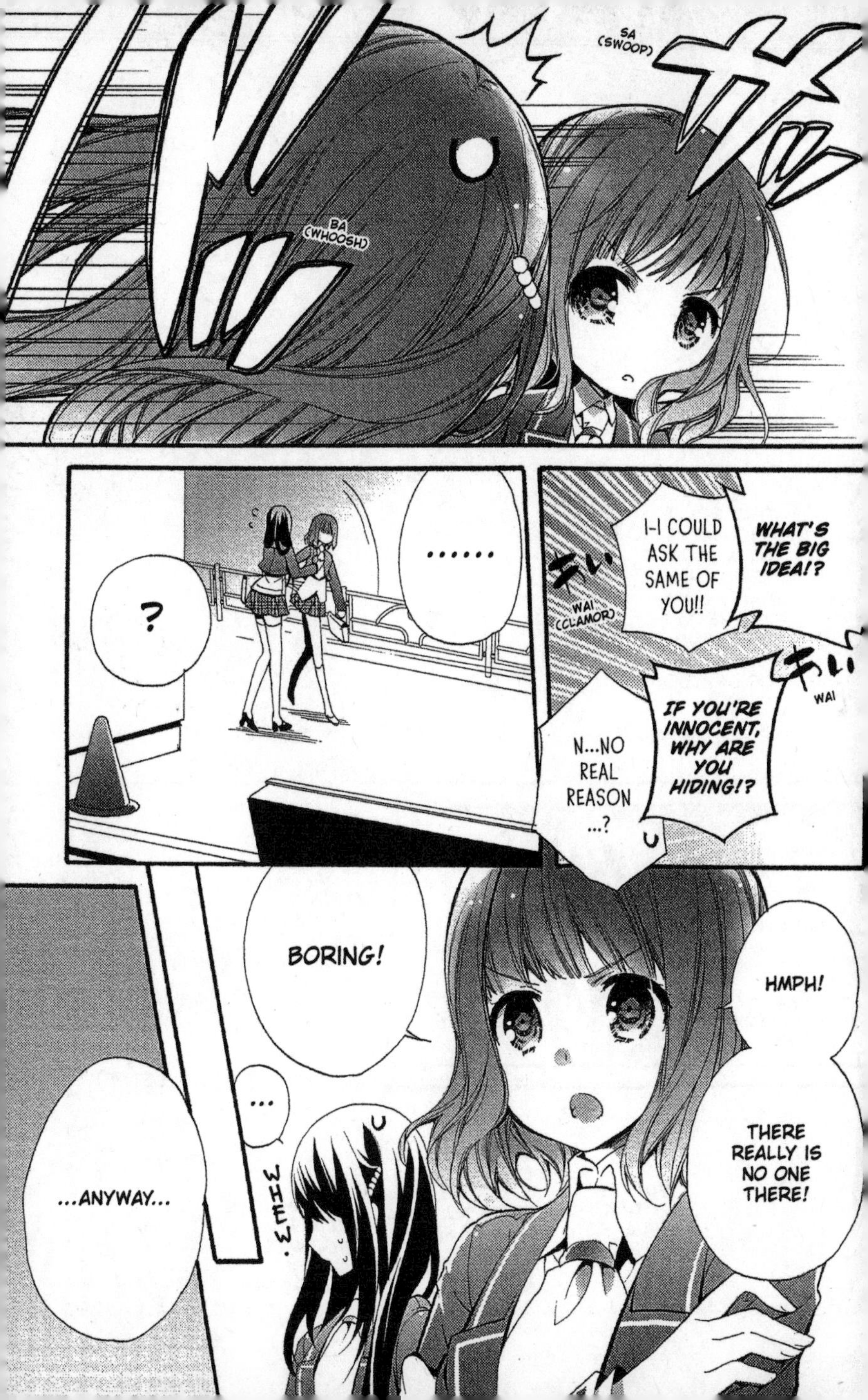
SA (SWOOP)
BA (WHOOSH)
WHAT'S THE BIG IDEA!?
I-I COULD ASK THE SAME OF YOU!!
WAI (CLAMOR)
WAI
IF YOU'RE INNOCENT, WHY ARE YOU HIDING!?
N...NO REAL REASON ...?
......
?
HMPH!
THERE REALLY IS NO ONE THERE!
BORING!
...
WHEW.
...ANYWAY...

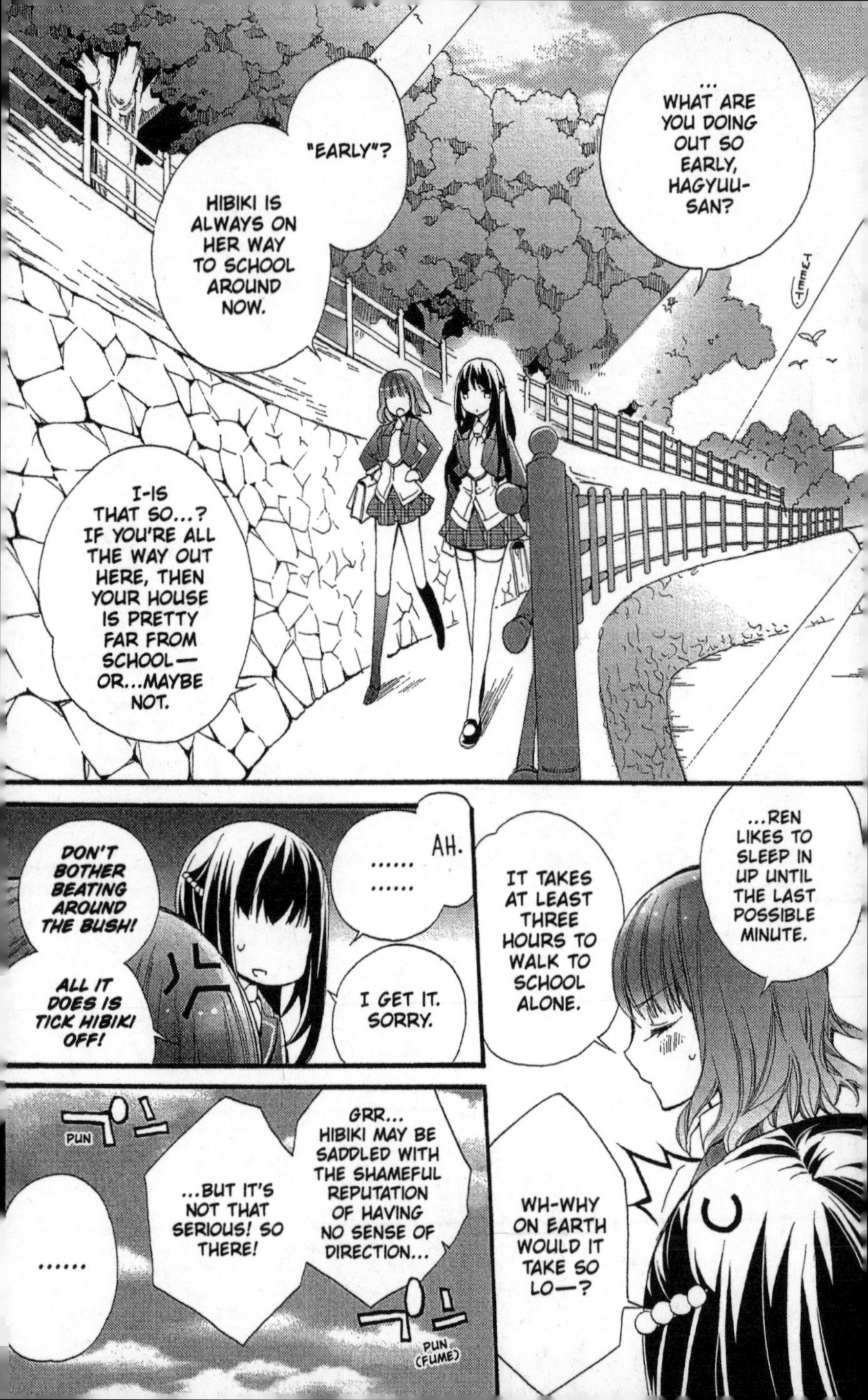
...
WHAT ARE YOU DOING OUT SO EARLY, HAGYUU-SAN?
"EARLY"?
HIBIKI IS ALWAYS ON HER WAY TO SCHOOL AROUND NOW.
I-IS THAT SO...? IF YOU'RE ALL THE WAY OUT HERE, THEN YOUR HOUSE IS PRETTY FAR FROM SCHOOL—OR...MAYBE NOT.
...REN LIKES TO SLEEP IN UP UNTIL THE LAST POSSIBLE MINUTE.
IT TAKES AT LEAST THREE HOURS TO WALK TO SCHOOL ALONE.
WH-WHY ON EARTH WOULD IT TAKE SO LO—?
AH.
......
......
I GET IT. SORRY.
DON'T BOTHER BEATING AROUND THE BUSH!
ALL IT DOES IS TICK HIBIKI OFF!
GRR... HIBIKI MAY BE SADDLED WITH THE SHAMEFUL REPUTATION OF HAVING NO SENSE OF DIRECTION...
PUN
...BUT IT'S NOT THAT SERIOUS! SO THERE!
PUN (FUME)
......

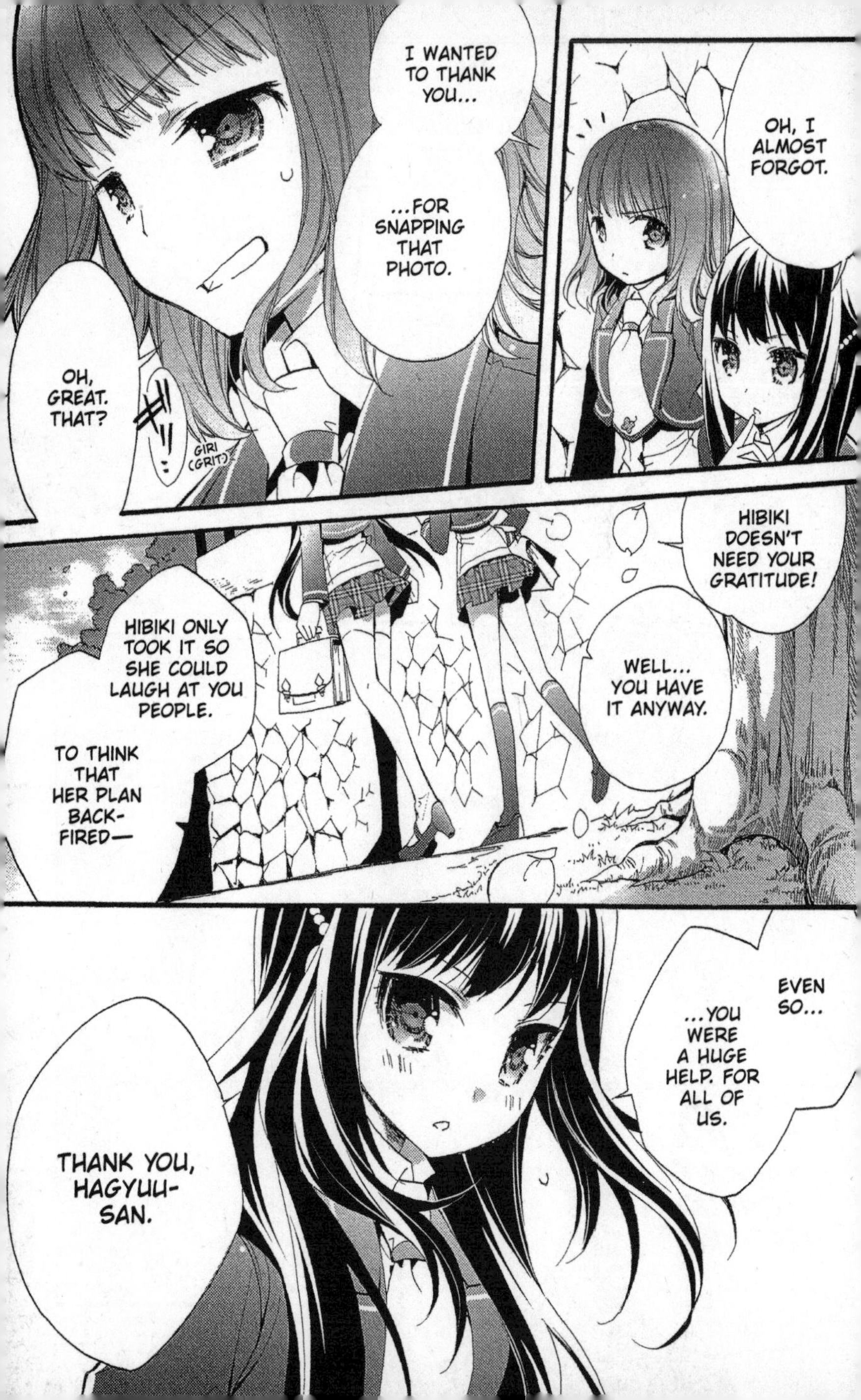
OH, I ALMOST FORGOT.
I WANTED TO THANK YOU...
...FOR SNAPPING THAT PHOTO.
OH, GREAT. THAT?
GIRI (GRIT)
HIBIKI DOESN'T NEED YOUR GRATITUDE!
WELL... YOU HAVE IT ANYWAY.
HIBIKI ONLY TOOK IT SO SHE COULD LAUGH AT YOU PEOPLE.
TO THINK THAT HER PLAN BACK-FIRED—
EVEN SO...
...YOU WERE A HUGE HELP. FOR ALL OF US.
THANK YOU, HAGYUU-SAN.

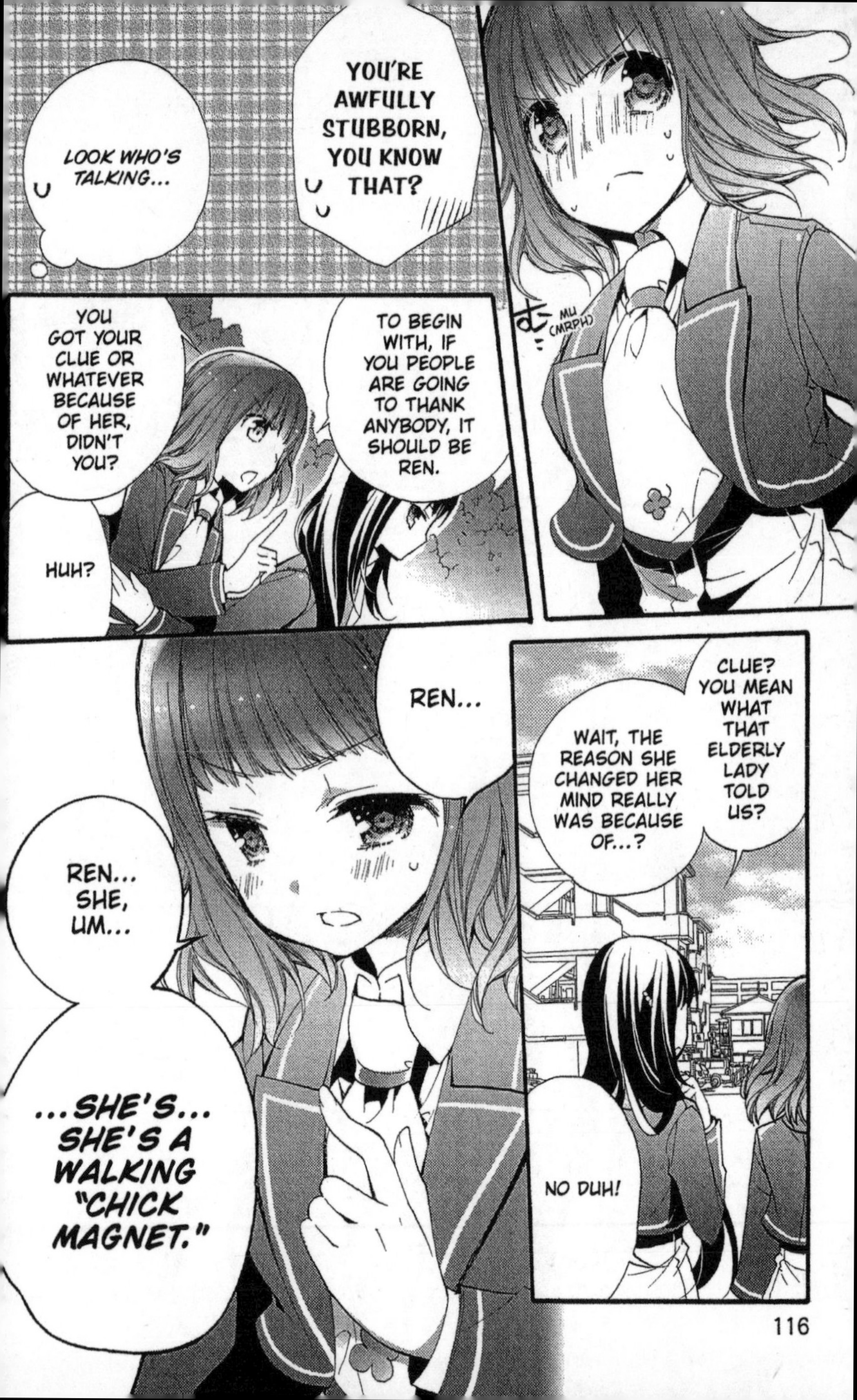
MU (MRPH)
YOU'RE AWFULLY STUBBORN, YOU KNOW THAT?
LOOK WHO'S TALKING...
TO BEGIN WITH, IF YOU PEOPLE ARE GOING TO THANK ANYBODY, IT SHOULD BE REN.
YOU GOT YOUR CLUE OR WHATEVER BECAUSE OF HER, DIDN'T YOU?
HUH?
CLUE? YOU MEAN WHAT THAT ELDERLY LADY TOLD US?
WAIT, THE REASON SHE CHANGED HER MIND REALLY WAS BECAUSE OF...?
NO DUH!
REN...
REN... SHE, UM...
...SHE'S... SHE'S A WALKING "CHICK MAGNET."

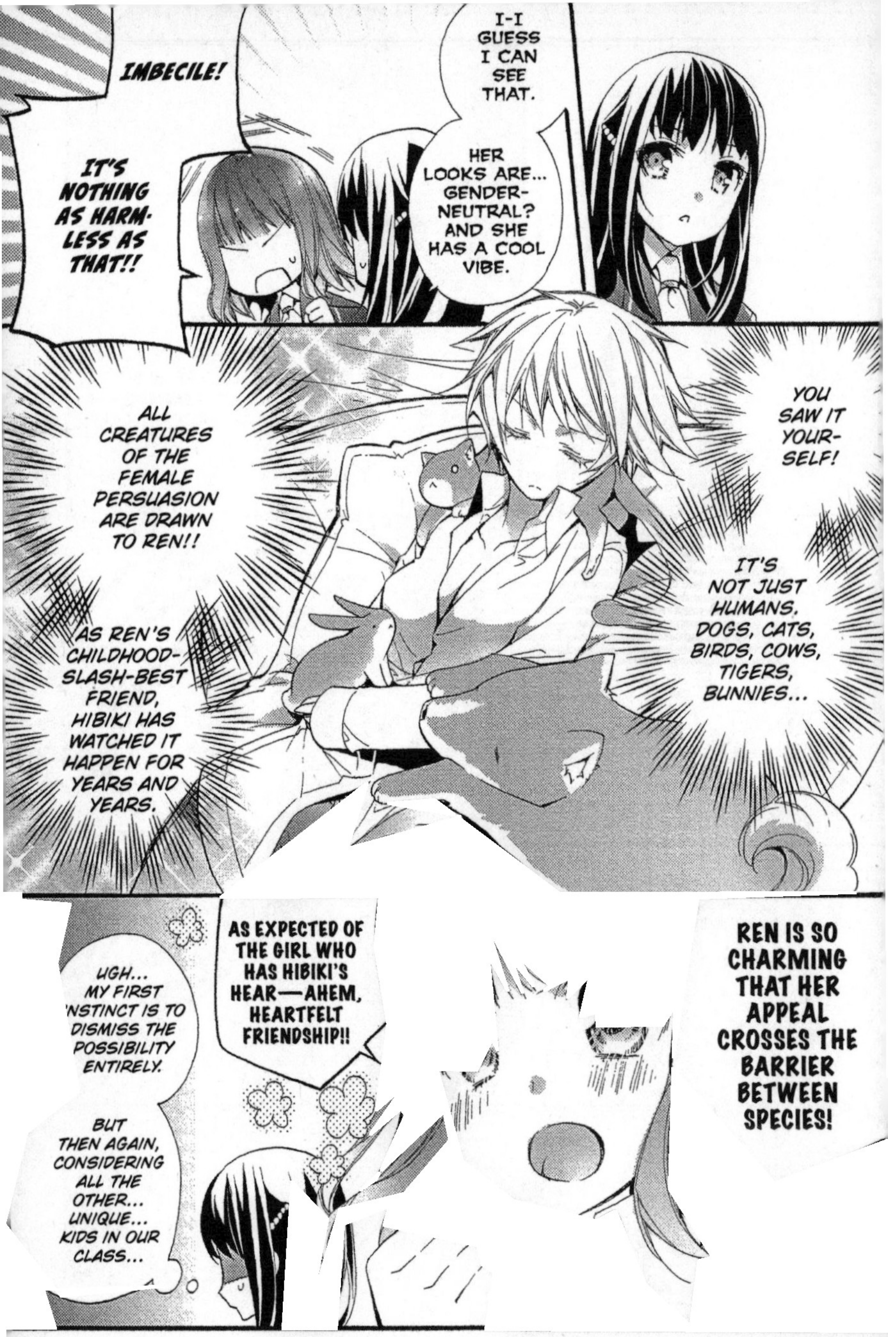
I-I GUESS I CAN SEE THAT.
HER LOOKS ARE... GENDER-NEUTRAL? AND SHE HAS A COOL VIBE.
IMBECILE!
IT'S NOTHING AS HARMLESS AS THAT!!
YOU SAW IT YOURSELF!
IT'S NOT JUST HUMANS. DOGS, CATS, BIRDS, COWS, TIGERS, BUNNIES...
ALL CREATURES OF THE FEMALE PERSUASION ARE DRAWN TO REN!!
AS REN'S CHILDHOOD-SLASH-BEST FRIEND, HIBIKI HAS WATCHED IT HAPPEN FOR YEARS AND YEARS.
REN IS SO CHARMING THAT HER APPEAL CROSSES THE BARRIER BETWEEN SPECIES!
AS EXPECTED OF THE GIRL WHO HAS HIBIKI'S HEAR—AHEM, HEARTFELT FRIENDSHIP!!
UGH... MY FIRST INSTINCT IS TO DISMISS THE POSSIBILITY ENTIRELY.
BUT THEN AGAIN, CONSIDERING ALL THE OTHER... UNIQUE... KIDS IN OUR CLASS...

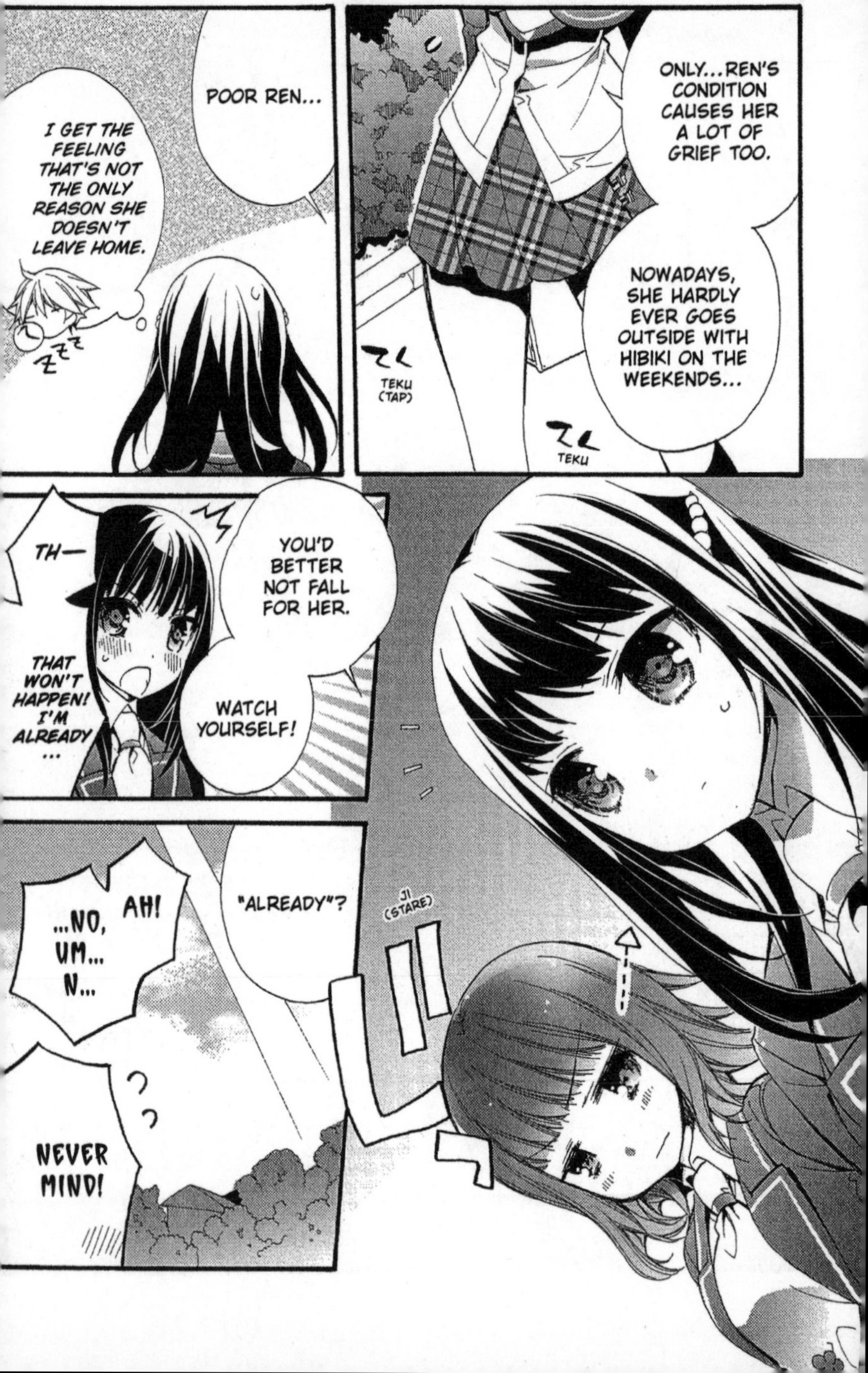
ONLY...REN'S CONDITION CAUSES HER A LOT OF GRIEF TOO.
NOWADAYS, SHE HARDLY EVER GOES OUTSIDE WITH HIBIKI ON THE WEEKENDS...
TEKU (TAP)
TEKU
POOR REN...
I GET THE FEELING THAT'S NOT THE ONLY REASON SHE DOESN'T LEAVE HOME.
JI (STARE)
YOU'D BETTER NOT FALL FOR HER.
WATCH YOURSELF!
TH—
THAT WON'T HAPPEN! I'M ALREADY ...
"ALREADY"?
AH!
...NO, UM... N...
NEVER MIND!

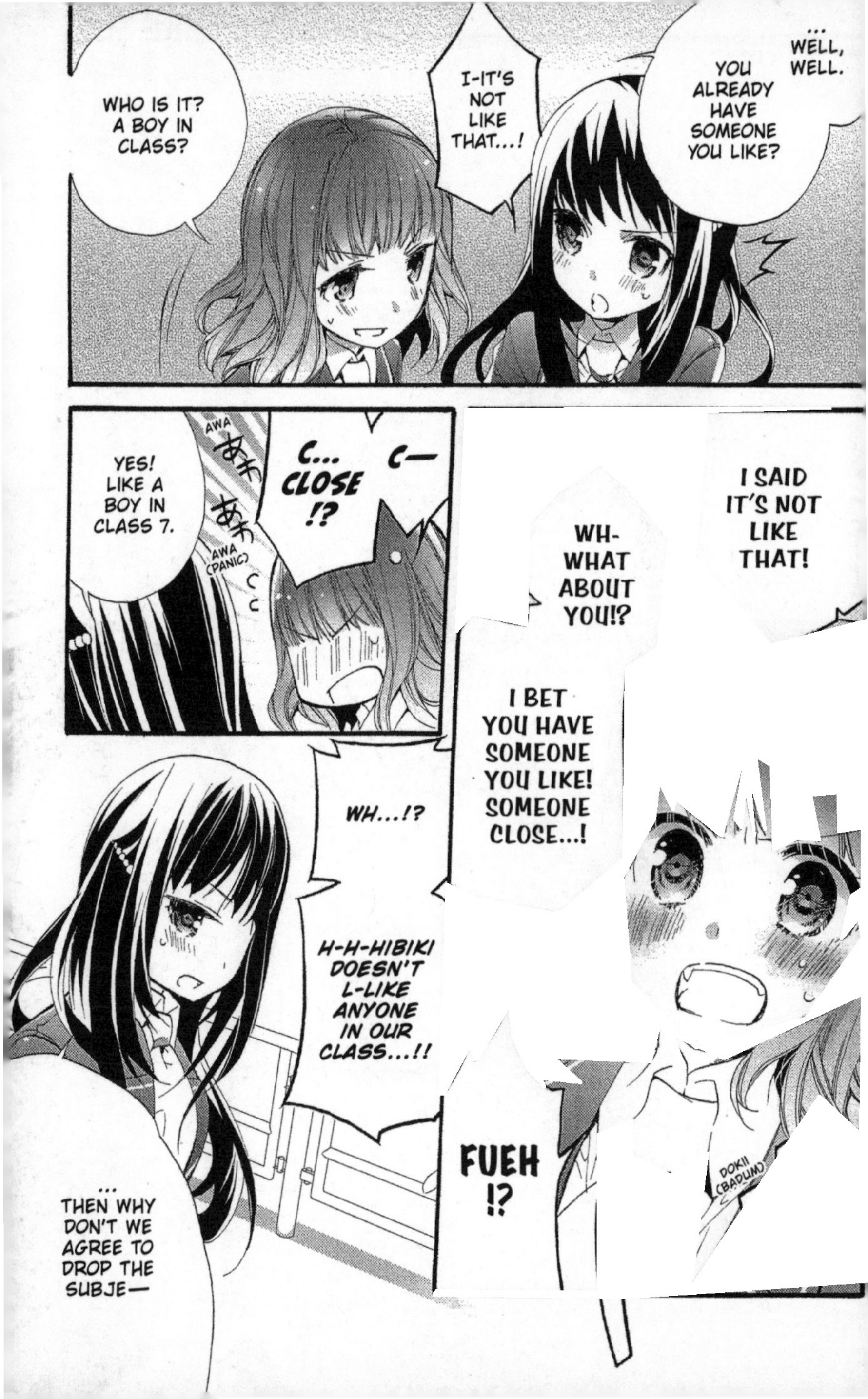
... WELL, WELL. YOU ALREADY HAVE SOMEONE YOU LIKE?
I-IT'S NOT LIKE THAT...!
WHO IS IT? A BOY IN CLASS?
I SAID IT'S NOT LIKE THAT!
WH- WHAT ABOUT YOU!?
I BET YOU HAVE SOMEONE YOU LIKE! SOMEONE CLOSE...!
FUEH !?
DOKI (BADUM)
C... C— CLOSE !?
AWA あわ AWA あわ (PANIC)
YES! LIKE A BOY IN CLASS 7.
WH...!?
H-H-HIBIKI DOESN'T L-LIKE ANYONE IN OUR CLASS...!!
... THEN WHY DON'T WE AGREE TO DROP THE SUBJE—

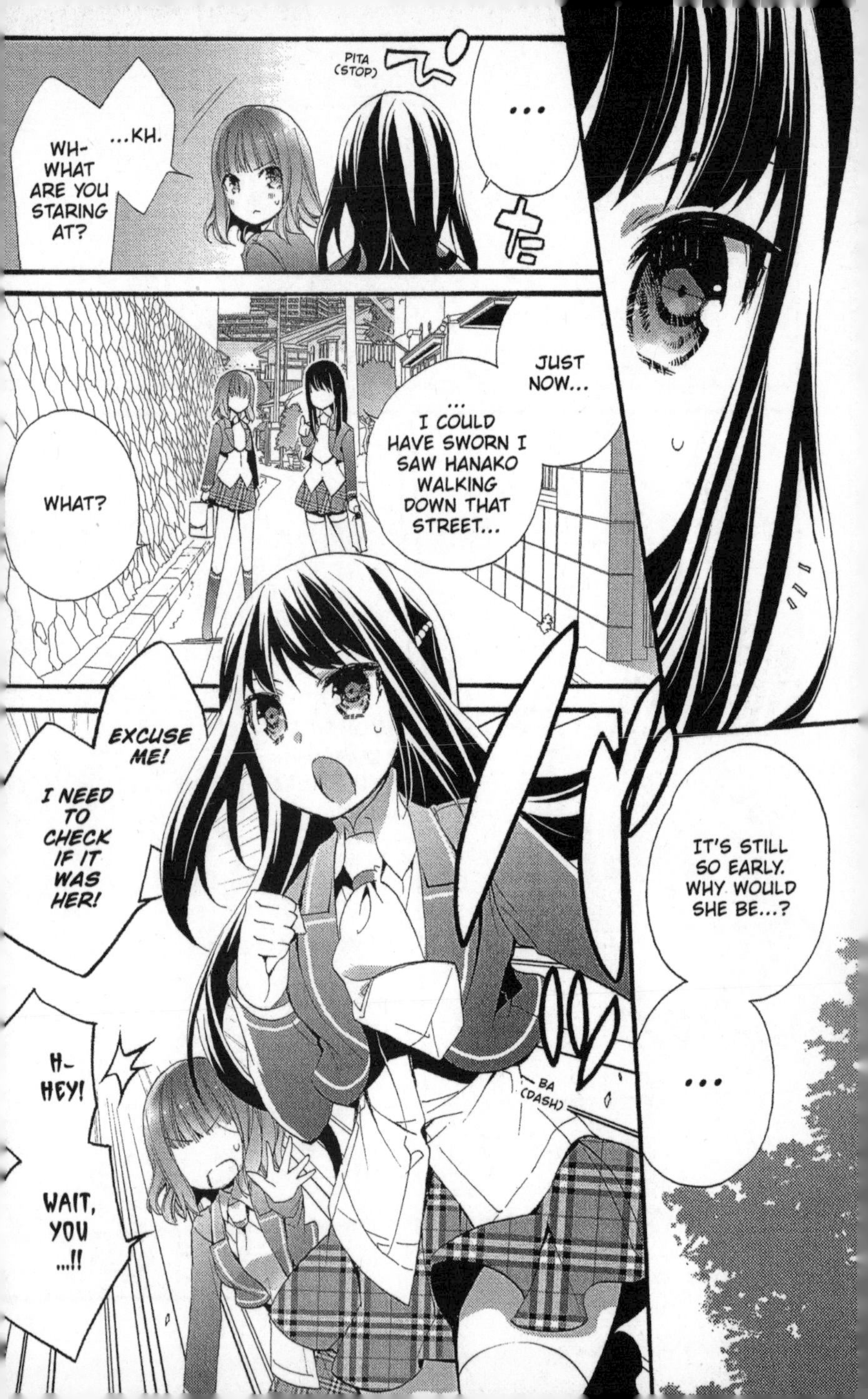
PITA (STOP)
...
...KH.
WH- WHAT ARE YOU STARING AT?
JUST NOW...
... I COULD HAVE SWORN I SAW HANAKO WALKING DOWN THAT STREET...
WHAT?
IT'S STILL SO EARLY. WHY WOULD SHE BE...?
...
EXCUSE ME!
I NEED TO CHECK IF IT WAS HER!
BA (DASH)
H- HEY!
WAIT, YOU ...!!

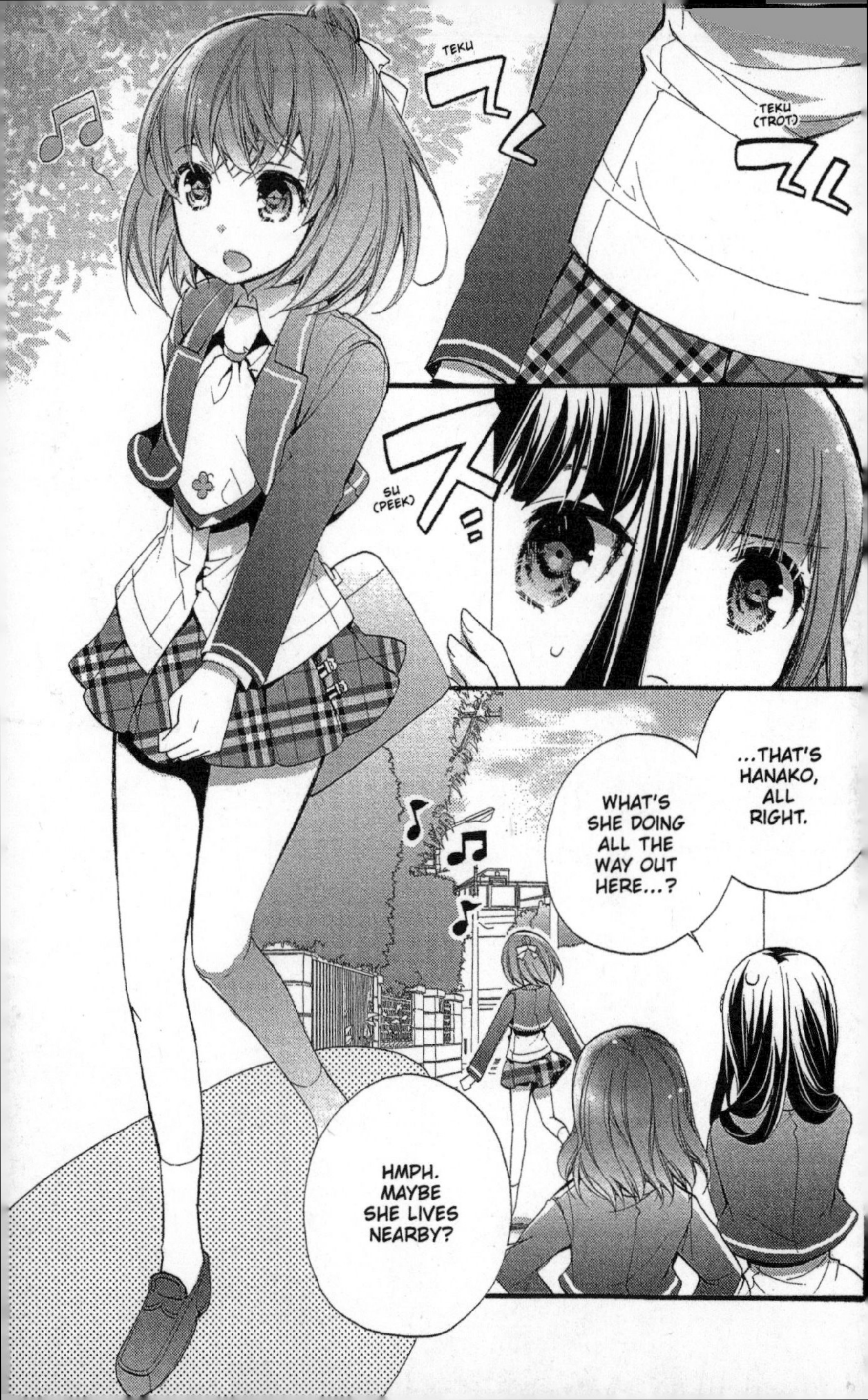
TEKU (TROT)
TEKU
SU (PEEK)
...THAT'S HANAKO, ALL RIGHT.
WHAT'S SHE DOING ALL THE WAY OUT HERE...?
HMPH. MAYBE SHE LIVES NEARBY?

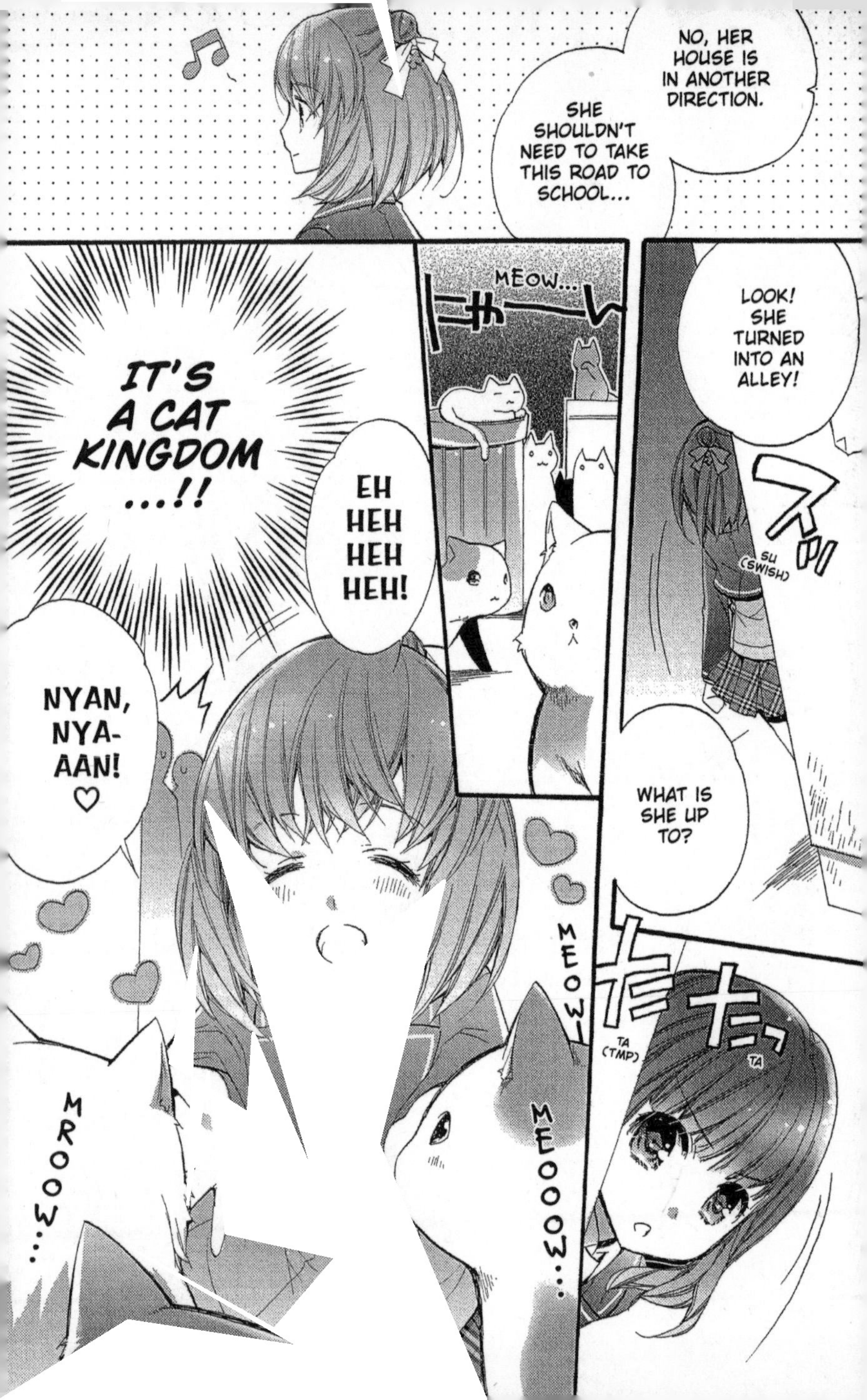
NO, HER HOUSE IS IN ANOTHER DIRECTION.
SHE SHOULDN'T NEED TO TAKE THIS ROAD TO SCHOOL...
LOOK! SHE TURNED INTO AN ALLEY!
SU (SWISH)
WHAT IS SHE UP TO?
TA (TMP)
TA
MEOW...
IT'S A CAT KINGDOM...!!
EH HEH HEH HEH!
NYAN, NYA-AAN! ♡
MEOW!
MEOOOOW...
MROOOW...

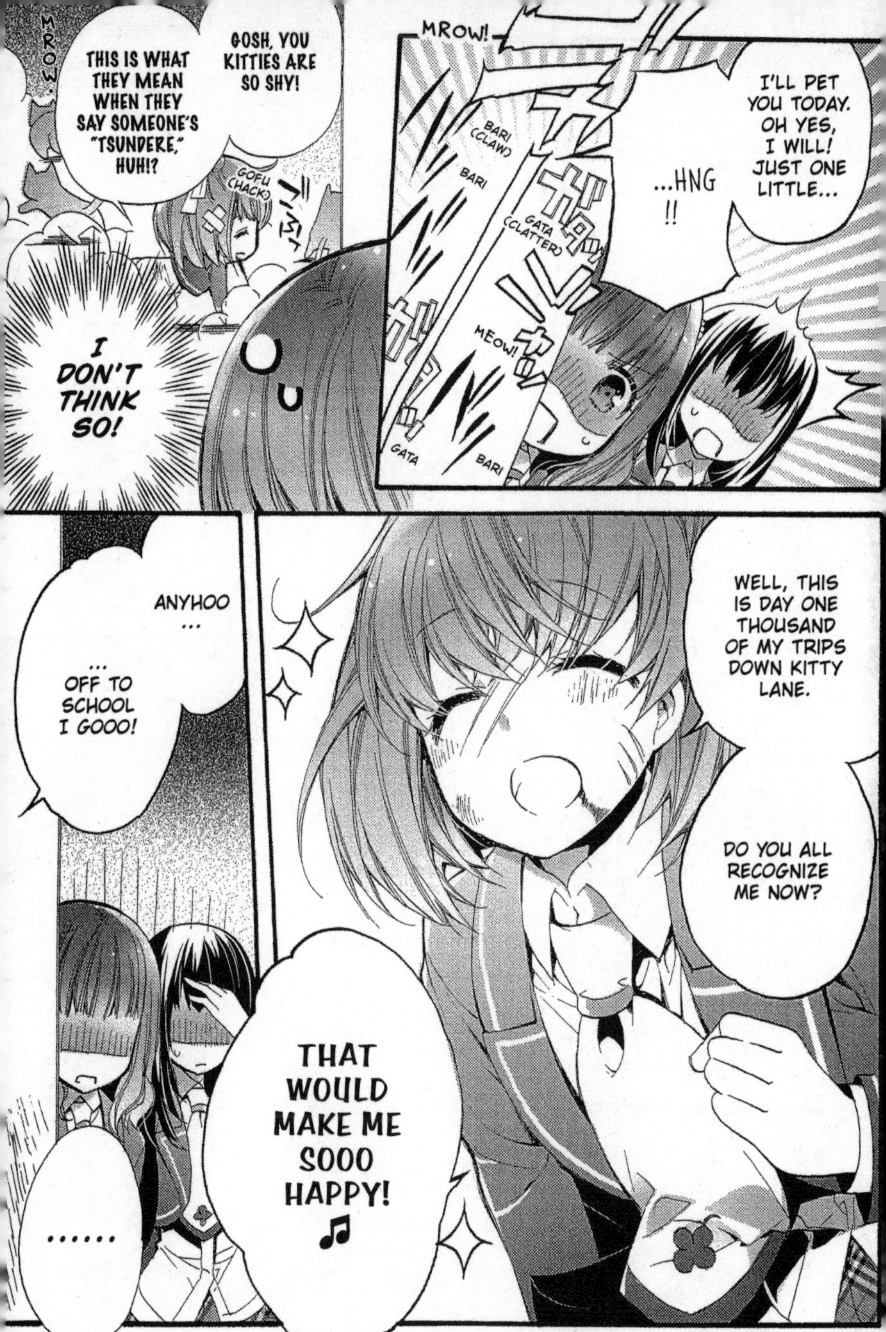
MROW!
I'LL PET YOU TODAY. OH YES, I WILL! JUST ONE LITTLE...
...HNG!!
BARI (CLAW)
BARI
GATA (CLATTER)
MEOW!
GATA
BARI
GOSH, YOU KITTIES ARE SO SHY!
THIS IS WHAT THEY MEAN WHEN THEY SAY SOMEONE'S "TSUNDERE," HUH!?
MROW.
GOFU (HACK)
I DON'T THINK SO!
WELL, THIS IS DAY ONE THOUSAND OF MY TRIPS DOWN KITTY LANE.
DO YOU ALL RECOGNIZE ME NOW?
THAT WOULD MAKE ME SOOO HAPPY! ♫
ANYHOO...
...OFF TO SCHOOL I GOOO!
......

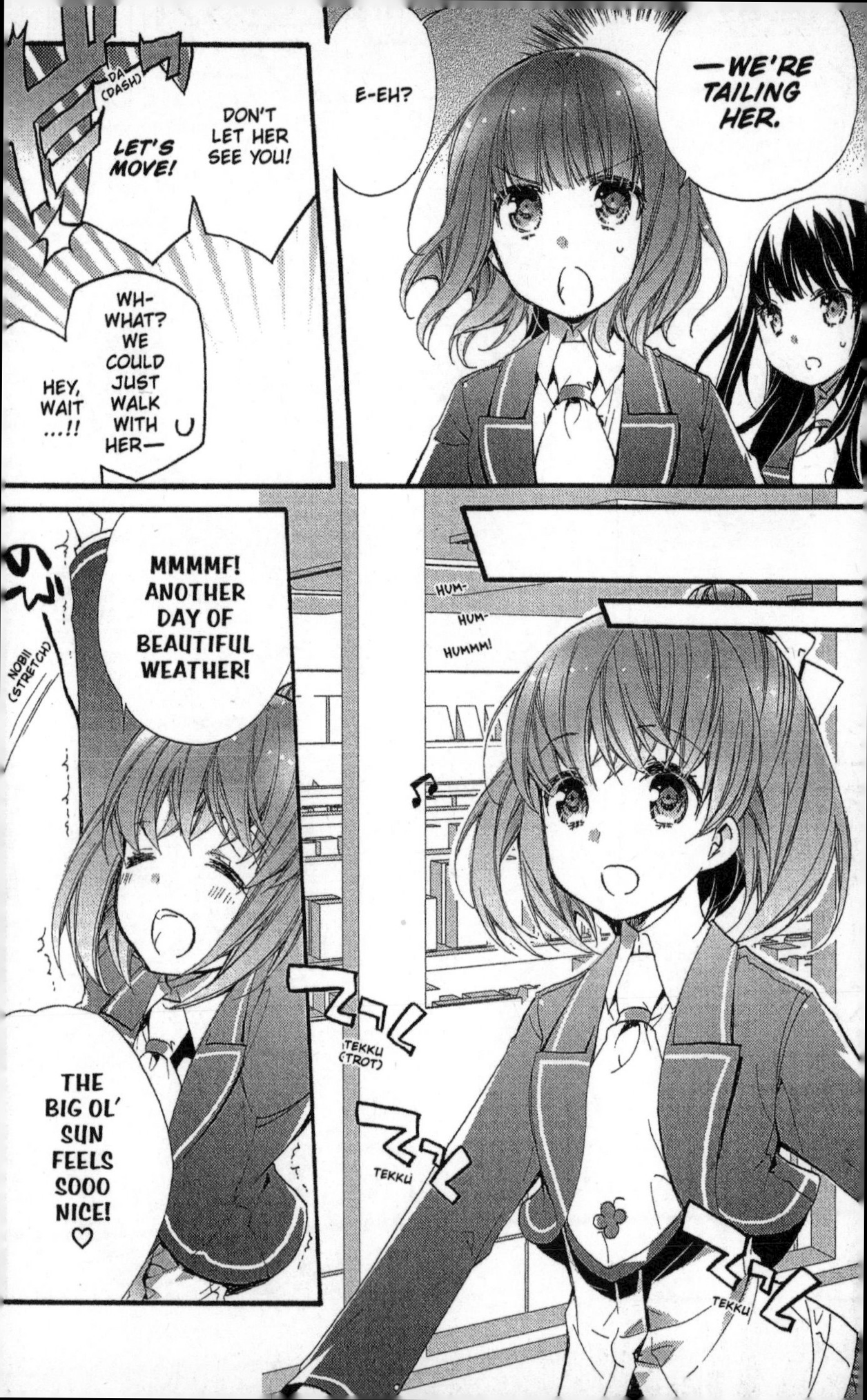
—WE'RE TAILING HER.
E-EH?
DON'T LET HER SEE YOU!
LET'S MOVE!
DA (DASH)
WH-WHAT? WE COULD JUST WALK WITH HER—
HEY, WAIT ...!!
HUM-HUM-HUMMM!
TEKKU (TROT)
TEKKU
TEKKU
MMMMF! ANOTHER DAY OF BEAUTIFUL WEATHER!
NOBII (STRETCH)
THE BIG OL' SUN FEELS SOOO NICE! ♡

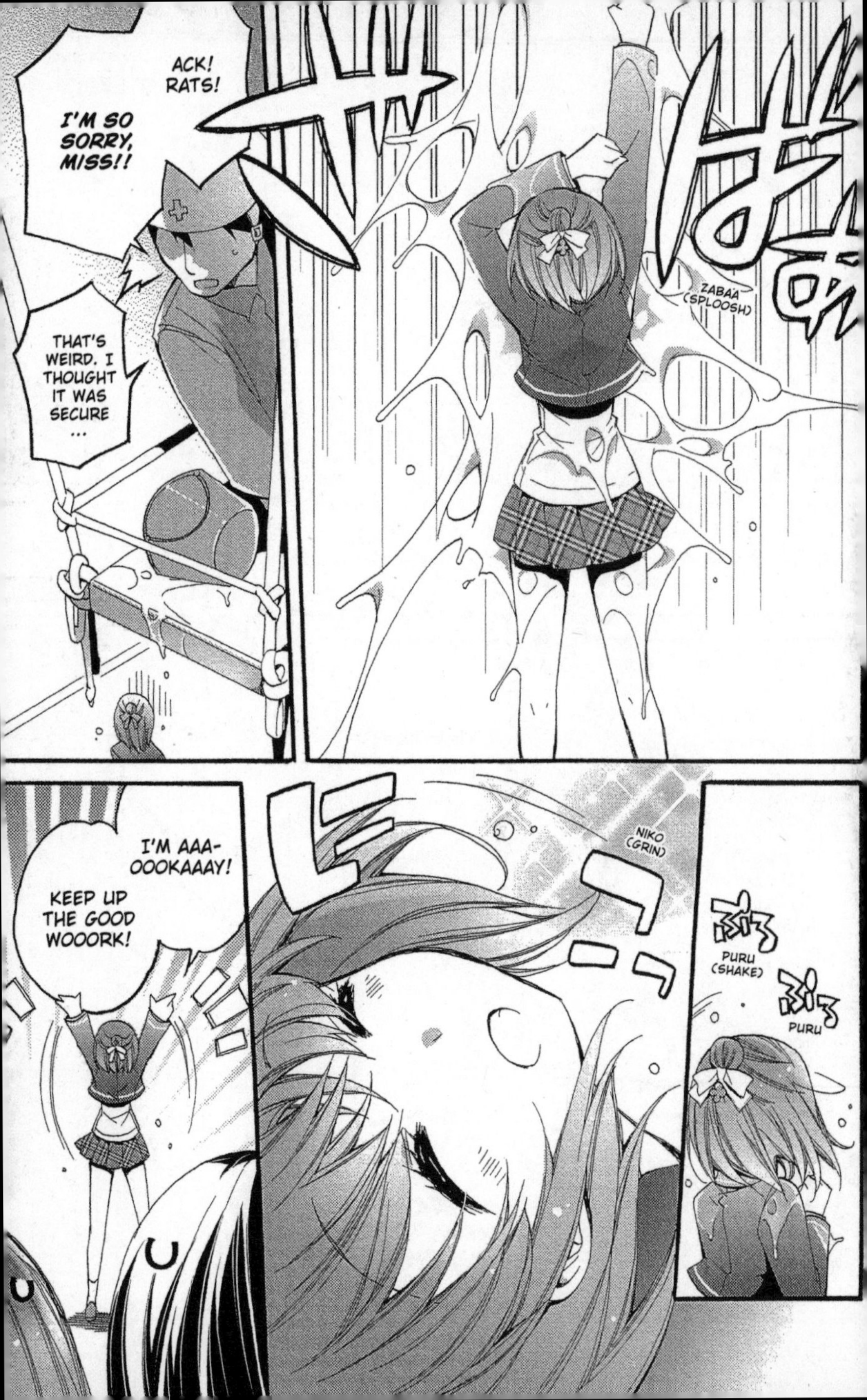
ZABAA (SPLOOSH)
ACK! RATS!
I'M SO SORRY, MISS!!
THAT'S WEIRD. I THOUGHT IT WAS SECURE ...
ぷる
PURU (SHAKE)
ぷる
PURU
NIKO (GRIN)
I'M AAA-OOOKAAAY!
KEEP UP THE GOOD WOOORK!

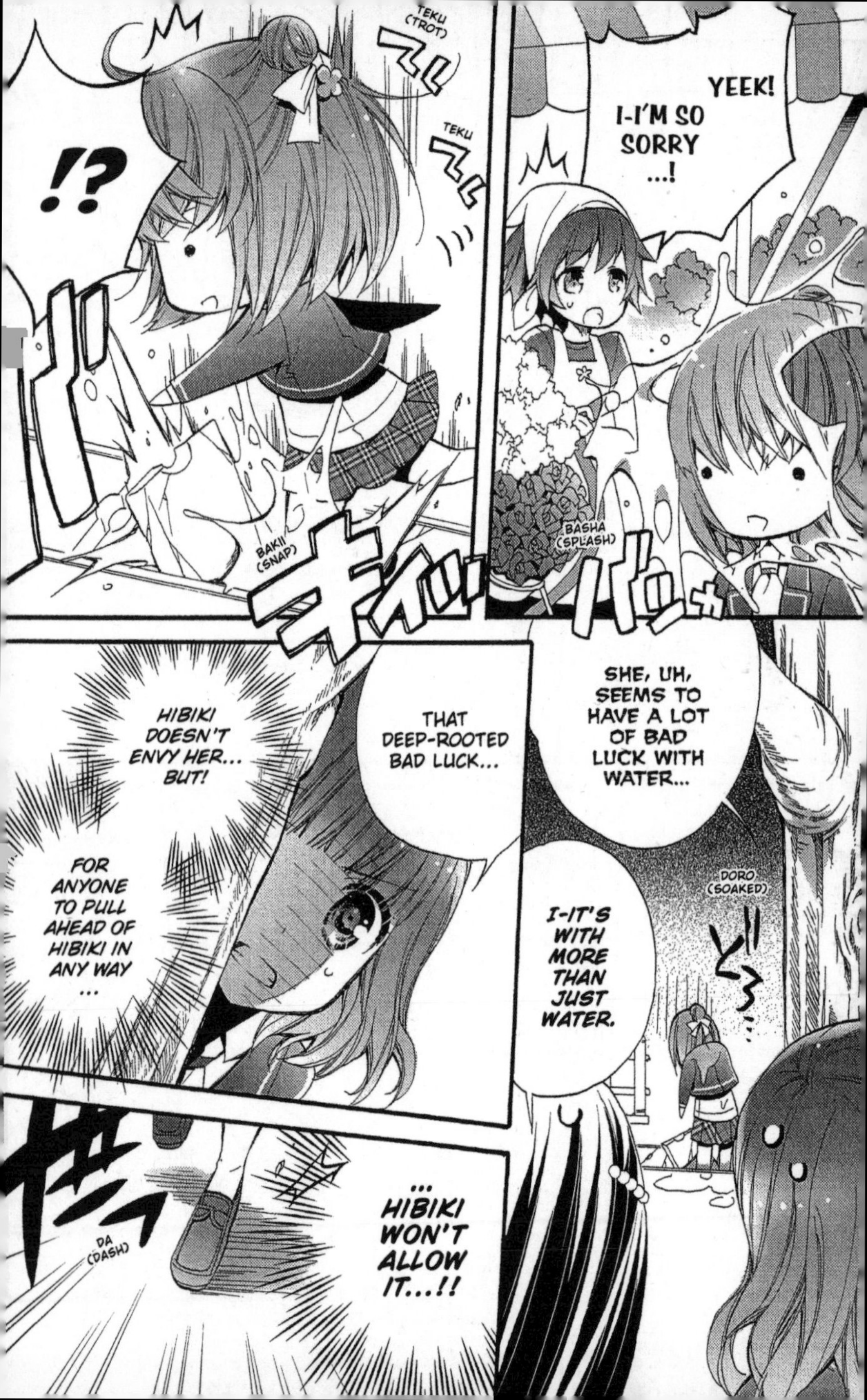
YEEK!
I-I'M SO SORRY ...!
BASHA (SPLASH)
TEKU (TROT)
TEKU
!?
BAKII (SNAP)
SHE, UH, SEEMS TO HAVE A LOT OF BAD LUCK WITH WATER...
THAT DEEP-ROOTED BAD LUCK...
HIBIKI DOESN'T ENVY HER... BUT!
I-IT'S WITH MORE THAN JUST WATER.
DORO (SOAKED)
FOR ANYONE TO PULL AHEAD OF HIBIKI IN ANY WAY ...
... HIBIKI WON'T ALLOW IT...!!
DA (DASH)

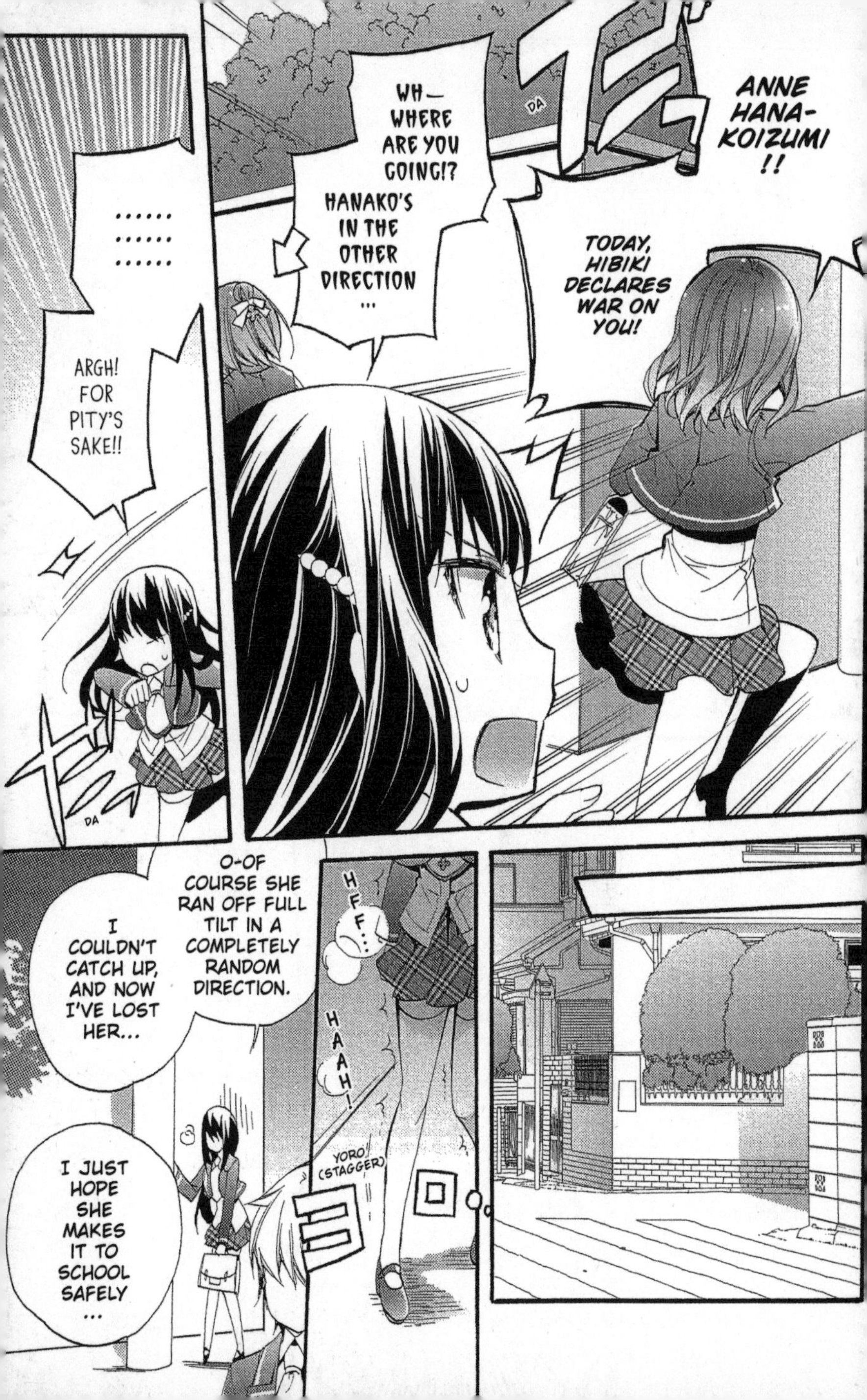
DA
ANNE HANA-KOIZUMI!!
TODAY, HIBIKI DECLARES WAR ON YOU!
WH— WHERE ARE YOU GOING!?
HANAKO'S IN THE OTHER DIRECTION ...
......
......
......
ARGH! FOR PITY'S SAKE!!
DA
HFF...
HAAAH!
YORO (STAGGER)
O-OF COURSE SHE RAN OFF FULL TILT IN A COMPLETELY RANDOM DIRECTION.
I COULDN'T CATCH UP, AND NOW I'VE LOST HER...
I JUST HOPE SHE MAKES IT TO SCHOOL SAFELY ...

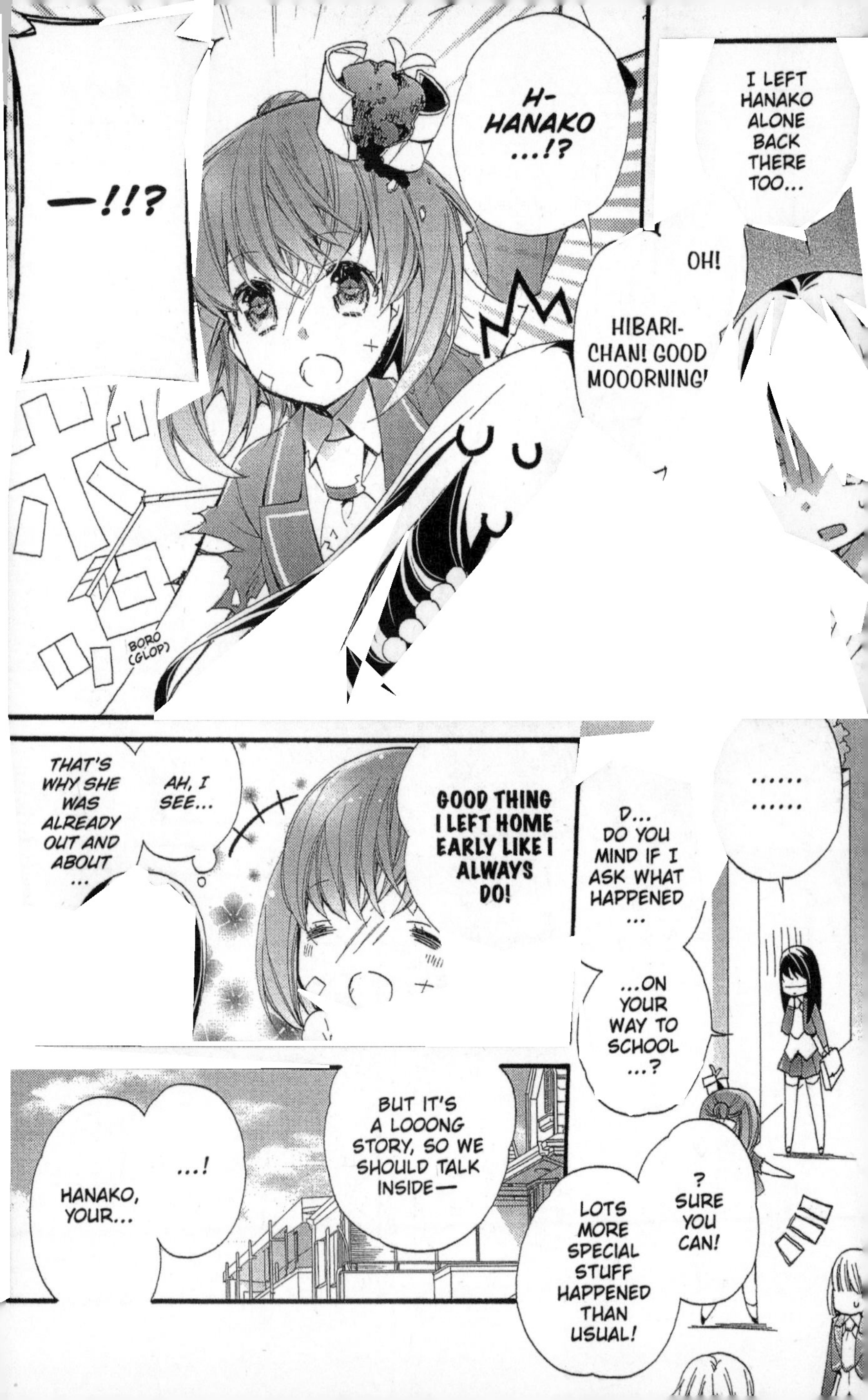
I LEFT HANAKO ALONE BACK THERE TOO...
OH!
HIBARI-CHAN! GOOD MOOORNING!
H-HANAKO...!?
BORO (GLOP)
—!!?
......
......
D... DO YOU MIND IF I ASK WHAT HAPPENED...
...ON YOUR WAY TO SCHOOL...?
? SURE YOU CAN!
LOTS MORE SPECIAL STUFF HAPPENED THAN USUAL!
GOOD THING I LEFT HOME EARLY LIKE I ALWAYS DO!
AH, I SEE...
THAT'S WHY SHE WAS ALREADY OUT AND ABOUT...
BUT IT'S A LOOONG STORY, SO WE SHOULD TALK INSIDE—
...!
HANAKO, YOUR...

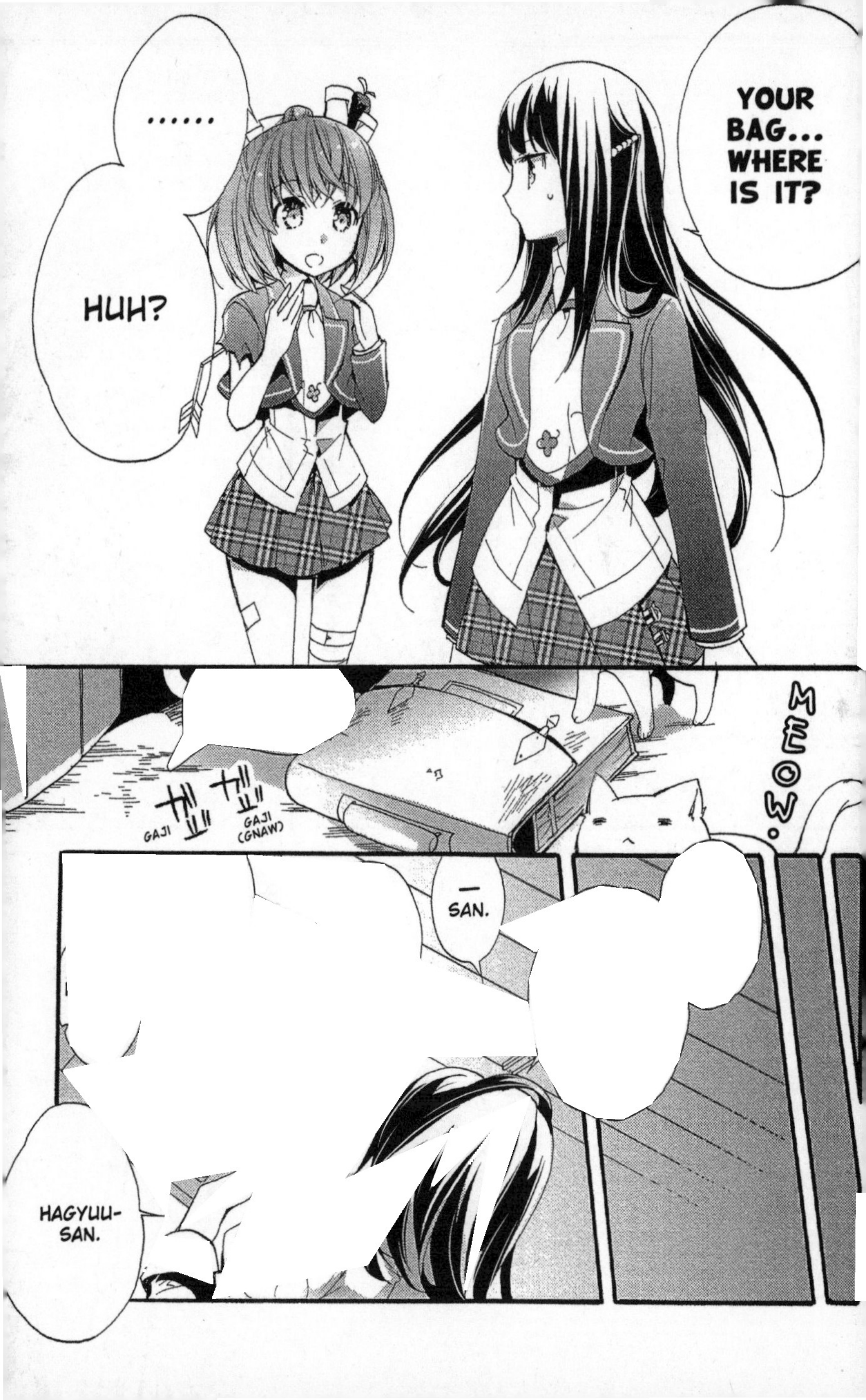
YOUR BAG... WHERE IS IT?
......
HUH?
MEOW.
GAJI
GAJI (GNAW)
—SAN.
HAGYUU-SAN.

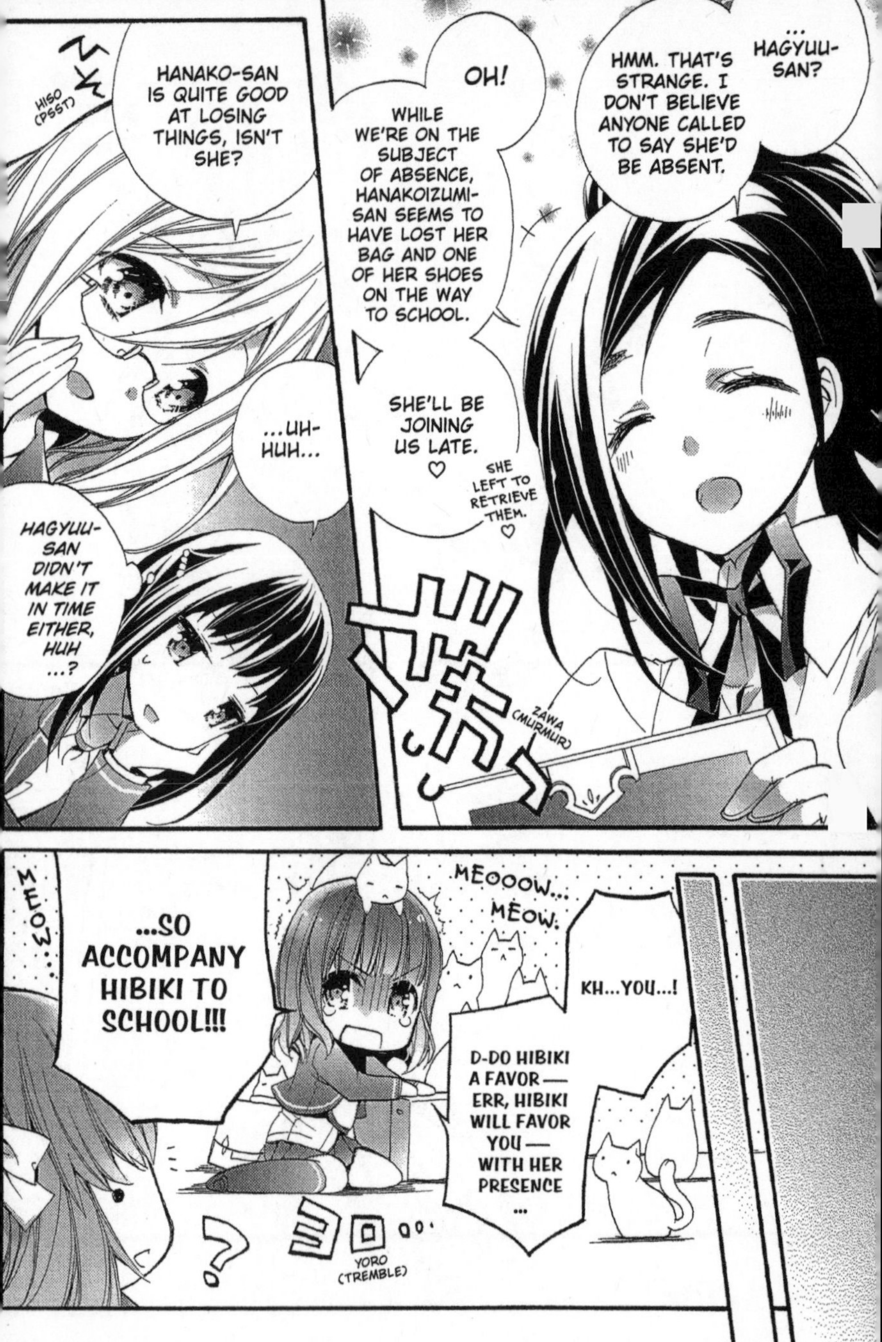
...HAGYUU-SAN?
HMM. THAT'S STRANGE. I DON'T BELIEVE ANYONE CALLED TO SAY SHE'D BE ABSENT.
OH!
WHILE WE'RE ON THE SUBJECT OF ABSENCE, HANAKOIZUMI-SAN SEEMS TO HAVE LOST HER BAG AND ONE OF HER SHOES ON THE WAY TO SCHOOL.
SHE'LL BE JOINING US LATE. ♡
SHE LEFT TO RETRIEVE THEM. ♡
ZAWA (MURMUR)
HISO (PSSST)
HANAKO-SAN IS QUITE GOOD AT LOSING THINGS, ISN'T SHE?
...UH-HUH...
HAGYUU-SAN DIDN'T MAKE IT IN TIME EITHER, HUH ...?
KH...YOU...!
MEOOOW... MEOW.
D-DO HIBIKI A FAVOR— ERR, HIBIKI WILL FAVOR YOU— WITH HER PRESENCE ...
...SO ACCOMPANY HIBIKI TO SCHOOL!!!
MEOW...
YORO (TREMBLE)

Anne Happy
unhappy go lucky!

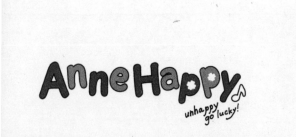

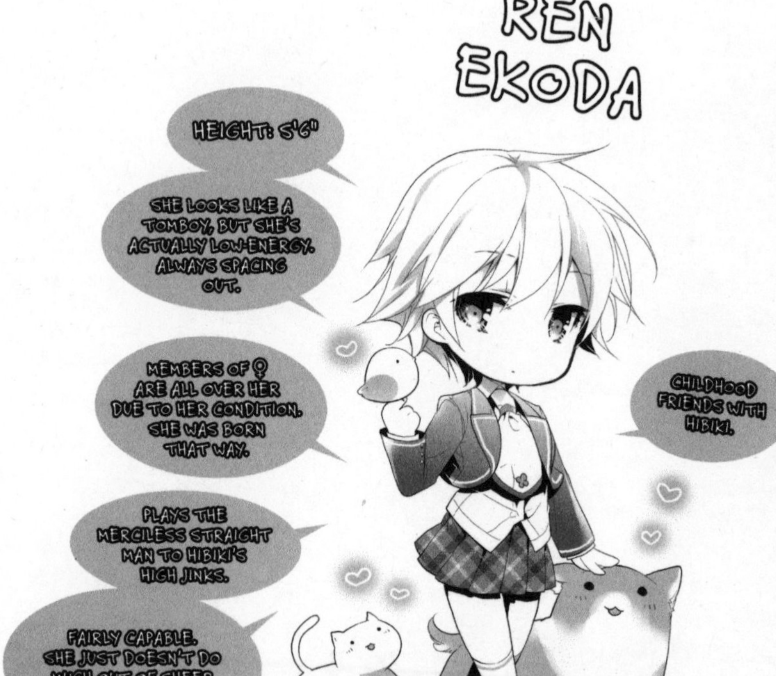
REN EKODA
HEIGHT: 5'6"
SHE LOOKS LIKE A TOMBOY, BUT SHE'S ACTUALLY LOW-ENERGY. ALWAYS SPACING OUT.
CHILDHOOD FRIENDS WITH HIBIKI.
MEMBERS OF ♀ ARE ALL OVER HER DUE TO HER CONDITION. SHE WAS BORN THAT WAY.
PLAYS THE MERCILESS STRAIGHT MAN TO HIBIKI'S HIGH JINKS.
FAIRLY CAPABLE. SHE JUST DOESN'T DO MUCH OUT OF SHEER LAZINESS.

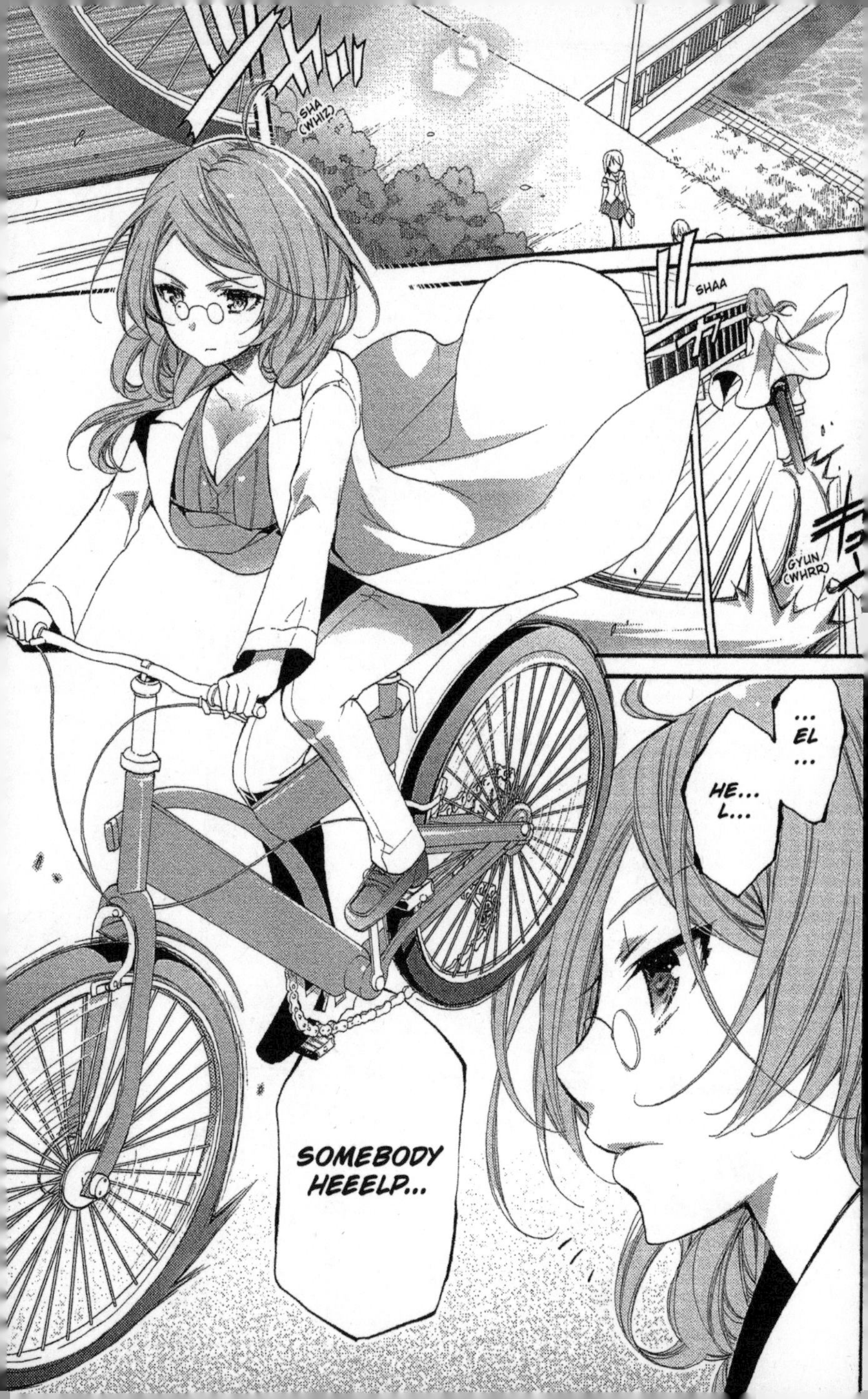
SHA (WHIZ)
SHAA
GYUN (WHRR)
... EL ...
HE... L...
SOMEBODY HEEELP...

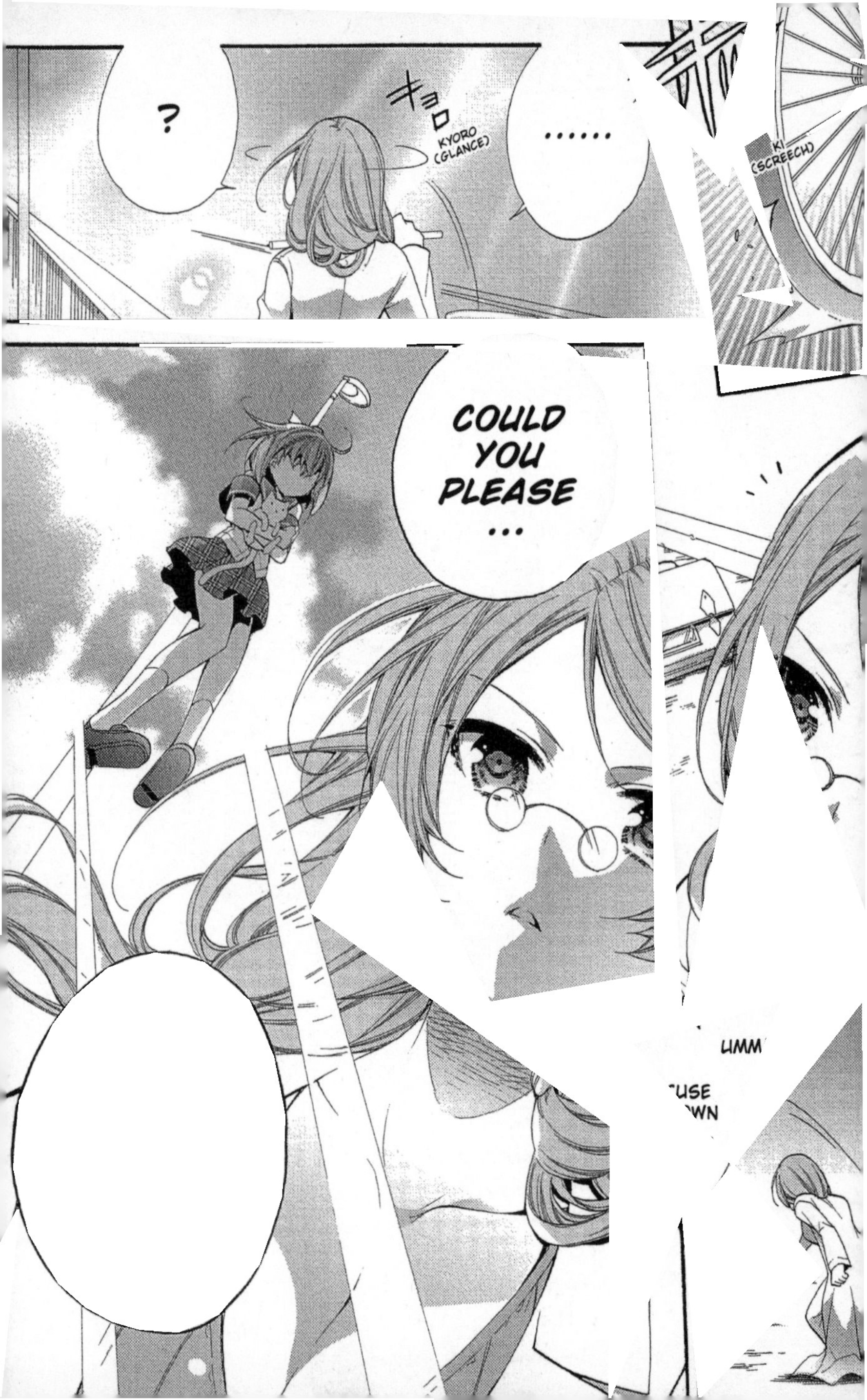
KI (SCREECH)
......
キョロ
KYORO (GLANCE)
?
UMM
COULD YOU PLEASE ...

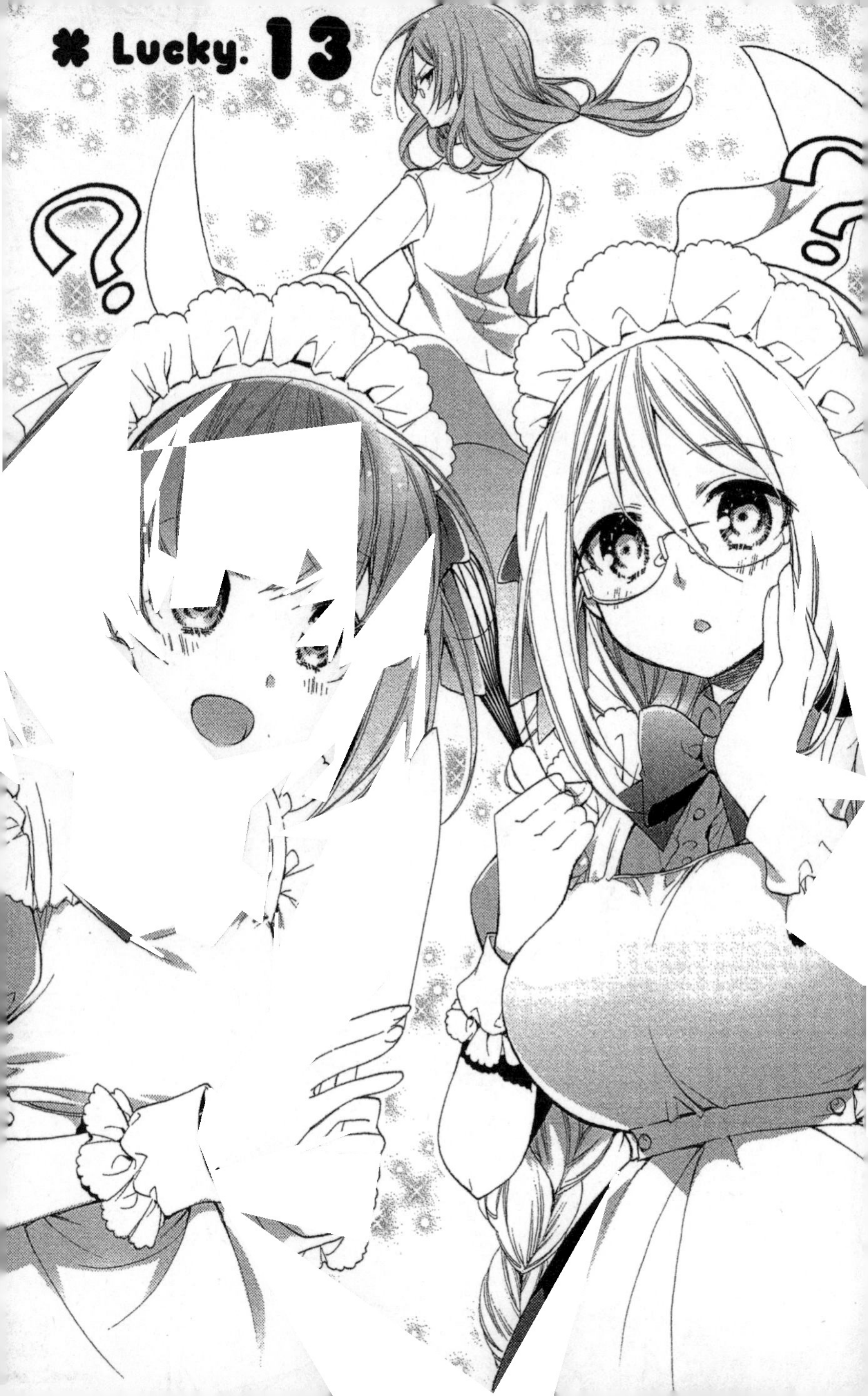
Lucky. 13
?
?

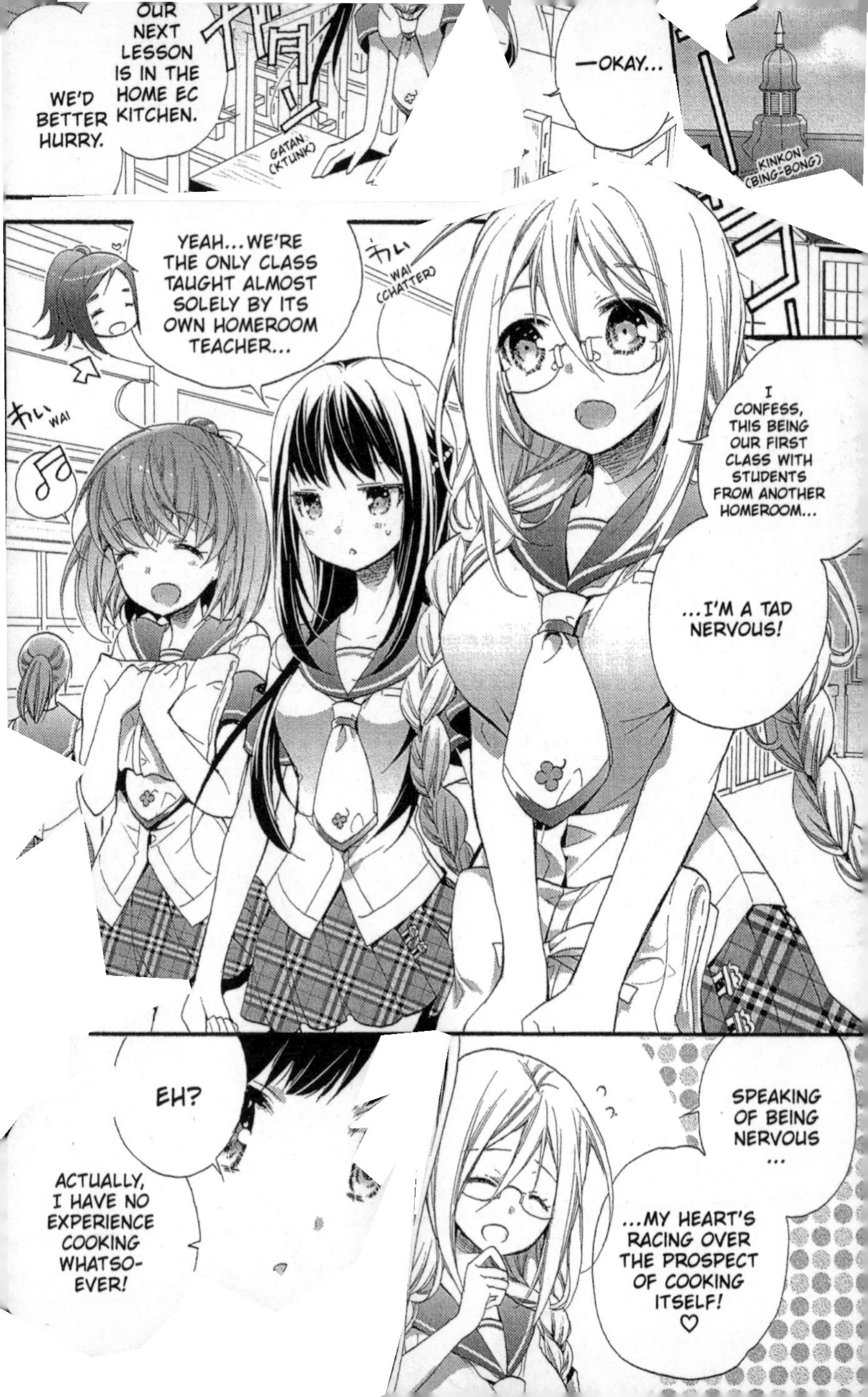
KINKON (BING-BONG)
OUR NEXT LESSON IS IN THE HOME EC KITCHEN.
WE'D BETTER HURRY.
GATAN (KTUNK)
—OKAY...
I CONFESS, THIS BEING OUR FIRST CLASS WITH STUDENTS FROM ANOTHER HOMEROOM...
...I'M A TAD NERVOUS!
わいWAI (CHATTER)
YEAH...WE'RE THE ONLY CLASS TAUGHT ALMOST SOLELY BY ITS OWN HOMEROOM TEACHER...
わいWAI
SPEAKING OF BEING NERVOUS...
...MY HEART'S RACING OVER THE PROSPECT OF COOKING ITSELF! ♡
EH?
ACTUALLY, I HAVE NO EXPERIENCE COOKING WHATSO-EVER!

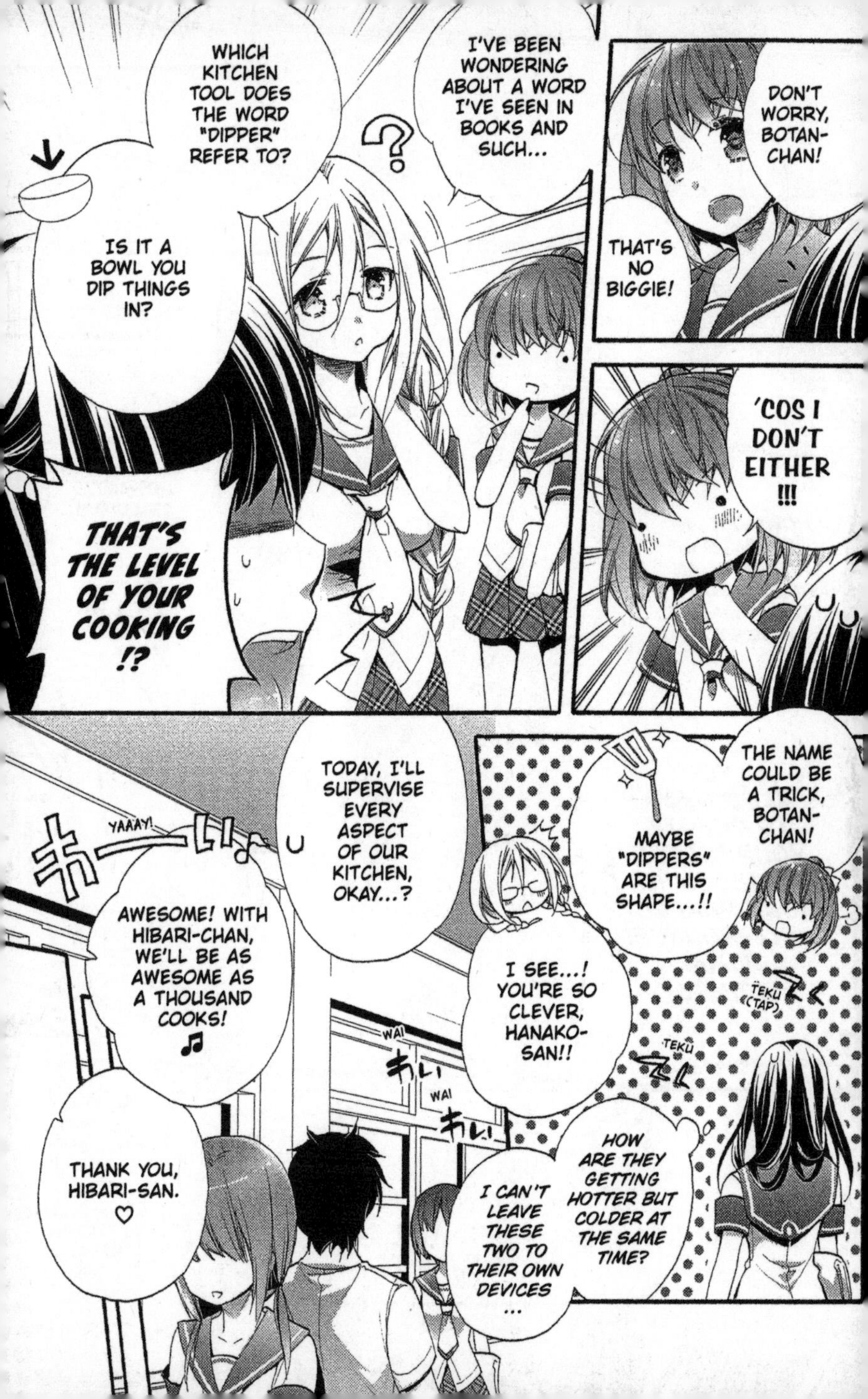
DON'T WORRY, BOTAN-CHAN!
THAT'S NO BIGGIE!
'COS I DON'T EITHER !!!
I'VE BEEN WONDERING ABOUT A WORD I'VE SEEN IN BOOKS AND SUCH...
WHICH KITCHEN TOOL DOES THE WORD "DIPPER" REFER TO?
IS IT A BOWL YOU DIP THINGS IN?
THAT'S THE LEVEL OF YOUR COOKING !?
THE NAME COULD BE A TRICK, BOTAN-CHAN!
MAYBE "DIPPERS" ARE THIS SHAPE...!!
I SEE...! YOU'RE SO CLEVER, HANAKO-SAN!!
TEKU (TAP)
TEKU
HOW ARE THEY GETTING HOTTER BUT COLDER AT THE SAME TIME?
I CAN'T LEAVE THESE TWO TO THEIR OWN DEVICES ...
TODAY, I'LL SUPERVISE EVERY ASPECT OF OUR KITCHEN, OKAY...?
YAAAY!
AWESOME! WITH HIBARI-CHAN, WE'LL BE AS AWESOME AS A THOUSAND COOKS! ♫
WAI
WAI
THANK YOU, HIBARI-SAN. ♡

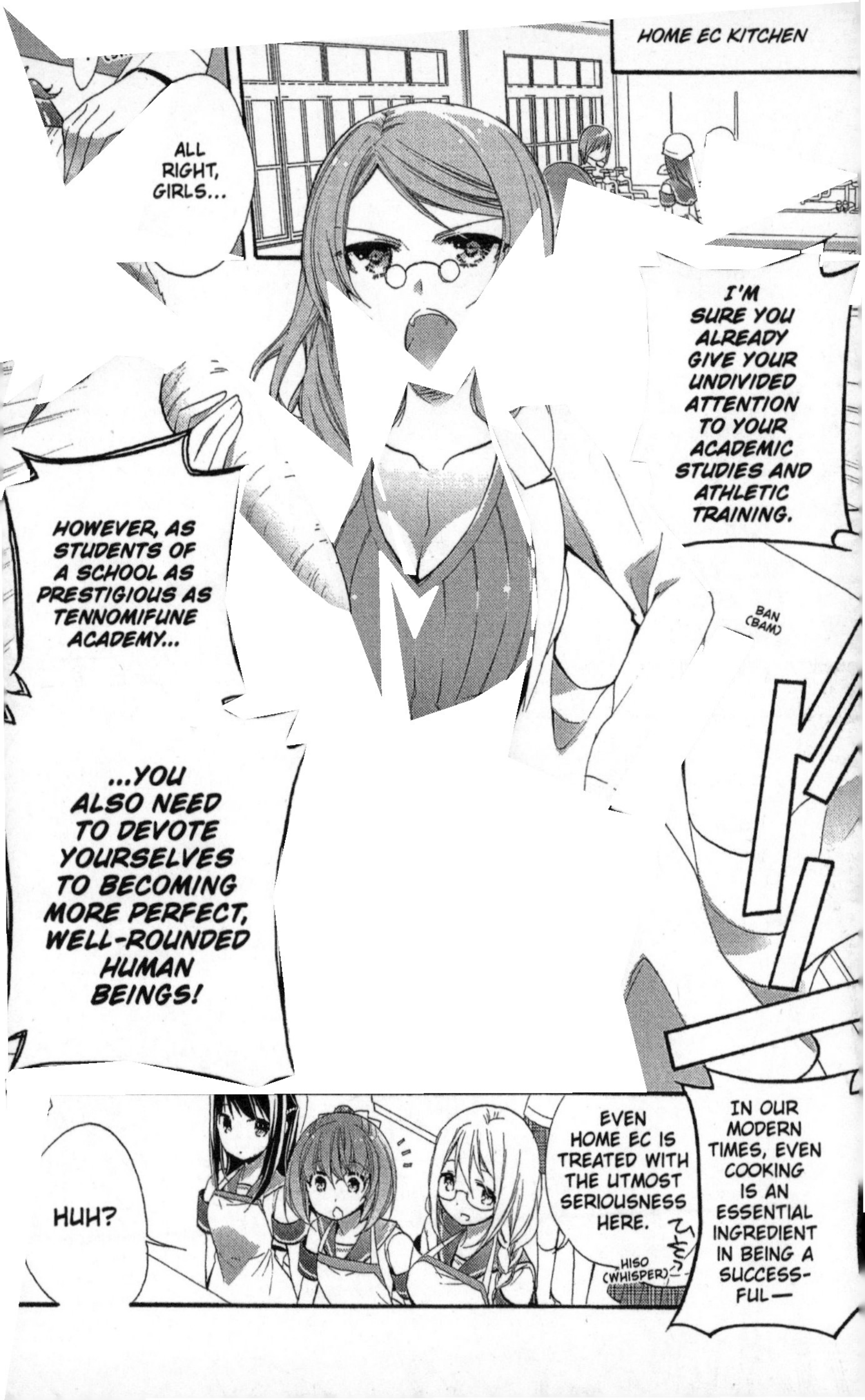
HOME EC KITCHEN
ALL RIGHT, GIRLS...
I'M SURE YOU ALREADY GIVE YOUR UNDIVIDED ATTENTION TO YOUR ACADEMIC STUDIES AND ATHLETIC TRAINING.
BAN (BAM)
HOWEVER, AS STUDENTS OF A SCHOOL AS PRESTIGIOUS AS TENNOMIFUNE ACADEMY...
...YOU ALSO NEED TO DEVOTE YOURSELVES TO BECOMING MORE PERFECT, WELL-ROUNDED HUMAN BEINGS!
IN OUR MODERN TIMES, EVEN COOKING IS AN ESSENTIAL INGREDIENT IN BEING A SUCCESS-FUL—
EVEN HOME EC IS TREATED WITH THE UTMOST SERIOUSNESS HERE.
HISO (WHISPER)
HUH?

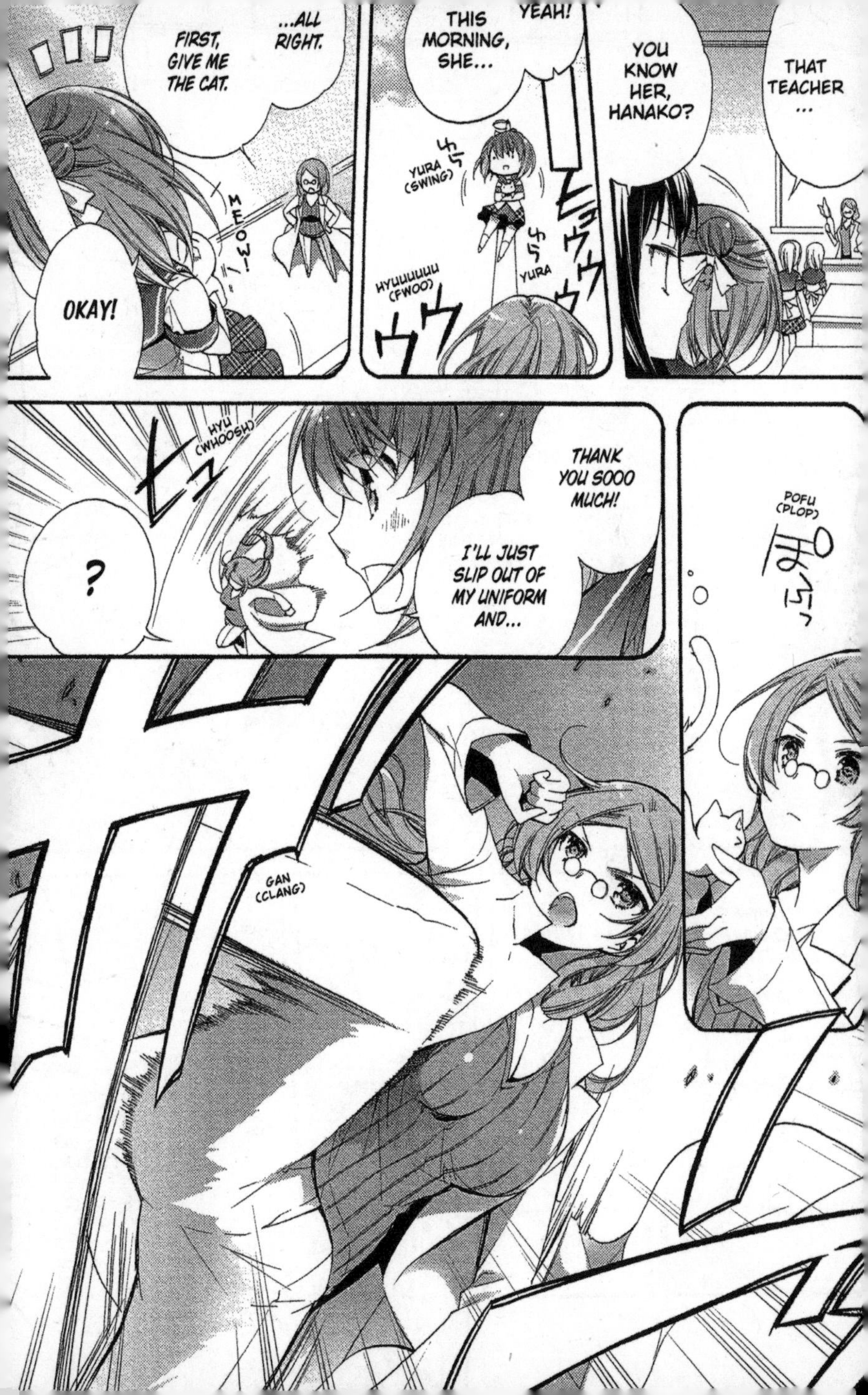
THAT TEACHER ...
YOU KNOW HER, HANAKO?
YEAH!
THIS MORNING, SHE...
YURA (SWING)
YURA
HYUUUUUUU (FWOO)
...ALL RIGHT.
FIRST, GIVE ME THE CAT.
MEOW!
OKAY!
POFU (PLOP)
THANK YOU SOOO MUCH!
I'LL JUST SLIP OUT OF MY UNIFORM AND...
HYU (WHOOSH)
?
GAN (CLANG)

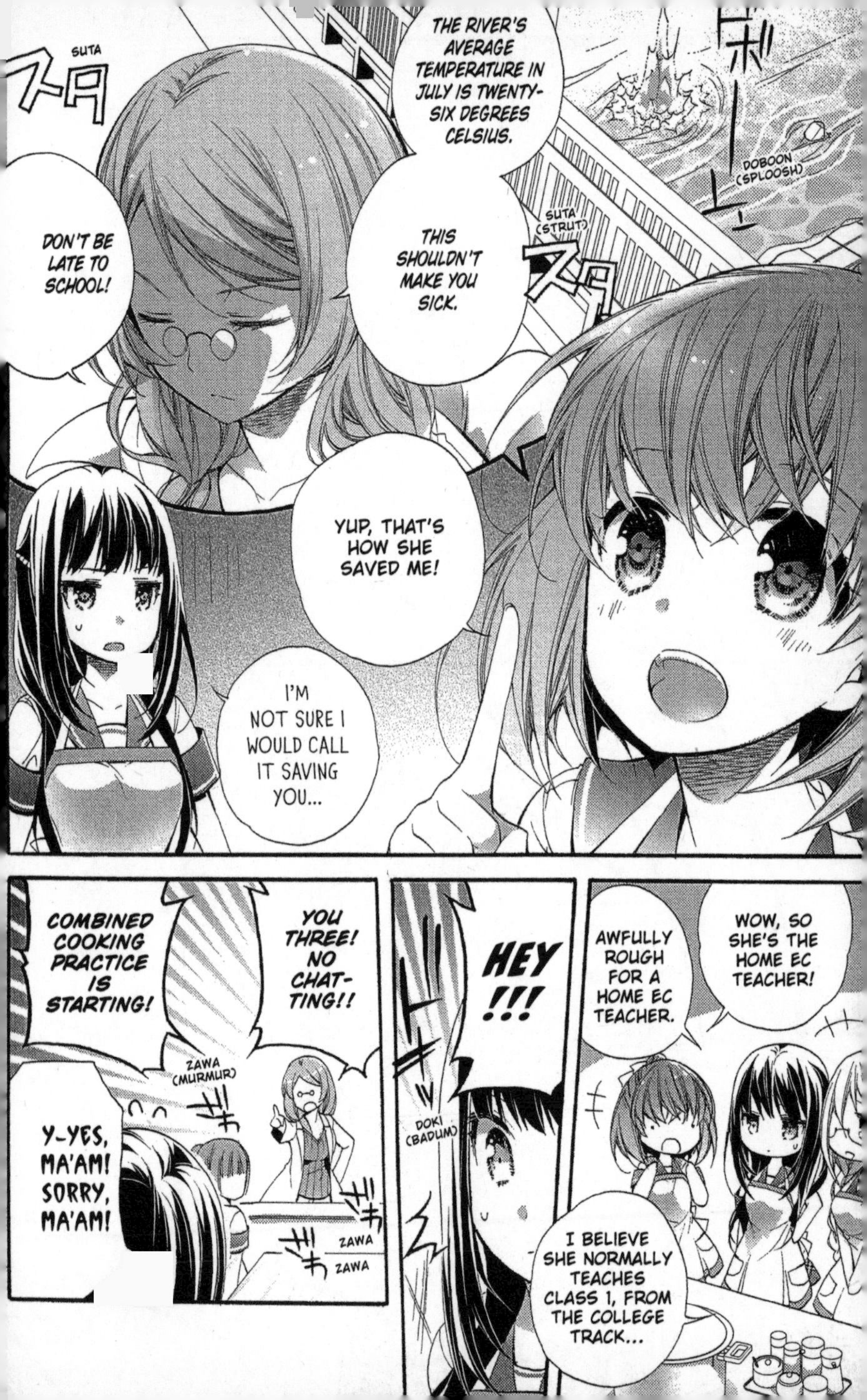
ドボーン
DOBOON (SPLOOSH)
THE RIVER'S AVERAGE TEMPERATURE IN JULY IS TWENTY-SIX DEGREES CELSIUS.
スタ
SUTA (STRUT)
THIS SHOULDN'T MAKE YOU SICK.
スタ
SUTA
DON'T BE LATE TO SCHOOL!
YUP, THAT'S HOW SHE SAVED ME!
I'M NOT SURE I WOULD CALL IT SAVING YOU...
WOW, SO SHE'S THE HOME EC TEACHER!
AWFULLY ROUGH FOR A HOME EC TEACHER.
I BELIEVE SHE NORMALLY TEACHES CLASS 1, FROM THE COLLEGE TRACK...
HEY!!!
DOKI (BADUM)
YOU THREE! NO CHATTING!!
COMBINED COOKING PRACTICE IS STARTING!
ZAWA (MURMUR)
ZAWA
ZAWA
Y-YES, MA'AM! SORRY, MA'AM!

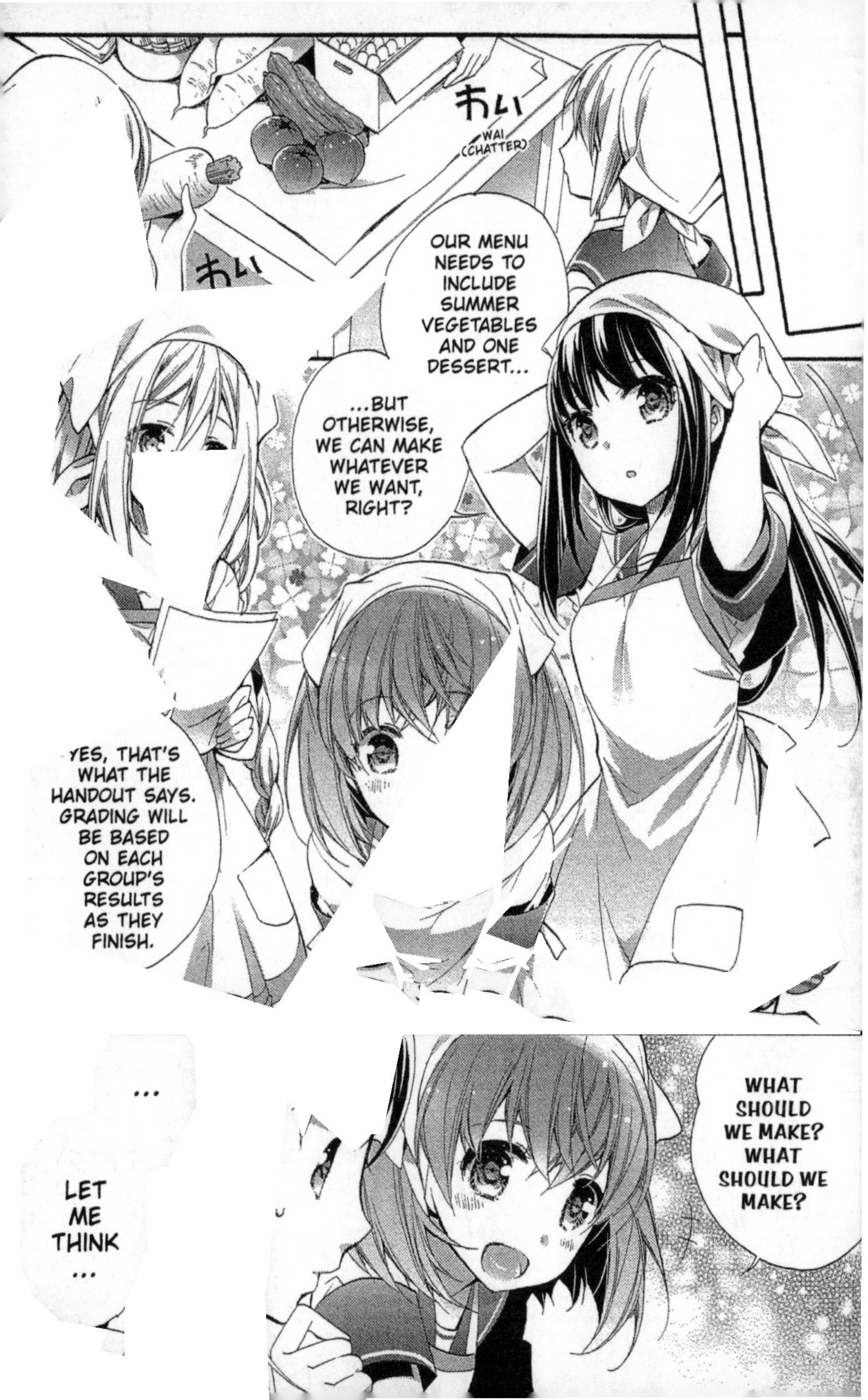
わい
WAI (CHATTER)
わい
OUR MENU NEEDS TO INCLUDE SUMMER VEGETABLES AND ONE DESSERT...
...BUT OTHERWISE, WE CAN MAKE WHATEVER WE WANT, RIGHT?
YES, THAT'S WHAT THE HANDOUT SAYS. GRADING WILL BE BASED ON EACH GROUP'S RESULTS AS THEY FINISH.
WHAT SHOULD WE MAKE? WHAT SHOULD WE MAKE?
...
LET ME THINK...

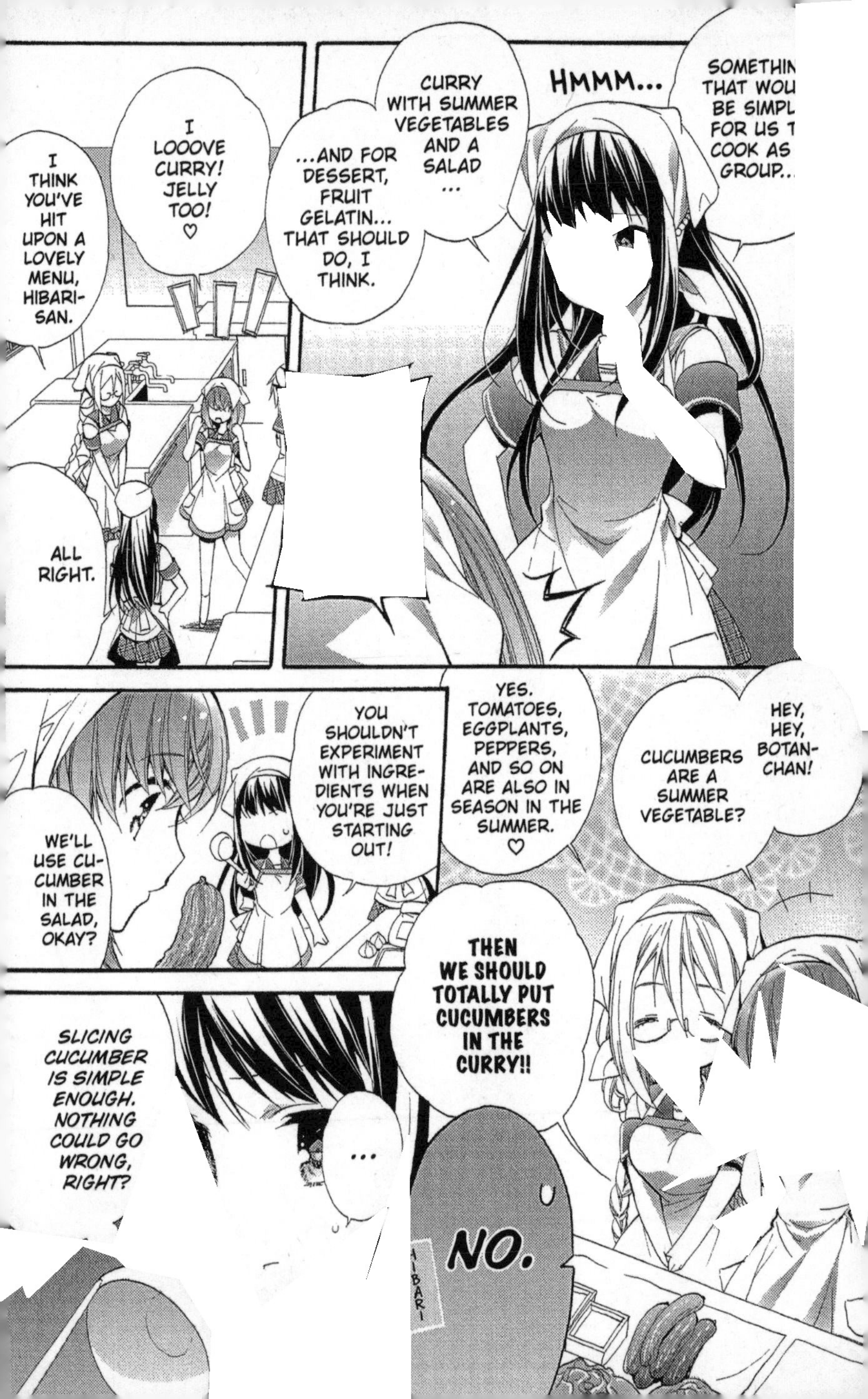
SOMETHIN THAT WOU BE SIMPL FOR US T COOK AS GROUP...
HMMM...
CURRY WITH SUMMER VEGETABLES AND A SALAD ...
...AND FOR DESSERT, FRUIT GELATIN... THAT SHOULD DO, I THINK.
I LOOOVE CURRY! JELLY TOO! ♡
I THINK YOU'VE HIT UPON A LOVELY MENU, HIBARI-SAN.
ALL RIGHT.
HEY, HEY, BOTAN-CHAN!
CUCUMBERS ARE A SUMMER VEGETABLE?
YES. TOMATOES, EGGPLANTS, PEPPERS, AND SO ON ARE ALSO IN SEASON IN THE SUMMER. ♡
THEN WE SHOULD TOTALLY PUT CUCUMBERS IN THE CURRY!!
YOU SHOULDN'T EXPERIMENT WITH INGREDIENTS WHEN YOU'RE JUST STARTING OUT!
WE'LL USE CUCUMBER IN THE SALAD, OKAY?
NO.
HIBARI
...
SLICING CUCUMBER IS SIMPLE ENOUGH. NOTHING COULD GO WRONG, RIGHT?

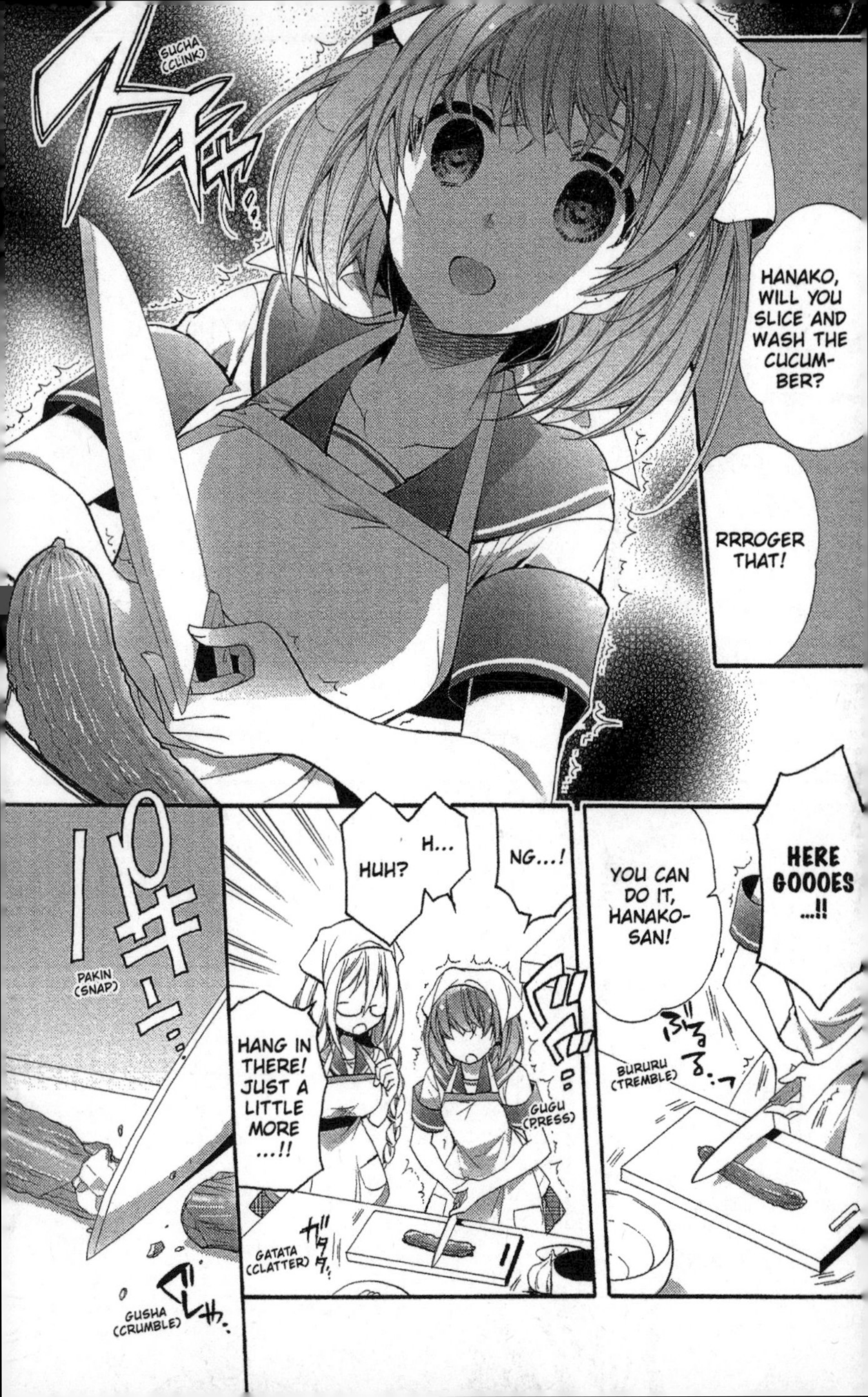
HANAKO, WILL YOU SLICE AND WASH THE CUCUMBER?
RRROGER THAT!
SUCHA (CLINK)
HERE GOOOES ...!!
YOU CAN DO IT, HANAKO-SAN!
BURURU (TREMBLE)
NG...!
H... HUH?
HANG IN THERE! JUST A LITTLE MORE ...!!
GUGU (PRESS)
GATATA (CLATTER)
PAKIN (SNAP)
GUSHA (CRUMBLE)

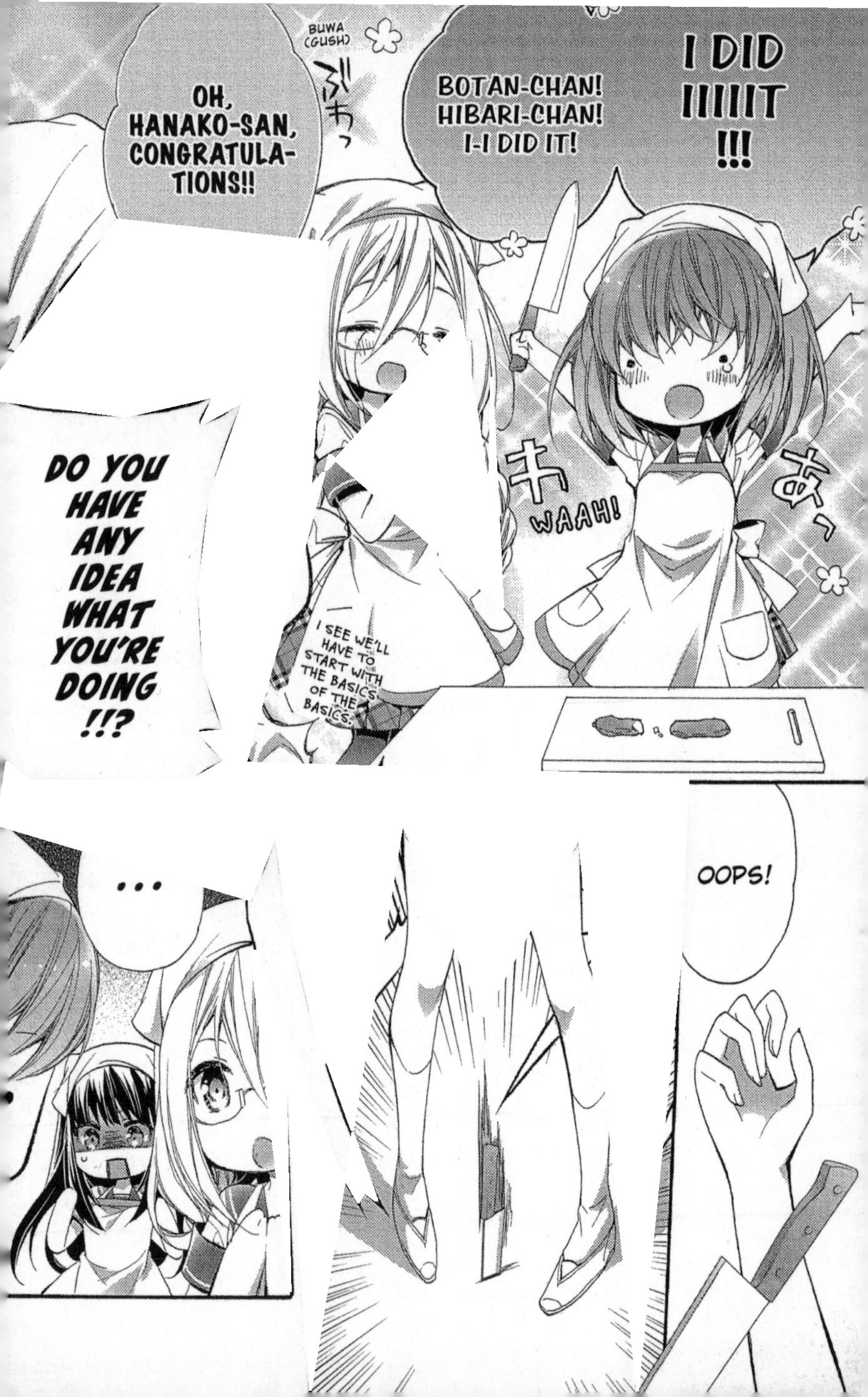
I DID IIIIIT !!!
BOTAN-CHAN! HIBARI-CHAN! I-I DID IT!
ぶわっ
BUWA (GUSH)
OH, HANAKO-SAN, CONGRATULA-TIONS!!
あっ
わ
WAAH!
DO YOU HAVE ANY IDEA WHAT YOU'RE DOING !!?
I SEE WE'LL HAVE TO START WITH THE BASICS OF THE BASICS.
OOPS!
...

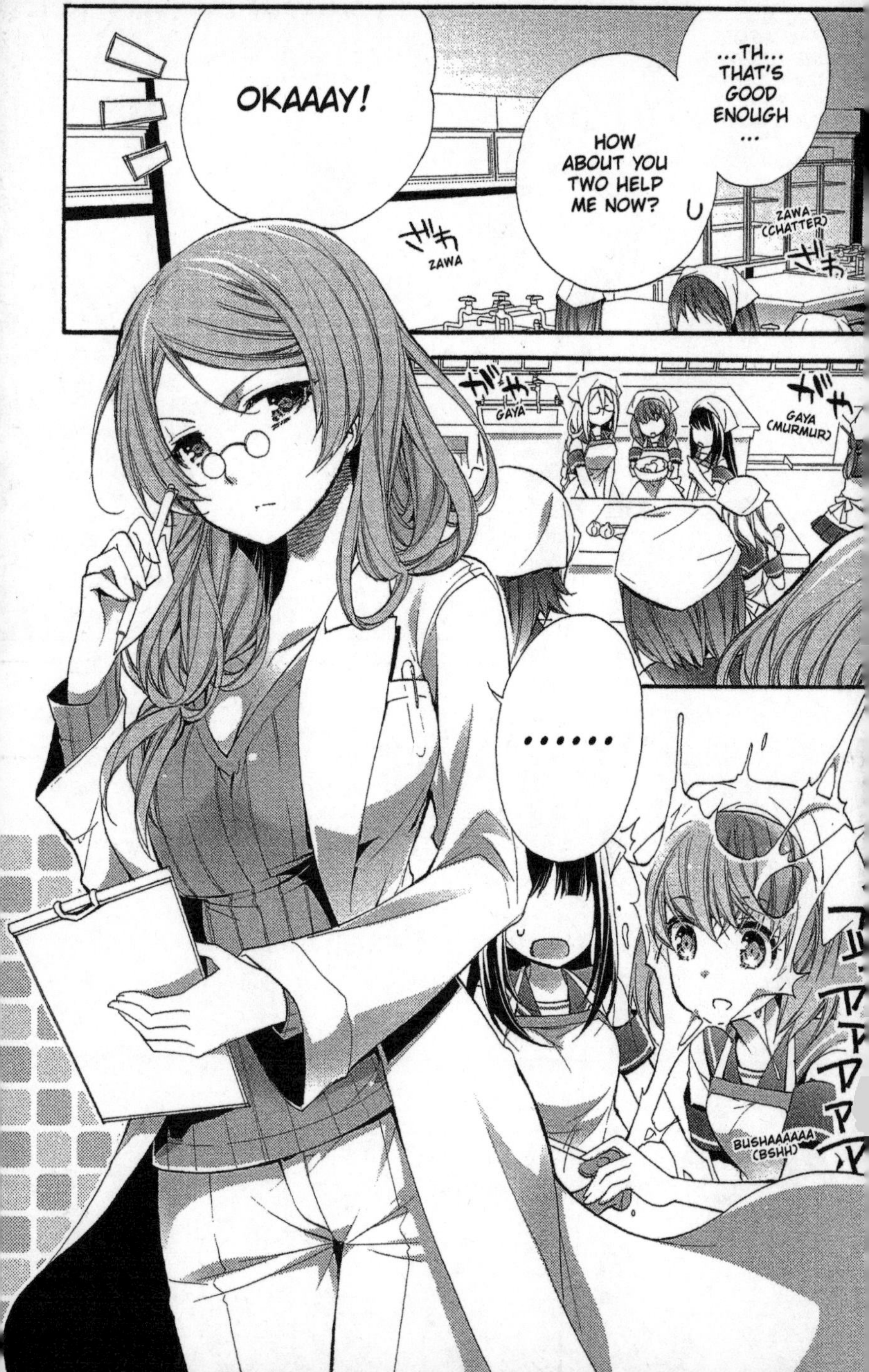
...TH... THAT'S GOOD ENOUGH ...
HOW ABOUT YOU TWO HELP ME NOW?
OKAAAY!
ZAWA (CHATTER)
ZAWA
GAYA (MURMUR)
GAYA
......
BUSHAAAAAA (BSHH)

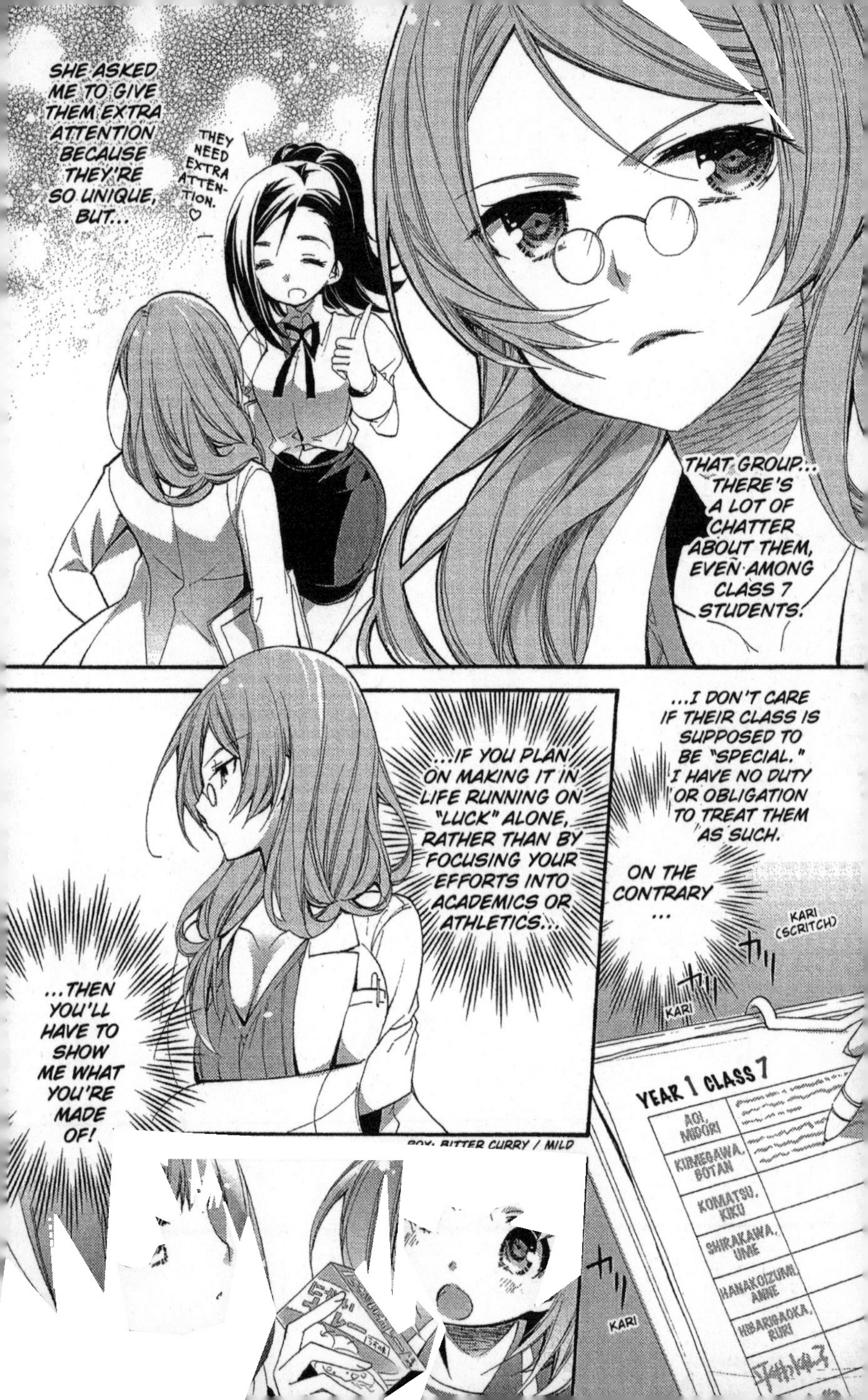
SHE ASKED ME TO GIVE THEM EXTRA ATTENTION BECAUSE THEY'RE SO UNIQUE, BUT...
THEY NEED EXTRA ATTENTION. ♡
THAT GROUP... THERE'S A LOT OF CHATTER ABOUT THEM, EVEN AMONG CLASS 7 STUDENTS.
...I DON'T CARE IF THEIR CLASS IS SUPPOSED TO BE "SPECIAL." I HAVE NO DUTY OR OBLIGATION TO TREAT THEM AS SUCH.
ON THE CONTRARY...
KARI (SCRITCH)
KARI
...IF YOU PLAN ON MAKING IT IN LIFE RUNNING ON "LUCK" ALONE, RATHER THAN BY FOCUSING YOUR EFFORTS INTO ACADEMICS OR ATHLETICS...
...THEN YOU'LL HAVE TO SHOW ME WHAT YOU'RE MADE OF!
BOX: BITTER CURRY / MILD
YEAR 1 CLASS 7
AOI, MIDORI
KIMEGAWA, BOTAN
KOMATSU, KIKU
SHIRAKAWA, UME
HANAKOIZUMI, ANNE
HIBARIGAOKA, RURI
KARI

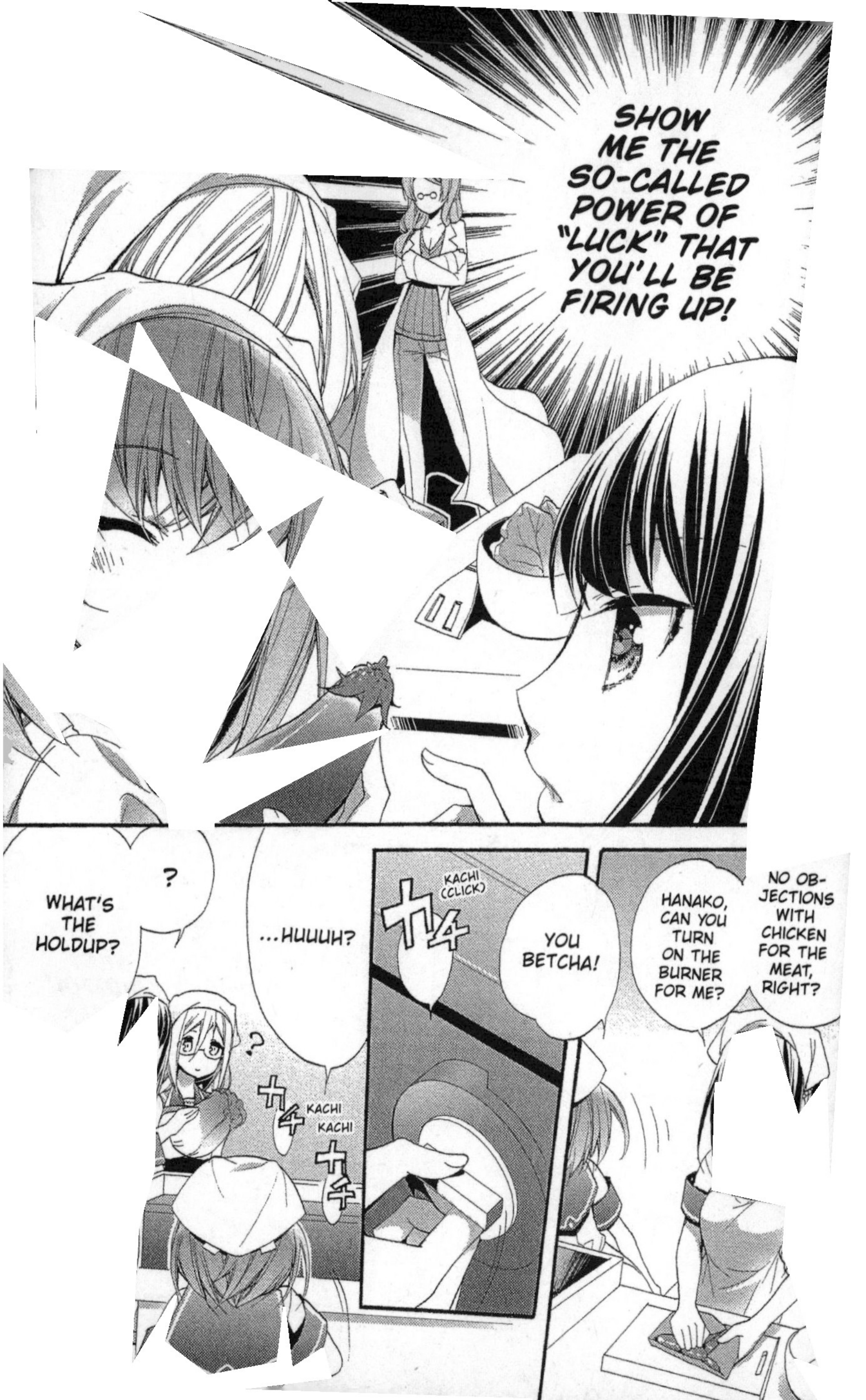
SHOW ME THE SO-CALLED POWER OF "LUCK" THAT YOU'LL BE FIRING UP!
NO OB-JECTIONS WITH CHICKEN FOR THE MEAT, RIGHT?
HANAKO, CAN YOU TURN ON THE BURNER FOR ME?
YOU BETCHA!
KACHI (CLICK)
...HUUUH?
?
WHAT'S THE HOLDUP?
KACHI KACHI
?

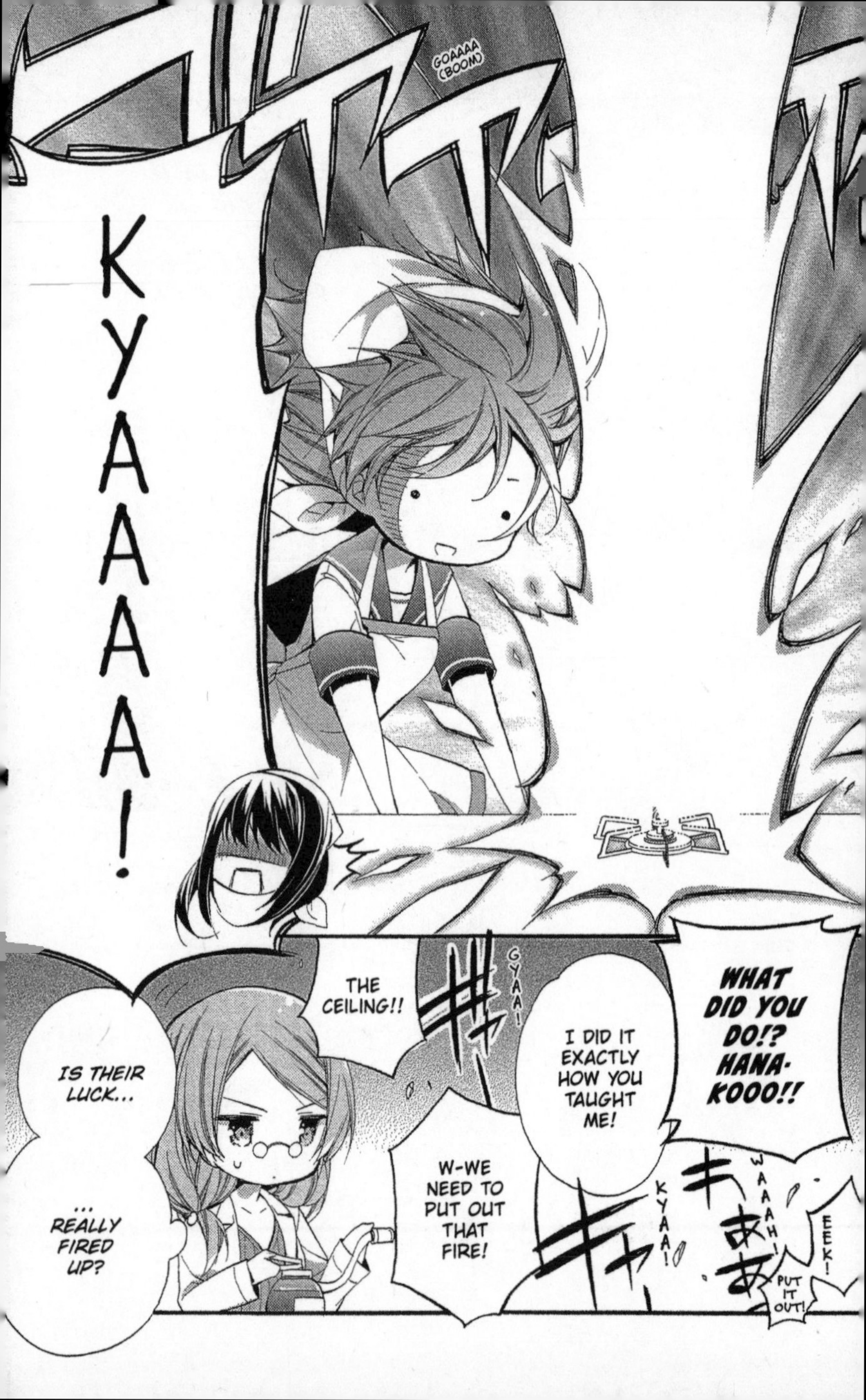
GOAAAA (BOOM)
KYAAAA!
WHAT DID YOU DO!? HANA-KOOO!!
I DID IT EXACTLY HOW YOU TAUGHT ME!
GYAA!
THE CEILING!!
EEK!
WAAAH!
KYAA!
PUT IT OUT!
W-WE NEED TO PUT OUT THAT FIRE!
IS THEIR LUCK...
...REALLY FIRED UP?

Anne Happy

unhappy go lucky!

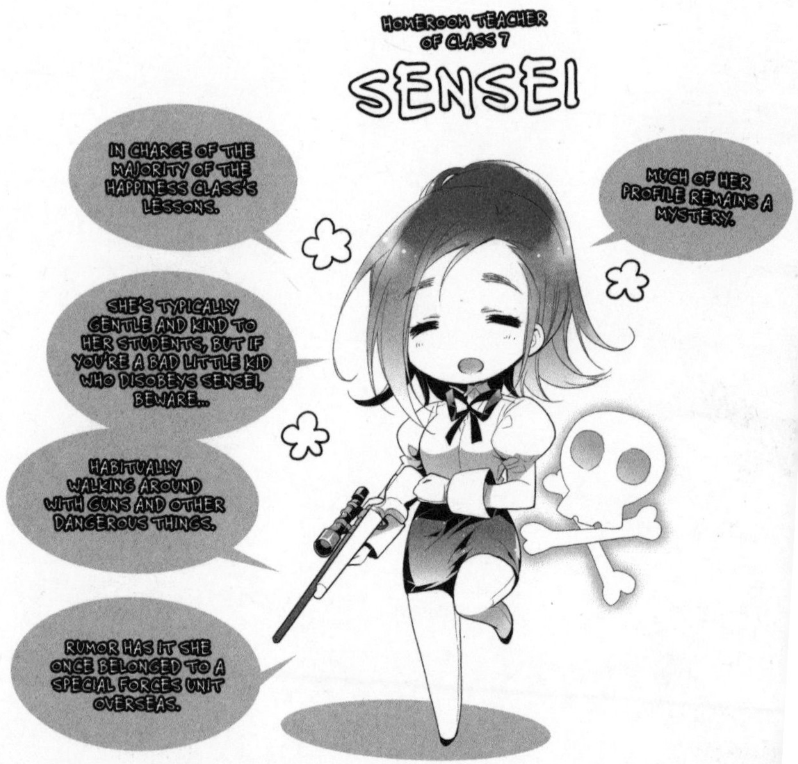
HOMEROOM TEACHER OF CLASS 7
SENSEI
MUCH OF HER PROFILE REMAINS A MYSTERY.
IN CHARGE OF THE MAJORITY OF THE HAPPINESS CLASS'S LESSONS.
SHE'S TYPICALLY GENTLE AND KIND TO HER STUDENTS, BUT IF YOU'RE A BAD LITTLE KID WHO DISOBEYS SENSEI, BEWARE...
HABITUALLY WALKING AROUND WITH GUNS AND OTHER DANGEROUS THINGS.
RUMOR HAS IT SHE ONCE BELONGED TO A SPECIAL FORCES UNIT OVERSEAS.

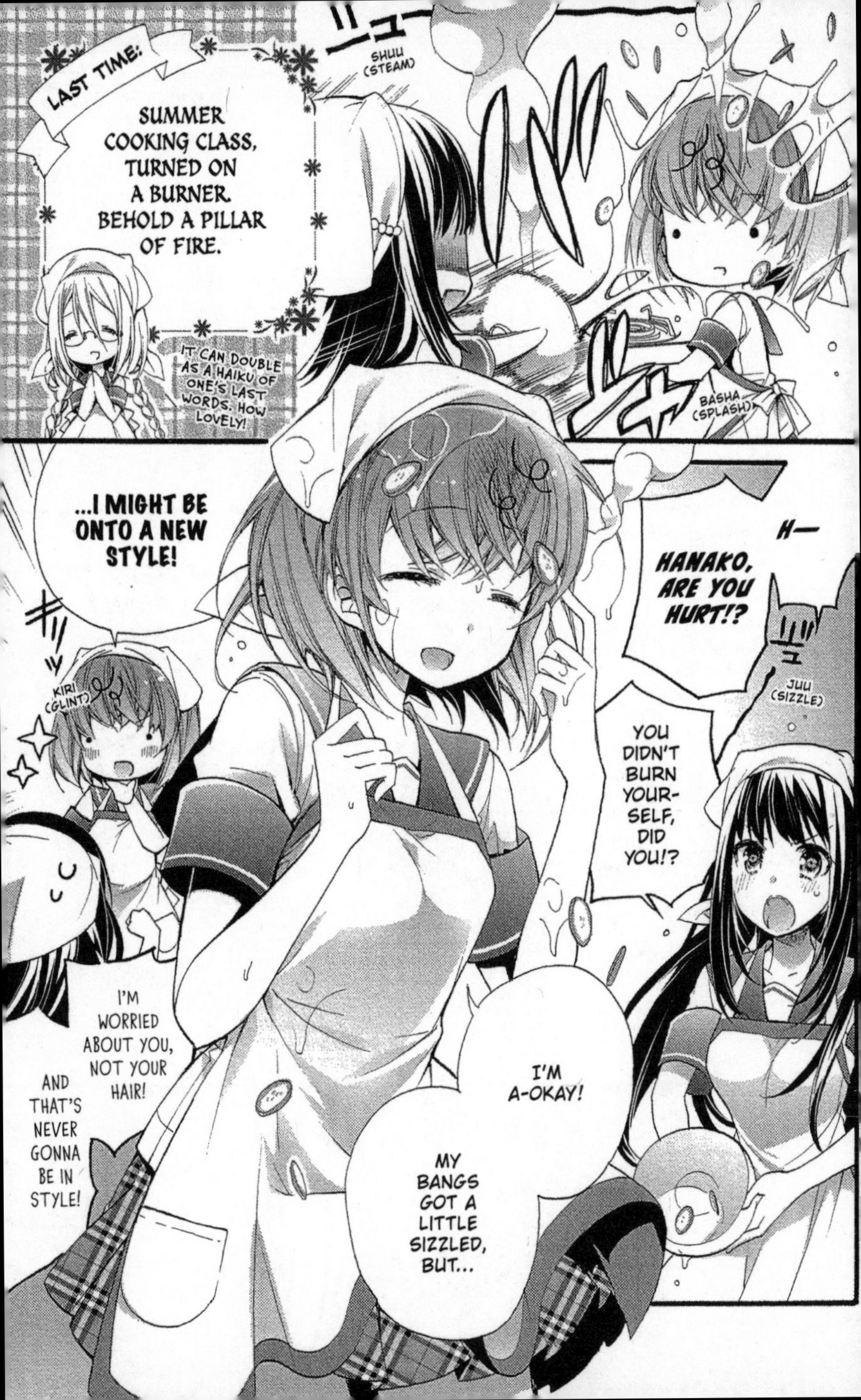
SHUU (STEAM)
BASHA (SPLASH)
LAST TIME:
SUMMER COOKING CLASS, TURNED ON A BURNER. BEHOLD A PILLAR OF FIRE.
IT CAN DOUBLE AS A HAIKU OF ONE'S LAST WORDS. HOW LOVELY!
H—
HANAKO, ARE YOU HURT!?
JUU (SIZZLE)
YOU DIDN'T BURN YOURSELF, DID YOU!?
I'M A-OKAY!
MY BANGS GOT A LITTLE SIZZLED, BUT...
...I MIGHT BE ONTO A NEW STYLE!
KIRI (GLINT)
I'M WORRIED ABOUT YOU, NOT YOUR HAIR!
AND THAT'S NEVER GONNA BE IN STYLE!

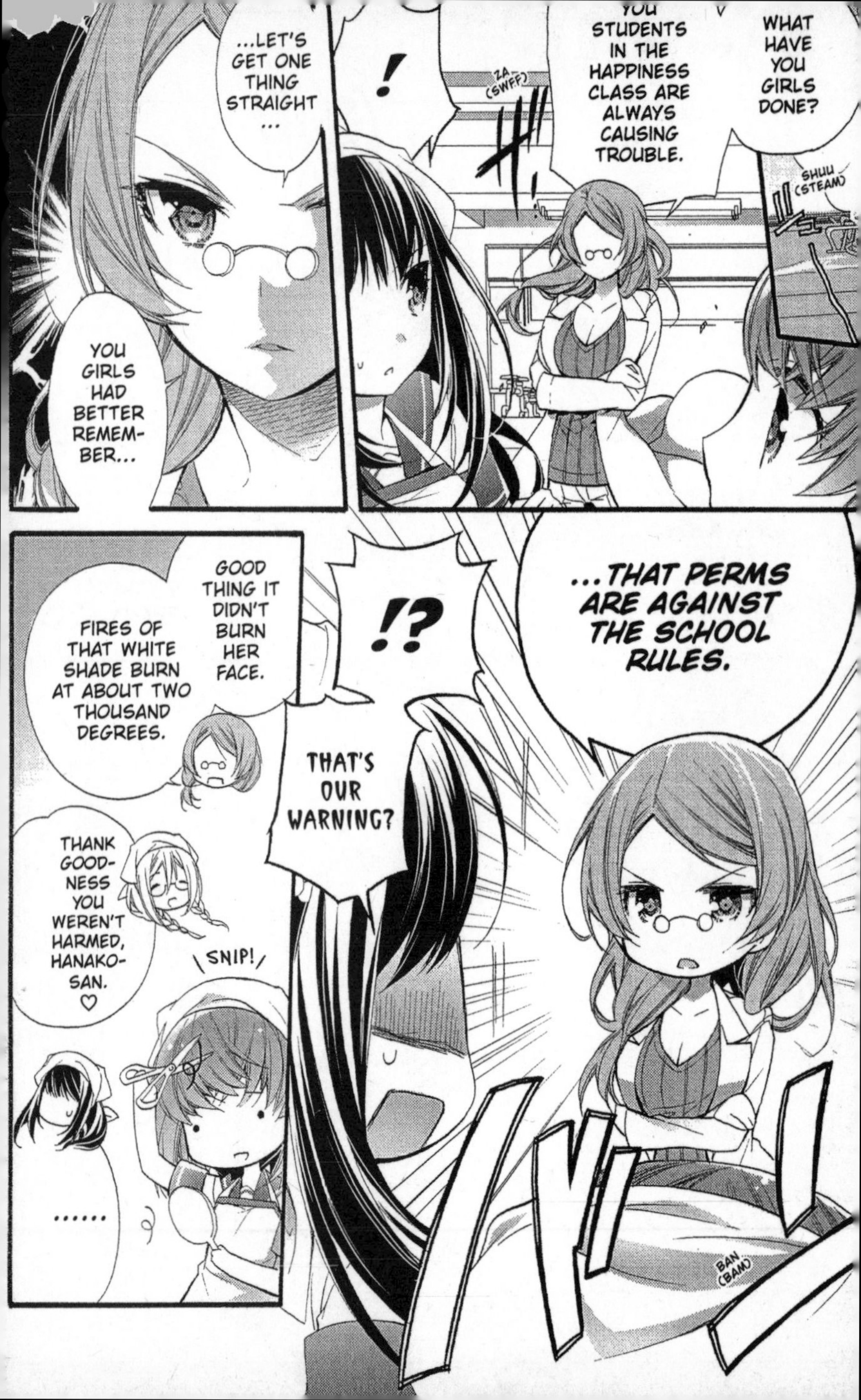
WHAT HAVE YOU GIRLS DONE?
SHUU (STEAM)
YOU STUDENTS IN THE HAPPINESS CLASS ARE ALWAYS CAUSING TROUBLE.
ZA (SWFF)
!
...LET'S GET ONE THING STRAIGHT...
YOU GIRLS HAD BETTER REMEMBER...
...THAT PERMS ARE AGAINST THE SCHOOL RULES.
BAN (BAM)
!?
THAT'S OUR WARNING?
GOOD THING IT DIDN'T BURN HER FACE.
FIRES OF THAT WHITE SHADE BURN AT ABOUT TWO THOUSAND DEGREES.
THANK GOODNESS YOU WEREN'T HARMED, HANAKO-SAN. ♡
SNIP!
......

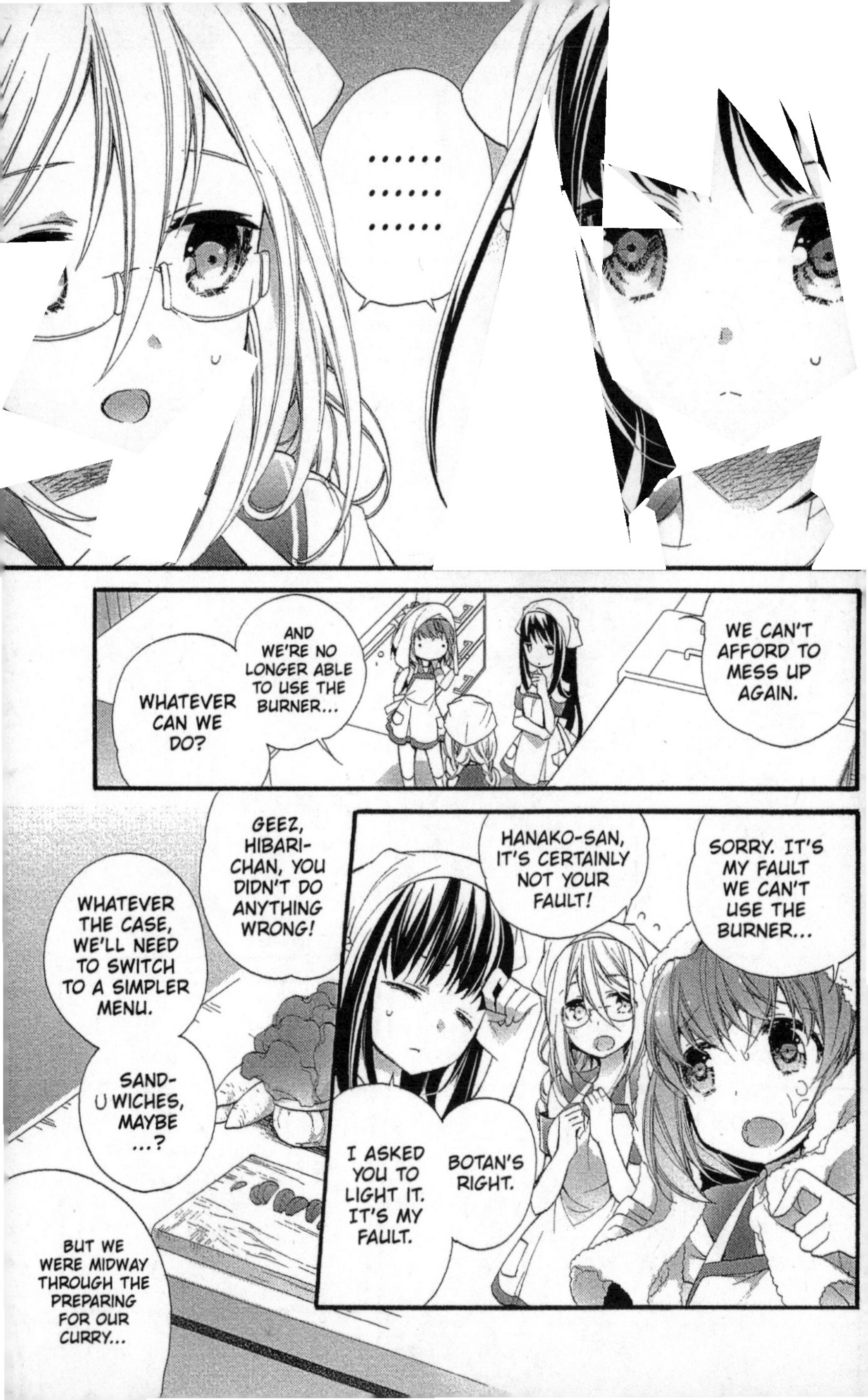
....
WE CAN'T AFFORD TO MESS UP AGAIN.
AND WE'RE NO LONGER ABLE TO USE THE BURNER...
WHATEVER CAN WE DO?
SORRY. IT'S MY FAULT WE CAN'T USE THE BURNER...
HANAKO-SAN, IT'S CERTAINLY NOT YOUR FAULT!
BOTAN'S RIGHT.
I ASKED YOU TO LIGHT IT. IT'S MY FAULT.
GEEZ, HIBARI-CHAN, YOU DIDN'T DO ANYTHING WRONG!
WHATEVER THE CASE, WE'LL NEED TO SWITCH TO A SIMPLER MENU.
SAND-WICHES, MAYBE ...?
BUT WE WERE MIDWAY THROUGH THE PREPARING FOR OUR CURRY...

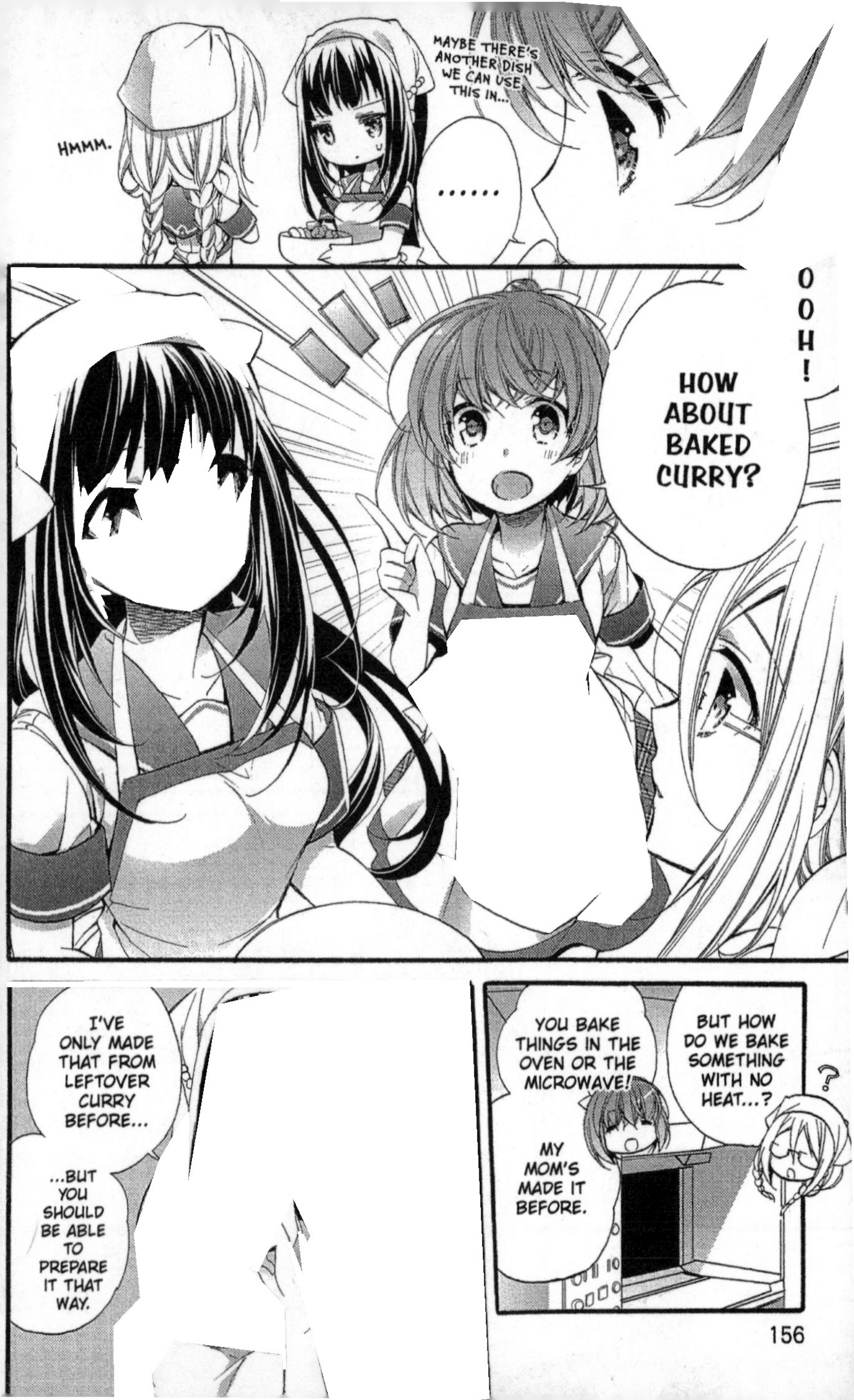
MAYBE THERE'S ANOTHER DISH WE CAN USE THIS IN...
......
HMMM.
OOOH!
HOW ABOUT BAKED CURRY?
BUT HOW DO WE BAKE SOMETHING WITH NO HEAT...?
?
YOU BAKE THINGS IN THE OVEN OR THE MICROWAVE!
MY MOM'S MADE IT BEFORE.
I'VE ONLY MADE THAT FROM LEFTOVER CURRY BEFORE...
...BUT YOU SHOULD BE ABLE TO PREPARE IT THAT WAY.

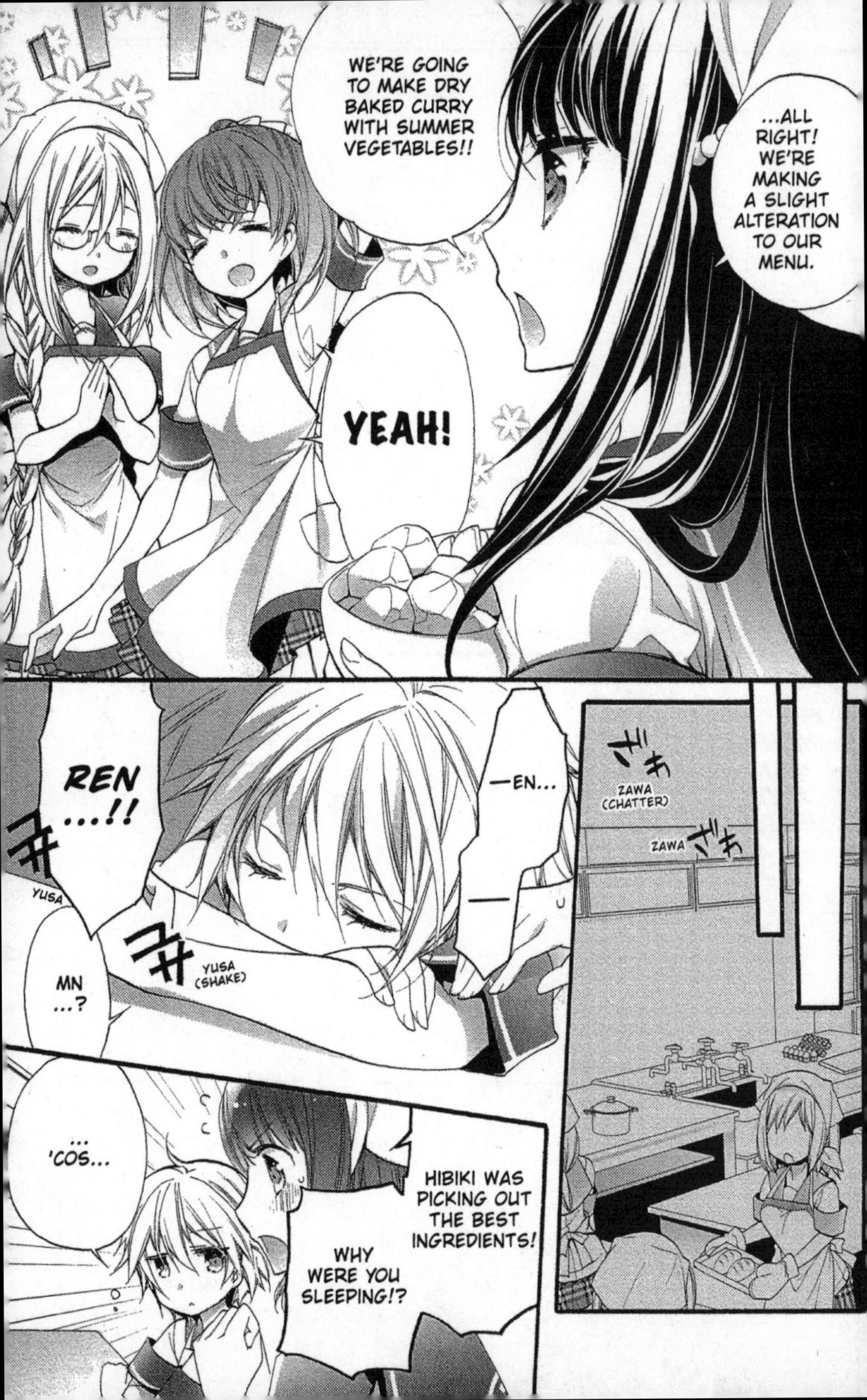
...ALL RIGHT! WE'RE MAKING A SLIGHT ALTERATION TO OUR MENU.
WE'RE GOING TO MAKE DRY BAKED CURRY WITH SUMMER VEGETABLES!!
YEAH!
ざわ
ZAWA (CHATTER)
ざわ
ZAWA
—EN...
—
REN ...!!
YUSA
YUSA (SHAKE)
MN ...?
HIBIKI WAS PICKING OUT THE BEST INGREDIENTS!
WHY WERE YOU SLEEPING!?
... 'COS...

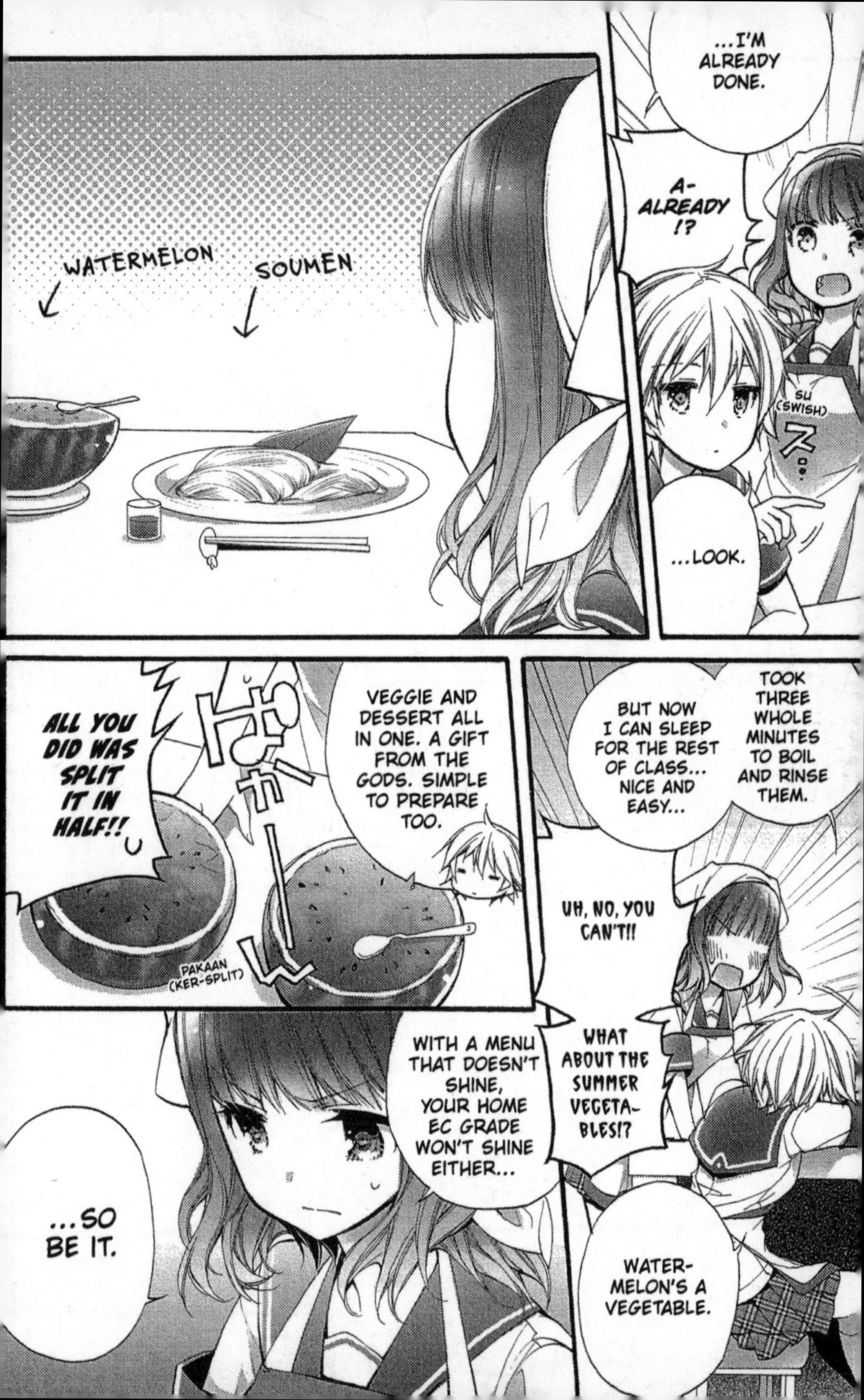
...I'M ALREADY DONE.
A- ALREADY !?
SU (SWISH)
...LOOK.
WATERMELON
SOUMEN
TOOK THREE WHOLE MINUTES TO BOIL AND RINSE THEM.
BUT NOW I CAN SLEEP FOR THE REST OF CLASS... NICE AND EASY...
UH, NO, YOU CAN'T!!
WHAT ABOUT THE SUMMER VEGETA-BLES!?
WATER-MELON'S A VEGETABLE.
VEGGIE AND DESSERT ALL IN ONE. A GIFT FROM THE GODS. SIMPLE TO PREPARE TOO.
ALL YOU DID WAS SPLIT IT IN HALF!!
PAKAAN (KER-SPLIT)
WITH A MENU THAT DOESN'T SHINE, YOUR HOME EC GRADE WON'T SHINE EITHER...
...SO BE IT.

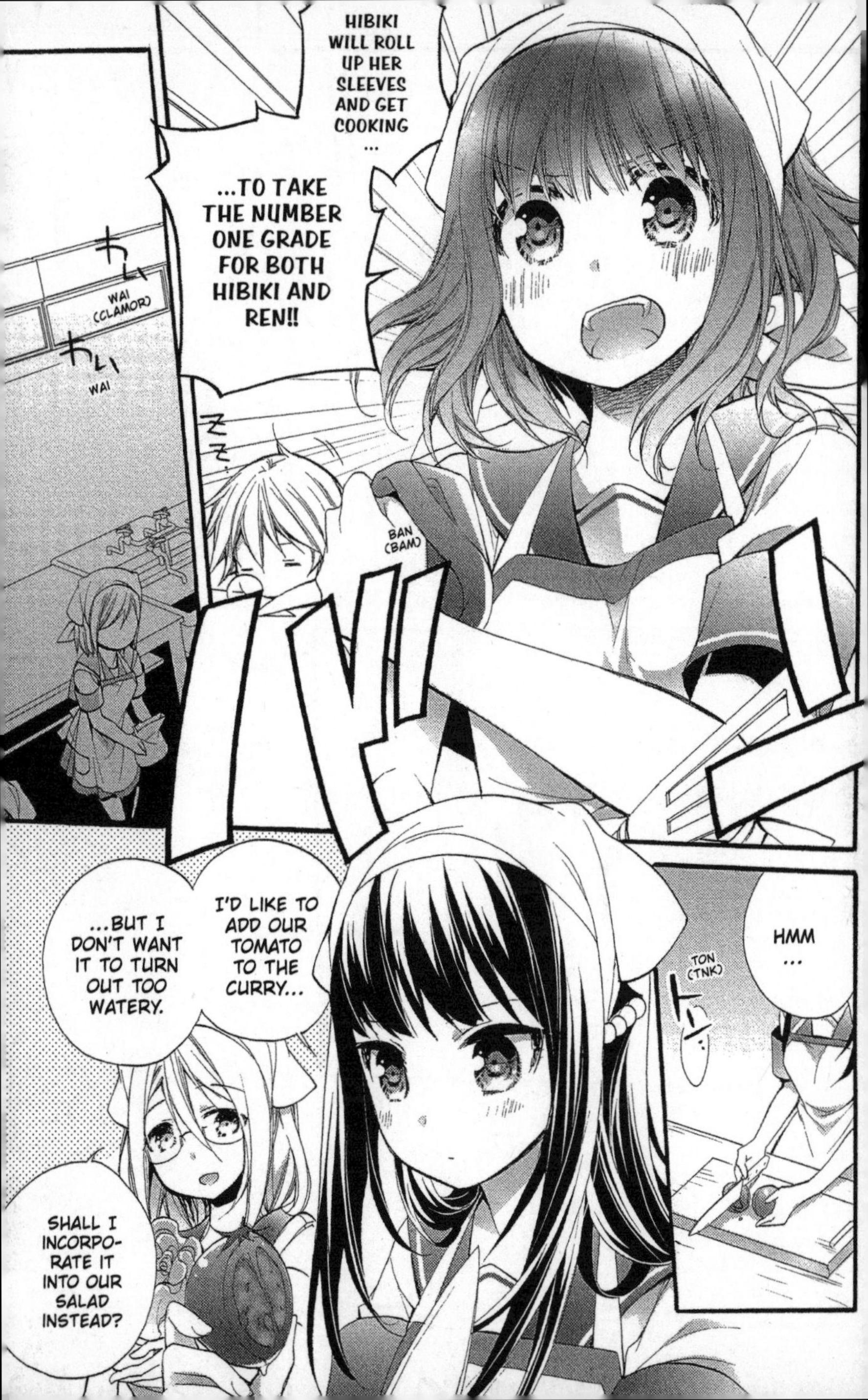
HIBIKI WILL ROLL UP HER SLEEVES AND GET COOKING ...
...TO TAKE THE NUMBER ONE GRADE FOR BOTH HIBIKI AND REN!!
わい
WAI (CLAMOR)
わい
WAI
BAN (BAM)
HMM ...
TON (TNK)
I'D LIKE TO ADD OUR TOMATO TO THE CURRY...
...BUT I DON'T WANT IT TO TURN OUT TOO WATERY.
SHALL I INCORPORATE IT INTO OUR SALAD INSTEAD?

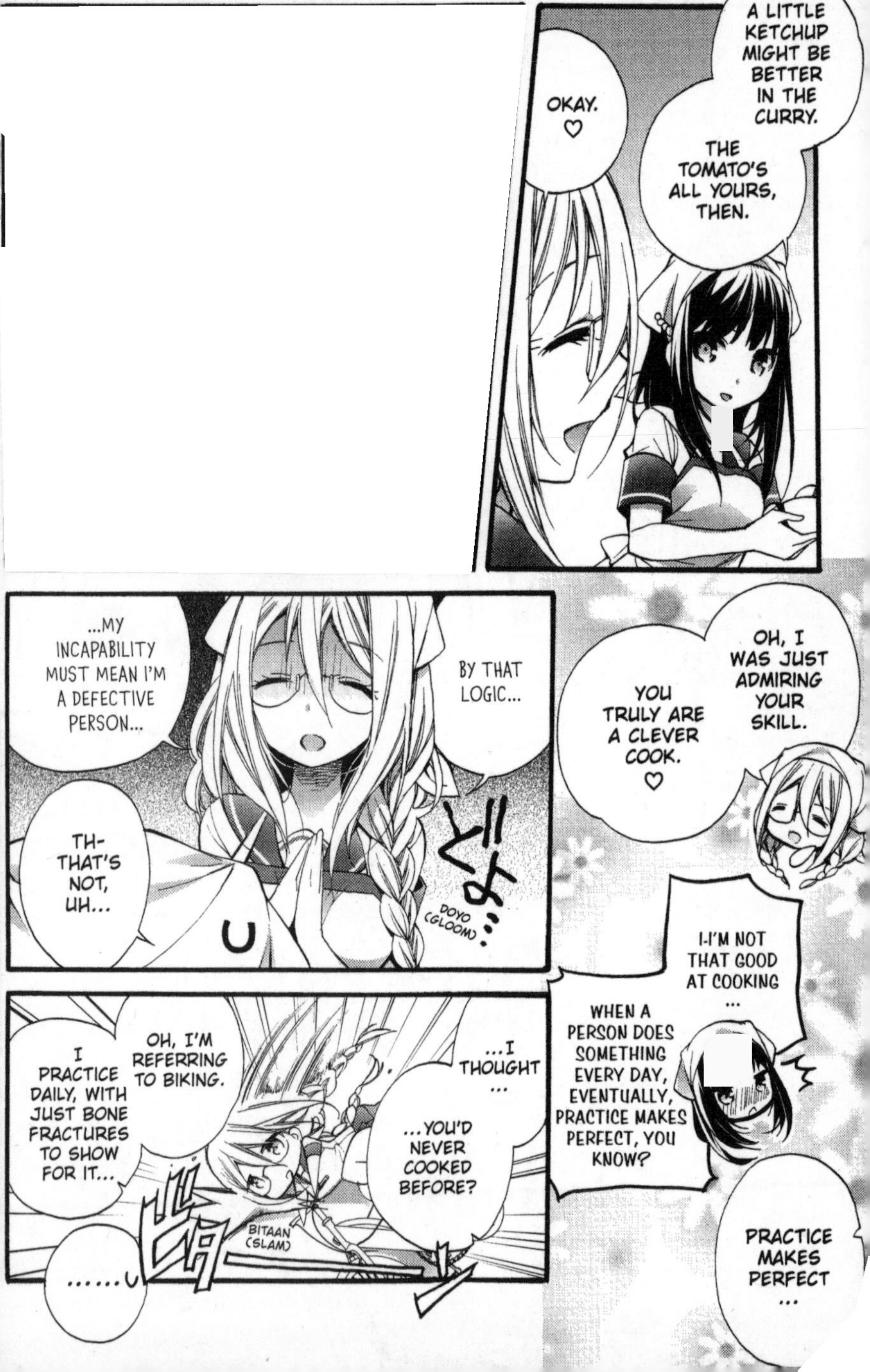
A LITTLE KETCHUP MIGHT BE BETTER IN THE CURRY.
THE TOMATO'S ALL YOURS, THEN.
OKAY. ♡
OH, I WAS JUST ADMIRING YOUR SKILL.
YOU TRULY ARE A CLEVER COOK. ♡
I-I'M NOT THAT GOOD AT COOKING ...
WHEN A PERSON DOES SOMETHING EVERY DAY, EVENTUALLY, PRACTICE MAKES PERFECT, YOU KNOW?
PRACTICE MAKES PERFECT ...
BY THAT LOGIC...
...MY INCAPABILITY MUST MEAN I'M A DEFECTIVE PERSON...
DOYO (GLOOM)
TH-THAT'S NOT, UH...
...I THOUGHT ...
...YOU'D NEVER COOKED BEFORE?
OH, I'M REFERRING TO BIKING.
I PRACTICE DAILY, WITH JUST BONE FRACTURES TO SHOW FOR IT...
BITAAN (SLAM)
......

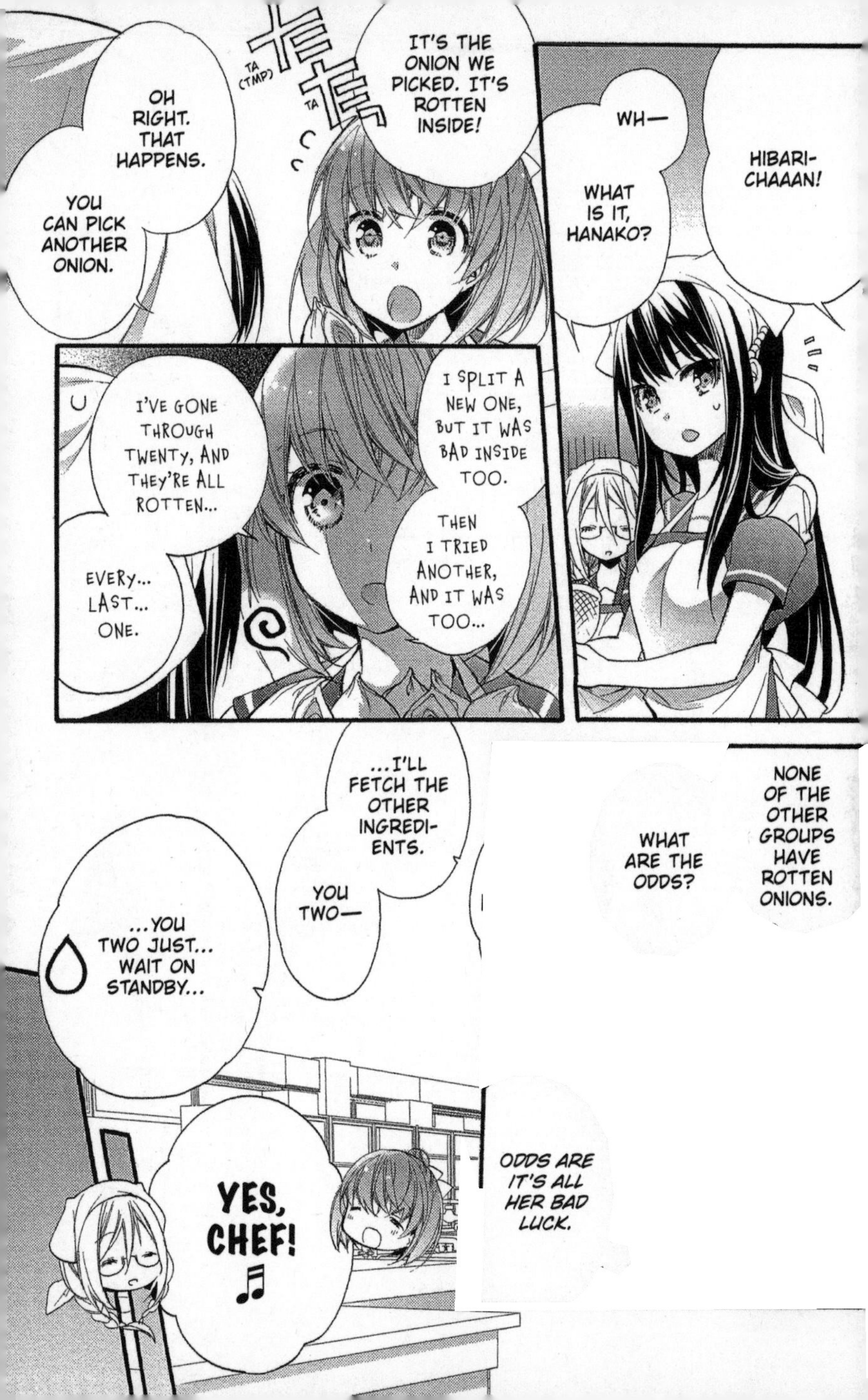
HIBARI-CHAAAN!
WH—
WHAT IS IT, HANAKO?
TA (TMP) TA
IT'S THE ONION WE PICKED. IT'S ROTTEN INSIDE!
OH RIGHT. THAT HAPPENS.
YOU CAN PICK ANOTHER ONION.
I SPLIT A NEW ONE, BUT IT WAS BAD INSIDE TOO.
THEN I TRIED ANOTHER, AND IT WAS TOO...
I'VE GONE THROUGH TWENTY, AND THEY'RE ALL ROTTEN...
EVERY... LAST... ONE.
NONE OF THE OTHER GROUPS HAVE ROTTEN ONIONS.
WHAT ARE THE ODDS?
ODDS ARE IT'S ALL HER BAD LUCK.
...I'LL FETCH THE OTHER INGREDIENTS.
YOU TWO—
...YOU TWO JUST... WAIT ON STANDBY...
YES, CHEF!

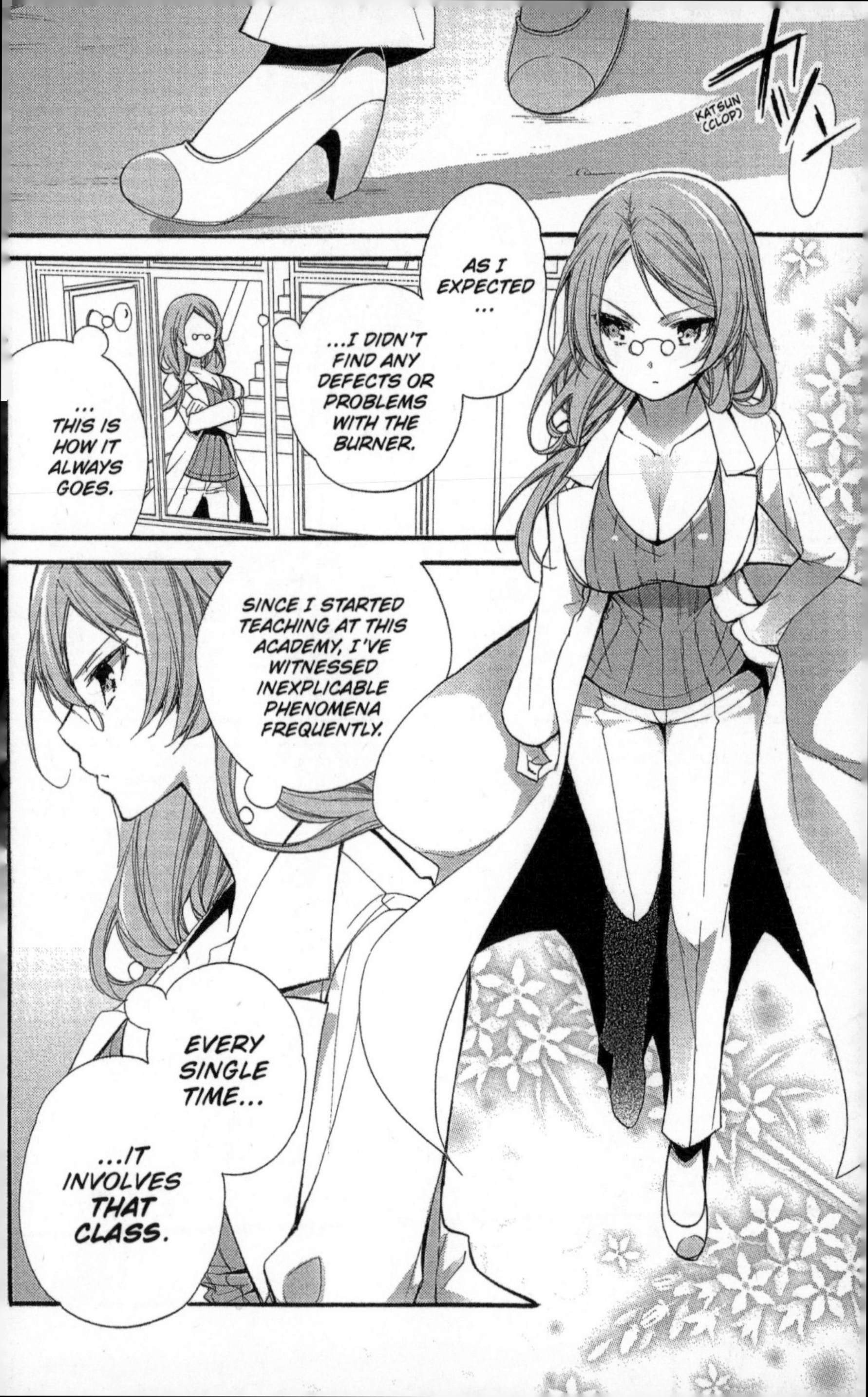
KATSUN (CLOP)
AS I EXPECTED...
...I DIDN'T FIND ANY DEFECTS OR PROBLEMS WITH THE BURNER.
... THIS IS HOW IT ALWAYS GOES.
SINCE I STARTED TEACHING AT THIS ACADEMY, I'VE WITNESSED INEXPLICABLE PHENOMENA FREQUENTLY.
EVERY SINGLE TIME...
...IT INVOLVES THAT CLASS.

WHY?
GIRI (CLENCH)
THIS IS A PRESTIGIOUS SCHOOL WITH HISTORY AND REPUTATION. THEY'RE FLOODED WITH APPLICANTS, BOTH LOCAL AND FROM OTHER PREFECTURES.
WHY GO OUT OF THE WAY TO FIND STUDENTS WHO, ON TOP OF HAVING NOTHING TO OFFER, BRING THEIR NEGATIVE KARMA TO SCHOOL WITH THEM?
KATSU
KATSU
KATSU
IS THERE SOMETHING MORE TO IT...?

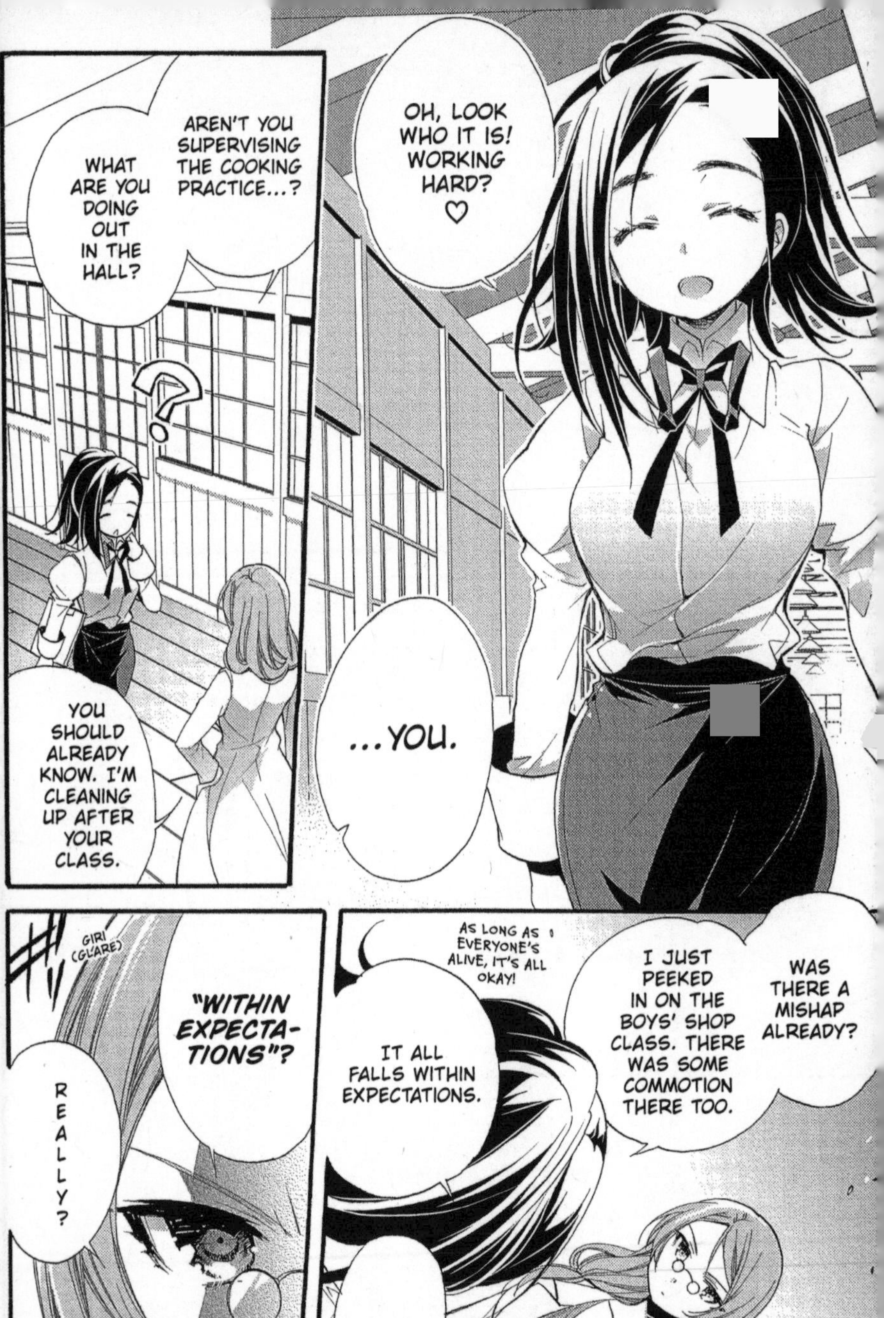
OH, LOOK WHO IT IS! WORKING HARD? ♡
...YOU.
AREN'T YOU SUPERVISING THE COOKING PRACTICE...?
WHAT ARE YOU DOING OUT IN THE HALL?
YOU SHOULD ALREADY KNOW. I'M CLEANING UP AFTER YOUR CLASS.
WAS THERE A MISHAP ALREADY?
I JUST PEEKED IN ON THE BOYS' SHOP CLASS. THERE WAS SOME COMMOTION THERE TOO.
AS LONG AS EVERYONE'S ALIVE, IT'S ALL OKAY!
IT ALL FALLS WITHIN EXPECTATIONS.
...
GIRI (GLARE)
"WITHIN EXPECTA-TIONS"?
REALLY?

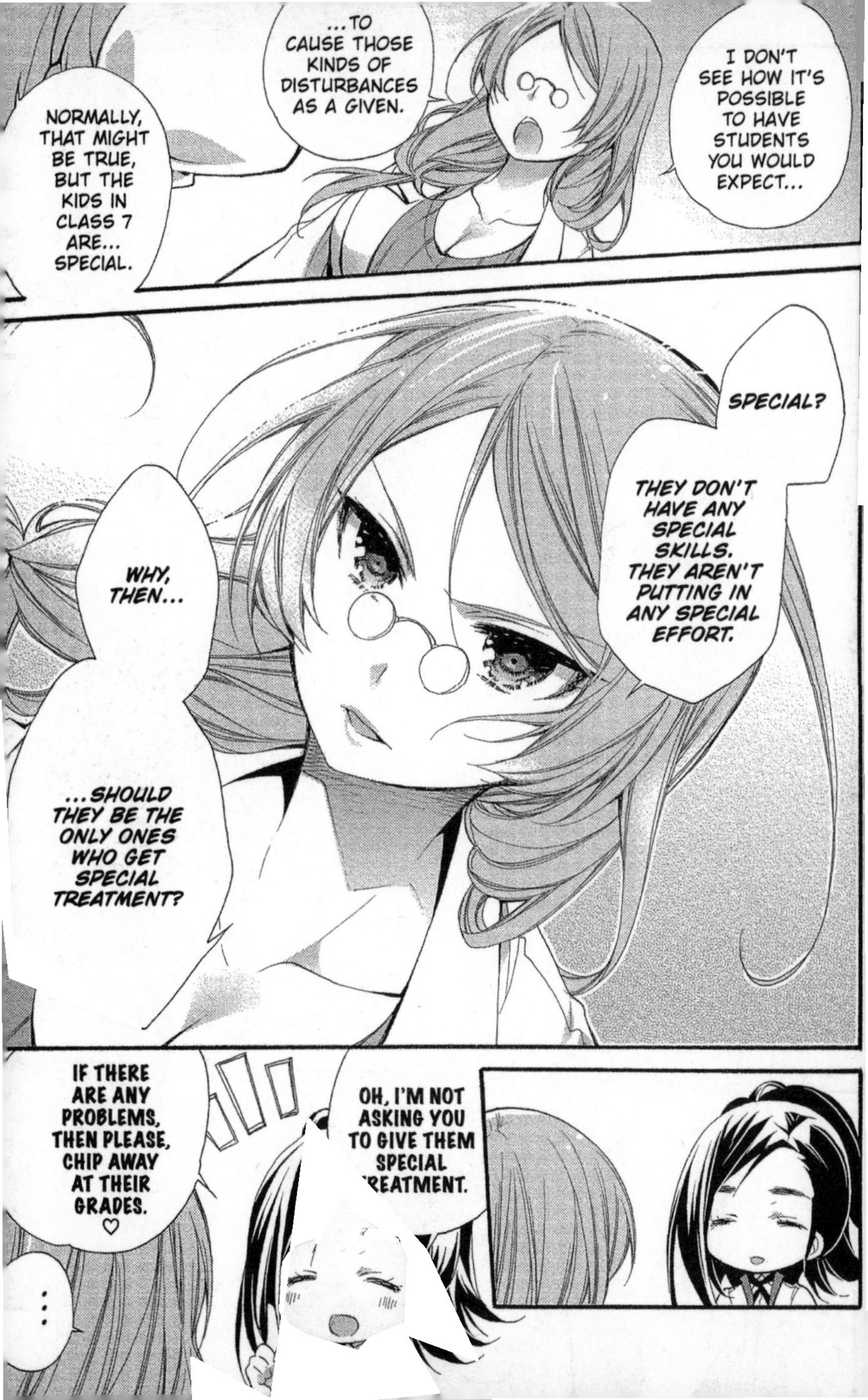
I DON'T SEE HOW IT'S POSSIBLE TO HAVE STUDENTS YOU WOULD EXPECT...
...TO CAUSE THOSE KINDS OF DISTURBANCES AS A GIVEN.
NORMALLY, THAT MIGHT BE TRUE, BUT THE KIDS IN CLASS 7 ARE... SPECIAL.
SPECIAL?
THEY DON'T HAVE ANY SPECIAL SKILLS. THEY AREN'T PUTTING IN ANY SPECIAL EFFORT.
WHY, THEN...
...SHOULD THEY BE THE ONLY ONES WHO GET SPECIAL TREATMENT?
OH, I'M NOT ASKING YOU TO GIVE THEM SPECIAL TREATMENT.
IF THERE ARE ANY PROBLEMS, THEN PLEASE, CHIP AWAY AT THEIR GRADES. ♡
...

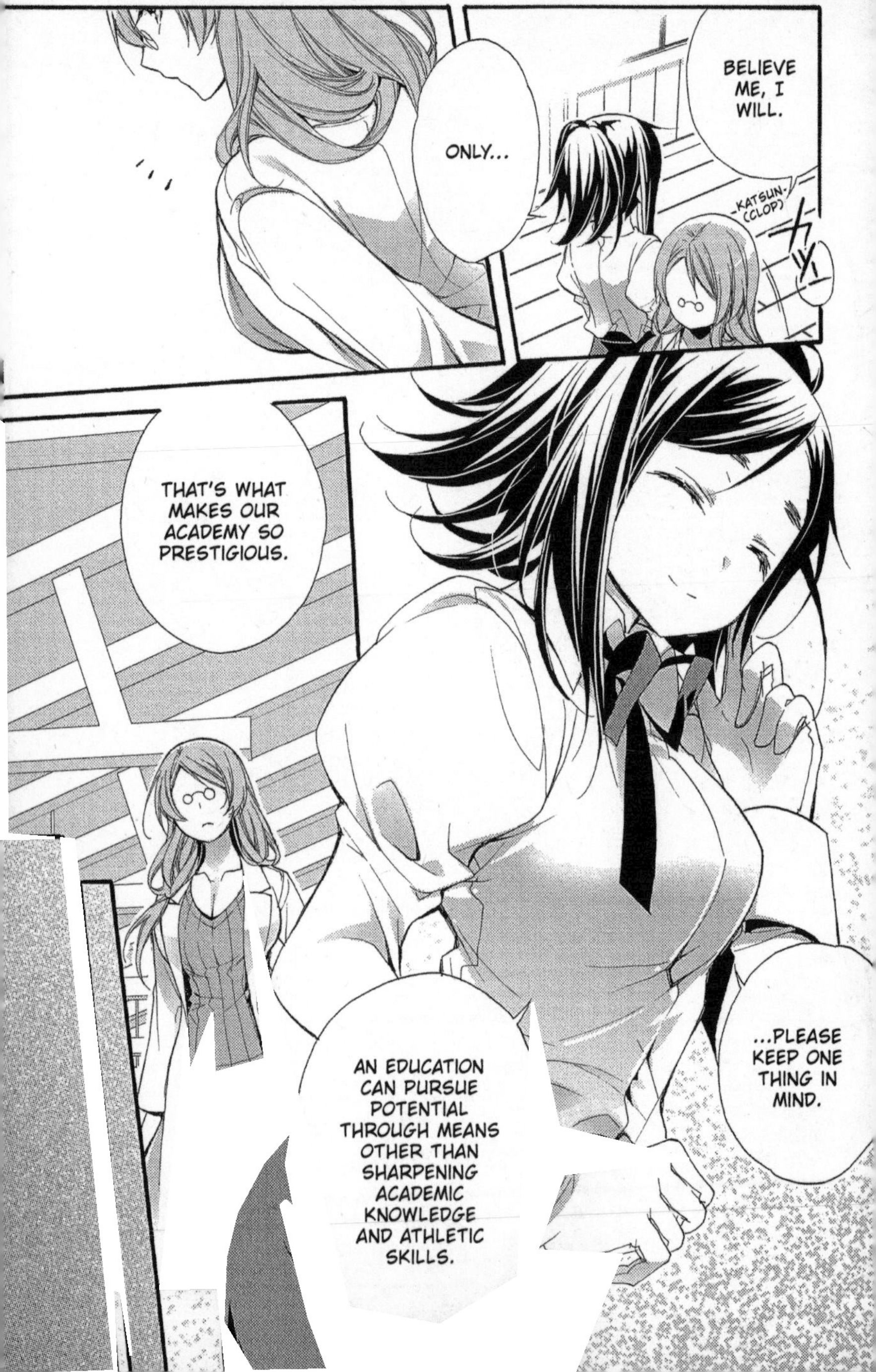
BELIEVE ME, I WILL.
KATSUN- (CLOP)
ONLY...
...PLEASE KEEP ONE THING IN MIND.
AN EDUCATION CAN PURSUE POTENTIAL THROUGH MEANS OTHER THAN SHARPENING ACADEMIC KNOWLEDGE AND ATHLETIC SKILLS.
THAT'S WHAT MAKES OUR ACADEMY SO PRESTIGIOUS.

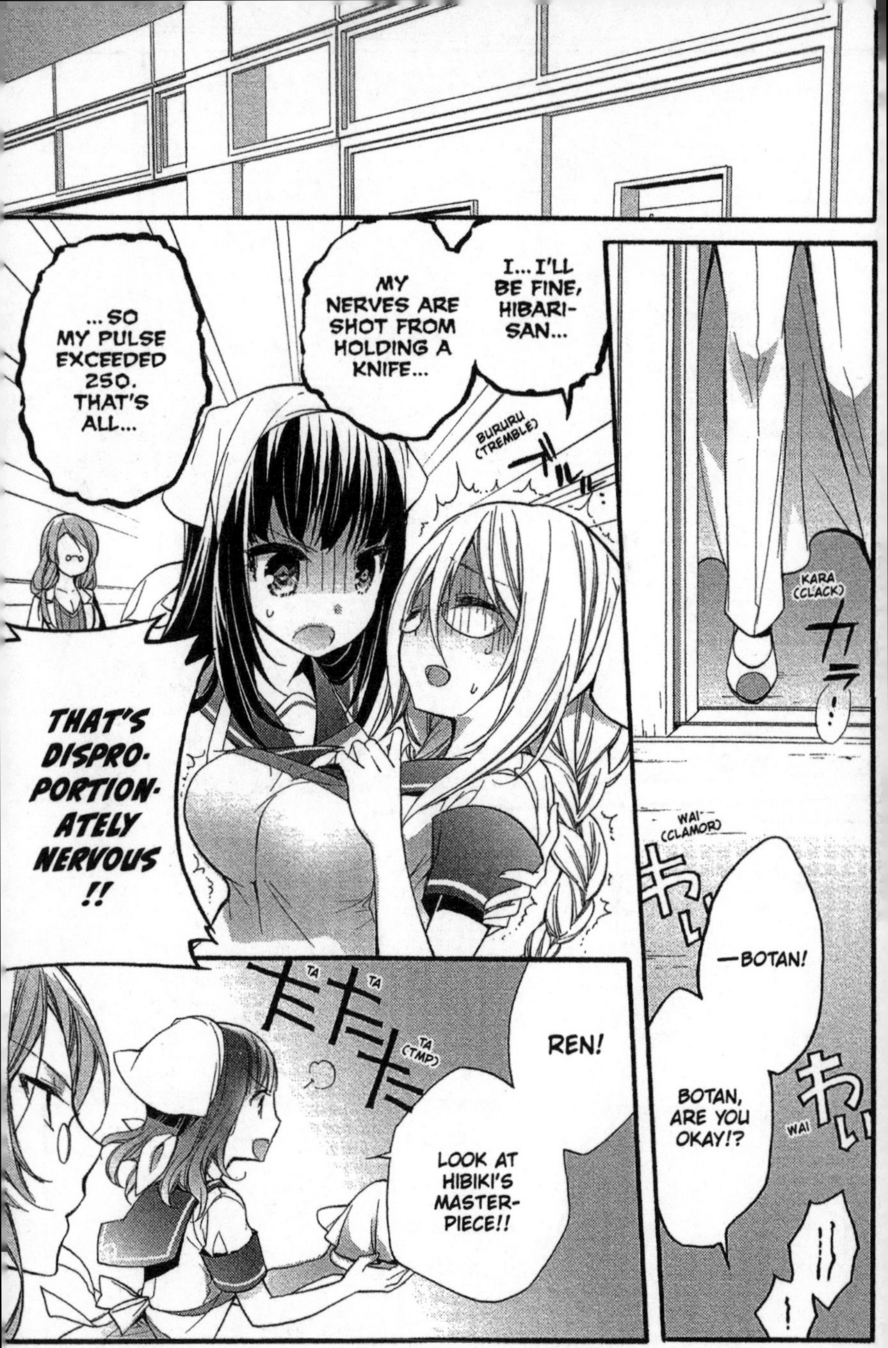
KARA (CLACK)
I... I'LL BE FINE, HIBARI-SAN...
MY NERVES ARE SHOT FROM HOLDING A KNIFE...
... SO MY PULSE EXCEEDED 250. THAT'S ALL...
BURURU (TREMBLE)
THAT'S DISPRO-PORTION-ATELY NERVOUS!!
WAI (CLAMOR)
—BOTAN!
BOTAN, ARE YOU OKAY!?
WAI
TA TA TA (TMP)
REN!
LOOK AT HIBIKI'S MASTER-PIECE!!

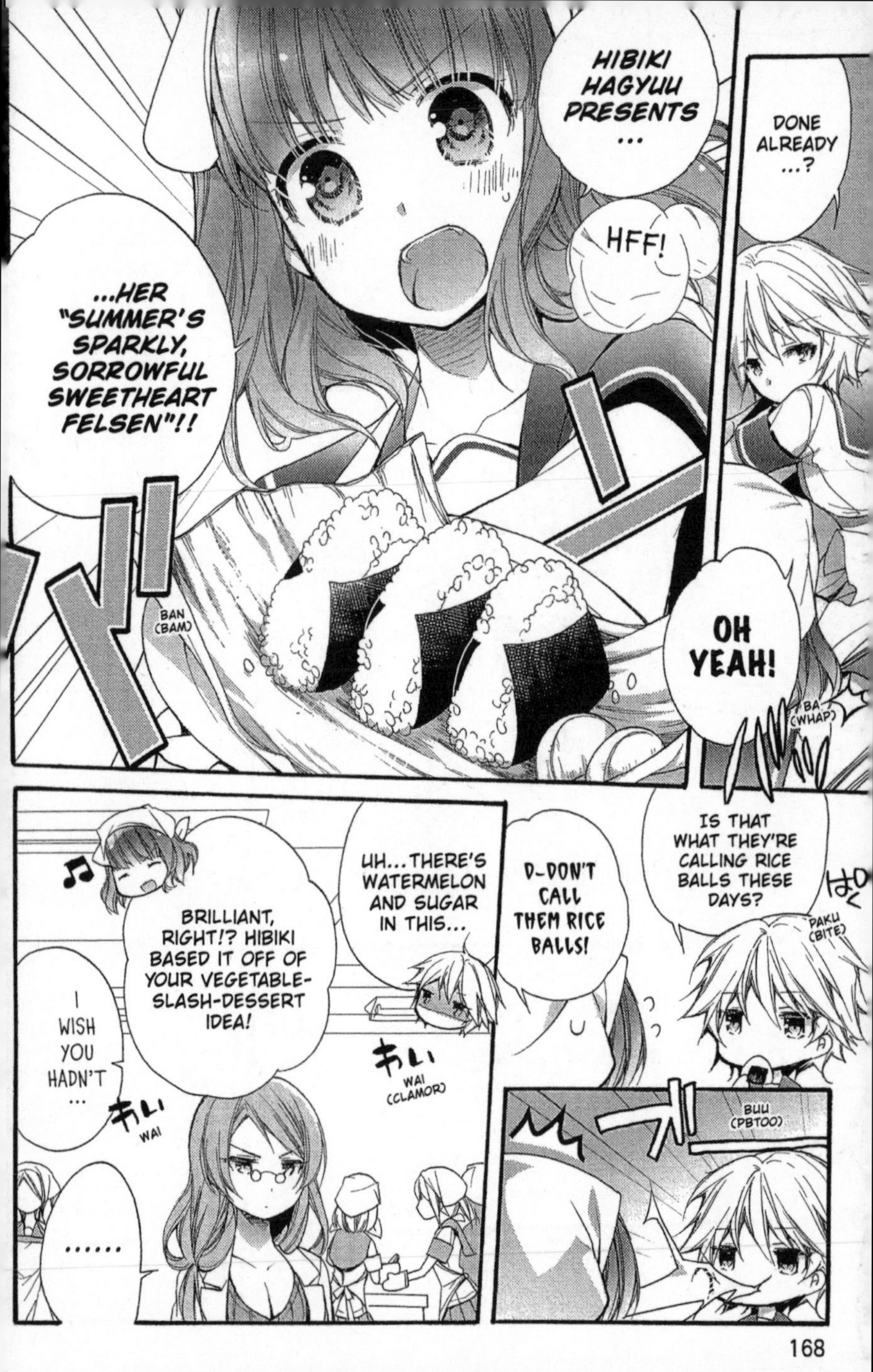
DONE ALREADY ...?
OH YEAH!
BA (WHAP)
HIBIKI HAGYUU PRESENTS ...
HFF!
...HER "SUMMER'S SPARKLY, SORROWFUL SWEETHEART FELSEN"!!
BAN (BAM)
IS THAT WHAT THEY'RE CALLING RICE BALLS THESE DAYS?
PAKU (BITE)
D-DON'T CALL THEM RICE BALLS!
BUU (PBTOO)
UH...THERE'S WATERMELON AND SUGAR IN THIS...
BRILLIANT, RIGHT!? HIBIKI BASED IT OFF OF YOUR VEGETABLE-SLASH-DESSERT IDEA!
WAI (CLAMOR)
I WISH YOU HADN'T ...
WAI
......

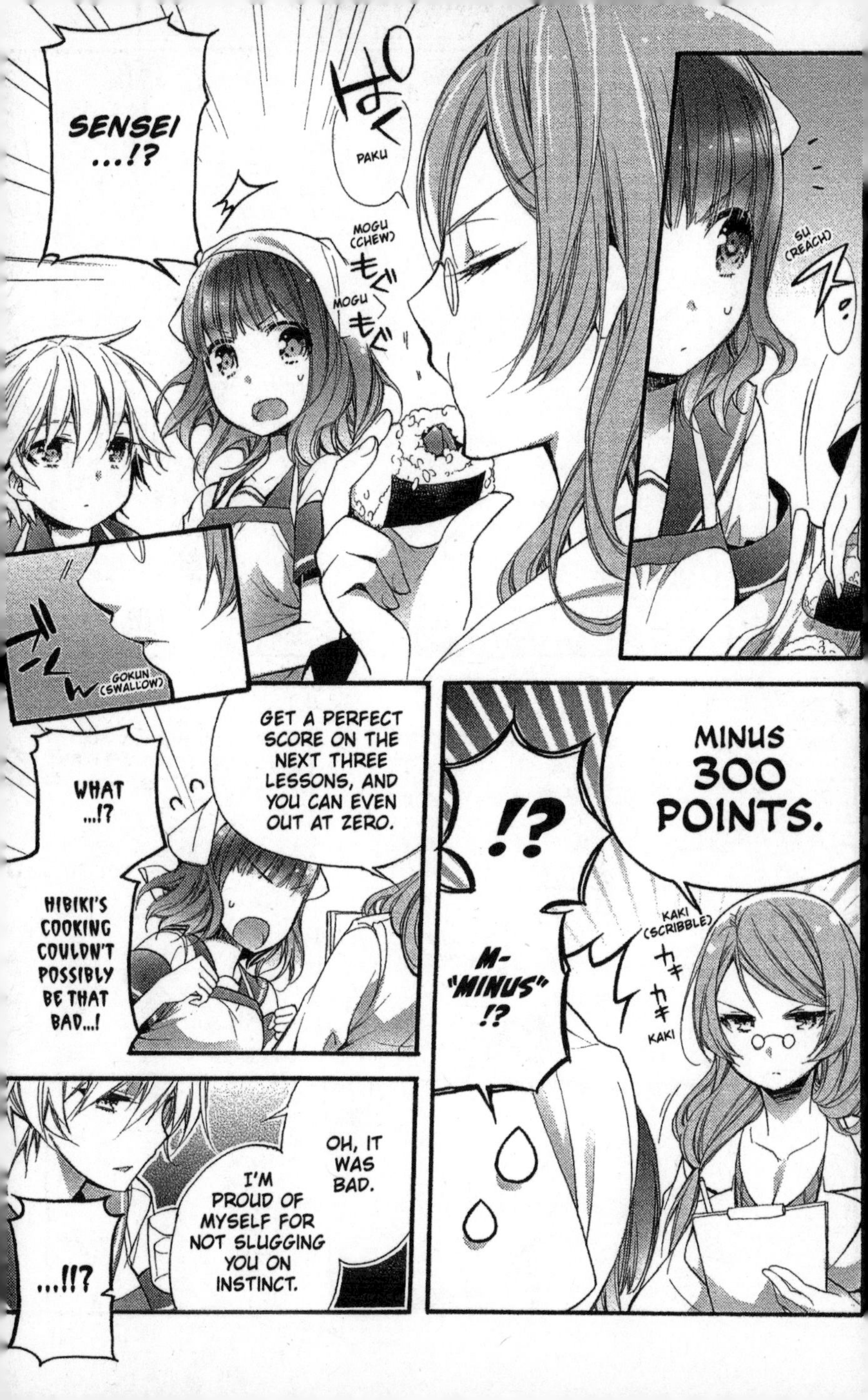
SU (REACH)
ス
ぱく
PAKU
MOGU (CHEW)
もぐ
MOGU
もぐ
SENSEI ...!?
GOKUN (SWALLOW)
MINUS 300 POINTS.
!?
KAKI (SCRIBBLE)
カキ
カキ
KAKI
M- "MINUS" !?
GET A PERFECT SCORE ON THE NEXT THREE LESSONS, AND YOU CAN EVEN OUT AT ZERO.
WHAT ...!?
HIBIKI'S COOKING COULDN'T POSSIBLY BE THAT BAD...!
OH, IT WAS BAD.
I'M PROUD OF MYSELF FOR NOT SLUGGING YOU ON INSTINCT.
...!!?

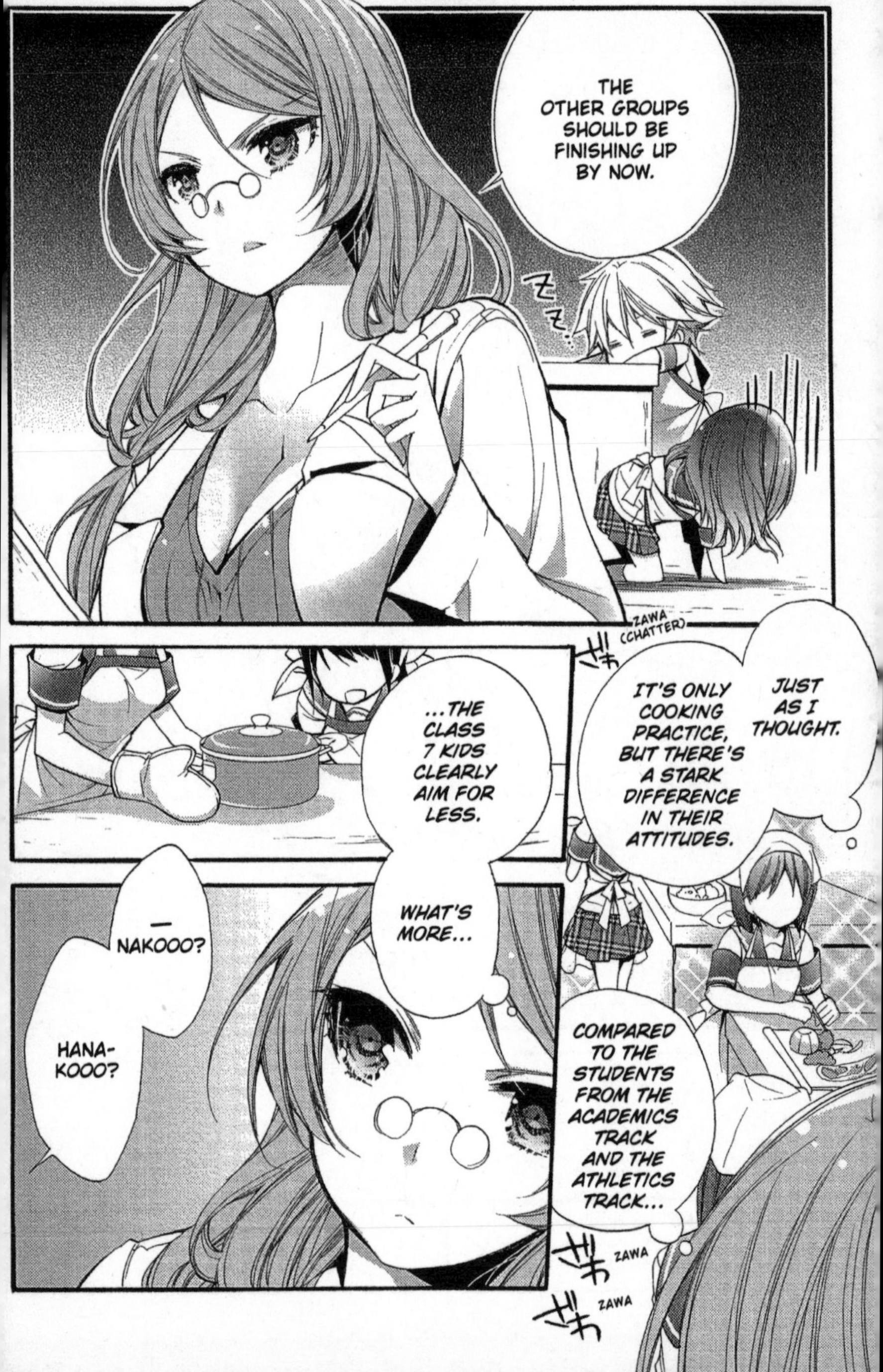
THE OTHER GROUPS SHOULD BE FINISHING UP BY NOW.
ZAWA (CHATTER)
JUST AS I THOUGHT.
IT'S ONLY COOKING PRACTICE, BUT THERE'S A STARK DIFFERENCE IN THEIR ATTITUDES.
...THE CLASS 7 KIDS CLEARLY AIM FOR LESS.
WHAT'S MORE...
COMPARED TO THE STUDENTS FROM THE ACADEMICS TRACK AND THE ATHLETICS TRACK...
ZAWA
ZAWA
—NAKOOO?
HANA-KOOO?

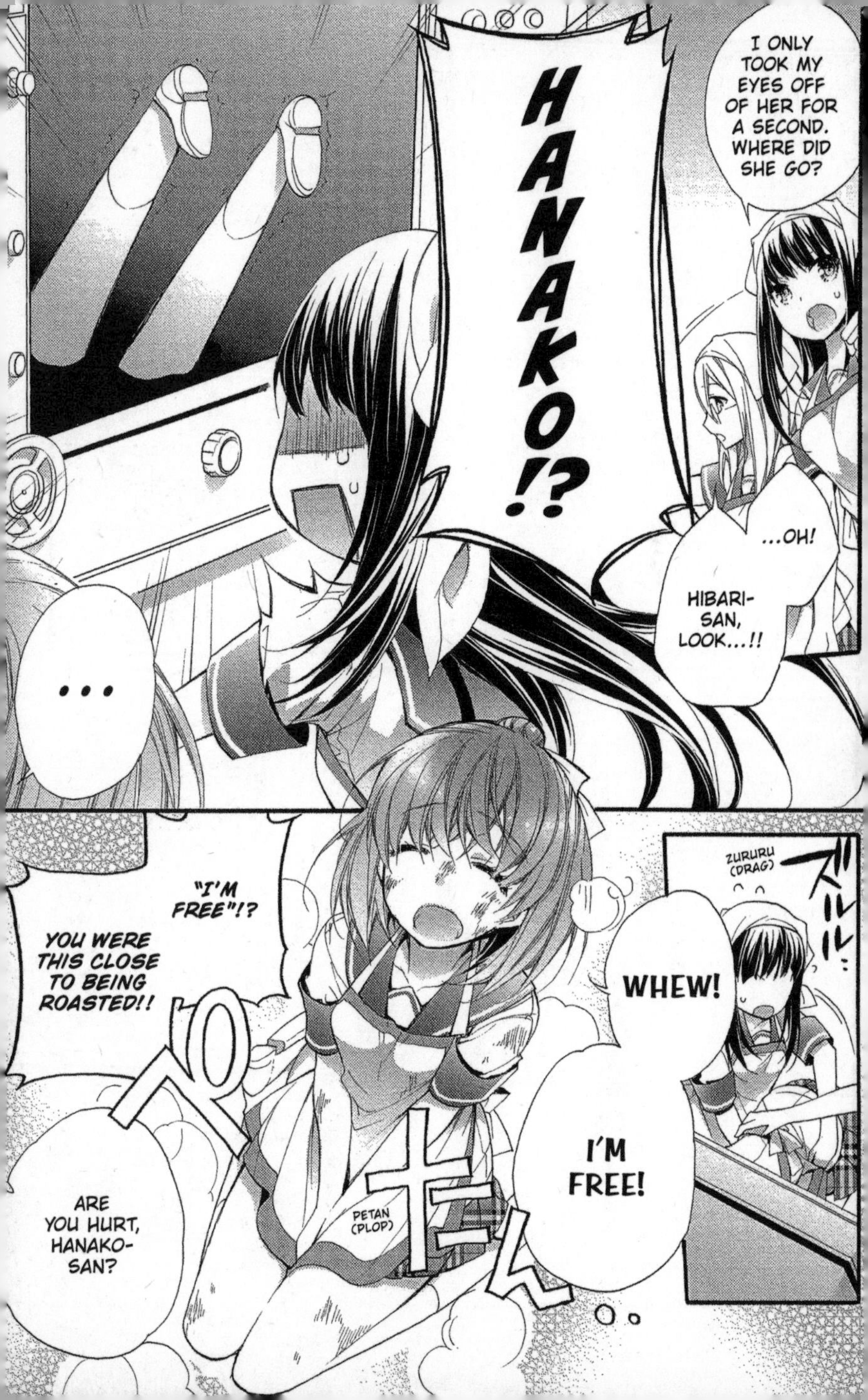
I ONLY TOOK MY EYES OFF OF HER FOR A SECOND. WHERE DID SHE GO?
HANAKO!?
...OH!
HIBARI-SAN, LOOK...!!
...
ZURURU (DRAG)
WHEW!
I'M FREE!
PETAN (PLOP)
"I'M FREE"!?
YOU WERE THIS CLOSE TO BEING ROASTED!!
ARE YOU HURT, HANAKO-SAN?

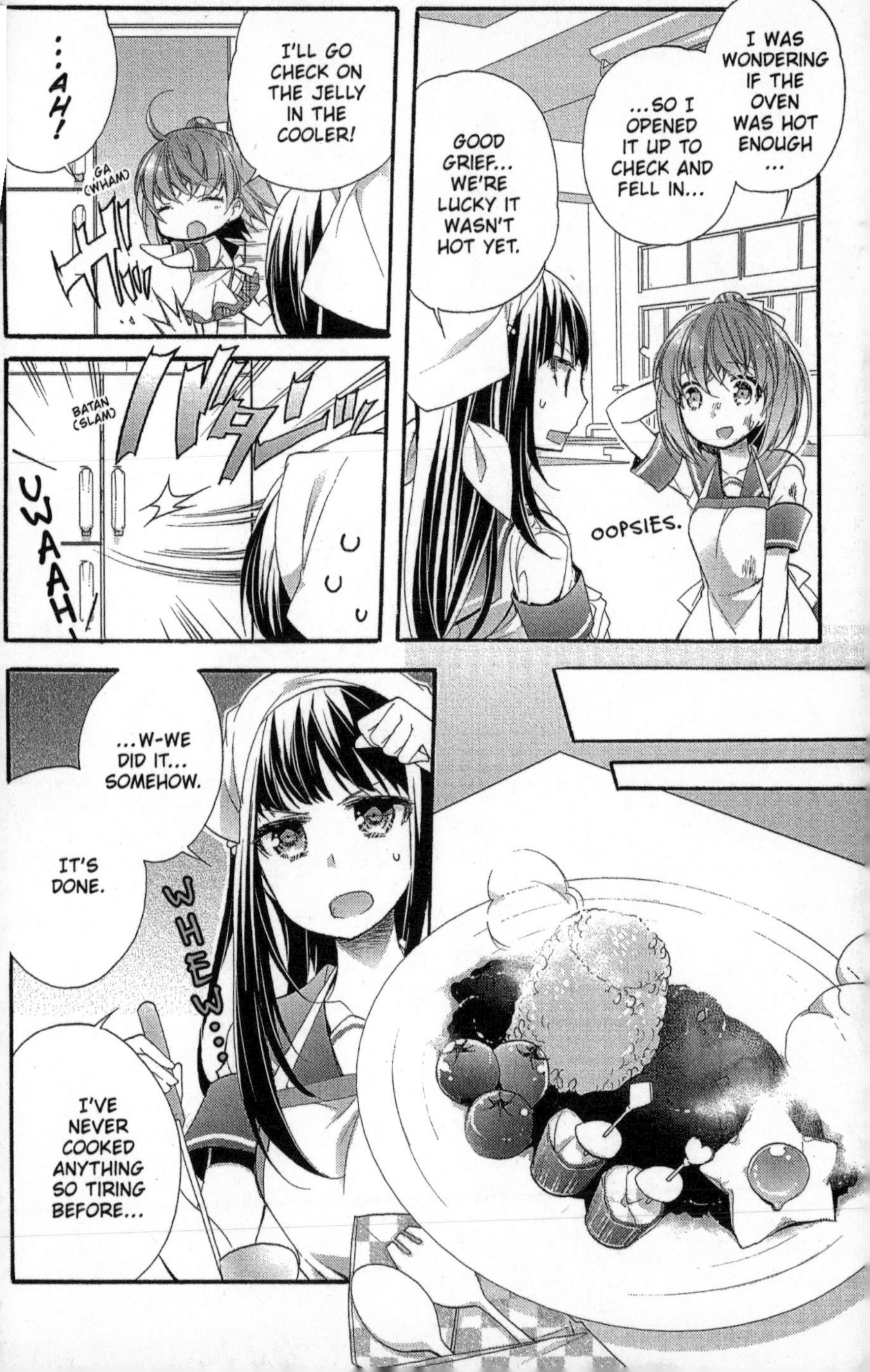
I WAS WONDERING IF THE OVEN WAS HOT ENOUGH...
...SO I OPENED IT UP TO CHECK AND FELL IN...
GOOD GRIEF... WE'RE LUCKY IT WASN'T HOT YET.
OOPSIES.
I'LL GO CHECK ON THE JELLY IN THE COOLER!
...AH!
GA (WHAM)
BATAN (SLAM)
UWAAH!
...W-WE DID IT... SOMEHOW.
IT'S DONE.
WHEW...
I'VE NEVER COOKED ANYTHING SO TIRING BEFORE...

HOMEROOM TEACHER OF CLASS 1

SENSEI

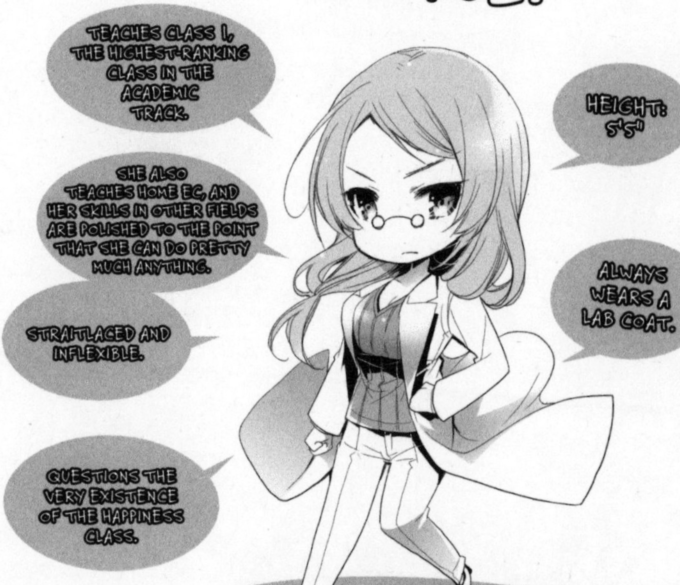

HEIGHT: 5'5"
TEACHES CLASS 1, THE HIGHEST-RANKING CLASS IN THE ACADEMIC TRACK.
SHE ALSO TEACHES HOME EC, AND HER SKILLS IN OTHER FIELDS ARE POLISHED TO THE POINT THAT SHE CAN DO PRETTY MUCH ANYTHING.
ALWAYS WEARS A LAB COAT.
STRAITLACED AND INFLEXIBLE.
QUESTIONS THE VERY EXISTENCE OF THE HAPPINESS CLASS.

Anne Happy

unhappy go lucky!

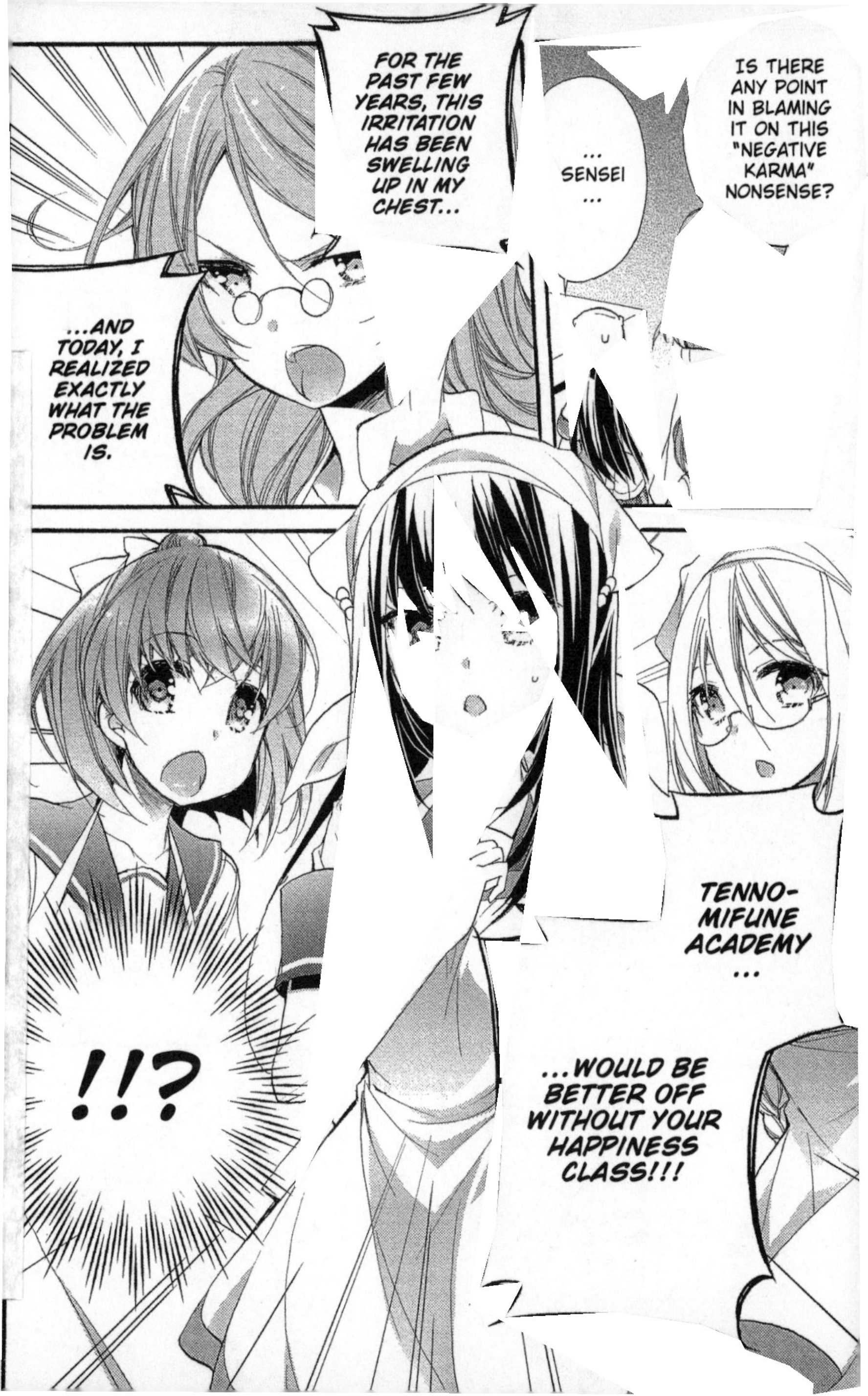
IS THERE ANY POINT IN BLAMING IT ON THIS "NEGATIVE KARMA" NONSENSE?
...SENSEI...
FOR THE PAST FEW YEARS, THIS IRRITATION HAS BEEN SWELLING UP IN MY CHEST...
...AND TODAY, I REALIZED EXACTLY WHAT THE PROBLEM IS.
TENNO-MIFUNE ACADEMY...
...WOULD BE BETTER OFF WITHOUT YOUR HAPPINESS CLASS!!!
!!?

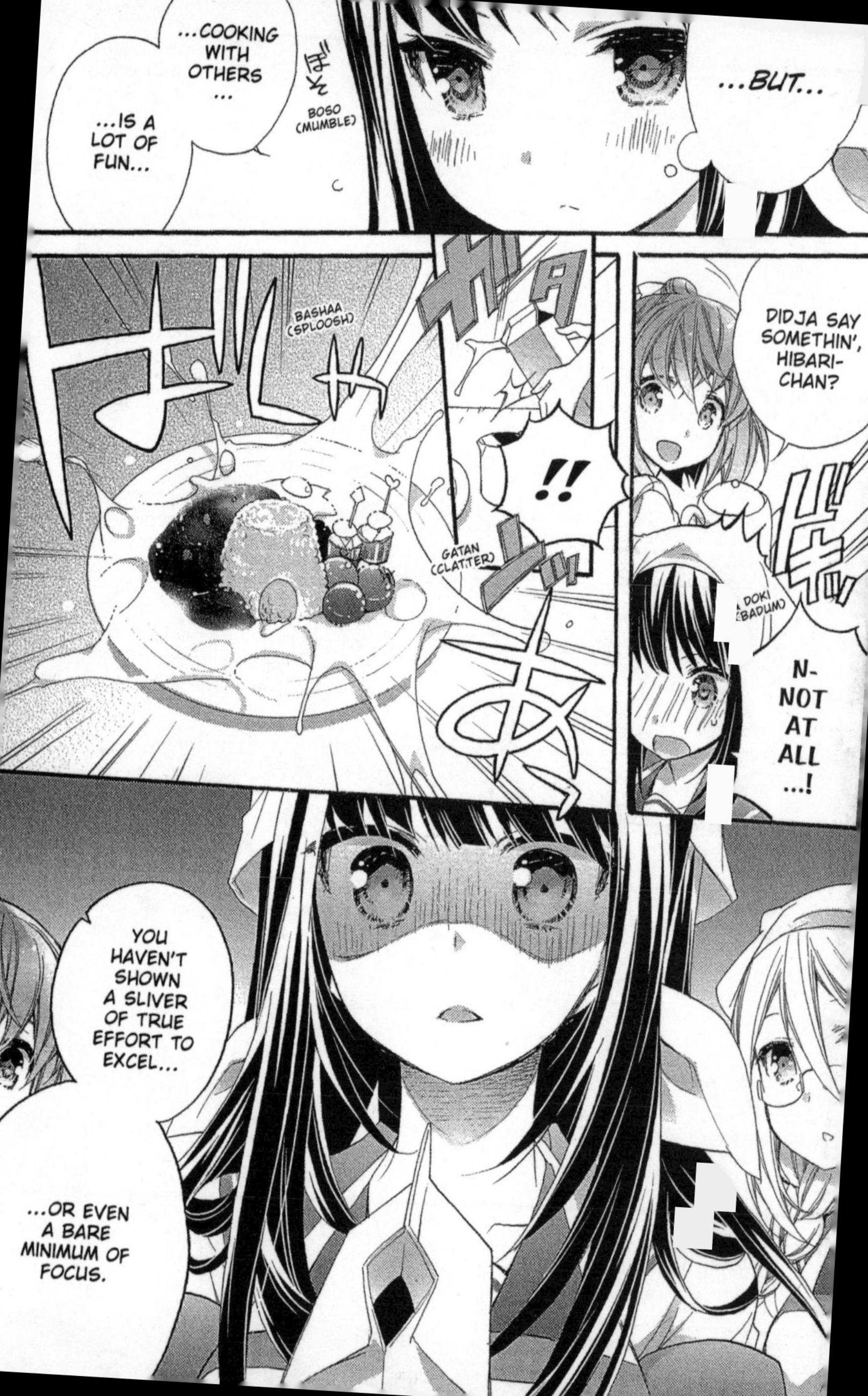
...BUT...
BOSO (MUMBLE)
...COOKING WITH OTHERS ...
...IS A LOT OF FUN...
DIDJA SAY SOMETHIN', HIBARI-CHAN?
DOKI (BADUM)
N-NOT AT ALL ...!
!!
GATAN (CLATTER)
BASHAA (SPLOOSH)
YOU HAVEN'T SHOWN A SLIVER OF TRUE EFFORT TO EXCEL...
...OR EVEN A BARE MINIMUM OF FOCUS.

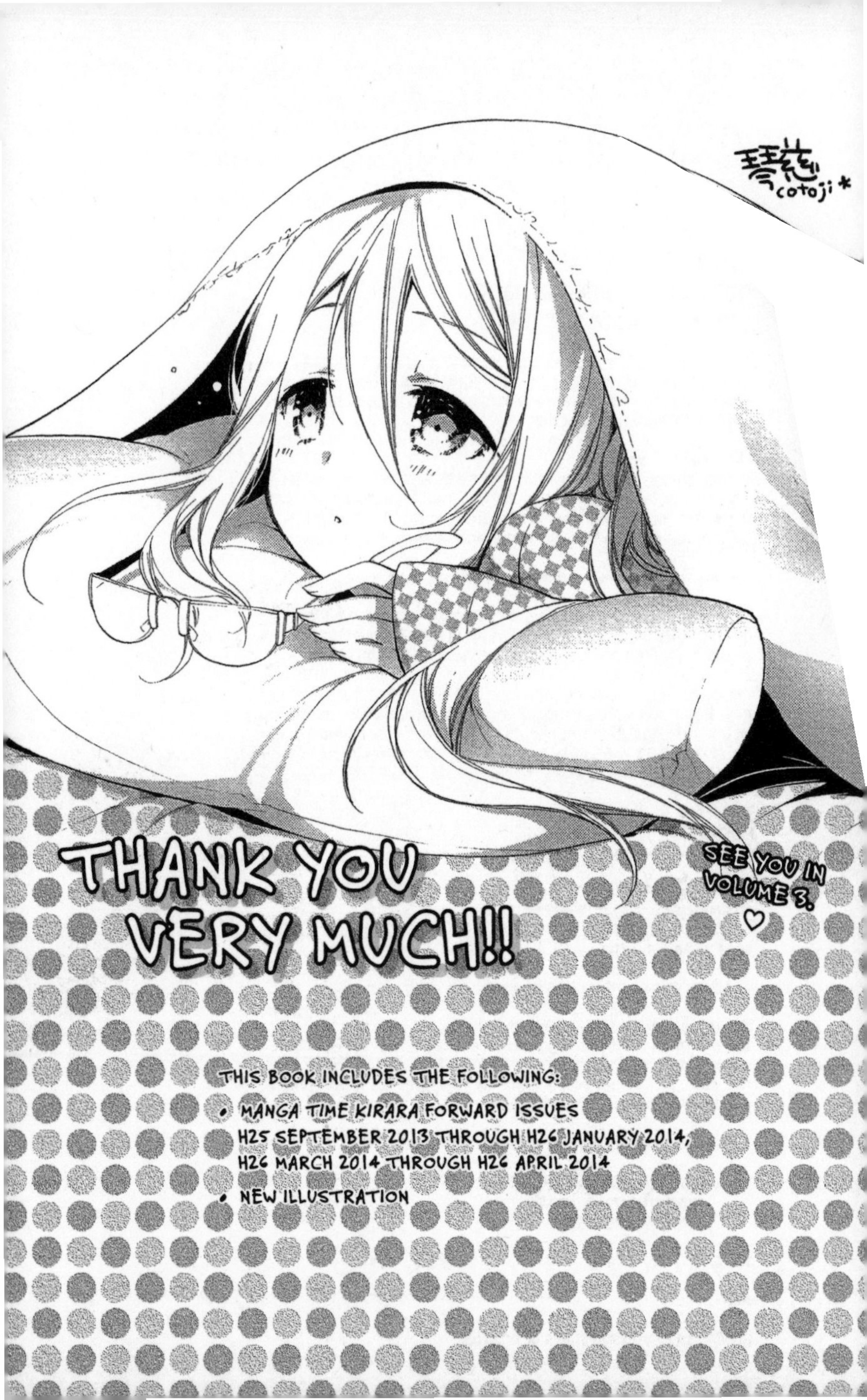
cotoji*
SEE YOU IN VOLUME 3. ♡
THANK YOU VERY MUCH!!
THIS BOOK INCLUDES THE FOLLOWING:
• MANGA TIME KIRARA FORWARD ISSUES H25 SEPTEMBER 2013 THROUGH H26 JANUARY 2014, H26 MARCH 2014 THROUGH H26 APRIL 2014
• NEW ILLUSTRATION

COTOJI

Translation: Amanda Haley
Lettering: Rochelle Gancio

ANNE HAPPY ♪ VOL. 2
© 2013 Cotoji. All rights reserved. First published in Japan in 2013 by HOUBUNSHA CO., LTD., TOKYO. English translation rights in United States, Canada, and United Kingdom arranged with HOUBUNSHA CO., LTD through Tuttle-Mori Agency, Inc., TOKYO.

English translation © 2016 by Yen Press, LLC

Yen Press
1290 Avenue of the Americas
New York, NY 10104

Visit us at yenpress.com
facebook.com/yenpress
twitter.com/yenpress
yenpress.tumblr.com

First Yen Press Edition: August 2016

Yen Press is an imprint of Yen Press, LLC.
The Yen Press name and logo are trademarks of Yen Press, LLC.

The publisher is not responsible for websites (or their content) that are not owned by the publisher.

Library of Congress Control Number: 2016931012

ISBNs: 978-0-316-27612-2 (paperback)
        978-0-316-31794-8 (ebook)
        978-0-316-31795-5 (app)

10 9 8 7 6 5 4 3 2 1

BVG

Printed in the United States of America